TREADING THE BOARDS

Actors and Theatres in Georgian Lincolnshire

By Neil R Wright

Published by
THE SOCIETY FOR LINCOLNSHIRE HISTORY AND ARCHAEOLOGY
2016

First published by the Society for Lincolnshire History and Archaeology 2016

© Society for Lincolnshire History and Archaeology

ISBN 978 0 903582 55 1

British Library Cataloguing in Public Data
A CIP catalogue record of this book is available from the British Library.

All rights reserved

No part of this publication may be reproduced or transmitted in any form or by any means, electronic or mechanical, including photocopying, recording, or by any information storage or retrieval system, without permission in writing from the publisher.

Designed by Ros Beevers

Printed in the United Kingdom by Local Printer Co, Blyton, Gainsborough

Cover illustration: Travelling actors at a turnpike toll gate, about 1825
From Pierce Egan, 'The Life of an Actor' (1825)

CONTENTS

List of illustrations	iv
Acknowledgements	vi
Foreword	ix
Preface	xi
1 Prologue – Foundations Laid	17
2 A Night at the Theatre	27
3 An Actor's Life	51
4 Go Forth and Multiply	80
5 Managers Galore	105
6 Wartime Prosperity	129
7 Twilight is Coming	155
8 Theatre Rural	171
9 A Shocking State of Destitution	205
10 Last of the Comedians	231
11 Epilogue – What Drama Did Next	253
Appendix 1 – Robertson family tree	261
Appendix 2 – Other relations of Fanny Robertson	262
Appendix 3 – Huggins family tree	262
Appendix 4 – Managers of Stamford theatre 1768–1847	263
Appendix 5 – Notes on theatres in the Lincoln circuit 1803	263
Appendix 6 – John Caple's *Corps Dramatique* 1848	264
Appendix 7 – Southwell theatre – surviving remains	265
Bibliography	266
Index	271

ILLUSTRATIONS

Cover picture – Travelling actors at a turnpike toll gate [Egan 1892]

Page	Subject
xiii	Places mentioned in the text – Lincolnshire
xiv	Places mentioned in the text – Britain (except Lincolnshire)
20	Portrait of Susannah Centlivre
22	Town Hall in Spalding that was used as a temporary theatre until 1745
27	Interior of Richmond Theatre - stage and proscenium arch
28	Stamford Theatre – Proscenium Door
31	Portrait of Edmund Kean
38	Spikes, candles, fruit and audience in a Georgian theatre
39	Interior of Richmond Theatre – view from the stage
40	A stage box, in 1810
51	Nicholas Nickleby with a company of comedians
55	Portrait of Anne Brunton (Mrs Merry)
61	Portrait of Thomas Grist
62	Portrait of William Betty, the 'Young Roscius'
64	Portrait of Ira Aldridge
73	Playbill, Spalding, 14 July 1780
75	Wide Bargate, Boston – extract from painting by George Northouse
78	Map showing location of Lincoln's first theatre
78	The surviving front wall of Lincoln's first theatre
78	Door bracket on front wall of Lincoln's first theatre
79	The Harlequin, Steep Hill, Lincoln
80	Playbill, Lincoln, 1754
81	Portrait of George Alexander Stevens
82	Map showing location of Lincoln's second theatre
82	278 High Street, in front of King's Arms yard, Lincoln
82	Arch into King's Arms yard, Lincoln
83	Lincoln theatre, 1805
84	Map of Stamford, showing location of theatres
84	Stamford theatre – basement plan
84	Stamford theatre – facade (drawing)
84	Stamford theatre – cross section of remains in theatre
88	Memorial to Cassandra Whitley in St John's church, Stamford
89	Nottingham theatre, 1805
89	Derby theatre, 1805
91	Plan of the Lincoln circuit, 1790
93	King's Lynn theatre, 1805
96	Map of Gainsborough, showing sites of theatres
97	Site plan of first Gainsborough theatre
98	Karl Wood watercolour of rear of Gainsborough first theatre
99	Gainsborough's first theatre being demolished c.1938
100	Map of Peterborough, showing theatre, 1888
101	Map of Newark, showing site of theatre
102	Boston 1777 theatre in the Market Place
107	Portrait of John Whitfield
109	Playbill, Spalding theatre, 31 August 1796, Lincoln company
112	Map of Alford, showing site of Windmill inn
113	Windmill Inn, Alford Market Place
115	Gainsborough Old Hall – external stairs to gallery of theatre
116	Plan of Gainsborough Old Hall showing theatre
117	Playbill, Gainsborough, 23 October 1788

118	Portrait of Mrs Frances Brooke
118	No.2, Northgate, Sleaford, where Mrs Brooke died
119	Plan of Louth, 1808, showing site of theatre
119	Louth Panorama, detail of panel by William Brown
120	Map of Wisbech, showing site of theatre
120	Site plan of Wisbech theatre, 1887
123	Portrait of Sarah Siddons
124	Cartoon of Lady Albinia, Countess of Buckinghamshire
125	Cartoon – Lady Albinia and Pic Nics attacked by actors
126	Playbill, Lincoln, 27 October 1798
129	Signature of Thomas Shaftoe Robertson
129	Signature of Robert Henry Franklin
131	Portrait of Benjamin Wrench
134	Mr Brunton and Miss Smith, 1806
136	Portrait of John Quick
138	Map of Spalding, showing site of White Hart inn
139	Spalding Market Place, 1 January 1822
140	Map of Huntingdon showing site of theatre
141	Huntingdon theatre, 1805
142	Map of Grantham showing site of Swinegate theatre
143	Grantham theatre, 1805
144	Grantham theatre, front elevation 1952
145	Newark theatre, 1805
146	Ipswich theatre, plan showing 1810 layout
147	Ipswich theatre, painting of interior in 1885
147	Newark theatre, site plan
148	Map of Boston showing sites of theatres
149	Lincoln theatre, interior after fire of 1892
150	Southwell theatre, exterior (2012)
151	Map of Southwell, showing site of theatre
152	Map of Horncastle, showing site of theatre
153	Horncastle theatre, 1979
154	Playbill, Lincoln, 10 September 1806
155	Debtors' Prison in Lincoln Castle
157	Portrait of Joseph Cowell
162	Playbill, Wisbech, 14 May 1819
162	Playbill, Grantham, 17 May 1828, for the widow Chesterton
165	Portrait of Miss Clara Fisher
166	Playbill, Stamford, 9 June 1826
174	Playbill, Louth, 26 December 1810
175	Playbill, Worksop, 29 May 1811
180	Map showing four tours by Smedley, 1810, 1812, 1814, 1815
181	Map of Grimsby showing site of Golden Fleece Inn
182	Playbill, Grimsby, 13 January 1826
182	Site Plan of Golden Fleece Inn – theatre was to the rear
183	Sleaford theatre
184	Map of Sleaford, showing site of the theatre
185	Map of Holbeach showing site of the theatre
186	Map of Bourne, showing site of Southgate
187	Playbill, Brigg, 19 February 1839
193	Playbill, Sleaford, 17 January 1844
197	The Great Hall, Irnham Hall, near Grantham
197	Playbill, Irnham Hall theatre, 8 October 1807
201	Playbill, Caistor, 2 April 1833
208	Playbill, Stamford, 9 April 1824

208	Portrait of Charles William Macready
212	Portrait of Henry Compton
213	Playbill, Louth, 25 November 1833
214	Wisbech theatre – reconstruction diagram of interior
214	Nicholas Nickleby - View from stage, 1838
230	Travelling actors at a turnpike toll gate, 1826
233	Peterborough Corn Exchange, on site of theatre
236	Stamford theatre, facade in 1948
239	Playbill, Stamford, 3 August 1849
240	Grantham theatre – Demolition in 1952 (west side)
240	Grantham theatre – Demolition in 1952 (north side)
241	Grantham theatre – Survey of ground floor in 1952
246	Independent Chapel, Red Lion Street, Boston
253	Portrait of Thomas William Robertson
254	Portrait of Madge Robertson
256	Former Newark theatre, 2012
256	Wisbech theatre, 2015

ACKNOWLEDGEMENTS

Information for this history of theatre in Lincolnshire in the Georgian period has come from many sources and I owe a great debt to people who have aided my research in various ways. I would particularly like to thank Helen Bates, Ray Carroll, Richard Cook of Huntingdon, Roger Dobson of Southwell, Hazel Frogett, Tom Grimes Hon Curator of the Spalding Gentlemen's Society, Richard Hillier, Ken Hollamby, Jean Howard of the Louth Naturalists', Antiquarian and Literary Society, Chris Johnson, Malcolm Knapp, John Manterfield, John Minnis, Maureen Nicholls, Chris Padley, Chris Page, Eileen Robson, David Saunders, Christine Waterfield and Bob Williams (Stamford Town Council), as well as staff of the National Archives, the British Library, Parliamentary Archives, Stamford Arts Centre, and libraries in Lincoln, Boston (Lincs), Boston (Massachusetts), Grantham, Grimsby, Gainsborough, Holbeach, Huntingdon, Newark, Southwell, Stamford, Peterborough and Wisbech. Andrew Walker and Chris Lester read the text and made useful suggestions for improvements, and I am responsible for any remaining errors and omissions.

We have obtained illustrations from various sources and would like to thank the Angles Theatre (Wisbech), the Bodleian Libraries of the University of Oxford, the British Museum, the Delvers of Gainsborough, English Heritage (RCHM), Gainsborough Library, Gainsborough Old Hall, Grantham Library, Grimsby Library, Houghton Library of the University of Harvard, Ipswich Library (Suffolk Libraries), University of Illinois Library, Library and Archives Canada, Lincoln Central Library, Lincolnshire Archives, Louth Naturalists', Antiquarian and Literary Society, National Portrait Gallery, National Trust, Nottinghamshire Archives, Peterborough Archives, John Pinchbeck, The Georgian Theatre Royal, Richmond, Spalding Gentlemen's Society, Stamford Town Council, Survey of Lincoln, Usher Gallery, Lincoln, the Walters Art Museum, Baltimore, and Vivacity (Peterborough) for their kind permission to use illustrations. While every effort has been made to trace copyright holders, this has not been possible in all cases. Any omissions brought to the attention of the publisher will be remedied in future editions.

Dedicated to Fanny Robertson (1768–1855)
Outstanding star of the Lincolnshire stage for many years

FOREWORD

History is important because of what we learn about others and about ourselves. This fine book casts light on a little-known aspect of theatre history as it tells the fascinating story of the lives of actors in and around Lincolnshire in the 18th and early 19th centuries. Much is known about theatrical life in Georgian London and this work shows us how the pleasures and challenges of live theatre came to stimulate and entertain people in a rural part of the East Midlands, remote from what Dr Johnson called 'the Great Wen'.

I find it a wholly fascinating study of a world of which I knew nothing. That said, for an actor of today to read of the trials and excitements of one's peers two hundred years ago one is inevitably made aware of the fact that whilst the world today is utterly different, the essentials of what makes people become actors, and the need they have to tell stories and entertain, often against the odds, are the same as they have ever been. My having a little local knowledge of some of the towns and sites of the venues made the connections even more telling.

Enjoy reading what has obviously been a magnificent labour of love.

Jim Broadbent
Actor
London

PREFACE

The colourful history of Lincolnshire's Georgian actors and playhouses has been sadly neglected. Books written about theatres in that period mainly look at London or the national scene, which are sometimes seen as the same, or at significant theatres in the rest of Britain. But the golden age of drama spread beyond the haunts of the rich and powerful. This book seeks to tell how drama arrived, flourished and died in a prosperous agricultural county. Local companies of comedians performed in this area for nearly a hundred years but none of their playhouses were grand enough to be called a Theatre Royal. The history of theatres in some Lincolnshire towns has been written up, but in the Georgian period theatre in this county was organised in circuits and each town tells but a small part of the whole. For the first time this work considers theatres and touring companies of comedians, as actors were then called, in the context of the whole county, and of Lincolnshire-based circuits that covered a wider area.

In the 1970s whilst I was researching the history of Lincolnshire towns and industry between 1700 and 1914 I came across numerous references to comedians and theatres. Books published in the Georgian period give some information on drama in Lincolnshire, and in the twentieth century Diana Clementson, G. Hemingway and B.J. Parker wrote academic theses on the Lincoln, Newark and Gainsborough theatres, but very little is written about other playhouses. Sybil Rosenfeld and John Richards wrote short pieces in numbers of the Theatre Notebook in 1952 and 1975. Lou Warwick wrote in the 1970s about theatres in Northampton that were sometimes served by the Lincolnshire companies of comedians. Articles on theatres in Nottingham published by the Thoroton Society, and William Senior's 1894 book on Wakefield theatre, also refer to Lincolnshire-based companies. In the last fifty years Jim Golland has written a little about his ancestor Tom Manly of Stamford, books by Mervyn Gould, Frank Hance and Eddie Sissons refer to theatres in Boston, Stamford and Gainsborough respectively and websites give brief histories of some other theatres, but even for those places there is still more that can be told.

From the 1760s to the 1840s Lincolnshire had a flourishing theatrical life and in this book I have tried to tell the unknown story of actors and theatres, prosperity and poverty. Actors would arrive in a town and for about a month would reveal to local people a wide world of tragedy, excitement, romance, comedy, farce, laughter, song and dance. The quality might not always have been good but it was lively, popular and joined people's consciousness to the wider world and the expanding British Empire. London stars like Kean, Macready and Sarah Siddons occasionally appear in this history but they are fiery comets flashing across the sky. In the main the cast in this book are less familiar but equally hard working characters, whose reputation and fame did not long survive their own passing. Some are better known in the history of American theatre than they are here.

I started more detailed research after I retired in 2010. My main local source has been the Stamford Mercury, possibly the oldest surviving newspaper in Britain and one that served most of Lincolnshire and parts of adjacent counties during the eighteenth and nineteenth centuries. It contained advertisements for theatres, reports of the marriages and deaths of actors and managers, and occasionally reviews of performances and news about theatres. In early 2011 I spent six months looking through the Mercury from 1714 to 1855 and copying the references to theatres and actors. Further details were obtained from playbills held in several local museums and libraries, and from records in the Lincolnshire Archives. Account books kept by two Lincolnshire-based actor managers in the early nineteenth century have been examined, though I have not found any such records for the main company run by the Robertson family. Books by Elizabeth Grice and Moira Field provide comparative material on the East Anglian circuits of this period and other works on theatre, drama and actors elsewhere in Britain were used to put the Lincolnshire scene in a wider context. After a brief interval that allowed me to digest the information I had collected, I set about writing the book you have before you. I have found the research and writing to be fascinating, and I hope that you will have as much enjoyment reading it.

Neil R. Wright
Lincoln
3 July 2015

EXPLANATION OF TERMS AND ABBREVIATIONS

Britain adopted decimal currency on 15 February 1971 in place of sterling. The following table illustrates the relation between the old and new currency:

1d = 1 old penny = 0.416p
2d = 2 old pence = 0.83p
6d = 6 old pence = 2½p
1/- (1s) = one shilling (12 old pence) = 5p
1/6 (1s 6d) = one shilling and six pence = 7½p
2/- (2s) = two shillings = 10p
2/6 (2s 6d) = half a crown (two shillings and six pence) = 12½p
3/- (3s) = three shillings = 15p
£1 = twenty shillings = £1
One guinea = one pound one shilling = £1.05

'The long eighteenth century' is a natural historical period from the Glorious Revolution of 1688 to the accession of Queen Victoria in 1837.

Britain currently uses both Imperial and Metric measurements.
1 inch = 2.45 centimetres
1 foot (12 inches) = 0.3049 metres
1 yard (3 feet) = 0.9144 metres
1 mile (1,760 yards) = 1.6093 kilometres

MAP OF PLACES MENTIONED IN THE TEXT — LINCOLNSHIRE

Drawn by Ken Redmore

MAP OF PLACES IN BRITAIN MENTIONED IN THE TEXT (EXCEPT LINCOLNSHIRE)

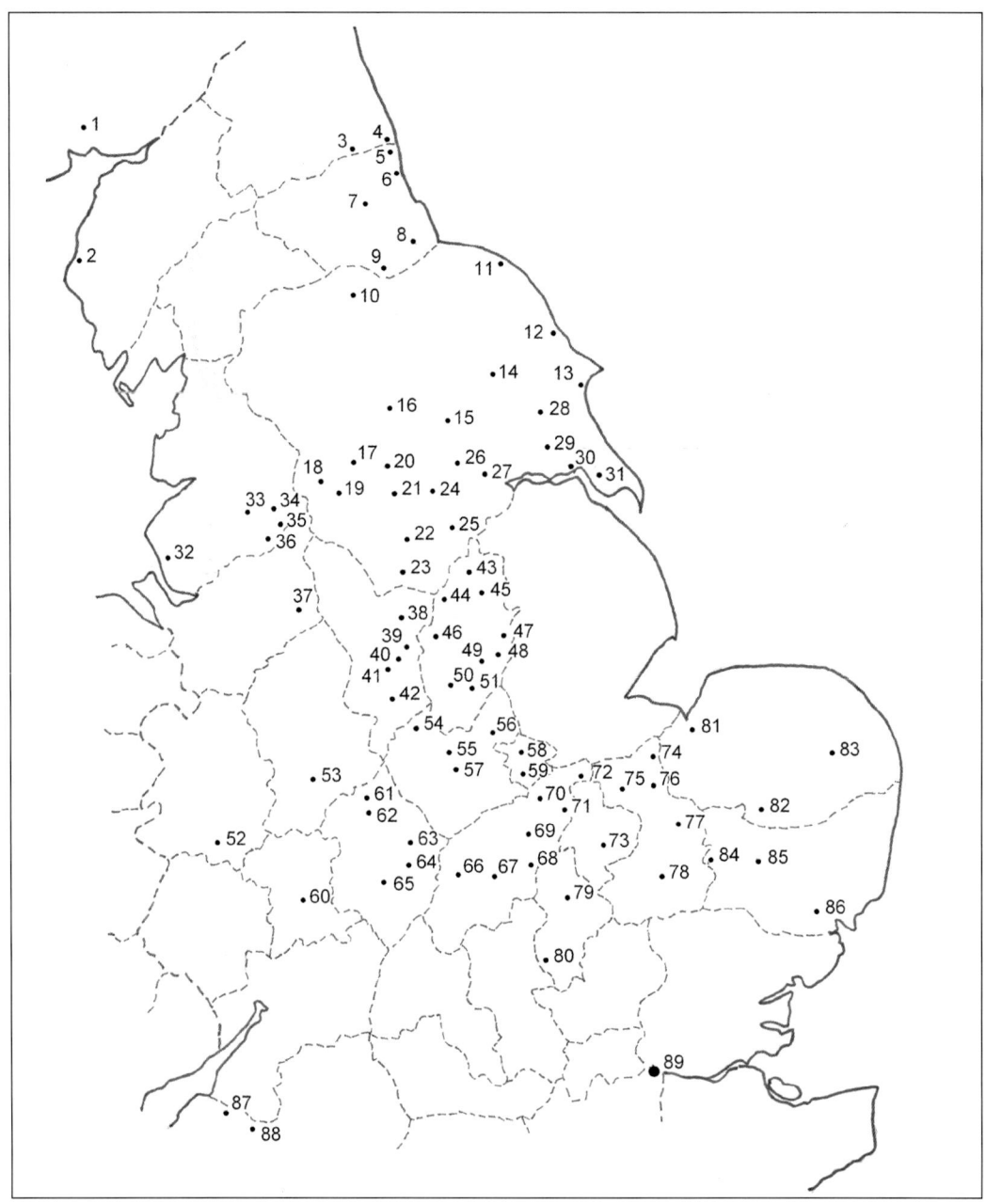

Drawn by Ken Redmore

INDEX TO PLACES MENTIONED IN THE TEXT - BRITAIN EXCEPT LINCOLNSHIRE

Alfreton – 39
Aston – 61
Barnsley – 22
Bath – 88
Bawtry – 43
Bedford – 79
Belper – 41
Beverley – 29
Bingham – 51
Birmingham – 62
Bradford – 17
Bridlington – 13
Brighton (Sussex) – off map
Bristol – 87
Bury (Lancs) – 33
Bury St Edmunds – 85
Cambridge – 78
Castle Donington – 54
Chesterfield – 38
Collingham – 47
Corby – 70
Coventry – 63
Darlington – 9
Daventry – 66
Derby – 42
Doncaster – 25
Driffield – 28
Dumfries – 1
Durham – 7
Edinburgh – off map
Ely – 77
Glasgow – off map
Great Driffield – 28
Halifax – 18
Harrogate – 16
Hedon – 31

Howden – 27
Huddersfield – 19
Hull – 30
Huntingdon – 73
Ipswich – 86
Kettering – 69
King's Lynn – 81
Leeds – 20
Leicester – 57
Leighton Buzzard – 80
Liverpool – 32
London – 89
Loughborough – 55
Ludlow – 52
Macclesfield – 37
Malton – 14
Manchester – 36
Mansfield – 46
March – 76
Melton Mowbray – 56
Newark – 48
Newcastle upon Tyne – 3
Newmarket – 84
Northampton – 67
North Shields – 4
Norwich – 83
Nottingham – 50
Oakham – 58
Oldham – 35
Oundle – 71
Peterborough – 72
Pontefract – 24
Retford – 45
Richmond (Yorks) – 10
Ripley – 40
Rochdale – 34

Scarborough – 12
Selby – 26
Sheffield – 23
South Shields – 5
Southwell – 49
Stockton – 8
Stratford upon Avon – 65
Sunderland – 6
Tenby (Pembrokeshire) – off map
Thetford – 82
Uppingham – 59
Wakefield – 21
Warwick – 64
Wellingborough – 68
Whitby – 11
Whitehaven – 2
Whittlesey – 75
Wisbech – 74
Wolverhampton – 53
Worcester – 60
Worksop – 44
York – 15

1

PROLOGUE – FOUNDATIONS LAID

THERE WAS a golden age of drama in the remote rural county of Lincolnshire during the Georgian period. It started about 1731, grew slowly at first, reached a peak in the stressful years when Britain was at war with Napoleon and expired in the 1840s. Live theatre is one of the most exciting cultural experiences, and in Lincolnshire it prospered more in that period than at any other time. From the 1760s to the 1840s there were more theatres in Lincolnshire, more professional actors working in the county and more plays put on each year than at any time before or since. Drama was organised in circuits, and one based in Lincoln included not only venues in southern Lincolnshire but also Newark, Peterborough, Wisbech and other towns on the fringes of adjacent counties, an area that may be referred to as 'greater Lincolnshire'. Towards the end of the period several towns in Yorkshire were also served by Lincolnshire based companies. But it did not last. Most theatres closed by the mid nineteenth century and music halls were opened to fill part of the vacuum. Lincoln theatre survived and others in Stamford, Sleaford, Wisbech and King's Lynn came back into theatrical use in the late twentieth century. Live drama in Lincolnshire is now provided by professional and amateur actors in theatres and other venues but, in contrast to the Georgian period, no professional actor can now earn a living just by working in and around the county without a public subsidy.

In 1714 King George I ascended the throne of Great Britain. There were then no theatres in Lincolnshire and troupes of actors who occasionally visited the county had to perform in barns or halls that had been set up as temporary playhouses. A hundred years later the scene was transformed – there were at least three companies of professional actors, called companies of comedians, making a good living touring Lincolnshire and adjacent places and a dozen towns had purpose-built theatres for them to perform in. But move on just another thirty years to the early part of Queen Victoria's reign and the scene has changed again – theatres had closed, many actors had left the county, and those still struggling on were facing real poverty and starvation. How and why did all this happen? Why was there so much drama in Georgian Lincolnshire, and what caused it to die so painfully? First let us consider what Lincolnshire had in the way of theatre before 1730.

The eighteenth century was not the first time that there had been dramatic performances in this part of the world. It is likely that the Roman city of Lindum Colonia (now Lincoln) would have had a theatre nearly two thousand years ago, though nowadays we do not even know where it was located.[1] There was then a

---
[1] Jones, M., *Roman Lincoln, Conquest, Colony and Capital*, Lincoln (2002), p.73.

long gap and from about 1235 there is evidence, including some play texts, of a rich religious dramatic culture in medieval Lincolnshire that involved both amateur and professional players. It is said that the religious plays of that time had certain features, such as the prominence given to the Virgin Mary, that appeared to be present throughout Lincolnshire and unique to the county. In the city of Lincoln itself the main period of medieval dramatic activity was from 1440 to 1500. Lincoln Cathedral had two plays performed on specific feasts in the church calendar: an Easter play replaced by 1457–58 by one performed on St Anne's Day, 28 July, and a Magi play replaced in 1490–91 by a play performed on Lady Day, 25 March.[2] Two plays marking the birth and death of Jesus Christ were replaced by two that dramatised the beginning and end of the adult life of the Virgin Mary.

The performances in the Cathedral appear to have influenced parish religious drama in Boston, Holbeach, Louth, Sleaford and other towns throughout the county. Local guilds in Lincolnshire towns were involved in the organisation and production of plays and processions. Though Lincoln Cathedral only staged two plays a year it appears that the guilds of the city produced a great variety of them. In the fifteenth century plays began to be performed in new venues away from churches, sometimes in dry moats outside town walls. It has been suggested that a circular depression in Lincoln about 60 feet across in the grounds of the Usher Gallery, on the line of the old city ditch, may have been such a performing space.[3] Some guilds in Boston, Louth and Stamford each had a schoolmaster as one of their chaplains, who would be university trained and so could have written plays. In Boston the wealthy and powerful Guild of St Mary arranged the town's Whitsuntide and Corpus Christi processions and entertainments, and paid professional performers ranging from civic waites to acting troupes, including the King's own company. In 1546 the new Boston Corporation absorbed the town's guilds and as late as the 1550s, William Harrison, one of nine guild chaplains of the former Guild of St Mary, was still known as 'Master of the Plaies'. Other places, such as Holbeach, Sleaford, Sutterton and Grimsby, also put on single plays run by guilds, most of them based on the life of the Virgin Mary. Louth started putting on 'cycle' plays about 1515, and by 1528–29 the town had a regular pageant house, instead of the old church of St Mary, which they had used in 1519–20. The house was in the lane now called Schoolhouse Lane and it belonged to the Holy Trinity Guild. Plays were last performed in Louth in 1556–57.[4]

From at least 1499 plays were put on by travelling troupes from London who were licensed professionals under the protection of various noblemen or the reigning sovereign. Those troupes visited the towns of Boston, Grimsby, Lincoln, Long

---

[2] Stokes, James (ed), *Records of Early English Drama – Lincolnshire*, Toronto (2009), pp.372, 404, 407; Kahrl, Stanley J., *Records of Plays and Players in Lincolnshire 1300-1585* (The Malone Society, Collections, Vol.VIII), Oxford (1974), p.21.

[3] Grigg, Erik, 'Lincoln's Lost Medieval Theatre', *Lincolnshire Past and Present*, No.67, Lincoln (2007), p.11.

[4] Stokes, *op. cit.*, pp.387, 393; Kahrl, *op. cit.*, pp.13, 14, 21, 23, 25.

Sutton, Louth, Market Deeping and Stamford, the monastery of Bardney Abbey and the households of Katherine Willoughby, Duchess of Suffolk, at Grimsthorpe Castle, and of Sir John, Lord Hussey, of Sleaford. However, it is difficult to draw many conclusions about the numbers of professional troupes who visited Lincolnshire in this period, the frequency of their performances, or the locations where they performed.[5]

The religious plays did not survive the Reformation, but much of the rich medieval culture of Lincolnshire continued well into the sixteenth century and there were many payments by Lincolnshire towns to players from villages and other towns in the county. Medieval plays enjoyed popular support and continued, with a change from sacred to secular subject matter, even after the dissolution of the religious guilds. In response to the Lincolnshire Rising in 1536, King Henry VIII installed three powerful magnates in Lincolnshire – the Duke of Suffolk, Lord Clinton, and the Earl of Rutland – and all three provided patronage to players and other performers.[6]

Between 1558 and 1575 Lincolnshire saw a great increase in the number of performances by troupes supported by nobles of Queen Elizabeth's court, but there was a noticeable decline in locally produced plays. By 1568, when all religious drama ceased in Lincoln and in most of the rest of Lincolnshire as well, the only players seen in the county were the professional companies of comedians from London.[7] A 1572 Act of Parliament decreed that all companies of players must be servants of either the Queen or a noble lord, and be authorised to play under a licence. On arrival in a town the licensed players had to present themselves to the Mayor, state whose servants they were and receive permission to perform. Players without a licence were deemed to be rogues, vagabonds and sturdy beggars and were turned out of town.[8] Puritans opposed traditional performances wherever they might occur and decried them as criminal activities. They had a temporary success in Boston in March 1577 when an injunction was passed that 'there shall be no more plays nor interludes in the church, nor the chancel, nor the hall nor the school house'. But that ban was cancelled in 1579 at the request of people in the borough; and annual religious plays were allowed in the hall until at least 1587.[9] Only in a few other places did local plays continue, for example, in Donington c.1563 (religious), Grimsby and Kirton in 1571–72 (unspecified topic), Louth in 1567–68 (perhaps a school play) and South Kyme in 1601 (satirical). Efforts at suppression continued during the early seventeenth century and in 1606-07 James Leeman, the curate of Wrangle, was charged with going 'mumeing in Boston in disguised apparell'. Money was paid to players in Boston in 1614, 1620 and 1624 though in 1620 this was

---

[5] Stokes, *op. cit.*, pp.438, 439.
[6] Stokes, *op. cit.*, pp.371, 379, 404; Kahrl, *op. cit.*, pp.30, 31.
[7] Stokes, *op. cit.*, pp.404, 439, 440; Kahrl, *op. cit.*, pp.21, 30, 31.
[8] Leacroft, Helen and Richard, The *Theatre in Leicestershire*, Leicester (1986), p.5.
[9] Kahrl, *op. cit.*, p.30; Thompson, Pishey, *History and Antiquities of Boston*, Boston (1856), p.211.

Susannah Centlivre (née Freeman) (1667–1723). This successful playwright was born in Holbeach.

Courtesy of the Rare Book and Manuscript Library, University of Illinois at Urbana-Champaign.

'to rid them out of the town'.[10] This cultural war culminated on 2 September 1642 when Oliver Cromwell issued an order closing all theatres and ending play acting. The only surviving vestige of old performances are some of the mummers' plays and plough plays that continued into the early twentieth century, or even later in some places.

The year 1660 witnessed the restoration of the monarchy and the beginning of a new lusty and licentious age. Puritanism was shrugged off, the theatres were reopened, modernised and the pit invented, and London launched itself into an era of elegant living and unrestrained indulgence. For the first time young women replaced boy actors on the stage. The title 'Theatre Royal' was granted to two London theatres, in Covent Garden and Drury Lane, in 1662, and they initially had a monopoly of the legitimate drama. The dramatists and actors suppressed during the Commonwealth were naturally royalists, and after the Restoration there was an anti-Puritan outburst.

At this time Lincolnshire was making little contribution to the theatrical scene. One exception was Susannah Centlivre (*née* Freeman) (1667–1723) who was born in Holbeach but moved to London and became the most successful playwright of her time, writing Restoration comedies.[11] A leading actor was Colley Cibber (1671–1757) whose mother came from Glaston in Rutland. He was born in London but attended the free school at Grantham from 1682 to 1687 before becoming an actor in Drury Lane in 1690 and then one of the first actor-managers. He wrote some 29 plays and even became poet laureate. Some of his children also went on the stage including his youngest daughter, Charlotte, who spent much time cross-dressed as a man off-stage as well as on. Plays written in this period by Cibber, Centlivre and others were to be regularly revived throughout the eighteenth century.

Theatre in Britain was changing and about fifty years later the first permanent theatre in Lincolnshire was to be built. From 1679, when there was a constitutional crisis, theatre in this country lacked royal and aristocratic support and was in upheaval until the accession of King George I. Royal support was replaced by commercial ownership, in contrast to the rest of Europe, and drama and other arts in Britain became open to a larger public. The new commercial managers offered a more varied evening's entertainment with singing, dancing, acrobats and comic turns between the acts, and sometimes added a second play or 'afterpiece' after the main play. Theatre, like music, was an art form that could be enjoyed by the illiterate and the cheapest seats were only 1/- or sometimes 6d for the second half of the evening. That was not beyond the means of an artisan earning about £50 a year and the middling sort could visit the theatre two or three times in a season. Only the ill-dressed, ragged and poor might be excluded from a playhouse.[12] Growing

---

[10] Stokes, *op. cit.*, p.459; Thompson, *op. cit.*, p.211.

[11] Sampson, George, *The Concise Cambridge History of English Literature*, Cambridge (1941), p.513.

[12] Brewer, John, *The Pleasures of the Imagination; English Culture in the Eighteenth Century*, Abingdon (2013), pp.2, 85, 289, 290.

refinement and culture in Lincolnshire was indicated by the formation of the Spalding Gentlemen's Society in 1709 and the founding of the *Stamford Mercury*, Britain's oldest surviving newspaper, in 1710.

The Georgian period was an age of revolutions – political, social, transport, agricultural and industrial – with an explosion of radical ideas and technological innovations. Britain grew to lead the world in wealth, industry and innovation and Lincolnshire prospered as a source of food for London and for the manufacturing areas of the Midlands and Yorkshire. The expanding economy brought prosperity to the middling sort, a layer of people between the workers and the nobility, who were starting to rise in power as well as prosperity. By the 1780s the middle ranks of English society, which ranged from minor gentlemen to well-off artisans, with a family income between £50 and £200 a year, comprised nearly 25 per cent of the population. England also became the most rapidly urbanising part of Europe and provincial towns were growing even faster than London. By 1801 more than one quarter of the inhabitants of England and Wales lived in towns.[13] The rising prosperity of the urban middle class and their desire to show their good taste led commercial entertainment to spread from London to the rest of the country, especially after 1760. Even small towns like Lincoln and Stamford gradually acquired the civilising influence of assembly rooms, libraries, theatres and pleasure gardens. Local elections, court sessions and race meetings were part of the existing social life of provincial towns and they became the occasion for plays, concerts, assemblies and balls. Many people attending theatres did so for self-improvement, to develop into civilised, sociable and cultured individuals.[14] Theatre became an essential part of fashionable life even in small country towns, adding colour and magic to the local social scene.

In the early eighteenth century strolling troupes of actors started visiting Lincolnshire again and performed in barns, halls or other rooms that they could adapt for their use. In the twenty-first century the word 'comedian' usually means a solitary performer who tells jokes, whether in theatres, clubs, arenas or on television but in the Georgian period the word 'comedian' was the job title used when any actor was mentioned in newspapers, bought property or appeared in court. Nowadays a troupe of actors can be called a 'theatre company' or sometimes a 'repertory company' but in the eighteenth and early nineteenth centuries they were always a 'company of comedians' whether performing tragedy, comedy or other categories of drama. These 'comedians' were bringing new cultural experiences to many people across Lincolnshire. People in the audience, as William Hazlett said, could identify with characters, feelings and experiences that were foreign to them and, at the same time, satisfy their curiosity, voyeurism and delight in novelty.

---

[13] Brewer, *op. cit.*, pp.9, 395.
[14] Brewer, *ibid.*, p.3.

The Town Hall in Spalding was a court building used occasionally as a temporary theatre until 1745.
Spalding Gentlemen's Society.

During the first half of the eighteenth century the demand for drama throughout the kingdom grew and was more than the London based companies could satisfy. The answer was to create new touring companies of comedians in the provinces, usually based in one town and touring a circuit of other nearby places. Before there were purpose-built theatres, inns were the natural locations for plays and other polite leisure services to grow, as they had food, accommodation, stabling and large public rooms. However, as drama became more popular the players had to adapt larger buildings such as barns or warehouses, and eventually entrepreneurs erected purpose-built theatres.

Stamford was an ancient borough and the southern entry into Lincolnshire on the Great North Road. In the second half of the eighteenth century its population rose from about 2,600 to about 5,000. It was a social centre and transport hub for adjacent parts of several counties, easily accessible to touring companies from London and elsewhere. In Stamford they made use of the Guildhall, which was in the corner of St Mary's Square, to the east of the present Town Hall. In September 1718 Thomas Keregan's company of comedians performed comedies at the Guildhall at the time of Stamford races.[15] Keregan had started his acting career with the Norwich company and later went on to build York's first theatre, which opened in 1734. John Gay's celebrated *The Beggar's Opera* (1728) was performed in the Stamford Guildhall in April 1728 and for two weeks from 18 March 1734 the famous Signiora (sic) Violante performed 'Italian rope-dancing' (ie rope-walking) in the same venue. In December 1737 Thomas Topham from Islington, near London, commonly called 'the Strong Man', performed feats of strength in Stamford Guildhall, starting at 5pm. Prices were 2/- at the front and 1/- at the back, which were to be the usual prices for admission to the pit and gallery in theatres in later years. His entertainment also included singing 'with a very masculine voice'.[16] The Guildhall was not the only venue for entertainment in Stamford. The Assembly Room was used in August 1744 for a subscription concert of music with, in the interval, a 'dramatic entertainment of dancing' called *The Loves of Mars and Venus* by performers from the Theatre Royal, Covent Garden in London, and Mr Essex's scholars. This was an early but sophisticated attempt to explore the dramatic possibilities of dance, and one of the first to attempt to convey a whole story. It was performed on Wednesday 8 August, and was advertised a month before in the *Stamford Mercury* to raise subscriptions. It started at 6pm and ended at 9pm, followed by country dancing. It was sufficiently popular to be repeated on Thursday 16 August.[17]

Plays were also performed in other Lincolnshire towns by amateur actors as well as by professionals. The courtroom in Spalding Town Hall was used regularly for theatrical performances in the early eighteenth century, some of the touring companies of comedians staying as long as a month. At least one of these was a local company, the 'Croyland players', who used the hall in 1703 but nothing more

---

[15] *Stamford Mercury*, 18 September 1718.
[16] *SM*, 18 April 1728, 14 March 1734, 15 December 1737.
[17] *SM*, 12 July 1744, 2 and 9 August 1744.

is known of them. In 1719 the 'young gentlemen' of Spalding Grammar School performed a play written by the master of the school in the 'Town House' where a stage had been set up with 'very fine and tall' scenery. 'Several suits of gay cloathes' were made for them, and a prologue was promised to be written by the 'Best poet in Cambridge'. The play was performed for a week and Mrs Heron and some other people of good fashion took lodgings in the town as the roads were bad in winter. In 1720 it was said that ladies and gentlemen of Spalding were again planning a week of plays for the season, as well as a week of horse races and a monthly Assembly for dancing and cards.[18] In 1745 the erection of proscenium arches and other temporary theatrical alterations was banned because the Town Hall had been renovated.

At the Falcon Inn, Strait Bargate, Boston, gentlemen amateurs performed an opera *The New World in the Moon* for three nights in January 1724. Plays or balls were often provided as evening entertainment during horse-race meetings and three-day cock-fighting events. In 1726 Philippa Mundy wrote that the race week at Lincoln was very disappointing with 'ill acted plays, a foolish medley and a dusty assembly'.[19] In May 1729, during races at Sutterton, Mr William Denny's company of comedians performed. There were three days of cock-fighting at the Red Lion inn, Boston, in January 1732 and each night young gentlemen amateurs of the town performed a play. A company of comedians performed in a building in that inn yard in 1740, and later a granary near the Packhouse Quay was adapted and used when needed until a theatre was built in 1777.[20]

The attendance of the new middle class was the main financial support of drama and it was not feasible to have a building designed specifically for the performance of plays until a town had sufficient numbers of local merchants, industrialists, doctors and lawyers, but its financial viability also needed the attendance of shopkeepers, journeymen, skilled craftsmen and others of the lower orders of society who could afford a shilling for admission to the gallery. The local gentry and nobility were fewer in number but their attendance was often the magnet that attracted more of the middle class to a particular performance. Bath had its first purpose-built theatre in 1705 and a second in 1723 but in most other towns purpose-built theatres came after 1731. York's was built in 1734, one next to the site of Stourbridge Fair at Cambridge in 1737, Nottingham in 1740 and Hull by 1742, but Norwich was not built until 1758. The city of Lincoln had a purpose-built theatre by 1731, one of the first in the country, and another, in Stamford, was built about 20 years later, but performances in other Lincolnshire towns had to make use of less sophisticated venues for a few decades more.

In 1737 the theatrical scene throughout the country changed significantly as a Licensing Act imposed controls on performances by touring companies of

---

[18] Honeybone, Diana and Michael, *The Correspondence of William Stukeley and Maurice Johnson 1714-1754*, Lincoln Record Society Vol.104, Lincoln (2014), pp.31, 41.
[19] Massingberd papers, Archivists Report 9 (1957/58), p.35.
[20] *SM*, 10 January 1724, 8 May 1729, 16 December 1731; Thompson, Pishey, *op.cit.*, p.211.

comedians. This was the government's reaction to a bold satire in 1736 by Henry Fielding on Sir Robert Walpole, the first Prime Minister. The Act required all theatres to obtain either letters patent from the King or a license from the Lord Chamberlain, who was to vet all new plays and alterations to old ones. The Act related to 'interludes, tragedies and comedies, plays and other entertainment on the stage done for hire, gain or reward' and Section 1 provided that players would still be deemed rogues and vagabonds if they had no legal settlement in the place where they performed and had no licence from the Lord Chamberlain. Even some of the greatest actors of the eighteenth century toured England under the threat of the imposition of this Act.

Under Section 2 of the Act no new plays or additions to old plays could be acted until they had obtained the approval of the Lord Chamberlain. Only the Drury Lane and Covent Garden theatres in London were excluded from his censorship. That duopoly was modified in 1766 when a patent to stage drama was granted to the Little Theatre in the Haymarket, but only during the summer when Covent Garden and Drury Lane were not performing. The official approval of plays endured until the abolition of the Lord Chamberlain's authority in the liberal 1960s. One effect of the 1737 Act was to discourage new plays and lead to the staging of many more revivals, including the plays of Shakespeare. Experiment and novelty in writing moved from plays to novels and essays. The new plays that were written tended to be safe drama, bland and formulaic – comedies and farces with stock plots and familiar devices. Musical comedies and operettas proliferated and Thomas Arne's *Love in a Village* (1762) and Samuel Arnold's *The Maid of the Mill* (1765) were both great hits and remained in the repertoire for years.

The 1737 Act rendered the unlicensed theatres technically illegal but it did not kill drama in the provinces nor inhibit the building of theatres here. One reason was that gentlemen in the country, magistrates among them, simply did not want to be deprived of the pleasures of the theatre. The new provincial playhouses operated in a twilight zone beyond the law for a number of years and relied on the tolerance of local magistrates and the enthusiasm of leading townspeople for stimulating entertainment. One way to avoid the penalties of the Act was to put on 'concerts' with 'free' dramatic interludes, though within a few years attitudes relaxed and dramatic performances no longer needed to be so disguised. There were, however, cases where the Act was brought into full and powerful effect. Jemmy Whitley's Stamford circuit included Nottingham and in 1763 one of his actors named Wheeler was arrested there when a 'certain Alderman (who has obstinately persisted in opposing all amusements of this sort) issued his warrants to four constables to take up Mr Wheeler for acting the part of *Portious* in the tragedy of *Cato*' (1712). A riot ensued when the actor was being taken to the House of Correction, during which he escaped, but the unfortunate Whitley 'fell in the fray and was carried in a very bloody, not to say dangerous condition to the House of Correction'.[21]

---

[21] *Nottingham Journal*, 8 January 1763, quoted in Payne, Michael, 'Mr Whitley and his Company of Comedians: Nottingham St Mary's Gate Theatre, 1761-1865', *Transactions of the Thoroton Society*, Vol.109, Nottingham (2005), p.113.

The legal situation was modified by the Local Licensing Act of 1752 that allowed magistrates in London and Westminster and within a radius of 20 miles to grant licences to places of amusement, but this did not help greater Lincolnshire. The accession of King George III in 1760 was followed by developments in all forms of leisure, stimulated by a booming economy after the end of the Seven Years' War (1756-63). Alongside the plays of Shakespeare and Restoration dramatists were new works portraying the ideas and interests of the age. The tone was set by King George and Queen Charlotte who were ardent lovers of the stage, and commanded over three hundred performances between 1776 and 1800. The actor David Garrick (1717-79) single-handedly transformed the theatre world, acting with unprecedented naturalism, producing with prodigious energy, and giving his profession a respectability it never had before. Success spread to the provinces, where plays and farces were performed soon after they appeared in the London theatres, and later actors and actresses undertook gruelling tours around the country when the major London theatres closed for the summer. It was in the 1750s or '60s that a Lincolnshire theatre circuit came into being.

By the end of the eighteenth century the flourishing British stage was unparalleled anywhere in the world. There was another national surge of theatre building – Bath 1750, Norwich 1758, Bristol 1766, Stamford and Lincoln 1768. During the 1770s theatres were built in several other Lincolnshire towns though elsewhere the companies still had to use temporary theatres. When the Haymarket theatre in London was granted a Royal Patent in 1766, this encouraged some provincial managers to use the title 'Theatre Royal', such as Bath and Norwich in 1768 and York and Hull in 1769, though none of them had any right to the title. The need for a royal patent (or licence) was ended by the Theatre Regulation Act 1843 but no Lincolnshire theatre regularly used the title 'Theatre Royal' until the 1860s. Though not 'Theatres Royal', the main theatres in this county did become an established part of the social scene in their respective towns.

Lincolnshire theatres gained some relief from the legal restrictions in 1788 with the Theatrical Representation Act that empowered magistrates away from London to license theatrical productions in the provinces for up to sixty days at a time, and so confer legitimacy, though no second licence was to be granted until eight months had elapsed after the first nor to any place within the same jurisdiction within six months. This encouraged annual seasons rather than several short visits in the course of a year. The 1788 Act also offered the equivalent of London patents to theatres in selected provincial towns, though none were in Lincolnshire. Another boom in theatre building followed and by 1805 there were 279 theatres or recognised places of theatrical entertainment in Britain.[22]

---

[22] Booth, Michael R., Southern, Richard, Marker, Frederick and Lise-Lone, and Davies, Robertson, *The Revels History of Drama in English*, Vol.IV 1750-1880, London (1975), pp.40, 41; Mackintosh, Iain and Ashton, Geoffrey, *The Georgian Playhouse: Actors, Artists, Audiences and Architecture, 1730-1830*, London (1975), items 311-16.

Actor managers seeking an annual licence had to be obsequious to the influential people even in small places. They submitted a respectful petition like this one to the Kesteven magistrates at their general quarter sessions held at Bourne on 3 July 1832:

> *The humble petition of Joseph Smedley, Comedian, sheweth that your Petitioner prays your worships, leave and licence to open the theatre at Market Deeping for the performance of such plays, farces, and other entertainments of the stage as have been, or may be, acted at the Theatres in Westminster and duly submitted to inspection of the Lord Chamberlain. To commence on or about the* [blank] *day of September next ensuing and to continue for the usual period made and provided for by Act of Parliament.*[23]

The Court then made an Order, such as this one issued by the Beverley magistrates in general Quarter Sessions on 13 July 1829:

> *Ordered that Joseph Smedley comedian be and he is hereby licensed to open a Theatre at Great Driffield in the said East Riding and to perform Theatrical Amusements therein from the 8th day of September to the 1st day of November next.*[24]

Approval of the petition was usually a formality and the results of a refusal for an established company on a regular circuit could be disastrous. In April 1803 the magistrates at Nottingham turned down the application by the managers of the Stamford company, until a current election was over, because they were 'apprehensive that the opening of the theatre might, at this period, be dangerous to the peace of the town'.[25] In January 1816 the Boston magistrates, 'in consideration of the depressed state of the times', refused a licence for Thomas Shaftoe Robertson to perform in the town, which was one of his main venues.[26] With no income for several weeks, but a company to support and rent to pay, this refusal must have been a major contribution to the manager finding himself in the Lincoln debtors prison a few months later.

The effects of such occasional refusals showed how central theatre had become to the local social scene. In terms of quantity, if not perhaps in quality, there was more live theatre in Lincolnshire in the long eighteenth century than at any time before or since. Not only was theatre more abundant in the Georgian period, it was also different from twenty-first century theatre in many other respects, as will be described in the next two chapters.

---

[23] Lincolnshire County Archives, KQS/F/Clerk'sPapers/9(1832)/10/5.
[24] Lincolnshire County Archives, LLHS/38/5/9.
[25] *SM*, 29 April 1803.
[26] *SM*, 12 January 1816.

2

A NIGHT AT THE THEATRE

WHAT WAS a night at the theatre like for an audience in Georgian Lincolnshire? It was certainly different from the sort of evening we are used to today. The excitement of actors performing live before an audience, with the risks and opportunities that involves, is the same in both periods, but it is perhaps only at pantomimes and shows by magicians and stand-up comedians that we get an echo of the lively interaction between Georgian actors and their audiences. Most of the time we now sit quietly in darkness to observe what is happening on the stage and to laugh and applaud in the right places. There will be just one play and it will be repeated for several successive nights.

How different it was in Georgian times. Then people would go for a whole evening's entertainment. Theatre audiences did not sit in darkness and silence as they do in the twenty-first century. House lights could not be turned down. Candles would blaze in the chandeliers all night, their smoke somewhat obscuring the view of the stage by the end of the programme. The night's entertainment would include at least two plays, which might be tragedy, comedy, farce or pantomime with dances, songs, music, comic turns, acrobats, performing animals or transparencies showing topical events before, between and after those plays. There was as much activity among the audience as on the stage. In the lighted auditorium there was talking, laughing,

Interior of Richmond Theatre, Yorkshire. Note the apron stage projecting forward and doors on each side in front of the proscenium arch.
Courtesy of the Georgian Theatre Royal, Richmond.

In 1946 this door was discovered in the cellar of Stamford theatre and was recognised as a Proscenium Door, the only one surviving in this country. The measured drawing is by H. F. Traylen, FRIBA.
From Richard Southern, The Georgian Playhouse *(1948).*

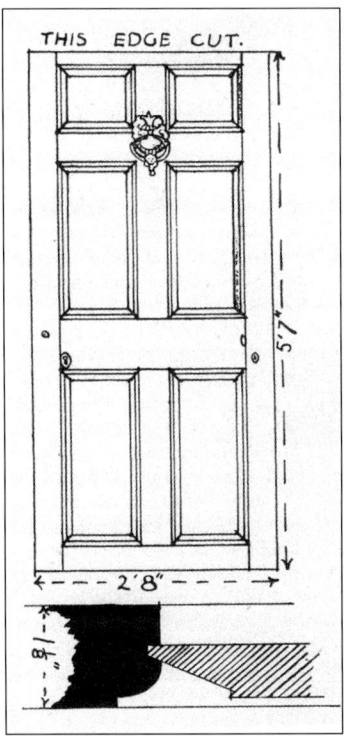

flirting, drinking, eating, walking about, applause, hisses, other distractions and inattention that gave life and colour to the house. Some people would attend for the first part of the programme, others for the second part, so there would be coming and going during the evening. Some of the audience actually had to walk across the stage to get to their seats in the boxes.

Most theatres were smaller than now and the architecture and lighted auditorium encouraged the audience to interact with the stage. Actors and audiences were much closer to each other, occupying a single space, and most acting was on the forestage that projected well in front of the proscenium arch with the audience on three sides of the performers. The audience could feel intimately involved, exchanging remarks with the players. The scenery was at first little more than an insipid background to the performance. Actors did not come on through the scenery, but through doors, one on each side of the stage, in front of the proscenium. In 1948 the remains of a door, believed to be one of these proscenium doors, was found in the cellar of Stamford theatre and is still on display in the Art Centre.[1] The style of acting was different, including a language of gesture and expression with less emphasis on naturalism. Much of the speech and action was given directly to the audience rather than to the other players on the stage. As the auditorium was lit the actors could see the reactions of the audience and respond to them.[2]

The Programme

The first rule for success in the theatre is to choose a play the public will pay to see. The plays could be tragedies, depicting man as the victim of destiny yet superior to it, comedies that differed from tragedy in having a happy ending, or farces that were popular comedy with horseplay and highly improbable situations. The eighteenth century was the Age of Enlightenment and thinkers were concerned to know how suffering and tragedy could be averted, so the drama they preferred were comedies and romances rather than classical tragedy where the good man did not always win. They wanted a happy ending so in *King Lear* (1605), as performed in this age, *Cordelia* did not die and *Romeo and Juliet* (1595) also ended well.[3] Plays of the late eighteenth century followed political trends in tending to replace unquestioning loyalty to a hereditary monarch by a newer, more democratic version of civic virtue that promoted the people's welfare. Many so called tragedies of this period were really romances, concerned to exhibit ideal virtue and they had a high-minded polished political rhetoric. In the early nineteenth century romantic tragedies often showed the state as a nightmare oppressor.[4]

---

[1] Southern, Richard, *The Georgian Playhouse*, London (1948), p.32.
[2] Taylor, David, 'Discoveries and recoveries in the laboratory of Georgian theatre', *New Theatre Quarterly* Vol.27, No.3 (2011), pp.236, 238, 240.
[3] Payne, Michael, 'Mr Whitley and his Company of Comedians; Nottingham St Mary's Gate Theatre, 1761-1865', *Transactions of the Thoroton Society*, Vol.109, Nottingham (2005), p.120.
[4] Booth, Michael R., *et al*, *The Revels History of Drama in English, Vol.IV 1750-1850*, London (1975), Susan Staves *Tragedy*, pp.89, 94, 95.

Comedy changed, leaving behind the acerbic wit and libertine cynicism of the aristocratic Restoration stage and underwent a 'sentimental revolution', adopting a more refined, polished and genteel tone that reflected the manners, follies and concerns of the serious-minded middle class that was rising in power and influence. To literate Georgians 'sentiment' meant the capacity to feel strongly, to have a sense of right and wrong in matters of morality and taste, and it influenced the search for the 'sublime' in religion, literature, architecture and natural scenery. What critics wanted were comedies with a moral tendency, or at least less offence to decency. The new genre of sentimental comedy was developed in contrast to the more traditional 'laughing comedy'.[5]

To the annoyance of serious playgoers, pantomime remained a successful popular entertainment throughout the Georgian period. It was different from what we now know by this name. It included characters from the Italian Commedia dell'arte – Harlequin, Colombine and Pantaloon – and had a serious story running through it but essentially included spectacle, acrobats, song, dance, travelogue, farce and special effects. Pantomime traditionally used body language, action without speech, although Harlequin did sometimes speak. It appealed to the senses rather than to reason, downplaying characterisation and plot development. During the Georgian period the Clown became the central character; Harlequin's role declined but his name continued in nearly every title. It also became more patriotic and nationalistic.[6]

There would be one theatre season each year, with plays every week for one or two months, but nothing for the rest of the year while the company of comedians visited other towns on their circuit. Performances were usually on four nights a week, Monday, Wednesday, Friday and Saturday, so with two plays per night they could put on eight different plays in a week. It was generally said that the main play of the evening was for the 'quality' and the afterpiece for the commoners. Afterpieces were often known as 'the farce' regardless of content and were frequently comedies.[7] Many of them had themes relating to servants' lives and social status, whether as tricksters or loyal servants. Sometimes the nights of performance might be changed, so in Race Weeks the company could stretch themselves to performances on each day that there had been a horse race. If a play proved popular in the early part of the season, it could be repeated later in response to public demand. The company had a repertoire of dozens of plays; a few were good and are still performed, but many quickly vanished leaving only an intriguing title. It was not an era of great writing for the stage, and the rewards for the dramatist were trivial in comparison with those of the successful novelist or

---

[5] Langford, Paul, *A Polite and Commercial People, England 1727-1783*, Oxford (1989), pp.461, 463, 466, 565.
[6] Booth, Michael R., *op. cit.*, O'Brien, John, *Pantomime*, pp.103-105, 108.
[7] Brewer, John, *The Pleasures of the Imagination: English Culture in the Eighteenth Century*, Abingdon (2013), p.264; Booth, Michael R., *op.cit.* Russell, Gillian, *Private Theatricals*, p.207.

even the admired poet. Audiences, like the actors, placed more emphasis on the interpretation of plays rather than on the words of the text.[8]

On 13 July 1781 the programme at Stamford included the tragedy *The Distress'd Mother* (1712), an interlude written by a local gentleman, then a second interlude taken from the farce *The Devil upon two Sticks* (1768), and finally the farce *The Deaf Lover* (1780). As on many occasions, there was a popular old play and a new one that had been a recent success in London together with some local material. In 1787 the playbill for the Gainsborough theatre included one play, tumblers, feats on the slack wire and 'The Egyptian Pyramid' of 'men piled on men'.[9] The local season could include some Shakespeare plays, 150-year-old Restoration comedies and recent plays that were 20 or 30 years old, but audiences also wanted to have the latest popular London plays that may be only a few weeks or months old. The educated part of the local audience would know about the newest plays appearing in the capital from reports and reviews in London newspapers, magazines and the letters of friends and would want to see these plays. In September 1778 Matthew Flinders, surgeon of Donington and father of the famous navigator, had started taking the monthly *Theatre Magazine*, of which each number contained a tragedy, a comedy, a farce and two good engravings.[10] To attract the knowledgeable audience to the local theatre the manager would go to the great expense of having the prompt book copied in London, if the play was not yet in print, and his cast would learn their parts in this addition to their repertoire.

Even as early as 1660 Shakespeare's plays were regarded as old fashioned and they were changed for the contemporary audience. In particular the actor/manager David Garrick (1717-79) modernised them for the Georgian taste and when he retired in 1776 he had restored the Bard to the very centre of the English stage. Seasons in each Lincolnshire town usually included at least one of Shakespeare's plays. During the late Georgian period the *Stamford Mercury* carried advertisements for 284 performances of his plays, and 161 of those were for just five plays – *Hamlet* (49) *Othello* (31), *Richard III* (28), *As You Like It* (28) and *The Merchant of Venice* (25). The large number of performances of those plays was in part due to visits to Lincolnshire by the London stars Edmund Kean (1787-1833) and William Charles Macready (1793-1873) who played the roles for which they were best known. The remaining 123 performances were for seventeen different plays, of which the most performed were *Cymbeline* (22) and *Romeo and Juliet* (20). There were only 19 performances of *Macbeth* but they were all in the latter part of the period, from October 1806. There were eleven performances of *Much Ado About Nothing*, ten

---

[8] Brewer, John, *op. cit.*, p.273.
[9] Parker, B.J., *The Theatre of Gainsborough. From 1772 until 1850*, thesis (1963) in Gainsborough library, p.53.
[10] Beardsley, Martyn and Bennett, Nicholas (eds), *Grateful to Providence. The Diary and Accounts of Matthew Flinders, Surgeon, Apothecary and Man-Midwife 1775-1802*, Vol.1 1775-1784, Lincoln Record Society Vol.95, Lincoln (2007), p.72.

Edmund Kean (1787–1833) was the outstanding star of his time and came to perform in Lincolnshire on several occasions. Painted by George Clint in 1820.
© *Victoria and Albert Museum, London.*

of *The Winter's Tale* and nine of *King John*. The latter play dealt with a war between England and France and so was topical at the time of the Napoleonic wars. Some plays that are now well known got few performances in Lincolnshire in the Georgian period. There were seven for *Henry IV,* five each for *King Lear* and *Twelfth Night* and two each for *Julius Caesar, The Tempest* and *Henry VIII*. In the whole period there was only one advertised performance of *The Merry Wives of Windsor*, in July 1834, and just one of *The Taming of the Shrew* as late as February 1842.

At the start of the nineteenth century a new form of drama appeared on the British stage, known as melodrama, in which a musical accompaniment emphasised the reactions of the characters at crucial moments in the play.[11] Some elements of

---

[11] Mackintosh, Iain and Ashton, Geoffrey, *The Georgian Playhouse: Actors, Artists, Audiences and Architecture, 1730-1830*, London (1975), item 29.

this new genre already existed and had appeared in *The Castle Spectre* (1797) by 'Monk' Lewis, but the distinctive melodramatic stage play really developed in France in the late eighteenth century. It was in part a response to the great revolutions and upheavals happening in the real world and reported in the newspapers. It was the theatrical expression of the romantic movement, which in poetry started in 1798 when Wordsworth and Coleridge published the *Lyrical Ballads*. Melodrama used black and white heroes and villains, without character development, was interested in the supernatural, aroused violent emotions and produced sensational effects, using the new developments in lighting and scenery. Some of Shakespeare's plays included ghosts, witches, fairies and the supernatural, which could bring a frisson of dramatic horror.

A play by Guilbert de Pixerecourt of 1800 was translated by the radical playwright Thomas Holcroft as *A Tale of Mystery* (1802) and was the first play performed in Britain to be called a 'melo-drama'. On 15 March 1799 *Blue Beard* (1798) performed at Stamford theatre was called a 'Dramatic Romance' but the first reference to 'Melo Drama' (sic) in the *Stamford Mercury* was to advertise a performance of *A Tale of Mystery* at Boston on 2 March 1803.[12] By 1816 melodrama had ousted tragedy as the dominant genre in the British theatre and Edmund Kean turned tragedies into melodramas that captured the spirit of the age. It was Kean's intensity that thrilled Regency audiences. Melodrama remained popular for several decades.

The stage could also present current events such as battles and the funerals of great men. On 9 April 1781 the Stamford theatre evening included 'a very grand and exact representation of the Sea-Fight off Scarborough between Paul Jones in the *Bonne Homme Richard* and Captain Pearson in the *Serapis*'. This battle on 23 September 1779 had ended the attacks on British ports by John Paul Jones of the United States Navy during the American War of Independence. Drama could be embellished by back-lit transparencies used for dramatic effects as well as to show current events such as the funeral of Lord Nelson in 1806. These transparencies were made by using translucent paint on loosely woven cloth such as gauze or scrim, which when lit from the front showed one picture, and produced a magical effect when the sheet was lit from behind. Until the end of the eighteenth century the effect was not very conspicuous, given the poor quality of the lighting and the fact that the auditorium itself was lit, but after 1785 the argand lamp was used and that increased light from oil three-fold.[13]

---

[12] *Stamford Mercury*, 15 March 1799, 25 February 1803.
[13] Rosenfeld, Sybil, *Georgian Scene Painters and Scene Painting*, Cambridge (1981), p.56; Booth, Michael R., *op. cit.*, Baugh, Christopher, *Scenography and technology*, p.52.

Music

Music was a central element in the Georgian theatre, owing in part to the popularity of a style of English ballad opera initiated by John Gay's *The Beggar's Opera*. That was first performed in London in 1728 and was staged in Stamford Guildhall in April that same year.[14] That style was in turn the basis of a new type of pastiche opera that enjoyed great success in the 1760s, including *Love in a Village* and *The Maid of the Mill*. Many other entertainments contained music to a greater or lesser extent and until 1800 pantomimes nearly always had continuous music, both vocal and instrumental. The works of Shakespeare as 'altered and improved', often had incidental music added. In addition there could be music and dancing between the acts of a play or the items of an evening's programme. Some actors could also play instruments and the theatre's orchestra would sometimes get extra help from local musicians, such as bands attached to militia units. At Peterborough theatre on 27 July 1807 'for this night only, by permission of the officers, the Harper of the Royal Anglesey Band will perform several favorite (sic) airs on the harp'.[15]

Songs and sketches with a local theme could be inserted into the evening's entertainment. At Grantham in January 1805 there was a new song called 'The Grantham and Gonerby Landlord's Defence Against Invasion, or no accommodation for the Emperor Bonaparte' that included reference to all the inn signs in the town. Eighteen months later in Stamford the evening began with 'A Pantomimical Prelude, called Harlequin's Trip from the Moon, or, A Visit to Stamford' with a comic song by James Robertson describing the town, Burghley, Wothorpe, the females, etc. as well as a description of Nottingham and a tribute to Lord Nelson and 'our Brave Seamen'. The season at Lincoln in 1820 included a comic song by Mr Raynor called 'The Humours of Lincoln Races'.[16]

Publicity and Bespeaks

To get people into the theatre the townsfolk and local gentry had to be told what was on offer each night. The manager would have posters and playbills printed by a local firm and that cost was significant. A hundred playbills cost only 1s 6d but fifty posters cost 10s. In the 1820s Thomas Manly paid the printer Drewery of Derby £17 8s 1d over a period of nine months.[17] Playbills were produced every day that the actors were performing and gave details of the coming evening's programme. The playbill man delivered them to the homes of likely customers and to shopkeepers to put in their windows. He was usually accompanied by a performer, no matter how severe the weather. In January 1826 Joseph Smedley said that playbills for Grimsby theatre were delivered not only to all houses in the town but also to thirteen named

---

[14] *SM*, 18 April 1728.
[15] *SM*, 24 July 1807.
[16] *SM*, 11 January 1805, 4 July 1806, 8 September 1820.
[17] Rosenfeld, Sybil, 'The Theatrical Notebooks of T.H. Wilson Manly', *Theatre Notebook*, Vol.7, No.1, London (October, December 1952), p.7.

local villages, and he asked people who did not regularly receive them to complain to him 'as persons are employed for the purpose'.[18] In February 1839 he gave the same message in a playbill circulated to villages around Brigg.[19]

Sometimes several members of the cast would parade the streets in costume, with a drummer to help drum up custom. Tate Wilkinson said that once in the 1760s the players in William Herbert's Lincoln company, when playing at Grantham, refused to parade the streets of the town with drum and trumpet, thinking it was beneath their dignity. The Marquess of Granby (1721-70), military hero and son of the Duke of Rutland of Belvoir Castle, sent for the manager of the troupe and said to him:

> *Mr Manager, I like a play, I like a player, and shall be glad to serve you. But, my good friend, why are you all so suddenly offended at and averse to the noble sound of a drum? I like it and all the inhabitants like it. Put my name on your playbill, provided you drum, but not otherwise. Try the effect on tomorrow night. If then you are as thinly attended as you have lately been, shut up your house at once, but if it succeeds, drum away.*

The manager reported this to his troupe, and after some debate, they voted *nem con* in favour of the drum. To their pleasant astonishment their little theatre was brimfull on the sound of the drum and Lord Granby's name.

> *After which night, they row-didi-dowed away, had a very successful season, and drank flowing bowls to the health of the noble Marquess.*[20]

Having a prominent local body or person like the Marquess of Granby 'bespeak' a play for one night was a device regularly used by country theatres in the Georgian period to boost attendance. At the start of the local season there would still be some dates for which a play had not yet been chosen and the manager would visit the principal inhabitants of the town and neighbourhood, and also local clubs and societies, and invite them to select a play. The name of the sponsor of a bespeak was always included in the advertising in order to attract the supporters and friends of the person or body. The pieces having been chosen, the patron or patrons attended on the night with their friends and followers, and each patron was given a playbill printed on white satin. Bespoke nights usually got large audiences but that could reduce attendance on other nights. They were sometimes a failure; stewards of races bespoke performances at Nottingham in 1821 that produced £43 8s 0d and at Derby in July 1826 £41 11s 0d, but at Stamford in 1829 only £8 11s 6d was raised.[21]

When local theatre was at the height of its popularity, from the 1790s through to the 1820s, the most regular sponsors of bespeaks in Lincolnshire were the militia, usually the officers of the local troops of volunteer infantry and cavalry. These

---

[18] Playbill, Grimsby Library, 4 January 1826.
[19] Playbill, Brigg, 19 February 1839, in Lincolnshire County Archives LLHS/38/5/4/2gii.
[20] Wilkinson, Tate, *Memoirs of his own life by Tate Wilkinson, patentee of the Theatre Royal, York and Hull*, Vol.2, York (1790), p.248.
[21] Rosenfeld, Sybil, *op. cit.*, p.9

militia had been raised to keep order within Britain during the war with France, but apart from a few locally controlled riots there was not much for them to do and they swiftly gained a reputation for being more interested in drilling and parties than in any kind of action. Some of the military sponsors included the privates as well as the officers, and one bespeak suggests some dissent in the ranks. When *The Hero of the North* (1802) and *Love Laughs at Locksmiths* (1803) were performed in March 1806 it was 'By Desire of the Non-commissioned Officers and the major part of the Privates of the Boston Loyal Volunteer Infantry'. Evidently some of the privates did not want to be associated with this event.[22] In August 1827 a night at Grimsby theatre was 'for the Officers and Crew of His Majesty's Revenue Cruizers (sic) *The Greyhound* and *Lapwing*'.[23]

The military were not the only ones to bespeak evenings at the theatre. Other bodies included, at different times, the Stamford Cricket Club, 'the Gentlemen Farmers and Graziers' who socialised at particular inns, 'the Young Ladies of Miss Winter's School at Collingham' at Newark, and 'the Young Gentlemen of Dr Orme's Academy' at Louth, 'the Ladies of Grimsby', Book Clubs and News Rooms attached to inns, and Gentlemen of the Amateur Harmonic Society of Grantham. Sometimes the group was defined as 'The Bachelors' of a particular town; on 13 October 1824 the 'Bachelors of Market Deeping' bespoke *To Marry or Not to Marry* (1806) by Elizabeth Inchbald and *How to Die for Love* (1814) by August von Kotzebue – we can see where their interests lay. One of the more unusual groups was defined as 'Members of Mr Green's Oyster Club' at Grantham in 1828. Another was 'Gentlemen of the Anacreontic Society' who met weekly at the Fleece in Louth to praise love and wine. From the 1840s there were also bespeaks by branches of the new Order of Odd Fellows. Very occasionally there were bespeaks by the Mayor or the Magistrates of particular towns and in 1845 during the railway mania one night at Lincoln theatre was at 'the Desire of the Cambridge and Lincoln, and Direct Northern' who were the supporters of two complementary railway schemes. The actor-managers James Shaftoe Robertson, Thomas Robertson and Joseph Smedley were Freemasons and used that to attract audiences. When Tom Robertson was in Wisbech each year he put on one night's performance for the 'Lodge of Strict Benevolence of the Ancient and Honourable Society of Free and Accepted Masons held at the Vine Inn, Wisbech', and the brethren all walked in procession from the inn to the theatre; the Epilogue was given by 'Brother and Sister Robertson'.[24] Joseph Smedley joined the St Botolph's Lodge of Freemasons in 1828.[25]

The companies of comedians also advertised in the local weekly newspapers. The earliest surviving copies of the *Stamford Mercury* date from the 1720s and by the end of the eighteenth century it was the main newspaper for all of Lincolnshire

---

[22] *SM*, 6 March 1806.
[23] Playbill, Grimsby Library, 8 August 1827.
[24] *SM*, 11 April 1806, 10 April 1807.
[25] Dixon, William, *A History of Freemasonry in Lincolnshire, being a record of all extinct and existing Lodges*, Lincoln (1894), p.239.

and adjacent parts. In the 1720s and 1730s there were one or two isolated notices for plays and operas in the *Mercury* and a few more in the 1770s, but from 1781 such advertisements started to increase. Between 1785 and 1829 there were advertisements for plays in one town or another nearly every week, with but few exceptions. The advertisements were at their most numerous and most detailed in the two periods 1791-96 and 1803-29 but in less prosperous times they were very short or omitted altogether.

The Auditorium

When any theatre opened for performances it would need to be aired, as out of season many of them had the pit floored over level with the stage and were used as warehouses or granaries, which could leave a musty smell. The notice for a performance at Stamford on 19 January 1784 said that 'particular care will be taken that the House is well air'd' but the problem never went away and for the performance on 14 March 1820 it was said at Stamford that 'The house will be thoroughly aired'.[26] Similar notices appeared at this and other local theatres in the intervening years. If the season started in winter the building would be cold and some years the managers stressed in their advertisements that the place would be heated and draughts excluded. In King's Lynn in Norfolk fires were lit on the stage for several days beforehand. In December 1802 to coddle his elite Grantham audience Robertson advertised that 'it having been suggested to him last year that the boxes admitted too great a current of air, so as to occasion it to be extremely cold' he had boarded up the Box Lobby at the theatre and erected a fireplace in it, then saying in November 1825 in Newark that 'fires have been kept constantly burning in the Stove that communicates with the boxes and the lower part of the theatre'.[27] As late as February 1848 it was said that people had avoided Gainsborough theatre because of its coldness, and to overcome that a new door had been added at the top of the stairs, and others made to fit, a new stove placed in the saloon and another in the centre of the theatre. Yet by the end of a successful evening the crowded theatre would be hot, smoky and airless, and ladies' fans were not only pretty but an essential evening accessory. Problems also occurred in midsummer. Audiences were reluctant to go into a theatre in hot weather as too many bodies crushed together could give the place a dank, sweaty smell by the end of the evening. Whitley at Stamford said, in June 1781:

> *As many friends to the theatre consider it rather a hardship to attend three times a week, particularly at this season, the company anxiously studious to remove every shadow of complaint, means to comply with their wishes and perform only two nights in each week.*[28]

In May 1787 Mr Pero was at Melton Mowbray theatre and advertised 'every method [has been] taken to make it as cool as possible'.[29]

---

[26] *SM*, 25 December 1783, 10 March 1820.
[27] *SM*, 10 December 1802, 11 November 1825.
[28] *SM*, 28 June 1781.
[29] *Leicester Journal*, 20 May 1787.

During most of the Georgian period theatres were lit by oil lamps and candles, either cheap tallow candles (rendered animal fat) though they were smoky and smelly, or wax candles, made from bees wax, which were more expensive but less prone to smell and smoke. During the course of the evening smoke gradually blurred the view of the stage. Gas lighting was first used to light a stage and auditorium in 1816 at London's Royalty, later the East London Theatre, in Wellclose Square, Whitechapel.[30] From the 1820s it was available in some towns of the Lincoln circuit. It was cheaper than wax candles, gave greater illumination and produced more easily graduated effects on the stage. A disadvantage of gas lighting was that it gave off acid that damaged paintings and tapestries, though people did not always understand that at the time. Derby theatre had gas lighting installed in May 1821 as did Wakefield theatre in October 1823, Halifax and Nottingham in 1824 and Stamford in 1828. The cost of gas at Derby was 8s 7d a night, but a small discount was allowed, and a season of twenty nights at Nottingham cost £9 (9s a night).[31] Boston theatre perhaps had gas lighting from 1826 when the works opened. When the theatre was advertised for sale in 1839 it was said that the whole of the gas fittings were nearly new but nine years later in October 1848 it 'had a narrow escape from being destroyed by fire, in consequence of the unsound state of the gas fittings'.[32] Lincoln gas works opened in 1829 and 'Mrs Robertson had 13 lights at the theatre and was charged 4s per night on the assumption that no more than five hours of lighting would be required each night on average'.[33] The streets of Newark were first lit by gas on Friday 21 December 1832 and 'Mrs Robertson's company of comedians were allowed the advantage of it during their performance on Wednesday evening'.[34] When Leicester theatre was first lit by gas in 1833 it was advertised that 'the oil, which, from its smell and smoke, has for so many years been a cause of great complaint, is *entirely removed* from the interior of the theatre'.[35] Gaslight in Sleaford was available from 1 October 1839 and Joseph Smedley applied for a gas supply to the theatre in April 1840, just a couple of months before he sold the building.[36]

In 1771 Sir Robert Talbot wrote that 'as it was in Athens ... the playhouse [in London] ... is for all classes of the nation. The peer of the realm, the gentleman, the merchant, the citizen, the clergyman, the tradesman, and their wives, equally resort thither to take their places, and the crowd is great'.[37] This was as true in Lincolnshire as it was in the capital. The leading patrons in any Lincolnshire town were the

---

[30] Merwe, Pieter van der, *Theatre in the Regency Era*, The Society for Theatre Research Conference Notes, London (2016), p.23.
[31] Rosenfeld, Sybil, *op. cit.*, p.7
[32] *SM*, 27 October 1848.
[33] Roberts, D.E., *The Lincoln Gas Undertaking 1828-1949*, Leicester (1981), p.9.
[34] *SM*, 21 December 1832.
[35] Leacroft, Helen and Richard, *The Theatre in Leicestershire*, Leicester (1986), p.16.
[36] Personal communication from Chris Page, quoting reference dated 14 April 1840 in Sleaford Gas Light Company minute book.
[37] The *Oxford Magazine*, quoted in Mackintoch, Iain and Ashton, Geoffrey, *The Georgian Playhouse: Actors, Artists, Audiences and Architecture, 1730-1830*, London (1975), after item 217.

This engraving of 1733 shows spikes around the orchestra pit, candles for illumination, and fruit sellers.
Engraving 'The Laughing Audience' by William Hogarth (1697–1764).

urban middle class, a small group of lawyers, merchants, doctors and clergy who were the magnates of the town. Farmers and gentry from miles around, together with the occasional aristocrat, crowded into towns for the short season. Many years later William Robertson reminisced about how many wealthy landlords and tenant farmers received friends and family visitors and made a few weeks holiday while they spiritedly supported the plays, dances and concerts of the season.[38] The audience was in three separate parts of the auditorium, reflecting the divisions of society, each with its own entrance along narrow corridors to the pit and boxes, and a separate staircase to the gallery. In the purpose-built theatres these parts were on different levels: the boxes were usually on three sides and level with the stage, the pit in front of them with backless benches was about three feet lower and

---

[38] Gould, Mervyn, *Boston and Spalding Entertainment and the Aspland Howdens*, Wakefield (2005), p.16.

a sloping floor, and above the boxes was steeply raked fixed seating in the gallery, referred to as 'the gods'. The rail at the front of the gallery could not be too high or it would obscure the view of the stage, and on at least one occasion this led to tragedy. On Monday 1 December 1800 a boy named Creasey fell from the gallery of Gainsborough theatre onto some iron spikes, and was so badly injured that he died three days later.[39]

Boxes were an essential feature of a 'proper' theatre but some of the early purpose-built Georgian playhouses on Lincolnshire circuits, such as those at Gainsborough, Wakefield and Grantham, lacked them at first and Grimsby never had them. Boston had boxes since it was built in 1777 and they were added to Spalding theatre about 1793 and to Grantham in 1797. A box could be taken as a whole or its seats sold separately. A low partition separated each box from its neighbours and later private boxes were developed with partitions ceiling high, their own door and even curtains at the front. The 'front boxes' were at the back of the theatre and had the best view of the stage, and the 'stage boxes' on each side were virtually on the stage itself. A few theatres had two tiers of boxes, the best ones level with the stage and cheaper ones above them. The upper classes sat in the boxes, the professional men, tradesmen and a general cross-section of the middle class on benches in the pit, and the working class, including servants, journeymen, apprentices and their women folk, in the gallery. It appears that some of the gentry might even have sat on the stage as in July 1780 playbills for performances at Spalding carried a notice that 'As many complaints have been made of the obstructions to the Performance by admitting Gentlemen on the Stage, 'tis hoped that they will not be offended

Interior of Richmond Theatre, Yorkshire, showing the pit and boxes with low dividing walls all around them and the gallery over the top.
Courtesy of the Georgian Theatre Royal, Richmond.

[39] SM, 5 December 1800.

Occupants of the stage boxes were as close as possible to the action, as shown here in 1810.
From National Trust magazine, No.101, Spring 2004.

at being positively refused admittance in future'.[40] Sometimes people would sit in different places; wealthy tradesmen might sit in boxes, and the lower middle classes were sometimes found, for economic reasons, in the gallery. As places devoted to the pursuit of pleasure, and open to nearly all ranks of society, theatres ran the risk that normal social conventions might be relaxed too far, encouraging unacceptable levels of high-spiritedness and rivalry. Some people found it disagreeable in a small theatre 'for persons of the first quality, and those of the lowest rank, to be seated

---

[40] Playbill, 17 July 1780, Lincolnshire County Archives, Misc. Don. 94/11/5.

on the same benches together'.[41] The proportions of seats in the different areas are indicated by Nottingham's 1760 theatre of which it was said in 1854: 'The Boxes will seat about 140 persons, two Stage Boxes 16, and two Private Boxes 8, the Gallery about 350, and the Pit about 260'.[42] That gave a total of 774 which when full produced a house of about £70, with prices of 3s, 2s and 1s.

People wanting a good view from the pit or the gallery needed to arrive soon after the doors opened to find the best places on the benches, though the more prosperous might send a servant to occupy a seat until they arrived. In King's Lynn servants were forbidden to keep seats for their employers after Act 1 of the main play. The richer patrons with reserved box seats would often arrive just before the evening's entertainment began, when the rest of the theatre was full. The stage boxes were entered via the stage so sometimes latecomers walked across it even if the play had started. In October 1800 the manager of the Lincoln theatre said that ladies and gentlemen crossing the stage to get into their seats in those boxes, which some did even during crowded scenes, was 'much complained of and frequently found to interrupt the performance', so he respectfully informed the public that 'in future, the entrance to the stage boxes will be exactly the same as to the side boxes'.[43] When nobility or leading gentry arrived in the theatre they often received applause from the audience, regardless of what was happening on the stage. At the end of November 1814 the young widowed Lady Monson with her son Lord Monson and friends attended Lincoln theatre and they arrived at 7 o'clock. Lord Monson, who was only four years old, 'appeared for a short time to labour under great apprehensions not unnaturally caused by the very flattering marks of applause which greeted the arrival of the party from Burton Hall, but his lordship shortly after appeared much diverted' once the pantomime *Fairy of the Forest* began.[44]

Mindful of being part of the theatrical experience the audience was boisterous, voluble and occasionally violent. All classes were together and all could express enthusiasm or hostility to the drama. The theatre, like British society, accorded much liberty to the ordinary man. The young men in the pit, who were probably the most attentive spectators, offered criticism and comment. During the Regency period in particular fashionable young men were not only highly tailored dandies, with wigs, stockings, stays and make-up, but they were raucous in modishly expressing intellectual passions and human sympathy. The audience in the gallery might have taken their places as soon as the doors opened, which could be as long as an hour before the performance, so boredom could lead to mischief and they had a reputation for drunken and unruly behaviour. Cheers

---

[41] Borsey, Peter, *The English Urban Renaissance: Culture and Society in the Provincial Town, 1660-1770*, Oxford (1991), p.302.
[42] Payne, Michael, 'Mr Whitley and his Company of Comedians: Nottingham St Mary's Gate Theatre, 1761-1865', *Transactions of the Thoroton Society*, Vol.109, Nottingham (2005), p.115, quoting *Nottingham Weekly Journal*, 20 January 1854.
[43] *SM*, 24 October 1800.
[44] *SM*, 2 December 1814.

and jeers could be expected from the 'gods', accompanied by songs, laughter and flying fruit, and even broken glass tumblers, metal and wood could rain down onto the stage. The aristocracy, gentry and fashionable society in the boxes were sometimes more concerned about seeing and being seen than about watching the play.

Even Tom and Fanny Robertson, the manager and star of the Lincoln circuit, suffered assaults in the theatre and in the early years of the nineteenth century three incidents appeared in the *Stamford Mercury*. At Newark on 6 December 1802 farmer John Renshaw threw a half-pint glass from the gallery of the theatre which struck Fanny Robertson violently on her hip. On 5 January 1805 Thomas Chantry assaulted Thomas Wright while he was receiving the admission money at the door of Grantham theatre, and then attacked Tom Robertson, as a result of which several people, due to the pressure of the crowd, got in without paying. In both cases the offender gave money to the poor, paid Tom Robertson's expenses and put a public apology in the *Mercury*. A tougher stance was taken on 14 January 1804 when John Martin, until recently employed by Robertson as 'stage-keeper' of Lincoln theatre, was fined five guineas for assaulting Robertson one theatre night during the previous season.

Very occasionally the companies of comedians reached people who might not be regular playgoers. In September 1777 the County Hospital was opened in Drury Lane, Lincoln, and by 13 October the governors had accepted an offer by Nat Herbert for his company to perform a play there.[45] In Februry 1842 the *Stamford Mercury* reported that about a dozen patients from the Asylum mental hospital in Lincoln had attended the 'comic' part of the performance one night 'and conducted themselves with as much propriety as the sane part of the audience'.[46]

In the twenty-first century theatre performances often start at 7.30pm and finish about 10pm. Georgian evenings had more content and usually lasted a lot longer. The usual time for starting performances in Lincolnshire theatres for most of the long eighteenth century was 6.30pm, and the doors opened about one hour earlier, as at Spalding in March 1813 and Boston in March 1824. In September 1787 the Gainsborough theatre opened at 5.00pm and the curtain rose at 6.15pm. In 1794 at Stamford it was declared that the performance was 'To begin at half past six o'clock, to whatever company are then in the house', so there was no delay for late-comers. During Race Week in June 1800 the manager had to be more accommodating to the gentry and it was advertised that the programme was 'To begin as soon as the Race is over'.[47] Sometimes the hour of performance advanced and in 1804 at Wakefield (then part of Smedley's circuit) it was 6.45pm, and in 1805 7.00pm. One of the latest start times was at Louth in March 1826 when the doors opened at 7.30pm for a

---

[45] Lincolnshire Archivist's Report 7 (1955-56), p.34.
[46] *SM*, 25 February 1842.
[47] *SM*, 27 June 1800.

start at 8.00pm. The long and varied programme could finish late despite the early start. At Stamford in 1782 the programme started at 6.45pm and would finish by 11.00pm. In 1789 the curtain rose at 7.00pm and it was said that the 'Performance will not exceed Half past Ten'. When J. Robson Daniel brought a company to Boston in 1848 he announced that 'Doors open at half-past Six, commence at 7, and terminate at 11 o'clock'.

The Takings – tickets and boxes

Price inflation is now accepted as a normal part of life but from about 1770 to 1840, the price of tickets for most performances in all the Lincolnshire theatres changed hardly at all, usually being 3/- in the boxes, 2/- in the pit and 1/- in the gallery. These were the prices at Grantham in 1792 and Stamford in 1795, and in 1803 it was said that these prices applied to all the theatres in the Lincoln circuit.[48] The box prices refer, of course, to seats (on benches) in the boxes, not to entire boxes. Ticket prices might be increased at special times such as horse-racing weeks or when a London star appeared at the theatre. During Stamford Race Week in 1795 the prices were 3/-, 2/6 and 1/- with only the pit price being an increase. Totally different were the prices in some of the temporary theatres that were set up when the players arrived in a town as they would consist only of 'pit' and 'gallery', and in 1801 prices at such a theatre in Sleaford were 1d in the gallery and 2d in the pit, though sometimes they charged the same price as the purpose-built theatres.

In those theatres with two tiers of boxes, seats in the ones level with the stage cost more than those above them. In 1800 the prices at Grantham were: Boxes 3/-, Upper Boxes 2/6, Pit 2/- and Gallery 1/-. In 1775 seats in boxes at Stamford had cost 2/6, raised to 3/- by 1795, and in 1805 when that theatre had two tiers of boxes their prices were: Boxes 3/-, Pit and Upper Boxes 2/-, and Gallery 1/-. The Lincoln theatre rebuilt in 1805/6 also had two tiers of boxes though it seems they charged the same price for each tier – 3/6 in 1840.[49] In 1820 the highest prices in Lincoln were 4/- for the Stage Boxes. Prices were higher in King's Lynn with 4/- for the lower boxes, 3/- upper boxes, 2/- pit and 1/- gallery. However much the price of seats in boxes might vary, the pit was usually 2/- and the gallery always stayed at 1/-.

People in the boxes who only came for the second part of the programme would pay half-price, sometimes referred to as '2nd price', and in 1803 it was said that applied to all theatres in the Lincoln circuit.[50] In 1763 the London theatres had tried to abolish half-price admission but they both backed down, Covent Garden after a riot wrecked it and closed it for a week. In 1814 at Stamford half-price applied from 8.30pm, in 1823 from 9.15pm and in 1849 from 9pm. In 1820 and 1840 at Lincoln half price for the Boxes was 2/-. At Stamford Race Week in 1824 '2nd Prices' of 1/- off were offered for all seats except those in the Gallery, the reduced prices being:

---

[48] Warwick, Lou, *Theatre Unroyal; Or, They called them Comedians*, Northampton (1974), p.31.
[49] Clementson, Diana W., *The Theatre Royal, Lincoln*, thesis (1960) in Lincoln Central Library, p.37.
[50] Warwick, Lou, *ibid*.

Boxes 2/-, Pit 1/6, Upper Boxes 1/6 and 'no half-price in the Gallery' (which was still 1/-).[51] At Lincoln theatre in September 1806 'Children under 10 Years of Age [were] admitted at Half Price' and Stamford theatre in 1814 said that 'children and schools [were] admitted at half-price from the commencement', though it is not clear if that was general or was special for those particular performances.[52] In 1848 J. Robson Daniel charged low prices at Boston: Boxes 2s 6d, Pit 1s 6d and Gallery 6d, with 'Second-prices' Boxes 1s 6d, Pit 1s, No half-price in the Gallery. Children were admitted at the start to the Boxes 1s 6d, Pit 1s.

The money taken if all seats were sold at full price was a measure of the capacity and value of a theatre. As indicated above, Nottingham theatre was a £70 house. In 1803 the takings at the Stamford theatre when full were said to amount to £60, and Lincoln £60 to £70. When the new theatre at Boston was built in 1805/6 the takings could amount to £100 and in 1803 a full house at Grantham would produce £50. In July 1803 Thomas Robertson undertook to give one night's takings at each of his theatres to the 'Patriotic Fund at Lloyds' 'for those who suffer or merit in the defence of their King and Country'. One year later he published the result, listing each theatre and the amount that had been raised on those particular nights. This was as follows:

> Lincoln - £29 11s 0d
> Spalding - £29 12s 6d
> Newark - £33 15s 0d
> Grantham - £19 14s 6d
> Boston - £15 1s 6d
> Wisbech - £17 18s 0d
> Northampton - £12 4s 6d
> Peterborough - £9 5s 0d
> Huntingdon - £8 3s 0d

making a grand total of £175 5s 0d.[53]

These takings are less, in some cases quite a lot less, than the figures quoted above for full houses and that might be due to those paying half-price. For this fund-raising effort he was called the patriotic manager, and he said that 'what will be a pleasure and gratification to myself is being able to give my aid to the Defenders of my King and Country!'[54]

In later years, when the theatres were anxious to get customers through the doors, they sometimes made a point of declaring that the usual prices would still apply and no extra charge would be made even when a star such as Edmund Kean was appearing. By the 1840s moral attitudes were discouraging theatre attendance and those theatres that were still open reduced their prices, which further worsened

---

[51] *SM*, 25 June 1824.
[52] Playbill, Lincoln, 15 September 1806; SM, 4 November 1814.
[53] *SM*, 10 August 1804.
[54] Richards, John, 'Thomas Shaftoe Robertson and The Theatric Tourist', *Theatre Notebook*, Vol. XXIX, No.1, London (1975), p.5.

their financial situation. In 1856 the prices at Lincoln theatre were: boxes 2/6, upper boxes 1/6, pit 1/- and gallery 6d. One of the most detailed descriptions of prices was given for Stamford theatre in 1849. This stated that 'Two Private Boxes have been constructed in the Dress Circle, admission 4/- or One Guinea for 6 Persons. Prices of admission – Boxes 3/-, Upper Boxes 2/-, Pit 1/-, Gallery 6d. 2nd price to Boxes only at 9 o'clock'.[55] When the Stamford theatre finally closed in June 1871 the prices were down to 2/-, 1/- and 6d.

On the night of a performance payments for admission could be made at the theatre, but before then the usual place to buy tickets was from the printer who produced the handbills. When an evening was for the 'benefit' of a member of the company, advance tickets could be bought from that person's lodgings. Newspaper advertisements indicate the ad hoc ticket sale arrangements at other times. In 1778 at Stamford tickets could 'be had at the Bull, the Crown, Printing-office in Maiden-lane and the George in St Martin's'. The following year they could be bought 'at the usual places, and of Mr Sailes at Mr Broughton's, Baker, near All-Saints Church'. In 1785 at Stamford tickets could also be obtained from 'Mr Spencer at the theatre each day from ten till one' and two years later the theatre was open to sell tickets from 10.00am to 2.00pm.[56] In 1794 it was said that tickets in Lincoln could be obtained 'at the usual places Up-hill and below'. In 1831 they could be bought 'at the principal inns' in Lincoln. When the theatre held a benefit in 1813 for Boston mariners in French prisons tickets could be had from 'all the Booksellers in Boston'. When J. Robson Daniel opened Boston theatre in 1848 he said that 'tickets could be had of the manager at his residence in High Street, or at the theatre from 12 to 2.00; or at Mr Joshua Beverley's bookshop in the Market Place'. Beverley was also the printer of the handbills.[57]

The elite members of society who sat in the boxes would send their servants to visit the 'box-keeper', usually a local trader in the town, who allocated the boxes and kept a record in the box-book. The premises of the traders who did this were referred to as the box-office. Customers could buy tickets at the same time as booking a box, or leave the ticket purchase until later. In 1788 the manager of the Stamford theatre received complaints that people had booked boxes but had not then taken tickets and did not attend, so they had stopped other people from using those boxes. To avoid this in future he asked that people should buy tickets at the same time as booking a box.[58] In September 1806 during Lincoln Race Week it was stated that 'No Places secured unless paid for at the Time of Taking'[59]. In 1775 the box-keeper in Stamford was Mr Sherwood in St Mary's Street, but by 1778 it had been taken

---

[55] *SM*, 23 March 1849.
[56] *SM*, 3 June 1785, 6 April 1787.
[57] Lincolnshire County Archives, 3/ANC/7/23/49; Letter No.13a.
[58] *SM*, 20 June 1788.
[59] Playbill, Lincoln, 10 September 1806.

back in-house and places could 'be taken at the Theatre from Ten o'clock till One, and at other Times of Mr O'Brien (only) at Mr Kitson's in St George's Street'.[60]

Some box-keepers and their families held those positions for long periods. In 1794 and 1798 the box-keeper in Lincoln was John Carrott, Breeches-maker, and by 1806, after his death, his widow Elizabeth took over; in 1813 her premises were in the Strait, about 100 yards north of the theatre. By 1821 the Box-keeper was Miss Carrott who was still in the Strait, where she had a circulating library. By 1833 she had moved to 'Butchery-street, adjoining the Theatre yard' suggesting that the box-office may then have been very close to the modern entrance to the theatre in that street, now part of Clasketgate. The box-keeper at Grantham for many years was Mr Joseph Codling, a tailor, who died in February 1815, aged 64. In Stamford the long serving box-keeper was Mr Rooe, a stationer and member of the Corporation, and in Boston Thomas Clarke, a bricklayer, had that honour for a long time. Mr Clarke died in 1821 and his wife carried on; when she died in 1834 it was said that she 'had kept the box-book of Boston theatre for 40 years' so she had handled that business for her husband all the time.[61] In 1798 the box-keeper in Wisbech was Mr Rust, and in 1819 and 1824 Mrs Rust of the Timber Market was handling tickets as well as places for the boxes. In 1820 the box-keeper in Gainsborough was Adam Stark (1784-1867) who had succeeded Mr Mozley as a bookseller and printer in the Market Place in 1815. He also printed the playbills for the theatre in the 1820s and 1830s and nowadays is best known as a historian of the town.

Moral Objections

What has been said so far was of interest to regular theatre-goers but for some people a night at the theatre was too wicked to contemplate. Theatre flourished in Lincolnshire in the long eighteenth century but ever since the Reformation there had been people who believed that the stage was immoral and profane. People who enjoyed theatre were colluding with the players in a pleasurable deception, but some devout Protestants viewed the stage as a place of trickery and deceit, full of illusions and magic similar to those which they believed the Roman Catholic church had used to bamboozle ignorant observers into becoming credulous believers. The high church cleric William Law, in his *The Absolute Unlawfulness of the Stage Entertainment fully demonstrated* (1736), declared that 'a player cannot be a living member of Christ, till he renounces his Profession'.[62] This underlying belief in the immorality of the stage grew stronger through the Georgian period, its adherents increasing in numbers and vehemence, and eventually it rose triumphant in the nineteenth century. Actors faced virulent hostility from Methodists and other anti-theatrical groups. John Wesley himself, the founder of Methodism, insisted

---

60 Playbills, Stamford, 29 March 1775, 19 June 1778.
61 *SM*, 30 March 1821, 28 February 1834.
62 Brewer, John, *The Pleasures of the Imagination: English Culture in the Eighteenth Century*, Abingdon (2013), p.268.

in 1764 that 'most of the present stage entertainments sap the foundation of all religion'.[63] According to the actor-manager Tate Wilkinson of York, the clergy and ministers' message was that 'every-one who entered a playhouse was, with the players, equally certain of eternal damnation'.[64] Other less vehement critics still saw theatre encouraging profanity and blasphemy, or threatening the long-established order of society, and some feared that luxury and refinement, of which theatre was part, would weaken the moral fibre of Britain.

Theatres enjoyed popular support during the stressful years of war with France but after 1815 the continuing astonishing rise and reach of Methodism and the revival of the Church of England led many middle class people to stay away from theatres and condemn in ever stronger terms the 'moral laxity' of those who still went to such places. Condemnation of immorality in plays, and of the morals of actresses, had changed to condemnation of theatres *per se*. In May 1823 in Derby the officers of the cavalry refused to bespeak a night at the theatre owing to non-conformist prejudice. Manly, the manager, wrote:

> *Bible societies, religious tracts and missionary meetings so debauched the minds of the Derbyshire gentry, that the most disgusting hypocrisy threw a gloom over their manners in Public. Forsaking the amusements of the theatre was considered a solemn proof of piety. O! the vile humbugs.*[65]

Robert Simpson in his *History of Derby* (1826) said of all theatres:

> *Happy will it be when these nurseries of vice and immorality no longer exist. The profaneness and blasphemy with which most of our tragedies abound, and the ribaldry, lewdness and obscenity of our comedies sufficiently indicate the malignant influence they will naturally have upon the morals of a people who are fond of such amusements.*[66]

Some managers fought back. In January 1826 Joseph Smedley put on *Pride Shall Have a Fall* by the Rev. G. Croly, attacking the follies of the so-called 'Crack Regiments', and in the playbills Smedley said that it 'tends to prove (in the words of Archbishop Tillotson) that "the Stage can put Vices out of Countenance which cannot be so decently reproved nor so effectually exposed and corrected any other way."'[67]

People like Simpson would no sooner go into a theatre than they would enter a brothel or an opium-den. In 1834 a Dr Lardner was due to give a lecture on the steam engine to the Lincoln Mechanics Institute and as they expected a large audience Tom Robertson offered them free use of his theatre. However Dr Lardner, a clergyman of the Church of England, objected to giving his talk in the theatre so the grammar school in the Greyfriars building was used instead. A similar issue arose

---

[63] Hammond, J.L., *The Age of the Chartists*, London (1930), p.258.
[64] Payne, Michael, *op. cit.*, p.122.
[65] Rosenfeld, Sybil, 'The Theatrical Notebooks of T.H. Wilson Manly', *Theatre Notebook*, Vol.7, No.1, London (October, December 1952), pp.9, 10.
[66] Warwick, Lou, *Drama that Smelled; Or, Early Drama in Northampton and Hereabouts*, Northampton (1975), p.128.
[67] Playbill, Grimsby, 13 January 1826.

in March 1848 in Gainsborough when it was proposed that the local Philharmonic Society should hold its future concerts in the theatre that had now been 'admirably adapted' for that purpose. However 'the religious scruples of certain parties will not allow them to listen to music in a Theatre'[68] and later that year the concerts moved to the newly opened Public Rooms in the Old Hall. In 1847 the *Stamford Mercury* suggested that Gainsborough did not need a theatre now that the best kind of literature was accessible to all classes and people could find rational amusement 'in the bosoms of their families' and did not need to seek entertainment in public.

In December 1842 the Gainsborough reporter of the *Mercury* said of the theatre and actors:

> *The moralist must consider it a melancholy thing to witness some dozen or fourteen rational beings, all wearing the human form divine, disguised in decorations* [costumes] *representing harlequins, scaramouches, and tom-fools, and others as a sort of nondescript animal with a beard and head having the appearance of an antiquated billy-goat, elevated on a stage playing 'fantastic tricks before high heaven,' and, as is often the case, to a crowd callous to the intent of the 'genteel beggars', but bent on giving vent to coarse jokes and licentious raillery, to the obstruction of the actors' profits.*[69]

In the eighteenth century the *Stamford Mercury* had advertised the programmes of theatres but had not commented on the morality of drama. During the 1820s the newspaper started publishing reviews of theatrical performances, written by people who enjoyed theatre, and in the 1840s commented on the religious opposition to drama. In November 1842 one contributor to the *Mercury* said that the decline in public taste for the stage was due to 'religious fanatics' whose zeal for the welfare of the soul after death had inspired them to condemn any pleasures in this world.[70] In April 1844 the *Mercury* noted:

> *Our Queen, as the 'defender of the faith', most generously supports the dramatic art, but some priests make it out to be an anti-Christian amusement; and (unfortunately for the* corps dramatique*) the major portion of their flock seem to be coming to the same opinion; Puseyism* [the Catholic revival in the Church of England] *teaches everything of Popery except its toleration of rational amusements.*[71]

While that writer might regret the condemnation of drama, since the 1830s the positive views in the *Mercury* had slowly been joined or replaced by negative reports by writers who welcomed news of theatre closures as signs of the moral improvement of society.

---

[68] *SM*, 10 March 1848.
[69] *SM*, 2 December 1842.
[70] *SM*, 4 November 1842.
[71] *SM*, 26 April 1844. Edward Pusey (1800-82) headed the Catholic revival in the Church of England.

A generation earlier, at the start of the nineteenth century, respectable people might condemn the immorality of the stage but they could still be amused by its productions. Even some clergymen had gone to theatres, but moral Victorians looked back on that as another sign of the decadence of the Georgian clergy. In November 1848 the *Stamford Mercury* stated, without comment, that 25 years earlier 'the then Vicar of Gainsborough was in the habit of going to theatre in his carriage'. When Thomas Tomlinson of Caistor died on 21 May 1849, at the great age of 97, it was said that he used to be very fond of plays...

> *...and once he (gratuitously) performed at Caistor theatre in* Douglas *(1785) along with some of his neighbours, two of whom afterwards were respectable clergymen of the church – one the late Rev. Robert Neesham, Perpetual Curate of Stainfield, near Wragby, and the other the present Vicar of Scopwick, near Lincoln* [the Rev. George Oliver, DD].

At least one older person defended the theatre-going of his youth by saying that drama had deteriorated since then. In 1856 Pishey Thompson (1785-1862) referred in his *History of Boston* to: 'This once polite and intellectual recreation in Boston, in which many of the best and wisest of its inhabitants had taken pleasure', and he contrasted it with what he called the 'degraded drama' of the 1850s.[72]

The defenders of the theatre in Lincolnshire did not say that the new moral standards of the day were wrong but instead reiterated the ancient and honourable claim that plays were moral and useful. The argument that theatre deludes was met by the counter argument that it showed the need to distinguish appearance from reality. They stressed that theatre was a rational amusement and a moral and political force as it could show servants and apprentices the rewards of virtue and the dreadful penalties of sin and misbehaviour. George Lillo's play *George Barnwell* (1731), a classic tale of the doom which afflicted a Londoner destroyed by greed and sexual passion, was often performed in Lincolnshire as well as elsewhere as late as 1834 to improve the minds of the lower classes with its self-evident impressive and instructive moral. In 1826 the manager Joseph Smedley at the opening of Sleaford's theatre season recited that 'this shall be my guide: my study, which I will through life pursue, to keep the Moral of the stage in view' and 'my effort's to aid fair Virtue's cause'.[73] In 1835 Thomas Manly, another local manager, declared to his audience in Halifax that: 'The religious and virtuous life is not impaired by an occasional engagement with Rational Amusements'.[74] It was also said that theatres could promote virtue and patriotism and encourage polite sociability. Theatres could preserve, rather than undermine, order and good government and could counter pervasive conservative fears of the spread of Methodism with its 'enthusiasm' and

---

[72] Thompson, Pishey, *History and Antiquities of Boston*, Boston (1856), p.211.
[73] Lincolnshire County Archives, LLHS/38/5/8/2.
[74] Golland, Jim, 'A Dramatic Discovery, or, A Manly Enterprise', *Local History Magazine*, No.42, Nottingham (1994), p.14.

religious fervour. In 1833 Mr Macarty brought a troupe to Caistor and, recognising who were his main opponents, stressed that his company's performances 'will have that moralizing and instructive tendency which will induce even the Methodistical part of the neighbourhood to give their interest and patronage'. However in 1845 the reporter for the *Stamford Mercury* also despaired about the stultifying effect on the local theatres of people only going to see morally acceptable plays. 'The fashion of the period is to patronise those amusements only to which patronage is courted by the clap-trap that there will be "nothing to offend even the most fastidious".[75]

The defenders of the theatre did not win the argument. By the 1840s it was too late to reverse a belief that had been there since the Reformation, had triumphed during the Commonwealth, went underground at the Restoration but had been growing ever since. In 1842 the *Stamford Mercury* said: 'The truth is, the players' occupations gone; public taste has experienced a withering change, which threatens to be fatal to the sock and buskin'.[76] The middle classes had been the financial mainstay of the stage, and their withdrawal from theatres in Lincolnshire was to prove fatal. Before that sad day the people of this county and its near neighbours had enjoyed over 80 years of entertainment.

---

[75] *SM*, 31 January 1845.
[76] *SM*, 20 May 1842. 'Sock and buskin' refers to comic and tragic drama in general.

3

AN ACTOR'S LIFE

Some of the Lincolnshire companies of comedians were similar in size and composition to Vincent Crummle's company, shown here in Charles Dickens' Nicholas Nickleby, *published in 1838–39.*

For over fifty years in the Georgian era it was possible for an actor to make a decent living performing in and around Lincolnshire, something that no actor can do in the twenty-first century without public subsidy. Though most actors moved around the country and the best succeeded in London, some then worked all their lives in greater Lincolnshire. The social position of provincial actors was very ambiguous. In financial and moral terms they were at a low level of society, yet they regularly performed before people of the highest rank, and rich and powerful young men expected to be able to go backstage and meet actresses in their dressing rooms. For many actors their family, friends and professional relations were geographically widespread. Even the humblest player would spend his year trudging about a county, many had played in widely dispersed British cities and towns, and some travelled overseas to perform in America or British colonies elsewhere. Some were born into the profession, being the children of actors, but others were young men who had been apprenticed to respectable trades or professions and ran away to join the theatre, such as Jemmy Whitley and James Shaftoe Robertson who became dynamic leaders of theatre in eighteenth century Lincolnshire.

The stars of the Lincolnshire stage could enjoy a lot of local support if, as some did, they stayed with the company for several years. They became well known to the public in the towns of their annual circuit. The audiences saw them in a variety of different roles, and came to know not only their styles of acting, but the details of their private lives. Though actors had to be ready to play any role when required they usually took on some particular 'stock character' and stuck to their special line of business in each of the plays put on during a season. The recognised leader was the Tragedian, who played *Hamlet* and *Macbeth* and might appear also in serious comedy. The Juvenile Tragedian played *Laertes* or *Macduff*, combining such roles with light comedy. The Juvenile Leads played the young lovers and the youthful heroes and heroines. The Old Man and the Old Woman appeared in such parts as *Sir Anthony Absolute* in Sheridan's *The Rivals* (1775) and *the Nurse* in *Romeo and Juliet*, while the Heavy Father (or Heavy Lead) played tyrants in tragedy and, from the 1800s onwards, villains in melodrama. The Heavy Woman played *Lady Macbeth* or *Emilia* in *Othello* (1603). The Low Comedian, who ranked next in importance to the Tragedian, played leading comic parts of a broad, farcical, or clownish type, together with minor roles in tragedy. The Walking Lady and Gentleman played the secondary parts, such as *Careless* in Sheridan's *The School for Scandal* (1777); they were usually beginners, and poorly paid. General Utility, or simply Utility, also poorly paid, played minor roles in every type of play, the Supernumerary, or Super, was engaged merely to walk on, had nothing to say, and was not paid at all.[1] The Low Comedian was the successor to the Elizabethan clown and fairground buffoon, and an ancestor of the modern stand-up comedian.

In a month-long season an actor could perform in up to 32 different plays, and actors could not be expected to handle all roles equally well. There could be square pegs in round holes: short thin Falstaffs and overage Romeos. Irish characters turned up in the most unexpected plays because there was always a popular Irish actor to play them. As long as the companies of comedians were the only actors to be seen locally, audiences would cheer or hiss what was presented to them and only a few widely travelled playgoers could compare local standards with those of London. In those days there were no schools of acting and all provincial companies

---

[1] Hartnoll, Phyllis and Found, Peter (eds), *The Concise Oxford Companion to the Theatre (New Edition)*, London (2nd edn 1992), p.483.

became recognised training grounds for young men and women to learn from the old stock actors, and in their heyday it was rare for a player to begin his career anywhere else.[2]

There is more to the theatrical life than the illusion presented on stage. A successful company also included musicians, prompters, set-builders, carpenters, sweepers and fruit-sellers. At Stamford the music was usually supplied by three fiddlers at 3s each per night and other instruments were employed from time to time, such as a bass viol, drums and a horn. For several years from 1821 the leader of the band was William Davis, an Irish comedian and melodist, but Thomas Manly the manager at Stamford had no ear and successful singer John Braham found the orchestra so bad that he refused to sing with it and preferred to accompany himself on the piano.[3]

Professional actors were part of a peripatetic subculture, moving around the country like gypsies, and mixing with others within that exotic life, though occasionally being joined by people from more respectable families outside the theatrical world. The companies of comedians were sometimes referred to as 'families' and this was true in more ways than one. Most companies had actors and actresses married to each other, and within a few years they produced numerous 'infant prodigies'. Thomas and Mary Manly of Stamford had eleven children and William and Margaret Robertson of Lincoln had 22 children. In the unbroken sequence of performance and travelling between towns there was hardly time for actresses to give birth. On Sunday 26 March 1809 Mrs Brooke, of the Lincoln company, while on her journey to perform in Wisbech,

> *was safely delivered of a child in her post-chaise, about four miles from that place. There were four females with her at the time.*[4]

The Robertsons were the leading family in the Lincolnshire theatrical world for three generations but even they experienced life in all its extremities. Their children were bundled about from town to town, nursed at the back of draughty stages, put to sleep in dressing rooms that were no more than curtained off recesses in the wings, or left in various towns of the circuit with people who would care for them for a fee. Later still, adult players had parents, siblings, aunts and uncles performing alongside them.

Being a theatre manager in Georgian times was not an easy life. He had to defend his theatre against moralists and reformers who wanted to shut down the place; he needed to placate and win over a vociferous, active and opinionated theatre-going public; he had to deal with actors, actresses and patrons whose conduct might well compromise his work; and he had also to work within the system of legal constraints imposed by the Crown. Above all, he had to try to make a profit.

---

[2] *Ibid.*, p.91.
[3] Rosenfeld, Sybil, 'The Theatrical Notebooks of T.H. Wilson Manly', *Theatre Notebook*, Vol.7, No.1, London (October, December 1952), pp.4, 5.
[4] *Stamford Mercury*, 7 April 1809.

The business of running theatres and companies of comedians was dominated by men and even in the playbills all male roles were listed before any of the female parts. In Lincolnshire in the Georgian period there are instances of women inheriting such businesses on the death of their husbands or fathers, but in each case it was expected that they would 'resign' control to a male relative. About 1770 Mrs Herbert inherited the Stamford circuit and in that case it may be understandable that she appointed George Stevens to run it since he had already been managing it for her late husband. However, when her son returned to claim the company the decision to let him have it was made by his mother, in return for a financial settlement. Jemmy Whitley died in 1781 and his business passed to his daughter Elizabeth and her husband Andrew Gosli, but they were more interested in receiving rents from the theatres than in running a company. When James Robertson died about 1781 he already had two partners and his widow Ann Robertson joined them as an equal, but when Miller replaced the earlier partners in 1787 Ann then called in her son Tom and gave him her share. William Taylor died in 1800 and his share of the Stamford company passed to his widow, but she seems to have played no part in its running and her business partner James Robertson was the effective manager. Sarah Richardson had inherited her father's theatres around Durham in 1785 and a few years later her husband William Huggins was running that circuit before transferring his interests to Lincolnshire. Fanny Robertson inherited the Lincoln circuit when her husband Tom died in 1831 and her nephew William helped to run it, but there was marked ambiguity about whose company it was. Newspaper reports sometimes referred to William as the manager and sometimes to Fanny in that role. The issue was only resolved when Fanny finally retired in 1843. A different situation arose in the Bullen company in the dying days of Georgian theatre, where Mrs Bullen took over from her husband who by 1845 seemed to be no longer capable of dealing with the dire poverty they were suffering.

The managers of several of the companies of comedians in Lincolnshire were related to each other, and to theatrical families elsewhere, by ties of blood and marriage. Tom Robertson (1765-1831) of the Lincoln company, sometimes called 'The Mogul', married in 1793 actress Frances Mary Ross (1768-1855), known as Fanny. A year earlier on 6 September 1792 in St Clement Danes in Westminster Fanny's younger sister Anna (1773-1849) had married John Brunton (1775-1849) of Covent Garden theatre whose father, also called John (1741-1819), was the successful manager of the Norfolk company of comedians from 1788 to 1800. John had started his acting career with the Lincoln company. In 1792 his sister Anne Brunton (1769-1808) married Robert Merry (1755-98), a gentleman and a poet, and had to give up her acting career. Merry spent all his inheritance and to support them both Anne happily accepted an invitation to cross the Atlantic and appear on stage in Philadelphia, then the capital of the United States, on 5 December 1796. She was slim, feminine and gifted with a melodious voice, lauded as 'the most perfect actress America has seen', and became a favourite with the Philadelphia audience. Following the death of Robert Merry she married

Mrs Anne Merry, born Anne Brunton, was related to Fanny Robertson of the Lincoln company of comedians as her brother was married to Fanny's sister. Mrs Merry went to America and was the first great actress in the USA.

Courtesy of the Rare Book and Manuscript Library, University of Illinois at Urbana-Champaign.

the ageing actor/manager Thomas Wignell but he died within a month and she became joint manager of the company by inheritance. The company had four theatres, in Philadelphia, Baltimore, Alexandria and Washington. In August 1806 Anne married actor William Warren and she died in June 1808, four days after giving birth to a still-born child. During her twelve years there this 'redoubtable actress' was the *grand dame* of tragedy on the American stage.[5]

John Brunton's youngest sister Louise (1785-1860) was also an actress, until she married the Earl of Craven on 12 December 1807 and retired from the stage. John and Anna's daughter Eliza Brunton (1799-1860) later married actor manager Henry Yates who in 1825, with a partner, acquired the Adelphi theatre in London. From 1802, if not earlier, John and Anna Brunton, Fanny Robertson's sister and brother-in-law, were acting in the Lincoln company. In 1806 Mrs Brunton was apparently a guest at the opening season of the new Boston theatre. Then in 1810 she was engaged by the Lincoln company 'for the season', playing *Ophelia* in *Hamlet* (1600) in February, and Mr Brunton 'of the Theatres Royal Covent Garden and Haymarket' was hired for three nights in 1814 and another few nights in 1815.[6]

Tom Robertson's brother James (1773-1831) was an actor with the Stamford company and in 1791 married actress Eliza Robinson (d.1806), whose actress mother was then called Mrs Taylor (1755-1837). The Taylors later came to Stamford and in 1795 James and his father-in-law became joint managers of the company. Following the death of William Taylor in 1800, his widow married a young actor Benjamin Wrench (1778-1843), and a little later they left Stamford and Mrs Wrench's share of the company was purchased by Thomas Manly (c1772–1840), another actor who was married to Mrs Wrench's other daughter Mary. For another decade James Robertson was joint manager of the Stamford company with his brother-in-law Thomas Manly, and Manly then ran the Stamford circuit on his own until 1839. James' children and grandchildren went on the stage, as did some of Thomas Manly's children.

Around the turn of the century other troupes of players started to tour Lincolnshire and adjacent parts, and several of those were formed by actors from the Stamford or Lincoln companies. Joseph Smedley (1784–1863) and his wife Melinda (1781-1870) both performed with the Lincoln players in the early 1800s; Melinda was born in Norwich and probably first appeared on the boards there with Brunton. Joseph ran his own company from 1807 to 1840. Melinda's maiden name was Bullen and another actor called Bullen ran a small troupe in Lincolnshire in 1841–45 as a successor to Smedley. The Huggins family who ran a company between 1796 and 1830 had also performed with the Stamford players. A short-lived independent company was formed in 1794 by William King who was married to the daughter of William Pero, manager of the Stamford company, to which King and his leading actors had belonged. If to the ties of blood and

---

[5] Hughes, Glenn, *A History of the American Theatre 1700-1950*, New York (1950), pp.78, 96, 112, 113. Alexandria is in northern Virginia, just six miles from Washington, and was part of the District of Columbia until 1847.

[6] Warwick, Lou, *Theatre Unroyal; or, They called them Comedians*, Northampton (1974), pp.28, 29; SM, 4 June 1802, 7 February 1806, 14 February 1806, 9 February 1810, 30 September 1814, 13 January 1815.

marriage was added the tie of employment, all of the longer serving actors in Georgian Lincolnshire can be seen to be closely linked to each other.

Financial insecurity

The life of an actor was precarious and unpredictable. Theatrical people knew that in order to survive and thrive in the consumer society of Georgian Britain they had to sell their wares in the cultural market place. Actors' wages were usually a pittance, their weekly 'share' of the takings barely paying current expenses, and in bad times they could really suffer the direst poverty. Sometimes the local troupes got full houses but often they sold barely enough tickets to make their performances worthwhile. If business proved bad everyone was unpaid and therefore unfed. Actors learnt their craft in provincial theatres but the best-paid jobs were in the capital and ambitious actors wanted to get on the stage there.

London had the largest theatres in the kingdom and they were profitable businesses. Drury Lane theatre employed about 150 people, of whom 80 were actors, spent about £40,000 a year and made a net profit of £3,000 to £6,000 a year. In 1774 two leading actors in Drury Lane earned £25 a week followed by two others on £12 and £8 respectively, with middle ranking actors earning £3 to £6 and those with minor parts receiving 12s to £2 a week. In 1797/98 some ten to fifteen leading actors in Covent Garden theatre earned between £20 and £15 per week, some ten actresses, £5 to £10, and some small part actors 15s a week.[7]

Most country towns had only one theatre each but in London there was competition and only the best talent could succeed. The vast London theatres with hundreds of seats needed a different style of acting to that in the small intimate country playhouses and actors had to adapt. Even Sarah Siddons, who became the greatest tragedienne of her age, failed on her first efforts in London. Mr E.H. Seymour (d.1819) joined the Stamford company in June 1804 and also played with the Norwich company. He wrote a book on Shakespeare's plays, but when he appeared on stage at Covent Garden in November 1812 he was a complete failure and the audience would not let him continue. Sophia McGibbon was in the Stamford company in 1810 before moving to York and Hull, and in September 1813 played *Mrs Haller* in Kotzebue's *The Stranger* (1798) at Covent Garden theatre. That performance received great applause but was not followed with entree to the London stage. She tried again six years later and played *Imogene* in the tragedy of *Bertram* (1816) at Drury Lane theatre on 17 December 1819 and it was said that 'she now seems to have risen into distinction'.

What little information we have about local wages shows that all except the lowest paid London players were earning more than any actor in greater Lincolnshire. Some financial information is available in account books kept by Joseph Smedley

---

[7] Brewer, John, *The Pleasures of the Imagination: English Culture in the Eighteenth Century*, Abingdon (2013), p.263; Brown, Susan, 'Manufacturing spectacle: the Georgian playhouse and urban trade and manufacturing', *Theatre Notebook*, Vol.64, No.2, London (2010), p.60; Rosenfeld, Sybil, *Georgian Scenery Painters and Scene Painting*, Cambridge (1981), p.9

in the 1810s and Thomas Manly in the 1820s. Unfortunately we do not have any information about the finances of the main Lincoln company. In 1809 Smedley recorded the salaries paid each week to the seven actors in his company, listing each family as one entry. Husbands and wives received a joint salary, and children appearing as pages, young princes etc from an early age were not paid until they were recognised as useful actors. The total for all the actors was usually about £10 10s 0d a week though it varied from £8 17s 0d to £11 1s 0d. The Smedleys as a family always received £2 2s 0d each week in the 1810s. The Tennant family received £2 13s 0d though at times that was divided into £1 17s 0d for 'Tennants' and a separate 16s 0d for 'Miss Tennant' so she was perhaps the best performer in the family. The highest paid individual in 1810 was 'Goldfinch' who usually received £1 16s 0d though one week she was paid £1 18s 6d, and another £2 5s 0d. The Kellys as a family usually received £1 10s 0d a week and there were three actors who each received less than a pound – Hodgson 18s, Spragg 16s and Smith 12s. By June 1810 the cast had been joined by Mr Somerville who was paid £1 a week; he had perhaps replaced Goldfinch who had gone by then. Another Spragg had joined by September and that family were then paid £1 5s 0d, and in October a Neville had joined and was paid £1 1s 0d. Later in the 1810s Smedley did not record the payments to individual actors but the weekly total of their salaries was still around ten guineas. Other weekly expenses were the cost of circulating playbills (from 8s to 17s) and the door-keeper (usually 4s).[8]

Thomas Manly's notebooks for the Stamford company in the 1820s usually only recorded individual salaries when an actor came or left, though an entry in Passion Week 1821 (when no one else was paid) shows that the Manly family got £3 13s 6d each week. Other individual salaries varied from 18s to 25s and as Manly had a larger company than did Smedley the total rose from £21 7s 0d a week in 1821 to £31 18s 0d in 1828. Walter Donaldson, who was in the company for a period, said that a guinea was the usual salary and the actor had to find boots, shoes, buckles, silk stockings, hats, feathers, gloves, swords, canes, wigs, modern dress, long hose and military costume, whilst singers had to furnish the parts of their songs for the band.[9] On occasion Manly lent money to his actors as advances of wages. The prompter was paid £1 or £1 1s 0d. Manly paid stage keepers about 11s a week and the leader of the band 25s. In addition to the regular salaries there were occasional payments to supernumaries such as sixteen soldiers for £3, soldiers in *Tekeli* (1806) 6s, two pugilists for two nights in *Tom and Jerry* (1821) £1 6s 0d. Door keepers and checkers were paid 1s a night, equivalent to Smedley's payment of 4s a week.

During each season the main players and some other theatre staff were allowed a 'benefit' to supplement their meagre wages. Benefits could take different forms. The manager could make a charge for the theatre for one night, all takings above that amount going to the player concerned; or the takings could be shared by manager

---

[8] Lincolnshire County Archives, Smedley Notebooks. LLHS/38/5/3.
[9] Rosenfeld, Sybil, 'The Theatrical Notebooks of T.H. Wilson Manly', p.4.

and performer after deduction of expenses. A third method was for the manager to give performers a certain number of tickets, which they had to sell and could retain half the money. The income from a benefit might be low if the attendance was poor, or nil if takings were less than expenses. But at Mr Fromow's benefit at Halifax on 11 February 1823 he received £33 4s 0d, and on Mr Freer's farewell benefit at Nottingham on 13 November 1826 he got £44 0s 0d. In 1821 Thomas Manly and his wife had benefits at most towns on their circuit and the joint total of their receipts was £251 9s 6d so they were not doing badly. On a successful night there could be a lot of cash at the theatre and that could become a target for thieves. In December 1808 two soldiers tried unsuccessfully to rob the treasurer of Hull theatre while on his way home. A few weeks later on 29 January there was a burglary inside that theatre itself. They found no money, but broke open boxes in the ladies' dressing room and stole some of Mrs Wrench's jewellery and ornaments worth, it was said, 'a considerable amount'.[10]

A four-week season in a town might see a company performing up to 32 different plays and it was essential to keep the troupe together so that each role was taken by an actor who knew his or her part in all the plays. When recruiting a new actor, a manager needed to discover what roles the actor already knew. In 1837 Joseph Smedley engaged a Miss Desborough and he requested one list of the characters she *had* performed and another which she had *not*, but *wished* to do. She later refused one role as it was 'insignificant' and Smedley said that: 'surely it cannot be the Manager's fault that the author has not made it *better.*' The actress had also objected to being given a new role that she would have to study and Smedley complained:

> *Tis clear she would not study, nor act a part in which she has studied, except such as had been so frequently done before, as to have lost their attraction. Novelty, an audience requires and have a right to expect. 'If we live to please, we must please to live'.*[11]

The whole troupe could be thrown into consternation if any actor left during the year, without due notice, as a replacement would need to know or learn a great many parts. When a Mr Thomas, 'otherwise Hilyard', left the employment of Tom Robertson on 14 March 1806 'contrary to his contract of a stated time of service', it was so unprofessional that Robertson put a notice in the *Stamford Mercury* so that 'such a character may be known to managers in general'.

Some actors stayed with the Lincolnshire companies for decades. John Peters was with Whitley's Stamford company for about thirty years until his death in October 1797, aged 55. He had started as an actor and was said to be 'a beloved pupil' of Whitley and in later years he was the prompter. Thomas Wright (1762-1808) was a native of Lincoln and was a member of the Lincoln company for over twenty years.

---

[10] *SM*, 16 December 1808, 3 February 1809.
[11] Lincolnshire County Archives LLHS/38/5/3/30. The quotation is from a line written by Samuel Johnson and spoken by David Garrick when he became manager of Drury Lane in 1727.

For the first few years he was the prompter, in 1792 a Mr Wright painted scenery and for eight years from about 1800 he was the Treasurer 'with the strictest integrity'; in 1804 he had a benefit. Mrs Norris with 'excellent comic talents' was a member of the Lincoln troupe from 1804 and finally retired in January 1822. A subscription was raised to provide her with 'a few of the comforts of life in the evening of her days'. Mr Scholey Sidney (1738–1815), who died on 15 March 1815 aged 77, was with the Stamford company for over forty years. It would appear that there were at least two Mrs Sidneys who performed with that troupe. The first starred as Patty in the *Maid of the Mill* performed on 14 June 1782, and in July 1783 sang 'How merrily we live' from *The Flitch of Bacon* (1779) with Messrs Hudson and Bell. The other Mrs Sidney (1762-1840) joined the company in the 1790s and played with them for nearly forty years before she had her farewell benefit at Nottingham on 3 July 1829. Ill-health had forced her to retire but she lived several more years and died in Lincoln on 17 October 1840 aged 78.

A talented comic actor who spent all his career in Lincolnshire was George Northouse. He was probably the George Northouse (1798-1844) christened in Hull on 24 January 1798 and is first referred to in the account books of Joseph Smedley, when he apparently had a benefit at Alford on 6 April 1815. Northouse had joined Huggins' company by March 1819 when he had a benefit in Louth, and in October of that year he married an actress with the company, Miss Mary Ann Stoker, whose father was leader of the band at Louth in February 1825. Northouse was a good low comedian and scenery painter who could also sing. He stayed with Huggins until the troupe was dissolved in 1830, and in 1831 joined the Lincoln company as successor to Mr Gurner who had gone to London. In 1838 Northouse's performance as *Weller senior* in *Pickwick Papers* (1837) received good reviews.

Acting could be dangerous. Audiences wanted excitement so managers gave them storms, sinking ships, waterfalls and full-scale battles with exploding bombs. The destruction of the mill in *The Miller and his Men* (1813) became famous. In November 1824 of a performance of *Ivanhoe* (1820) at Lincoln it was said that:

> The scenery throughout met with high approbation, particularly the last coup d'oeil, *in which Miss Marinus as* Ulrica *was enveloped in flames!*

Fireworks were widely used and Thomas Manly's account books include recipes for making red and blue fire. On 2 August 1826 Manly had a serious accident at Nottingham theatre when a Roman candle was set off, to represent cannon fire, but the recoil hit Manly in the face, temporarily blinding him. It also set fire to the dress of Miss Strutt on the stage, and her burning clothes had to be torn off her; luckily she suffered no injury although understandably she was 'in the highest state of agitation and alarm'. Other accidents could occur. On 15 November 1826 Mr Neville, formerly of Tom Robertson's Lincoln company but by then at Sheffield theatre, took a pistol from his belt which exploded and shattered one of his hands.

An unusual accident occurred on 16 November 1841 at Peterborough, though as it involved a drug overdose it has a modern ring. Mrs Martyn, a performer with Robertson's company, had visited her injured husband in Stamford and on her return was chilled by the weather and depressed about her husband and was advised to take laudanum. This at first had the desired effect, but she had taken too large a dose and while performing on stage she fell senseless. A stomach-pump was applied 'and she was kept in constant exercise for several hours' to correct the effects of the drug. She was still too ill to perform the next day but had recovered enough to appear in Wisbech two days after that.[12]

When actors became aged or suffered ill-health they could end up in the parish workhouse or in prison for debt. They had no greater security than anyone else in Georgian Britain, even when theatre was at its most prosperous. In 1811 Mr Degville was in prison for debt, and on 30 October a benefit in Lincoln theatre was held in his absence to raise some funds for 'his unfortunate pecuniary embarrassments'.[13] On 18 June 1814 Edmund H. Armstrong, aged 62, 'who had long been a travelling comedian', died in the workhouse at Lincoln, and his poor widow was left disconsolate. As recently as March 1814 he had played *Mark Anthony* in Boston theatre. More successful in terms of financial security was Thomas Grist (d.1808) who started his career in London in 1775–77 but then spent the next thirty years performing in the provinces, appearing at Stamford in the 1780s and '90s and later with Butler and King in Gainsborough. In November 1804 the *Stamford Mercury* noted 'that the veteran Grist ... had made a very capital engagement at Manchester, not with a manager, but with a wife, who has brought a tolerable portion of grist to his mill – report says £23,000'.[14] It is thought that Grist had known Elizabeth Nevill for many years before their marriage, and was probably the father of her daughter Ann born in 1784.

Thomas Grist (d.1808), an actor who played in Stamford and Gainsborough theatres in the late 18th century.
© *National Portrait Gallery, London*

London stars

During the reign of George III actors became more significant than the play and theatres came to use stars to attract audiences. Through newspapers and magazines people all over Britain could read about the stars of the London stage and be keen to see them. London theatres closed for the summer and after 1800 the faster transport system provided by stage coaches on turnpike roads allowed actors to travel easily and perform anywhere in the country. The stars moved around alone and expected to find in each place a supporting company capable of playing with them with minimum rehearsals. Actors such as Sarah Siddons, Edmund Kean and William Charles Macready could visit Lincolnshire and other provincial theatres for engagements of a few nights only. Visiting stars usually received one third or one half of each night's takings with half of the benefit night. In August 1821 Macready received £51 4s 0d for three nights and a benefit, and in April 1827 Maria Foote

---

[12] *SM*, 19 November 1841.
[13] *SM*, 25 October 1811.
[14] *SM*, 2 November 1804.

William Henry West Betty, 'The Young Roscius', (1791–1874). He toured Lincolnshire in 1807 and 1808.

Painting by James Northcote, RA, 1804, in the National Trust collection, Attingham Park.

(1797?–1867) received half of the takings for three nights at Stamford amounting to £82 6s 0d. No star got more than she did at this theatre during the 1820s.[15]

The phenomenally successful 'Infant Roscius', William Henry West Betty (1791–1874) visited Lincolnshire in 1807 and the theatres doubled their prices. For five weeks at Stamford in 1807 he was paid the huge sum of £800 which was more than it cost to build a theatre in Lincolnshire at that date. He then went direct to Boston for three nights, following the benefit of the popular Fanny Robertson which produced takings of £81 for her. Master Betty received £182 18s 6d, being half the takings of his three nights. When he came again in 1808 the prices were

---

[15] Rosenfeld, *op. cit.*, pp.8, 9.

not so high, but still more than usual.[16] Edmund Kean came to Lincoln in April 1824 to play six parts in six nights. In two of those plays Fanny Robertson had the wonderful opportunity to perform with Kean, playing *Portia* to his *Shylock* in *The Merchant of Venice* (1596) and *Desdemona* to his *Othello*. At the same time the other great actor of the period, William Charles Macready, was also playing *Othello* in Stamford on 6 and 7 April 1824.

Ira Frederick Aldridge (1804-67) was an African American who, confronted with persistent discrimination against black actors in the United States, had come to Britain in 1824 and made his debut on the London stage in 1825. He played the major Shakespearian roles of *Romeo, Hamlet, Othello* and *Macbeth*, and later *King Lear*. After the death of Edmund Kean in 1833 while playing *Othello*, Aldridge took his place in that role at Covent Garden but was driven from there after only two performances due to hostility from the pro-slavery lobby. Though only tolerated in the minor London theatres he was lauded in the provinces and visited Lincolnshire several times in the 1840s. When he appeared at Lincoln theatre in February 1842 the audiences for his performances were exceedingly small which was normal at that time. He was in the county again in 1847 and 1849 and in the latter year the *Mercury* commented that 'those who think of Africans as an inferior race of beings, should particularly see this highly accomplished gentleman: it might sweep away the vanity that concludes that the intellectual can consist only with a white skin', Ira Aldridge is the only African American to have a bronze plaque among the 33 actors honoured at the Shakespeare Memorial Theatre at Stratford on Avon.[17]

Dresses and morals

New costumes or 'dresses' would be advertised in playbills as they were as important as scenery in making the theatre a place of spectacle. In 1824 it was said of a performance by Fanny Robertson at Lincoln that 'Mrs T. Robertson's *dress* was only exceeded by her *acting* in the character of *Rebecca*'. While performing, actresses prided themselves in dressing fashionably, regardless of the specific part they played. A chambermaid could look like a lady. There was much debate about consistency and historical accuracy of costumes in plays that mixed together 'Old English' style and contemporary dress. A successful company of comedians would have an extensive and valuable wardrobe, as well as a library of music and scripts. In the costume store the glittering robes of kings lay next to those of Christian saints, and fine dresses of Roman emperors mingled in democratic fashion with rags of paupers and shepherdesses. The wardrobe keeper was a valued member of the company, and on Sunday 21 July 1816 Mrs Golding, wardrobe keeper to

---

[16] *SM*, 13, 20 and 27 March 1807, 13 and 20 May 1808. 'Roscius' refers to Quintus Roscius Gallus (d.62BC) who was a Roman comic actor of such celebrity that his name became an honorary epithet for any particularly successful actor, such as Master Betty.

[17] *SM*, 26 January 1849. In 2012 Aldridge's life was the subject of a play, *Red Velvet* (2012), performed in London.

Ira Aldridge (1804–67) as Othello, painted about 1847 when he performed the role in Spalding.
© *Victoria and Albert Museum, London*

Robertson and Manly of Stamford, was stopped by three men on the field-road, near Langham, between Oakham and Melton Mowbray, who robbed her of 24 shillings, with which they got clear away.[18]

Highly popular among male supporters of the Georgian theatre were the 'breeches roles' for actresses. In an age when women wore full-length dresses all the time, the actress who cross-dressed in boys' clothing, as when playing Shakespeare's *Rosalind* or *Viola*, or in dozens of similar roles in eighteenth century comedies, revealed to the public the shape of a female leg. On 31 March 1794 the 25-year-old Fanny Robertson played the Dauphin, the young male heir to the French throne, in *Louis*

[18] *SM*, 2 August 1816.

the Unfortunate (1793) at Stamford. But such exposure of females to the male gaze tended to reinforce the old stereotype and associate actresses with prostitution regardless of their behaviour off stage. Several plays, such as Oliver Goldsmith's *She Stoops to Conquer* (1773), included plots in which prostitutes and ladies were mistaken for each other. Actresses wore make-up, as did prostitutes, but respectable women did not and it was well-known that the theatre in London's Drury Lane was surrounded by gaming dens and brothels.

Male actors could also play roles in the other gender but that did not have the same sexual frisson. They could be dames in pantomimes or farces, a tradition that still continues in modern theatre, but in July 1782 the Lincoln company performed *The Beggar's Opera Reversed* in Spalding, with all the male roles performed by actresses, and actors playing the ladies of the town. In 1778 13-year-old Tom Robertson played a black girl in two separate plays.

The actress Harriet Mellon (1777-1837) described the actor's life as

> *all cheerfulness, all high spirits – all fun, frolic and vivacity; they cared for nothing, thought of nothing, beyond the pleasures of the present hour, and to those they gave themselves up with the utmost relish.*

Their lives were filled with drinking, impulsiveness and a casual attitude to the marriage vows. The low opinion of actresses' morals was reflected in an apocryphal tale told in the *Stamford Mercury* in 1795:

> *At a country theatre, a few weeks ago, the heroine of the play was closely besieged by her lover in one of the scenes, and modestly checked his warm solicitation of mutual love. A drunken Squire called out to the actor from his box: 'Do not be so sheepish, my good friend offer her a guinea, as I did last night, and she will soon comply'.*

It is said that when Casanova's mother, Zanetta Farussi, eloped with Gaitona Casanova, an actor and dancer, in 1724, her father, who was a shoemaker, died of shame, such was the status of the acting profession at that time. Sarah Siddons (1755-1831), the leading actress of the Georgian era, almost single-handedly made leading actresses respectable in this country, but for most actresses the old image as mere courtesan still persisted.

The fate of Emma Sarah Love (1798–1881) endorsed the popular view. She was a London actress, and an even better singer, who performed with both the Lincoln and Stamford companies. Emma was at Newark for three successive nights in January 1828, and at Boston and Wisbech for four and two nights respectively in April. In July 1828 she appeared at Nottingham, Derby and Peterborough. While at the latter theatre she was proposed to by Captain Granby Hales Calcroft and they married on 10 November 1828, but the marriage had to be kept secret as they would both lose financially if it became known. Then on 18 July 1829, while

---
[19] *SM*, 18 December 1807.

performing with Manly's troupe at Nottingham, she eloped with the 6th Earl of Harborough (1797–1859) who built a cottage for her in the grounds of his mansion, Stapleford Park near Melton Mowbray. Emma had three sons by the Earl but she was unable to get a divorce from Calcroft so the Earl married Mary Eliza Temple of Stowe who took up residence in the hall. Emma continued to live in her cottage until the Earl died in 1859 when Lady Eliza immediately had it pulled down, though the best stones were reused to build a new cottage for Emma in the nearby village of Whissendine.

Some actresses, like Emma Love, became the mistresses of noble lords, and a favoured few married into the aristocracy. In 1774 Whitley's Stamford company included Miss Farren who later married the Earl of Derby. In 1807 two such marriages had Lincolnshire connections. On 30 April Robert Heathcote of Lobthorpe, Lincolnshire, brother of Sir Gilbert Heathcote of Normanton, Rutland, married Elizabeth Searle of Covent Garden theatre at St Martin's in the Fields, Westminster. Then on 12 December the Earl of Craven married Louise Brunton, also of Covent Garden, whose brother was married to Fanny Robertson's sister, and Fanny was one of the female relatives who received a marriage 'favour' from Louise, Fanny's being 'a very elegant one of white and silver'.[19] Another marriage occurred on 16 June 1827 when Harriet Mellon, by then the rich widow of Coutts the banker, married the 9th Duke of St Albans, whose father had made Redbourn Hall in Lincolnshire the family seat in 1816. When actresses married into the nobility they had to leave the stage, but many of them married actors and continued working in the theatre, though now with their husband's company if different from their own.

At the bottom of the acting profession were the much despised strollers, not attached to the regular theatres, but performing in inns, barns, tents, or wherever they could find a room. In 1798 they were also the subject of an apocryphal story in the *Stamford Mercury*:

> *A party of strolling players entering a country town, were met by a* chimney-sweeper's *boy, who ran home exclaiming – 'Master, Master, here's the* actor folk *come to town!' 'No reflection, ye young dog,' cried the* knight of the brush, *'you know not what you may come to, ere you die!'*

Chimney sweeps were at the bottom of normal society, their boys below them, but strolling players even lower still. However, at the highest level some actresses could marry into the nobility, and at the end of the eighteenth century the drama was sufficiently established in counties like Lincolnshire for the play-going public to take pride in their local company's leading performers as belonging to and reflecting credit on their town.

The need for a positive image of actors was not helped in 1807 by the case of John Granger, alias Sauceman, who led three labourers to break into the home of Richard Fox in Killingholme and steal a gold watch, 20 guineas in gold and three bank notes worth 15 guineas. They were caught and the three labourers sentenced to death, but though Granger was their 'captain' he turned King's evidence and was spared the gallows. Granger had been employed by a company of strolling players, and used his theatrical skills to disguise the gang in various ways with night-gowns, bonnets, false beards and ruddied faces. Not only was Granger let off but on the same day that the other three were to hang, he married the woman he had been co-habiting with for six or seven years. The judge did not want Granger to get off scot-free, so the following day Granger was sent to Nottingham to be sent abroad as a soldier, but the commanding officer refused to have him and he was returned to prison in Lincoln Castle. The authorities did not give up and four days later he was taken by a detachment of the 79th regiment to their depot on the Isle of Wight 'to serve his Majesty as a soldier in one of his foreign settlements'.[20]

The Acting Space

The purpose-built playhouses in Georgian Lincolnshire were smaller than modern venues, and had virtually no front of house space. They were generally plain functional buildings on the outside, usually of brick though Stamford had an elegant stone facade. A bit more theatrical was the Gainsborough Old Theatre which was said to be in the Egyptian style. The interiors were more decorative and probably followed the standard pattern for Georgian country theatres. The inside was brightly lit and usually highly decorated, the traditional colour being pale green with bright red for the hangings in the boxes. The first Lincoln theatre in Drury Lane was 66ft long by 24ft wide[21] and the medieval hall that contained Gainsborough theatre was 58ft 3in by 26ft 8in, very similar to the surviving theatre in Richmond, Yorkshire, which is 58ft 4in by 24ft 0in. Wisbech theatre was also similar in size to Richmond. The Stamford and Lincoln theatres of the 1760s were both larger than Richmond; they had a similar width though the former was longer – Stamford 92ft by 37ft and Lincoln 75ft by 38ft. A bit larger still were the Boston 1806 theatre at 80ft by 45ft and the Horncastle theatre in a converted barn at 94ft by 42ft. At Horncastle the auditorium was about 52ft long and the backstage about 42ft, separated by a proscenium arch 25ft wide. How large these were in human terms may be judged by the fact that the auditorium and stage of the present Theatre Royal in Lincoln together occupy the same space as the 1760 and 1806 Lincoln theatres. The foyer, box-office, bar, toilets, green-room, offices and twisting corridors and stairs of the present Lincoln Theatre Royal were added in the last 100 years or so and lie between the original theatre site and Clasketgate.

The auditorium of any Lincolnshire theatre was often the largest secular indoor space in the town where men and women of all ages and social classes could meet together. In church and chapel they could meet sedately but in theatres they could talk and socialise without inhibition. There they could hear and see moral, intellectual and historical ideas different from those expressed by priests or ministers.

---

[20] *SM*, 13, 20 and 27 March 1807.
[21] Clementson, Diana W., *The Theatre Royal*, Lincoln, thesis, (1960) in Lincoln Central Library.

Theatres could also show Britain's imperial role in distant military conflicts and the adventure of colonial expansion, and local spectators could imagine themselves as imperial citizens. Behind, beside and below the stage was a shadowy labyrinth of scenery, machinery and ropes with store rooms, dressing rooms, stairs and passages. In some of the purpose-built theatres, such as Stamford, the backstage area was larger than the auditorium. A 'proper' theatre also included facilities for the fitting of tight-ropes, slack-wires, trapezes and similar equipment as well as machinery for special effects such as a shower of snow on the Gainsborough stage or a thunder box. Fire was always a hazard in the age of candles and inflammable costumes and scenery, and Whitby theatre was completely destroyed by fire on 25 July 1823 (without loss of life). Luckily no Lincolnshire theatre burnt down in this period, though that nearly happened in Boston in 1848 and Lincoln did suffer that fate in 1892.

The drama only occupied each Lincolnshire theatre for about one or two months a year, and the rest of the time the buildings could be used to produce income in different ways. Quite often the pit was covered over to create a floor level with the stage and make a convenient granary or warehouse that could be rented out. A 21-year lease dated December 1800 between the Lincoln company's managers and the owner of Grantham theatre shows how this could work. As in most leases the managers were responsible for the 'Seats, Boxes, Pillars, Stage' and other interior fittings, and the landlord for the exterior. Then, unusually, the landlord was also liable to 'repair any damage or breaches ... made [when the company was not there] to or in the Seats, Boxes, Pillars, Stage or other the inside'. The lease said that the managers would perform 'one season only in every year at such part of the year and for so long time as they shall think proper'. When they were not performing in or making use of the theatre, the owner could use or let the premises

> *to whom and in what manner and for what purposes he may think fit and proper, doing no Damage or Injury to the Scenery or other Property and Effects ... which may remain or be left therein, Provided that the theatre shall not be let ... to any other Company of Comedians or to any person for the performance of Dramatic Pieces.*[22]

So the company had a 21 year monopoly of this playhouse for drama, able to choose the date and duration of the season, and the landlord could use or rent out the building for the other eleven months of each year.

Finances

Some theatres were owned by the managers of the companies of comedians, but most in Lincolnshire were rented from the local corporation or an individual, and all would have the same sort of joint use shown in the Grantham lease. In theatres that they owned managers could receive some income from renting them

---

[22] Lincolnshire County Archives, 3-GM/4/4.

to itinerant showmen, though not usually to other companies of comedians, or amateurs. Thomas Manly charged what he could get and in the 1820s that included five guineas from Buck for one night at Nottingham theatre, four guineas from Lloyd for three nights at Chesterfield, and five pounds from Master Grossmith for two nights at Stamford. Manly also received about 2/- a night for farming out fruit selling in his theatres. It seems that Manly received the income from subletting Stamford theatre even though that was owned by Lord Exeter. Joseph Smedley said that in theatres he owned:

> I let the Dressing Rooms and Money Taker's Room with the one opposite as Tenements for £9 per annum – and have the use of them to Dress in while the Theatre is open beside.

He said that at Howden in Yorkshire it was proposed to make a Billiard Room under the stage; 'first because tis wanted and next because twill pay better than the Tenement'.[23] Smedley's Sleaford theatre had four tenements underneath the auditorium, and pig-styes in the adjacent yard.

The surviving account books kept by Manly for the 1820s and Smedley for the 1810s give us a little information about the finances of the drama in Georgian Lincolnshire. They show that the rents the managers paid for theatres varied considerably. In the 1820s Nottingham was the most expensive on Manly's Stamford circuit and cost him £230 paid in quarterly instalments. He paid £121 to Mrs Crockford for Retford theatre, £100 later reduced to £80 to Rothwell for two months at Halifax, £40 to the Marquess of Exeter for Stamford and £30 to £35 for Chesterfield. Altogether he paid £721 in rent in 1821 and in addition had to pay poor, church, highway and street lighting rates and land taxes that varied from town to town. On 1 May 1773 Whitley and Herbert leased a newly-built theatre in Newark for 21 years, including 'new Dressing Rooms at the East End thereof', for £36 per annum to be paid in two instalments, half on 5 June and half on 5 December.[24] Under the 21-year lease of Grantham theatre Robertson paid £52 10s 0d per annum from January 1801 and when he took Boston theatre in 1806 on a thirty year lease he was to pay £176 per year.[25]

Smedley was appearing in smaller towns and even villages and his theatres were usually temporary playhouses so his rents were on quite a different scale. They were usually in guineas, one guinea being £1 1s 0d. In 1810 the most he paid was £12 12s 0d for Grimsby followed by £7 7s 0d for Alford, which were perhaps his only purpose built theatres, poor though they were. At Upwell and Brandon on the edge of Cambridgeshire he paid £5 5s 0d at each place. At Mildenhall nearby he did well and seems to have paid £2 0s 0d at first and then a further £3 13s 6d. At 'Stoke',

---

[23] Lincolnshire County Archives, LLHS/38/5/3/14.
[24] Hemingway, G., *The Robertson Family and the Lincoln and Nottingham Theatrical Circuits*, thesis (1976) in Lincoln Central Library, ref.UP 7467, p.66.
[25] Lincolnshire County Archives, 3-GM/4/4; SM, 3 September 1813.

probably Stoke Doyle near Oundle, he only paid half a guinea (10s 6d), but then had to pay £1 2s 0d for insurance of the barn! Back in Lincolnshire he paid £4 4s 0d for his venue in Crowland. For later years we have two more figures. In 1814 he paid £10 10s 0d for Melton Mowbray, but that may have been the cock-pit that he used in 1828 so would have been a better quality building than a barn. In 1830 he was encouraging supporters to build a theatre for him in Selby, Yorkshire, and he said it could be built for £500 and he would guarantee 2½% of that cost for his occupation 'two months in two years or 5 weeks a year', which would be £12 10s 0d.

These few surviving account books also throw a little light on the part that the companies of comedians played in the local economy. Theatres in Lincolnshire were on a smaller scale than those in London and only open for a short season in each town, so could not give the same level of support to local shopkeepers and craftsmen that was found around Covent Garden and Drury Lane. However the Lincolnshire companies would be valued customers for the period they were in a town, not only for printing and candles but for other purchases and lodgings for members of the company. In December 1840 Smedley said that each of his theatres in Yorkshire was amply stocked with scenery, machinery, properties, costumes and a library of scripts and music 'such as few can boast of'[26] and much of this would have come from local suppliers over the years. Secondhand clothes shops and shoe makers could provide items for the wardrobe, and new stockings would regularly be needed from the hosier. The local linen drapers could provide cloth and haberdashers sell buttons, ribbons and other items for the company's own seamstresses to make or repair costumes. The tin-man would be used to repair candle-holders, lamps and light reflectors for the illumination of the stage. In the cold months there would be fires to heat the theatre and the local coal merchant and chimney sweep would get business. As gas lighting became available in the 1820s and 1830s, that would produce income for the local gas company. In places where temporary theatres were erected the company of comedians would provide a significant job for local timber merchants, carpenters and painters. The repair and maintenance of purpose built theatres would need the same trades, as well as bricklayers, ironmongers, plasterers, plumbers, masons, glaziers, colourmen to provide paints, and upholsterers. Some purchases would also be needed to maintain and renovate the scenery. Occasionally the company might need other services, and on 14 November 1794 reference was made in the *Stamford Mercury* to a Mr Spencer, hairdresser of Stamford, 'who distinguished himself some time since at our theatre' – which probably means that he had produced spectular hair-dos for a play.

Some entries on the expenditure side of Smedley's notebook only gave the name of the person paid with no indication as to what the payment was for, but a few were more detailed. In 1810 Smedley's total expenditure for the year was £911 10s 0d of which about £500 was on salaries for himself and his actors.

---

[26] Lincolnshire County Archives. LLHS/38/5/6/2.

Most of that would be spent on food, lodging, clothes and other living expenses in the towns where they were performing. The rest was spent on such items as rent of theatres, printing posters and playbills, large quantities of candles for lighting the theatres, coal for heating in the winter and hire of horses and carriages to move the company and its paraphernalia from one town to another. During the two months they were in Grimsby in 1810 Smedley paid £13 11s 0d to Mr Morton for printing. In 1814 he spent a total of £14 14s 5d on tallow and candles to light the different theatres.

Other specific expenditure by Smedley in 1810 was small and included the purchase of boards and nails, payments to carpenters for work in some theatres, a guitar for £1 1s 0d, and a desk for 14s in Alford. The accounts also cover 1812 and 1814 and some references to 1815. In 1812 his expenditure included 10s on 'canvas armour' in Grimsby, in 1814 he spent 10s 2d in Bingham on velvet and silk for a tunic and 5s in Bawtry for a 'chariot', and in January 1815 he bought binding and gunpowder in Grimsby for 5s. Some of the venues where Smedley played in the 1810s were little more than villages and many times he spent more than he received; his company was in Crowland for four weeks and he spent £65 0s 6d (including wages) but the theatre only took £42, and in tiny Mildenhall in Suffolk he was down by £18 1s 0d.

Manly was operating on a larger scale than Smedley and in 1820 his expenditure was over £3,000 including about £20 a week on his actor's salaries. There were also payments to 'board boys' to advertise the shows, charwomen to clean the theatres, door keepers and 'scene-men' to move the scenery and operate any machinery. Other expenditure was on music, candles and lamp oil as well as the payment of rates and taxes on each theatre he owned. In one week in March 1822 at Stamford he spent £4 4s 7d on oil and candles, and £6 1s 5d on painting the theatre when the average wage for each of his actors was £1 1s 0d per week. He occasionally bought music and 'ale for the band' as well as stockings and shoes. The note books show only small amounts spent on repairs to the theatres as in rented premises the landlords would be responsible. Work paid for by Manly included repairing the roof of Nottingham theatre £3 1s 6d, the pit 7s 8½d, and the gallery stairs and pit £5, plastering and repairing the gallery at Stamford 8s, and covering the pit seats there 11s 4½d. The conclusion at the end of Manly's account book was that the stage was a hard life with little financial reward for the manager – the final page shows him several hundred pounds in the red and he comments that 'there is desolation in my bank'.

Scenery

The style of production in theatres changed during the Georgian period and scenery became more significant. In the mid eighteenth century the main acting area was on the forestage in front of the proscenium arch and the emphasis was on the play and players rather than on the decor. England at this time had a unique system of scene changing, the scenery splitting in the middle and sliding in grooves to the side of the stage in view of the audience. The system was never widely used elsewhere but suited the English type of play with many quick-changing scenes. Often the scenic effects were painted in a false perspective, which is why the action took place at a distance in front so as not to spoil the illusion. The scenery was a background, not a frame, and there was a feeling that too much scenery drew attention away from the actors. As the Lincoln company might perform up to 32 different plays each month it would be an expensive and difficult matter to supply different scenery for each play in a number of theatres. Stock scenery in each theatre that could be used for many plays was a practical necessity. In 1790 Tate Wilkinson said that even in London one scene at Covent Garden had been used repeatedly since 1747.[27]

Scenery started to change after 1773 when David Garrick employed Philippe Jacques de Loutherbourg at Drury Lane. The rise of the Romantic movement led to a shift from architectural to pictorial scenery and De Loutherbourg established England's lead in romantic scenery, introducing grandeur in the form of mountains and torrents of natural wilderness illuminated by dramatic light and shade to produce sublime effects. The Argand lamp gave a more brilliant and less flickering artificial light, and was used for the first time at Drury Lane in February 1785. The lighting was more controllable and allowed shadows, which were good for melodrama. Better lighting also allowed actors to play visibly with looks instead of audibly with words. With improved lighting and brighter paint colours developed by chemists, the scenery was no longer a poorly-lit decorative neutral background and became a surround with the actor performing in it. The developing taste for spectacular pieces and demands of the actors for better opportunities for display changed the form of the theatre itself. Playwrights provided material for the star to glitter in and the old platform-stage became the modern picture-stage framed in the proscenium arch. The audience could more convincingly be deceived and imagine themselves transported to the places represented on the stage.

The skill of scenery painting became ever more important and was closely linked to the operation of stage machinery. The patent theatres in London were constantly being rebuilt on an ever larger scale and the emphasis was increasingly on scenery and spectacular backdrops. Provincial theatres had to follow suit, even though they were more intimate than the huge London venues. De Loutherbourg worked by constructing maquettes which could easily be sent to other theatres that wanted to follow his sets. When 'new and appropriate' scenery was produced for a new play, that would be advertised in the press and handbills and might well get a comment in a review. Such new scenery would travel the circuit with that play until it was relegated to the stock in one playhouse.

Sometimes the Lincolnshire companies employed painters from London or other major theatres, but mostly they used local artists or actors in their own company.

Far Right: Playbill, Spalding, 14 July 1780. New scenery had been painted by Mr Hilton and the cast included James Shaftoe Robertson and Nat Herbert, the joint managers of the company.
Lincolnshire Archives Misc/Don 94/3

---

[27] Rosenfeld, Sybil, *Georgian Scene Painters and Scene Painting*, Cambridge (1981), p.12

(Not performed here these Four Years)

At the THEATRE in SPALDING,
On Friday Evening, July the 14th. 1780, will be performed
A COMEDY, call'd,

A Word to the Wife,

OR

ALL FOR THE BEST.

Captain DORMER, Mr. ROWSWELL.
Sir John DORMER, Mr. TANKERVILLE.
WILLOUGHBY, Mr. ROBERTSON.
VILLARS, Mr. MADDOCKS
JOHN, Mr. SIMMANS
WAITER, Mr. WATSON.
Sir George HASTINGS, Mr. KING.
Mrs. WILLOUGHBY, Mrs. READ.
Miss WILLOUGHBY, Miss FRODSHAM.
Miss DORMER, Mrs. MADDOCKS.
Miss Montague, Mrs. KING.

To which will be added A FARCE, called

The [French] INVASION,

OR A TRIP TO

BRIGHTHELMSTONE.

(With New SCENERY, painted by Mr. HILTON.)

Sir John EVERGREEN, ~~Mr. ROBERTSON.~~ Sidney
Charles EVERGREEN, Mr. ROWSWELL.
BEAUFORT, Mr. MADDOCKS.
DRILL, Mr. JACKSON.
TATTOO, Mr. WATSON.
ROGER, Mr. HERBERT.
CAMELION, Mr. KING.
BRUSSELS, Mrs. READ.
EMILY, Miss FRODSHAM.
Lady Catherine ROUGE, Mrs. MADDOCKS.

One of the first Lincolnshire references to a painter of scenery was in March 1784 at Stamford, when scenery for the successful new musical *Rosina, Or, Harvest Home* (1782) was 'by that celebrated artist' de Loutherbourg himself.[28] In 1785 Mr Pero, the manager of Stamford theatre, employed Mr Stanton from the Theatre Royal, Covent Garden, who had been a pupil of de Loutherbourg, as painter of scenery and producer of machinery and other effects for several plays from March to July. These included Dryden's adaptation of Shakespeare's *The Tempest* (1611), Cumberland's *The West Indian* (1771) and O'Keefe's *Peeping Tom of Coventry* (1785). The painters also produced transparencies that could be illuminated from behind. On 8 July 1785 the entertainment at Stamford included a view of Burghley House, and a view of Naples and Mount Vesuvius with moving lava. In September Stanton's view of Burghley, engraved by a Mr Cook, was published in Stamford at the price of 1s. Stanton produced scenery for the pantomime *Magician of the Rocks* in March 1786 and he was back in April 1791 to paint the scenery for the 'Grand Pantomimic Ballet d'Action' called *The Death of Captain Cook* (1791) as it had recently been performed in London and Paris.

In July 1792 a Mr Wright produced the scenery for Stamford's production of *Richard Coeur de Lion* (1786) by General Johnny Burgoyne. The advertisement for Mrs Manly's Benefit Night at Stamford on 14 July 1820 said:

> ...on this Evening there will be a Miniature Representation of the intended Coronation [of King George IV]; the figures painted by Westmacott, attired in correct costume.[29]

This suggests the theatre was displaying an actual painting by Charles Molloy Westmacott (1788-1868). The last mention of painters at Stamford in the *Mercury* was in 1823 when 'Mr Lawrence and Assistants' prepared the scenery for the farce of *Monsieur Tonson* (1821). The account books for the Stamford circuit in the 1820s gave other references to scenery and they frequently referred to the purchase of paint, canvas and colours. In 1822 a Mr Stretton was paid £14 15s 0d for painting for the company, and on 1 August 1828 Mr Phillips displayed his scenery at his benefit in Nottingham. Carriage bills indicate that some scenery was moved from town to town, such as Nottingham to Halifax by water, but other scenery was made for particular theatres. In 1830 a wagon carrying scenery failed to reach Stamford in time so the opening was postponed.

Companies also made use of local artistic talent. Between 1792 and 1817 the Lincoln company advertised at least once a year that they had 'new scenery by Mr Hilton of Lincoln' for one or more of their new productions, though a playbill as early as 14 July 1780 refers to 'new scenery by Mr Hilton' for a Lincoln company performance at Spalding.[30] That artist was William Hilton (1752-1822) who was a professional painter living in the Bail, near the Cathedral. He came from Newark

---

[28] *SM*, 19 March 1784.
[29] *SM*, 7 July 1820.
[30] Playbill, Lincoln, 14 July 1780. Lincolnshire County Archives Misc. Don. 94/3.

Extract from print of Wide Bargate, Boston, by George Northouse, and published in 1844. It is the only known surviving example of the artistic skills of local scenery painters in Lincolnshire.
(Author's collection).

and by 1786 had moved to Lincoln where his son William was born.[31] William junior followed the same profession as his father and achieved national success as an artist, becoming Keeper of the Royal Academy in 1827. In September 1803 the new popular play *Alfonso, King of Castile* (1801) was put on at Spalding with scenery 'modelled from London' and painted by Mr Hilton. The principal scenes were the garden of Alphonso's palace, a perspective view of the romantic part of the country adjacent to Burgos, the capital of Castile, the chapel of St Juan, and the Claudian vaults. The last task that William senior undertook for the Robertson company in Lincoln was in autumn 1817 when they announced that 'the theatre has been ornamentally painted by Mr Hilton of Lincoln'.[32] He had produced scenery for *The Forty Thieves* (1806) earlier that year, but in September 1817 the scenery for Morton's *The Slave* (1816) had been painted by 'Mr Connor of the Theatre'.

Other painters were used for quite short periods, to judge by the advertisements in the *Stamford Mercury*. On one occasion in 1794 Tom Robertson, manager of the Lincoln company, produced a grand transparency of the recent battle of Valenciennes.[33] In 1796 Mr Curtis of Newark painted the theatre in that town in an 'ornamental' manner, and in 1804 he was employed to do the same in Grantham theatre.[34] When a new theatre was opened in Northampton in 1806 it was said that 'The colour of the boxes is green relieved with fancied embellishments in white, designed and executed by Mr Merrick (and assistants) from the Theatre Royal, Drury Lane.'[35] Mr Brown, Fanny Robertson's stepfather, was an actor who had a benefit at Lincoln theatre on 27 October 1809 and, as well as performing in the 'petit ballet' of *Robinson Crusoe* (1805), he had also designed and painted the scenery for the piece. The skill of painting for the theatre was also of value outside the playhouse. In September 1795 Matthew Flinders, surgeon of Donington, took advantage of the skills of an actor/scenery painter and had the passage walls and staircase of his home painted 'in imitation of paper' by 'Craven the Player', also called 'Craven, Junr', for which he paid 5s.[36]

One actor who could paint excellent scenery worked for Smedley, Huggins and then the Lincoln company for several years. He has left us the only known example of work by a Lincolnshire scenery painter of the Georgian period. This was George Northouse who as early as 1820 had painted a whole set of scenery for Huggins and in 1823 produced the scenery for *The Law of Java* (1822) at Louth.[37] He joined the

---

[31] De Wint, Harriet, 'A Short Memoir of the Life of Peter De Wint and William Hilton, R.A.' in Lord, John (ed), *Peter De Wint 1784-1849*, Aldershot (2007), p.79.
[32] *SM*, 12 September 1817.
[33] *SM*, 6 June 1794.
[34] *SM*, 28 October 1796, 14 December 1804.
[35] Warwick, Lou, *Drama that Smelled; Or, Early Drama in Northampton and Hereabouts*, Northampton (1975), p.192.
[36] Beardsley, Martyn and Bennett, Nicholas (eds), *Grateful to Providence. The Diary and Accounts of Matthew Flinders, Surgeon, Apothecary and Man-Midwife 1775-1802*, Vol.2 1785-1802, Lincoln Record Society Vol.97, Lincoln (2009), p.156.
[37] Parker, B.J., *The Theatre of Gainsborough. From 1772 until 1850*, thesis (1963) in Gainsborough Library, p.60. SM, 7 February 1823.

Lincoln company in 1831, and that November they exhibited three new scenes he had painted. It was said that 'their effect as paintings (one of them is a copy from Claude) is said to surpass by far anything ordinarily produced as stage scenery'.[38] In 1833 he painted more scenery including a 'splendid scene of Grantham Market Place' and the 'interior of Peterborough Cathedral'. Northouse retired from the stage about 1840 and settled in Red Lion Street, Boston. He died on 23 February 1844 and on 24 May it was reported that prints of his painting of the sheep fair in Wide Bargate were selling well; copies can still be bought in the twenty-first century. He was not the only painter in Smedley's company as in January 1826 Mr Reeve produced new scenery for *Ivanhoe*, based on Walter Scott's celebrated novel, and also for the classic melodrama *The Castle Spectre*.[39]

James Robertson, a later manager of the Stamford company, was a good painter as well as an actor. The scenery for *St David's Day* performed on 11 August 1800 included 'a transparent Gothic window, painted for the occasion by Mr Robertson'.[40] In 1802 he painted new scenery for their performance of *The West Indian*. and in 1814 he produced a scene representing rejoicing in Halifax. After he retired from the Stamford company in 1818 he became involved with his brother's Lincoln troupe and between 1820 and 1827 painted scenery for several plays that toured their circuit. These included Colman's *Aladdin, or the Wonderful Lamp* (1819), Planche's *The Vampire* (1820) and Pocock and Bishop's popular musical drama *The Miller and his Men*. James Robertson's print of Nottingham Market Place, sold at half a guinea, was said to be a competent piece of work.[41] On 20 October 1826 'Mr Fraser and Assistants' produced the scenery for a 'dramatic spectacle' of *The Battle of Trafalgar, Or, The Death of Nelson* and James Robertson operated 'the mechanism of the shipping'. This Mr Fraser and his assistants painted scenery for the Lincoln company on a number of other occasions between 1825 and 1827. Some scene painters were also employed to decorate the playhouses and to paint pictures on the ceilings and box fronts as in Mr Hilton's last job. During this period Fraser's team also undertook the 'ornamental painting' of the theatres at Lincoln, Grantham, Newark and Peterborough, and also probably Wisbech. In November 1825 Mr Fraser was actually called 'Artist of the Theatre'.[42]

The form of theatre that flourished during the Georgian period, and which is described in this and the previous chapter, was a new experience for Lincolnshire people and was different from what was to follow in mid and late Victorian times. For the first time it brought professional actors to the main towns of the county on an annual tour and eventually led to the erection of several purpose-built theatres.

---

[38] *SM*, 11 November 1831.
[39] Playbills, Grimsby, 9 and 18 January 1826.
[40] Hemingway, *op. cit.*, p.20
[41] Wood, A.C., 'Nottingham 1836-1865, 1.The Borough 1835-65', *Transactions of the Thoroton Society*, Vol.LIX, Nottingham (1955), pp.33, 34.
[42] *SM*, 4 November 1825.

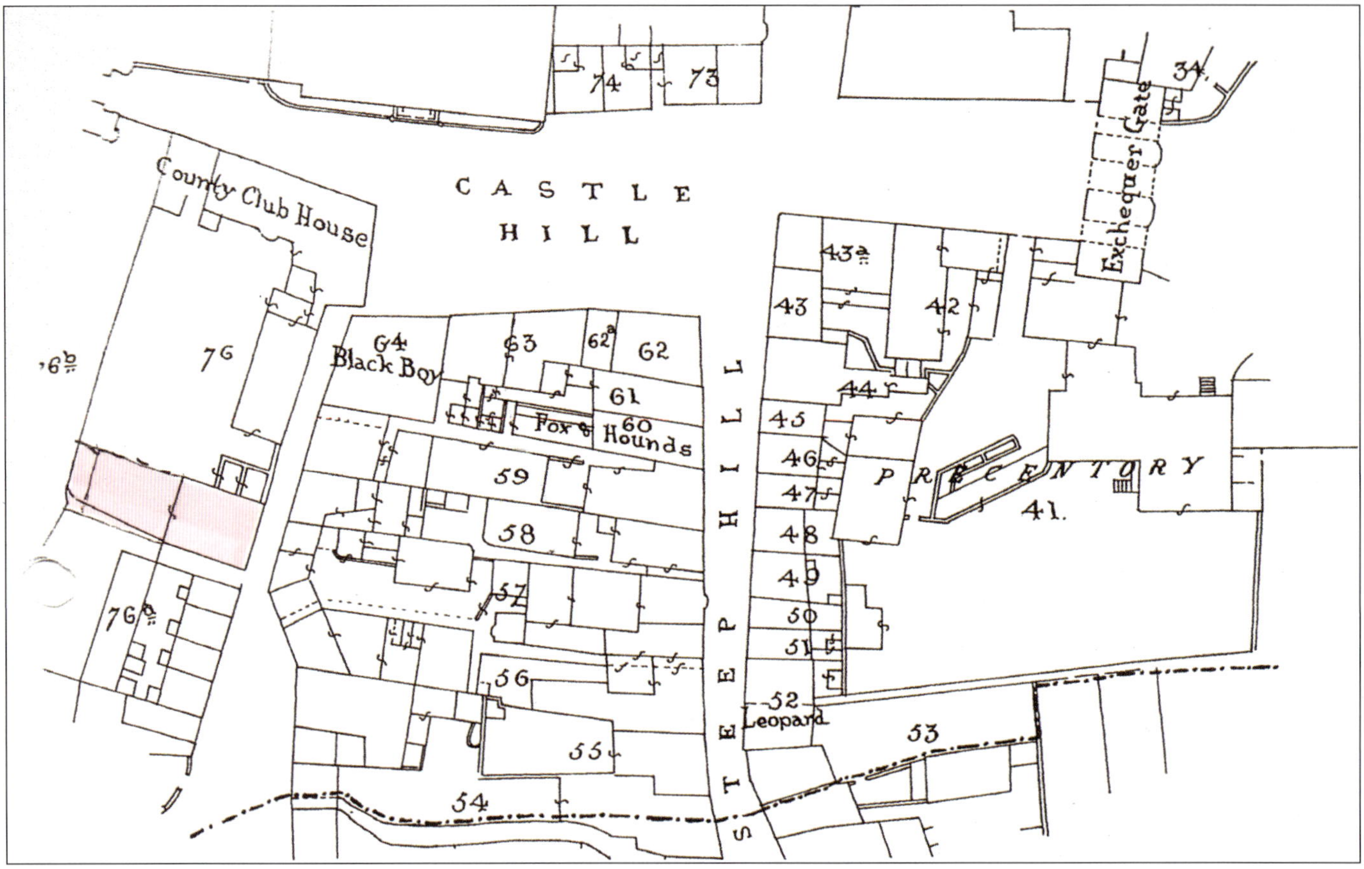

Above: Extract from Tithe Map, St Mary Magdalene parish, with Lincoln's first theatre marked in red. Built about 1731, it was located in the narrow section of Drury Lane close to Castle Hill.
Lincolnshire Archives ref: DIOC/Tithe Award/E659

Photographs May 2016

Left: Lincoln's first theatre closed about 1760 but a small part of the east wall, with a door opening, and the lower part of the stone south wall (left) still survive in Drury Lane.

Right: The door frame of the 1731 theatre still has an old bracket on the inside, which may date from that time.

Opposite page: The Harlequin on Steep Hill, Lincoln, was a pub in Georgian times used by the actors from the theatre in Drury Lane.

4

GO FORTH AND MULTIPLY

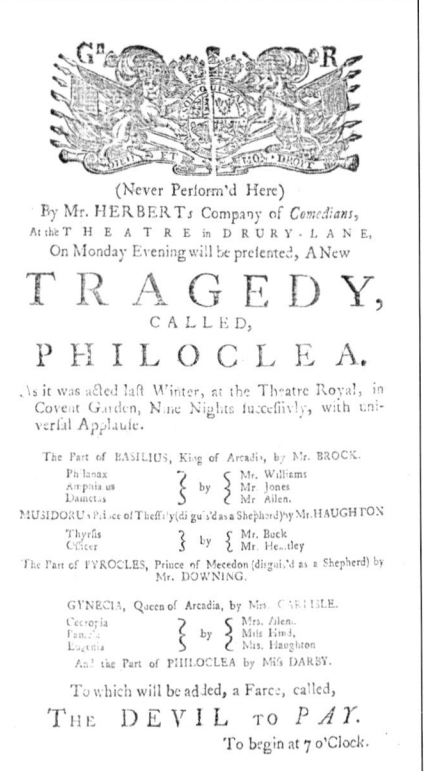

Playbill, Lincoln, 1754. The earliest playbill for a Lincolnshire theatre related to the first theatre on Drury Lane. It has the royal coat of arms but otherwise is less elaborate than later playbills.
(Lincoln Public Library)

Lincoln theatre, Herbert

For the first thirty years of the eighteenth century there were no purpose-built theatres in Lincolnshire and touring companies of comedians had to use various buildings as temporary playhouses. However, as drama became popular and demand grew it became feasible to erect buildings designed for use as theatres. Erasmus Audley (1684-1741), a joiner, carpenter and cabinet maker in Lincoln, had a vision that drama was here to stay and in about 1731 he took the gamble of erecting a theatre in a narrow lane, just below the walls of Lincoln Castle. The lane is now called Drury Lane and, like the locations of Liverpool's Georgian theatre and of Durham's second theatre, the lane was probably named after London's main theatre. To be a financial success a purpose-built theatre had to attract an audience from all levels of society, in the boxes, pit and gallery, and such a building could only succeed where there was likely to be full support on a regular basis, from the middle class in particular. Lincoln was not only the largest town in the county, with a population of about 4,500 in 1750, but was also a cathedral city and a venue for court sittings and horse race meetings, so the gentry from much of Lincolnshire would regularly visit the city for days at a time. We do not know what guarantees Audley had, if any, that actors would regularly use his theatre, and he certainly had no guarantee that audiences would keep coming. He was taking a big gamble, but he was ushering in a cultural revolution in Lincolnshire. Once this form of entertainment was planted in the county it took root, flourished and spread.

The theatre in Lincoln was the first to be built in the county since Roman times (depending on whether the late medieval pageant house in Louth may be regarded as a theatre) and for twenty years or so it was the only one. It was at the southern end of the modern car park off Castle Hill, and the only vestiges of the theatre are the stone south wall and a small portion of the brick east wall at the entrance to what is now Cask Restaurant and Brewhouse. The theatre was 66ft long and 24ft wide, though by 1888 the building had been reduced to half its original length as the structure shown on the 25in Ordnance Survey plan was only about 30ft long. That end of Drury Lane was too narrow for carriages so ladies went to the theatre in sedan chairs.[1] A few yards east of the theatre, on Steep Hill, is the fifteenth

---

[1] Hill, Sir Francis, *Georgian Lincoln*, Cambridge (1966), p.16.

century building later an inn called the Harlequin as it was often frequented by actors. It is now, in 2016, a bookshop. We have no indication which companies of comedians used that theatre in the 1730s or 1740s. They were probably touring companies from London or elsewhere. The boys of the Cathedral choir in their surplices were allowed to perform the chorus in *Romeo and Juliet* in that theatre, and Lady Deloraine is said to have seen a puppet play there.[2] Two comedians, Edward Maddesley and James Smith, are recorded as having been buried at the nearby church of St Mary Magdalene in 1740 and 1741 respectively.[3] Audley himself died in 1741, his will being proved on 18 April.[4]

In 1750 the Lincoln theatre was taken over by Dennis Herbert (c1695-1770), usually known as William Herbert, who started to develop a circuit of towns in south and west Lincolnshire and places just across the county boundary. In May 1751 they were in Spalding for at least a month and Maurice Johnson, founder of the Gentlemen's Society there, noted that 'they have no Harlequin, singers, nor dancers, so are more tolerable than mere Monkeys'. On 10 August 1753 they were there again and a 'suitable prologue' was written and spoken by George Stevens.[5] A playbill for the Drury Lane theatre in Lincoln has been dated to 1754, but otherwise there is little information about actors in the county at this time. When Robert Haddelsey married Jane Wray in Caistor in September 1755 his occupation was given as 'player' so he could have been with Herbert's Lincoln company, and may have been related to the actor named as Maddesley.[6]

William Herbert was sometimes called 'Dr Herbert' as he had been trained as a surgeon and apothecary.[7] He was performing in Newcastle in 1728, Leeds 1729 and King's Lynn from 1743 to 1748.[8] He was accustomed to drink great quantities of beer in a day, but luckily he had a provident wife who kept hold of the cash and paid his tradesmen's bills punctually. William was so absent-minded that when fighting a duel on stage he was known to forget which combatant was to succumb. One night he played *Douglas* in *Henry IV*, and Nathaniel, his son, *Sir Walter Blunt*. In the fifth act where *Blunt* is slain, William Herbert, who seldom attended to either the words or business of his part, fell down, instead of Nathaniel. A voice from behind, cursing his old soul, and telling him of his error, caused him to spring up and renew the combat, when Sir Walter expired amidst the shouts and acclamations of the audience.[9]

George Alexander Stevens (1710–80) son-in-law of William Herbert and effective manager of the Lincoln company in the 1760s when the new theatre was opened in the King's Arms yard. (Wikipedia)

---

[2] Hill, *ibid*.
[3] Hartnoll, Phyllis (ed), *The Oxford Companion to the Theatre*, London (3rd edition 1967), p.578.
[4] Jones, Stanley, Major, Kathleen, Varley, Joan and Johnson, Christopher, *The Survey of Ancient Houses in Lincoln, IV, Houses in the Bail, Steep Hill, Castle Hill and Bailgate*, Lincoln (1996), p.50.
[5] Honeybone, Diana and Michael, *The Correspondence of William Stukeley and Maurice Johnson 1714-1754*, Lincoln Record Society Vol.104, Lincoln (2014), pp.172, 187-8.
[6] Saunders, David, *More Portraits of Caistor*, Lincoln (2007), p.114.
[7] Hartnoll, *op. cit.*, p.578.
[8] Hemingway, G., *The Robertson Family and the Lincoln and Nottingham Theatrical Circuits*, thesis (1976) in Lincoln Central Library, ref.UP 7467.
[9] Winston, James, *The Theatric Tourist*, London (1805, facsimile 2008), p.62.

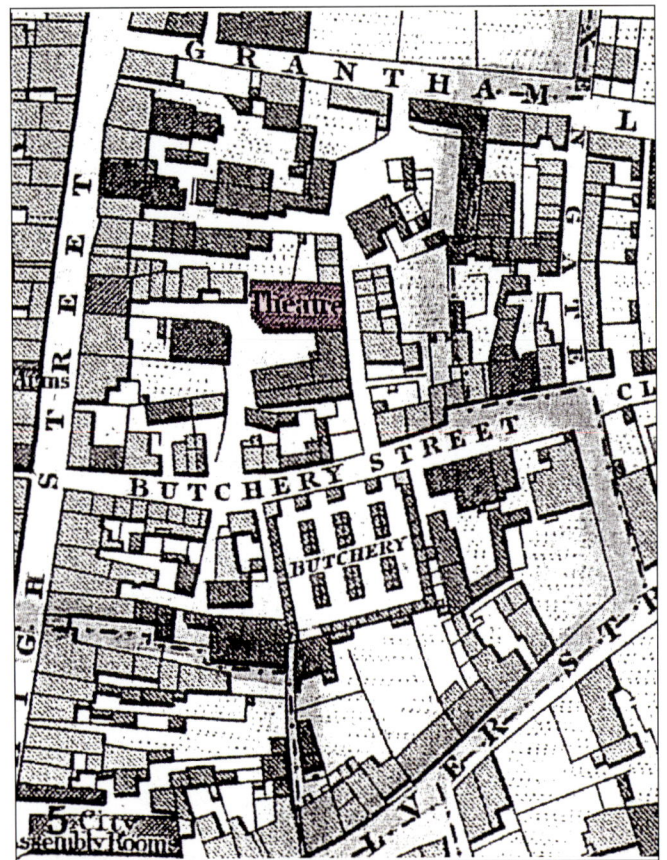

Clockwise from top left:

Lincoln's new theatre, established about 1768, was in the King's Arms Yard off High Street, shown here in a map of 1842. In 2016 the stage and auditorium of the Theatre Royal are still on the same site as the 1760s theatre.
Extract from Padley's 1842 Plan in Historic Town Plans of Lincoln 1610–1920, *Lincoln Record Society.*

The facade of No.278 High Street, Lincoln, still includes an archway leading to the King's Arms yard.
Photograph by Neil Wright, 2 January 2014

Through the archway can be seen the Theatre Royal, on the site of Lincoln's second theatre, in the King's Arms yard.
Photograph by Neil Wright, 21 August 2012

Opposite page:

This view of 1805 shows the main door of Lincoln theatre leading to boxes and the pit, with a staircase, left, leading up to the gallery. The corner position of the main door is clearly shown on the 1842 Plan above.
Houghton Library, Harvard University

William Herbert had three sons and a daughter. Nathaniel, the eldest son (d.1787) was apprenticed to a butcher but became an actor, and in about 1764 went with a company of comedians to the West Indies until 1769.[10] In the middle of the eighteenth century Jamaica had many wealthy planters who led a luxurious life and shortly before 1740 a playhouse was built in Spanish Town and a set of actors employed. William Herbert's second son, called Dennis, was placed in the Counting House of Mr Hogg in Lynn, and eventually became the principal merchant in Biggleswade, Bedfordshire. The youngest son held an office for several years in the Custom House in Lynn. Herbert's daughter Elizabeth (1728-1813) was an actress and on 25 February 1746 she had married George Alexander Stevens (1710-80) in Norwich. Stevens performed in several places. He was in Norwich by 1741, Lincoln 1750 (with Herbert's company), Bath 1751 and Dublin from September 1751 to May 1753. He was then in Lincoln again from 1753 to 1761, where he was frequently in debt, before going to Drury Lane theatre in London.

---

[10] Hemingway, *op. cit.*, p.40

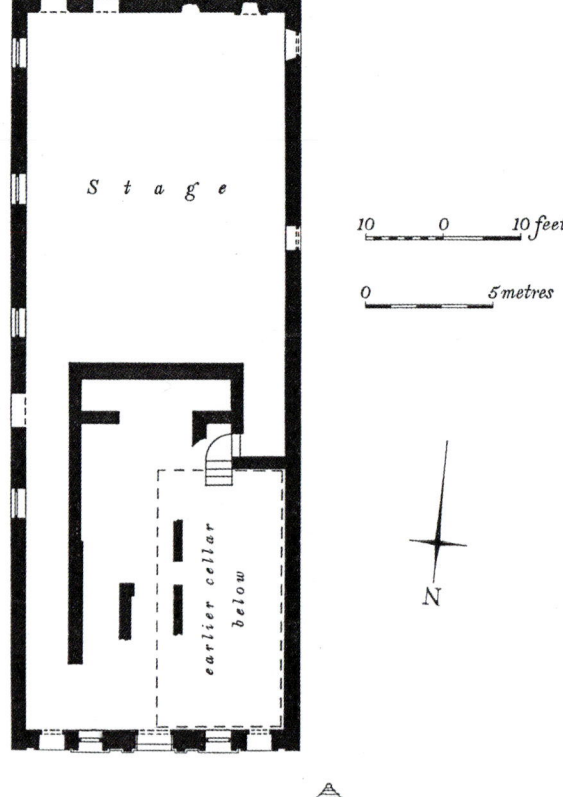

In Stamford the first theatre was in Broad Street behind the Nags Head inn, and the second was in St Mary's Street.

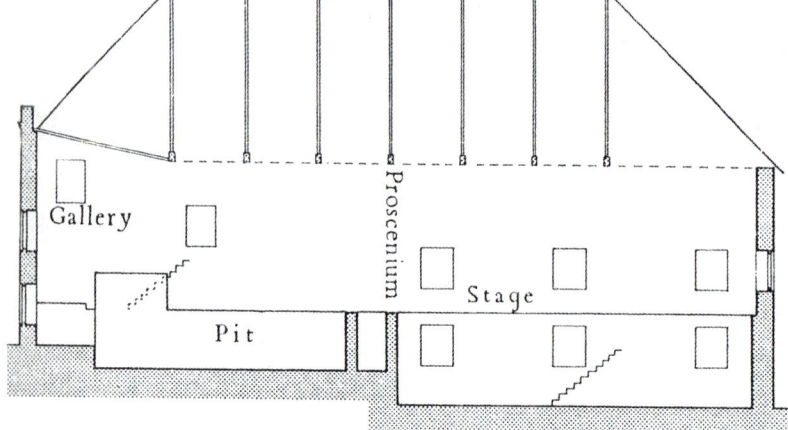

Top left:

Extract from Ordnance Survey 25in Plan, 1887, showing Stamford, with the locations of the first and second theatres highlighted.

Clockwise from top right, from Historic England, from RCHME Stamford Inventory Volume, 1977 (© Crown copyright. HE):

Plan at basement level of the second Stamford theatre, which opened on St Mary's Street in 1768.

Theatre on St Mary's Street, front elevation.

Theatre on St Mary's Street, diagrammatic section showing former arrangement.

Stevens was back in Lincoln in 1766. The Duke of York, raffish younger brother of George III, attended the Drury Lane theatre in Lincoln on Monday 29 September 1766 while returning south from Doncaster races. At his request the actors, referred to as 'Mr Stevens' company', put on *Midas*, (1592) by John Lyly, followed by a play of their choice. The Duke stayed for the first item and then went to a ball in the Assembly Rooms. The *Stamford Mercury* reported that:

> His Royal Highness seemed vastly pleased at the regularity and neatness of the house, and brilliancy of the company, and expressed much satisfaction at the performance of the piece.[11]

By this date William Herbert was about 70 years of age, and his son-in-law was evidently managing the company for him.

The elite area around Lincoln Castle and the Cathedral was in the northern part of the city, and about 1768 William Herbert, or more likely his son-in-law, left the theatre in Drury Lane to create a new one nearer to the centre. They adapted some buildings in the yard of the King's Arms tavern in High Street and this is still the site of the Theatre Royal auditorium some 250 years later.[12] In 1775 it was still being called the New Theatre. The original access to the yard of the King's Arms is still a right of way through an archway off High Street, next to a charity shop occupied in 2016 by the Red Cross. It is said that the old theatre in Drury Lane was then converted into two cottages.[13] Those cottages were later added to the large garden of No.4 Castle Hill and in 1843, when that house and land was sold, the building was referred to as 'one tenement now used as a stable and coachhouse formerly as a playhouse'. The surviving eastern half of the theatre is shown as a squarish building on the Tithe Map of 1851. The house and its garden, including the former theatre, was acquired by Lincoln City Council and demolished in 1938/39 to create a garden and car park, but these plans were postponed indefinitely on 1 April 1941 and instead the site was used as an emergency reservoir of water for fire fighting. It was later converted into a small car park.[14]

Stamford theatre, Whitley

Well before Lincoln theatre moved downhill, there was a second purpose-built playhouse in Lincolnshire. That was in Stamford, which was a social centre for south Lincolnshire and adjacent parts of other counties, and also an important staging post on the Great North Road. Its population in 1750 was about 2,500. It is not known when that theatre was built but it was perhaps before 1752 as the *Manchester Mercury* reported an Epilogue of thanks to the ladies and gentlemen, spoken by Mrs Stanford in

---

[11] *Stamford Mercury*, 9 October 1766.
[12] Warwick, Lou, *Drama that Smelled; Or, Early Drama in Northampton and Hereabouts*, Northampton (1975), p.188.
[13] Warwick, Lou, *op. cit.*, p.195.
[14] Jones, Stanley, Major, Kathleen, Varley, Joan and Johnson, Christopher, *The Survey of Ancient Houses in Lincoln IV: Houses in the Bail, Steep Hill, Castle Hill, and Bailgate*, Lincoln (1996), pp.49, 50; Tann, Geoff, 'Second World War Tanks for Uphill Lincoln', in *Lincoln Castle, Bail and Close* (Survey of Lincoln Vol.11), Lincoln (2015), p.64.

Jemmy Whitley's company of comedians on 21 April 1752 at the theatre in Stamford. It was located in an inn yard in Broad Street, referred to in one 1766 source as 'in the Corn Market at the Nag's Head' and as 'near All Saints Church' in April of that year.[15] The Nag's Head inn was two doors east of Browne's Hospital, opposite the junction with Ironmonger Street, and backed onto North Street. Numbers 5 to 8 Broad Street now stand on the site and the alley down the side is still called Nag's Head Passage.[16]

James Augustus Whitley (c1724-81) dominated the theatre in Stamford for over twenty years and was one of the leading provincial managers of the eighteenth century. In 1774 the *Nottingham Journal* referred to his company as 'the best travelling company at this time in England'.[17] His last name was variously spelled Whitly, Whitley or Whiteley though his first name was usually plain Jemmy. As a young man he worked for a solicitor in Dublin and when the lawyer was in gaol for debt Jemmy had to visit him there to arrange his work. On one of these calls Jemmy met an actor who was also 'visiting', Joe Elrington, and obtained an introduction to the Smock Alley Theatre in that city, writing out parts and later becoming prompter's call boy.

In 1742 Whitley left Dublin to join the widow Cassandra Parker (c1718-69) and her company of comedians in Galway in the west of Ireland. Their relationship quickly developed into something stronger. He married Mrs Parker and so started his career as a theatre manager. Poor receipts led them to leave Galway, eventually reaching Liverpool, and within a short time he had Manchester, Wolverhampton and Doncaster theatres in his hands. He built up an extensive empire of provincial theatres and the *Thespian Dictionary* of 1802 stated that Whitley had 'the most extensive Midland Circuit ever known in England'. That included Stamford and, at various times, Worcester, Bedford, Cambridge, Wolverhampton, Derby, Nottingham, Newark, Retford, Chesterfield, Wakefield, Leeds and other places. Henry Lee, another theatre manager, wrote that:

> *I believe Mr Whitley, with the exception of myself, built more theatres than any other manager in the kingdom. Building was less expensive than it has ever been since: besides Mr Whitley had the address to get the public to build theatres for him, and left them under his own direction.*[18]

He was said to have a pleasing voice as well as a generous heart. Winston said he was:

> *an actor of indifferent merit, zealous for the ancient school, had an unseemly twitch in his deportment, grave and sententious on all occasions, and a strict adherent to the measured cadence of te ti tum, and tum ti te.*

He had a violently passionate personality, and when in his passions he was vulgar, rude, boisterous, and, perversely, he so abhorred hypocrisy that he laboured to make himself appear as bad as possible. He would ridicule and abuse his actors

---

[15] Warwick, Lou., *op. cit.*, pp.164, 165; *SM*, 24 April 1766.
[16] Smith, Martin, *Stamford Then and Now*, Stamford (1992), pp.32, 52, 72.
[17] *Nottingham Journal*, 9 July 1774.
[18] Hodkinson, J.L. and Pogson, R., *The Early Manchester Theatre*, Manchester (1960), p.52.

in a whimsical, foulmouthed way like a Billingsgate fishwife, but would allow no one else to do that, and would give his players substantial benefits. He strongly promoted the dignity of his company and it has been suggested that 'puffing' or extravagant publicity may have been invented or at any rate developed by him.[19]

There were many anecdotes about Whitley. In a journey to Stamford, to save expenses, he walked, and carried his portmanteau on his arm. Within a few miles of his destination, he saw a hearse, and bargained with the driver to take him up. Being weary, he got into the interior and fell fast asleep, having previously desired *Jehu* to call him when he approached the town. The arch whip anticipating the pleasure of a joke, drove into the inn-yard of the George at Stamford, and collecting together as many of Whitley's friends as he could muster, told them he'd *show'm fun* – then, opening the door, he waked the snorting manager with news of his journey's end. Jemmy got out, and to his astonishment, saw himself surrounded with a number of acquaintances, who all at once said 'Ah, Master Whitley! How do you do? Welcome to Stamford'. To which the disconcerted actor replied, in his usual phrase – you lie you lie you thieves – 'I am *not* Master Whitley; I don't know any such person'; and coolly walked off with his portmanteau.[20]

In April 1766 Whitley and his company performed the comic opera *Love in a Village* in the theatre 'near All Saints Church' but he did not have a monopoly of that theatre.[21] On 28 November 1766 Mr Goodhall's company of comedians performed *The Distress'd Mother* for the benefit of Mrs Granger, a widow, and her five children, on the last night of their stay there. But the end of that theatre was near. In 1766 the Earl of Exeter, who lived in Burghley House on the edge of Stamford and dominated the town, leased to Whitley and Alderman William Clark, mason, for 99 years at £6 per annum, a piece of land in St Mary's Street, 110ft 8in by 43ft 6in, with the stipulation that they were to build a theatre on it. It was in the manner and style of the London theatres and was fitted with boxes, pit and gallery, and dressing rooms in the basement. The Earl had a private box with his coat of arms on it. By the time the theatre was finished it had cost £806 and was described as 'one of the compleatest in the kingdom'.[22] It was a simple classical building of local stone in the distinctive Stamford style, in a wide residential street rather than a commercial part of the town. In 1836 it was described as 'a plain looking edifice, but neatly and very commodiously fitted up in the interior'.[23] The diagrammatic section of the former arrangement shows that the stage occupied half the theatre, the floor of the side boxes was level with the stage, and that the ceiling over the gallery was higher at the back than at the front. The shell still survives, part of Stamford Arts Centre and

---

[19] *The Mirror of Taste, and Dramatic Censor*, Vol.1, No.5, May 1810; Gilliland, Thomas, *The Dramatic Mirror: containing the History of the Stage*, London, 1808, p.612.
[20] Winston, James, *op. cit.*, p.61.
[21] SM, 24 April 1766.
[22] Warwick, Lou, *op. cit.*, pp.165, 177; SM, 9 June 1768.
[23] Saunders, John, jun., *Lincolnshire in 1836*, Lincoln (1836), p.104.

once more in use as a theatre. The new theatre was opened on Monday 13 March 1768 when Whitley's company repeated *Love in a Village* that they had performed two years earlier. While the opening performance was being given there was some competition at "the old playhouse in the Corn Market at the Nag's Head" where the Sadlers Wells company from London were performing 'for the fair week only and positively no longer on account of going to Grantham Fair'.[24] After that nothing more is heard of the Broad Street theatre.

The opening of the new theatre must have given Jemmy Whitley great satisfaction, but within eleven months he faced a personal tragedy. His wife of 26 years, she who had given him his start as a manager, passed away. She is buried in St John's church, Stamford, where a marble monument was erected with the following wording:

> On the Tenth of February 1769 was entomb'd Cassandra, Wife of James Whitley, Gent., who amply possess'd all the good Qualities that accomplish the best of Women:
>
> The Silver Moon shall wither in her Prime
> The Golden Sun himself shall yield to Time
> The Stars grow dim but Chastity and Truth
> Shall ever flourish in immortal Youth.[25]

Above:
Memorial to Cassandra (d.1769), wife of Jemmy Whitley, in St John's church, Stamford.
Photograph by Neil Wright, 31 August 1998.

Opposite page:
Top: Nottingham theatre in 1805. Built by Jemmy Whitley and for long part of the Stamford circuit.
Houghton Library, Harvard University.

Bottom: Derby theatre in 1805. Also built by Jemmy Whitley and part of the Stamford circuit until the 1840s.
Houghton Library, Harvard University.

Circuits

Most companies of comedians in Britain could not make a living by performing in just one town. They each needed a circuit of other towns, which they could visit in a regular calendar of local 'seasons', usually at the time of race meetings, fairs or assizes when the potential audience was at its most numerous. From the middle of the eighteenth century travel was made easier as main roads all over the country were being improved by turnpike trusts. No longer would a few days of heavy rain turn highways into muddy quagmires that would delay carriages and wagons. These better roads enabled actors and their paraphernalia of costumes, scenery and props (then called dresses, scenery and decorations) to move more easily from town to town. Fairly quickly these circuits became established on a long term basis as purpose built theatres were erected in the main towns and the companies came to control these playhouses, owning them or having them on long leases, and so could exclude other companies from those buildings. The value of opening theatres at the time of special events such as marts and races was shown by the returns. In Wakefield in 1779 the theatre opened before the town's races started and on 6 September the theatre only took 30s. In 1822 Stamford mart brought in £55 2s 0d the first week and £160 19s 0d the second, and the race week that year brought in £78 16s 0d followed by only £24 0s 6d the next week. Tate Wilkinson once said

---

[24] Warwick, Lou., *op. cit.*, p.165.
[25] Warwick, Lou., *op. cit.*, p.166.

that stars had to be brought to attract people into the theatre before race week, but during that week the audience 'were wont to stare at one another and the stock company sufficed'.[26]

Whitley's circuit embraced several large towns over a wide area but Stamford was the only Lincolnshire town included. That theatre had two seasons, one in March and April around the Mid-Lent Fair and the other in June and July to include the races. Whitley's circuit was quite fluid. He built and owned the theatres in Nottingham, Derby and elsewhere but other towns left the circuit over the years and some new ones were added. In the early stages of establishing circuits there could be clashes between competing companies, as in Wakefield in 1774 where Whitley was unsuccessful and the town became part of Tate Wilkinson's York and Hull circuit.[27] Nottingham was the largest town in the East Midlands, with a population of 17,771 in 1779 that rose to 28,861 by 1801. The theatre there was built by Whitley about 1760, in St Mary's Gate and was partly on the site of an older theatre that had been converted from an old barn about 1740, and partly on land purchased from Alderman Fellows.[28] Derby was smaller with a population of 10,826 in 1801. Whitley built a theatre there in 1773 on the site of a former malthouse in Bold Lane; before that a room in Irongate was used for theatrical performances. He also built theatres in Wolverhampton in 1779 and Worcester (1780). Leicester did not get a permanent theatre until 1800 although its population in 1750 was about 9,000 and by 1801 had risen to about 17,000. From December 1759 Whitley's company performed in a temporary theatre in the first floor Assembly Rooms at Coal Hill, next to the site of the later clock tower, and until March 1766 they played alternate seasons there with Mr Durravan's company. Whitley returned to Leicester in 1770 and 1771, with Nat Herbert in the latter year, and every year from December 1776 to January 1781. Fitting up a temporary theatre was a considerable operation; in 1771 work on the Coal Hill Assembly Rooms started by 2 March but the first performance was not given until 8 April.[29] Whitley's circuit was split up after his death but Nottingham, Derby and Stamford stayed linked together for most years until the 1840s.

By the late 1760s the Lincoln company under William Herbert had also developed a circuit and was visiting towns in greater Lincolnshire, an area embracing southern Lincolnshire and the fringes of adjacent counties, on a regular basis. An advertisement dated 18 March 1796 indicated that the Lincoln circuit then comprised theatres at Lincoln, Boston, Newark, Grantham, Huntingdon, Spalding, Wisbech and Peterborough. The circuit was smaller than Whitley's and its individual towns were each smaller than those in the Midland circuit. There is not a full list

---

[26] Senior, William, *The Old Wakefield Theatre*, Wakefield (1894), pp.34, 39; Rosenfeld, Sybil, 'The Theatrical Notebooks of T.H. Wilson Manly', *Theatre Notebook*, Vol.7, No.1, London (October, December 1952), p.9.
[27] Senior, William, op. cit., pp.9, 23, 26.
[28] Payne, Michael, 'Mr Whitley and his Company of Comedians: Nottingham St Mary's Gate Theatre 1761-1885', *Transactions of the Thoroton Society*, Vol.109, Nottingham (2005), 115, 124.
[29] Leacroft, Helen and Richard, *The Theatre in Leicestershire*, Leicester (1986), pp.8, 10, 11, 15.

of the Lincoln circuit before this date but there are signs that by the 1760s it was already in the form recorded in 1796 and 1829. In 1751 they visited Spalding in May but two years later they were there from 10 August.[30] In 1756 the Kesteven Justices at Bourne sessions issued an order to the chief and petty constables of their area referring to:

> *several idle persons commonly called strollers having come lately into their parts and county, who had acted for hire or reward plays and other entertainments in open defiance of the law.*

No details were given and in the following years no proceedings were taken against actors so the constables perhaps turned a blind eye.[31] In 1767 the season at Lincoln was about eight weeks from September to November, as in later years. In 1772 and 1774 the company was at Peterborough in July at the time of the races, and in January 1776 their goods were moved from Grantham to Boston. In 1771 the actor Thomas Snagg (alias Wilks) performed with Mrs Herbert's Lincoln company in King's Lynn and Fakenham, but the latter town did not become part of their permanent circuit. The 1753 date in Spalding and those 1760s and 1770s dates at Lincoln, Grantham, Boston and Peterborough are the same as in 1796.[32]

Plan of the annual circuit of the Lincoln company in the 1790s. It changed little between the 1760s and 1820s, apart from King's Lynn being replaced by Huntingdon, and Oundle being added in late years.
Drawn by Ken Redmore

From 1786 the *Stamford Mercury* also had advertisements for plays in other towns and in 1829 the timetable of the Lincoln circuit was then little changed from that of 1796, although Oundle had been added by the latter date and some towns' seasons had moved by up to four weeks. Each town was visited once a year, the chief towns usually during race or assize weeks. The length of the season varied from two weeks to eight weeks or longer, depending in part on the size of the town and the potential audience. It seems that there were very few changes to the Lincoln circuit between 1770 and 1830, in marked contrast to the Stamford circuit. Later on, particularly after 1800, new companies of comedians toured more informal and adaptable circuits in Lincolnshire and adjacent counties and these mainly served the smaller towns that could not support a purpose built theatre. It was only in the 1830s that the circuit system collapsed as the popularity of theatre declined.

In the 1790s the annual tour of the Lincoln company started with Grantham in late December for about five weeks, some years arriving there before Christmas,

---

[30] Honeybone, op. cit., pp.187-8
[31] Varley, Joan, *The Parts of Kesteven – Studies in Law and Local Government*, Sleaford (1974), p.75.
[32] Warwick, Lou., *Theatre Unroyal; Or, They called them Comedians*, Northampton (1974), p.30; SM, 9 July 1772, 14 June 1774, 25 January 1776, 18 March 1796; Grice, Elizabeth, *Rogues and Vagabonds*, Lavenham, Suffolk (1977), p.22.

then moved to Boston in late January for about six weeks and to Wisbech from the beginning of March until about the end of April. From May to the middle of June there was a gap and it is not clear where the company may have been for that period of six weeks or so. In 1811 they were at Whittlesey for three weeks in June, and in 1828 at Oundle for the same season, but for this period in earlier years there are no advertisements in the *Stamford Mercury*. Even though these were not the hot and humid days of midsummer, which were the worst times for indoor entertainment, still it seems that this period was perhaps used as a break to learn new plays and prepare costumes and scenery. For the whole of July the Lincoln company were in Peterborough, then to Huntingdon for the first two weeks in August, and to Spalding for two or three weeks. From about the second week of September until about the middle of November they had nearly eight weeks in Lincoln, and they were then in Newark until the middle of December and finally down the Great North Road to Grantham, and so to start the circle again. By the time the circuit was fixed it was rare for them to perform anywhere else.

The theatre in Drury Lane was at first the only purpose built playhouse in the Lincoln circuit and elsewhere the actors still had to adapt warehouses or other buildings for their use. During the 1770s more theatres were built and by 1820 nearly all of the main towns in Lincolnshire had one. In the early days another theatre used by the Lincoln company was in King's Lynn, which was similar in size to Derby with a population of 10,096 in 1801. The Norwich company of comedians had been visiting Lynn regularly since 1750 and in 1766 they persuaded the Corporation to build a permanent theatre. The large medieval guildhall of St George was converted at a cost of £450 and it was also used by Herbert's Lincoln company. It had two tiers of boxes as well as a pit and gallery and was said to be very pretty. From the 1760s the Lincoln company visited Lynn regularly in August, but sometime before 1796 a dispute between the joint managers led to their losing the town after nearly forty years, and the magistrates passed the licence to the Norwich company. In 1815 the King's Lynn theatre was replaced by a new playhouse but in the twentieth century the Guildhall became a theatre once again. The Lincoln company added Huntingdon to their circuit in place of Lynn.[33] Another change to their circuit was the loss of Gainsborough in 1790 after about eighteen years.

The theatrical life of Lincolnshire was not parochial. It drew resources of plays, actors and scenery from London and in 1804 when Tom Robertson put on the splendid spectacle of *Cinderella* in Lincoln he got 'several parts of the machinery' from the capital; that got attention and this provincial production received 'a very high eulogium' in the London papers in October.[34] Actors, and sometimes plays, also came from major provincial cities such as Norwich, Dublin, Edinburgh, York

---

[33] Warwick, Lou., *Theatre Unroyal*, p.25; Lynn may have been visited by the company in August, which is the time when they later visited Huntingdon, but the time of the Gainsborough season in the old theatre is not yet known.
[34] *SM*, 28 September 1804, 26 October 1804.

King's Lynn theatre in 1805. Built in the medieval St George's Hall in 1766 and visited by the Lincoln company until the 1790s.
Houghton Library, Harvard University

and Bath. In turn greater Lincolnshire provided new actors not only for those places but also for London, North America and the West Indies. Even the people of a small town like Donington could enjoy the world of the theatre. Matthew Flinders, father of the famous navigator, visited theatres in Boston and Spalding in the late eighteenth century. Sometimes players came to Donington and in 1784 he wrote:

> *In the latter half of October and beginning of November we have had a small Company of Comedians with us. I went 3 or 4 times and once or twice was tolerably entertained – tho' the accommodations were but indifferent, being a cold Barn in the Church Street. Saw the Quaker's Wedding [1723] & Mayer of Garret [sic] [1763] very decently done. They came from Tattershall here and left us for Swineshead, but there I hear dissentions took place among them & they have separated.*

93

Fourteen years later in 1798 he noted:

> *During the greatest part of October we have had a small company of comedians at the Bull. They fitted up a snug small Theatre. The Fair helped them, otherwise they would have done very poorly.*

As early as January 1776 he had noted in his accounts 'gave some distressed Players 3s.'[35]

Although the companies of comedians were regularly on the move they did stay a number of weeks in each place so it was not worthwhile to tie up money in wagons to move their goods about. Sometimes they could move scenery and other goods by canal but usually they hired drivers and wagons. In January 1776 Nathaniel Herbert hired a van to take his goods from Grantham theatre to Boston. The goods were delivered safely, but on the return journey the wagon, now loaded with coal, overturned in the snow at Garwick (between Swineshead and Heckington) and the driver and his passenger were both killed. Luckily such accidents were rare. Fifty years later, in June 1824, John Billings, a youth employed by the manager of the Stamford company, was leading a wagon from Derby to Nottingham with the company's baggage, when he tried to get on the shafts. Unfortunately his cloak got caught in the front wheel, dragged him down and the wheel passed over his body. He was severely crushed and died the next morning.[36] Both of those entries do suggest that a single wagon was enough to move the company's goods between towns, though it is known that the Norfolk company on circuit used three wagons each holding six tons of equipment and drawn by teams of six horses, reduced to two wagons in summer. For most actors the usual mode of travel was on foot, trailing behind the company's wagons. About 1770 Thomas Snagg said that among the most respectable of the troop, three would hire a post chaise, 'making one of them a purse-bearer', which usually cost 9d a mile.[37]

In the 1820s Thomas Manly, then manager of the Stamford company, often travelled, presumably on horseback, for 1s 3d per mile, paid a man and ostler 4s 6d, and in addition had to pay tolls on the turnpikes. At other times he travelled by chaise for which in 1827 he paid £6 6s 0d from Stamford to Chesterfield; or by coach as he records for 2 March 1830:

> *On Wednesday morning 7 o'clock by coach from White Swan Halifax to Doncaster, one inside 17s two out 19s. From Doncaster on to Stamford one inside £1 15s, two out £2, Coachman etc 12s. Got into Stamford at 1 o'clock morning!*

While the manager travelled in comfort the players tramped. Walter Donaldson, one of Manly's actors, reckoned that they walked five hundred miles during the year. For this reason, he said, Manly never engaged older people and rarely married couples.[38]

---

[35] Beardsley, Martyn and Bennett, Nicholas (eds), *Grateful to Providence. The Diary and Accounts of Matthew Flinders, Surgeon, Apothecary and Man-Midwife 1775-1802*, Vol.1 1775-1784, pp.30, 127, 162, Vol.2 1785-1802, p.101, Lincoln Record Society Vol.95 and Vol.97, Lincoln (2007 and 2009).
[36] *SM*, 25 January 1776, 11 June 1824.
[37] Field, Moira, *The Lamplit Stage*, Norwich (1985), p.33; Grice, *op. cit.*, p.34.
[38] Rosenfeld, Sybil, 'The Theatrical Notebooks of T.H. Wilson Manly', *Theatre Notebook*, Vol.7, No.1, London (October, December 1952), p.3.

The Robertson family arrives

The second stage in the history of drama in Lincoln came to an end about 1770 when William Herbert died, not long after the theatre had moved downhill. His death led to a conflict which was to usher in 75 years of Robertson family domination of theatre in Lincolnshire. William Herbert's son Nathaniel returned to England from Ireland where he had been performing and hoped to take over the Lincoln company, being not only the eldest son but the only son on the stage. Nat Herbert had a considerable reputation as a country actor, particularly in coarse comic characters and clowns in pantomimes. Robertson said:

> *He was a man of not very polished manners, fond of society and loved a cheerful glass. When manager, he was noted for being very bustling and straightforwardly hasty behind the scenes when he had to perform, so that he oftener confused than aided.*[39]

However his mother, to whom William had left the company in his will, had given control to her son-in-law, George Alexander Stevens, who in turn had appointed Mr Dyer, one of his principal performers, as manager. Stevens had developed a satirical entertainment called *Lectures on Heads* in which he used a series of busts to make witty comments about characters of the day. *Heads* was first performed in 1764, became an immediate success and Stevens was earning more by taking that around Britain and Ireland and also to Boston and Philadelphia in the American colonies.[40] In the eighteenth century there were very few theatres in north America and the actors came from London and British provincial theatres. A company of comedians managed by Daniel Douglass toured between 1758 and 1774 and built theatres in Philadelphia, New York, Charleston and Providence, but there was no purpose built theatre in Boston until after 1800.[41] Stevens died in Baldock, Hertfordshire, in 1780.

Nat Herbert, frustrated in his hopes of getting the Lincoln circuit, tried to set up an opposition theatrical company but it did not succeed. At last, friends of the family intervened and an agreement was reached. His mother transferred the property and management to him for an initial payment and a yearly income. Nat found the necessary funds to pay his mother from the nearest wealthy theatre manager, selling a share in the company to Jemmy Whitley in 1772. Being busy with his other commitments Whitley appointed James Shaftoe Robertson (c1723-80), who was working at the York theatre at the time, as his deputy in the Lincoln partnership.[42]

James Robertson's family came originally from Perthshire in Scotland, but his father became a senior servant of Baron Clive or the Earl of Powis in the area

---

[39] Hemingway, *op. cit.*, p.38, 41; Gilliland, *op. cit.* pp.212-13.
[40] Brewer, John, *The Pleasures of the Imagination: English Culture in the Eighteenth Century*, Abingdon (2013), p.310; Warwick, Lou, *Drama that Smelled*, p.187.
[41] Henderson, Mary, *Theater in America*, New York (1996), pp.11, 12.
[42] Gilliland, *op. cit.*, p.212.

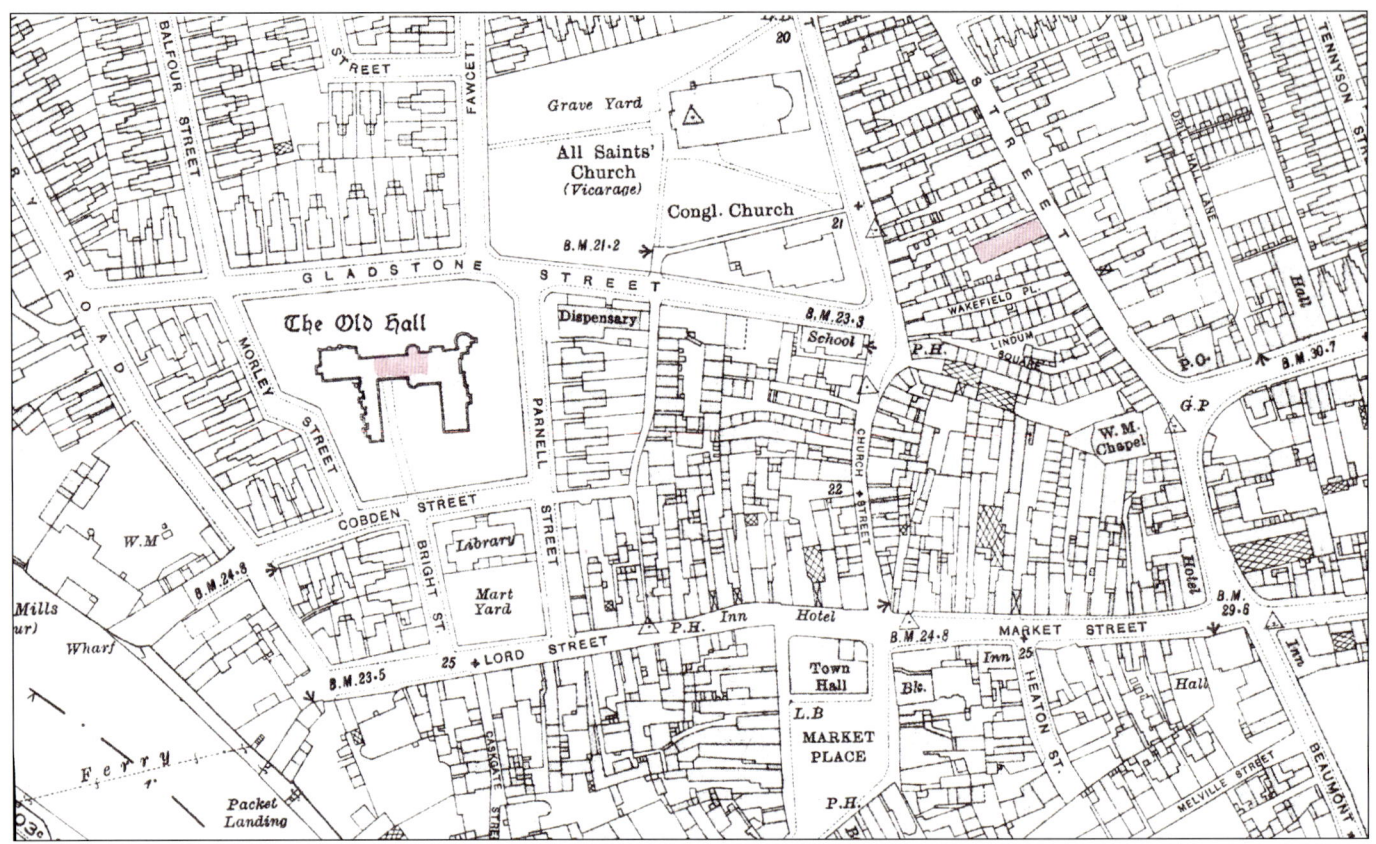

Gainsborough. The first theatre was in Back Street (now North Street), usually approached from Church Street, and the later theatre was in part of the medieval Old Hall. Extract from Ordnance Survey 25in Plan, 1921.

of Ludlow, Shropshire, where James was born, probably in 1723. James went to Ludlow Grammar School but ran away at seventeen to go on the stage. In the early days his life was not easy. One day travelling between towns, with a Mr Bensley, lately of Drury Lane, he found their united funds amounted to a single penny. With this they agreed to toss up for the purchase of a mutton pie, the winner alone to eat it. Robertson winning, Bensley, 'during the other's luscious banquet, stamped and swore like a truly hungry and irritated son of Thespis' On another journey with Henry King they suffered almost three days abstinence until they hit on the idea of cutting off their hair, at that time worn long, and selling it to buy food. As that left them nearly bald they had to use part of the money to buy a couple of 'cherry-tree wigs, vulgarly so called, which they wore to the no small entertainment of their brethren'[43]

A 'Mr Robertson' appeared with Durravan's company at Leicester in 1760 and 1764, and was also there with Whitley in 1761 and 1765. While acting in Loughborough in 1765 James Robertson married Miss Ann Fowler. They were performing in Lincolnshire that year if not earlier, for their son Thomas was born in Alford in 1765, and James also appeared with William Herbert's company at King's Lynn while Tom was young. Tate Wilkinson of York employed James and Ann in 1767, and as

---

[43] Richards, John, 'Thomas Shaftoe Robertson and The Theatric Tourist', *Theatre Notebook*, Vol. XXIX, No.1, London (1975), p.6; Winston, James, *op. cit.*, p.36.

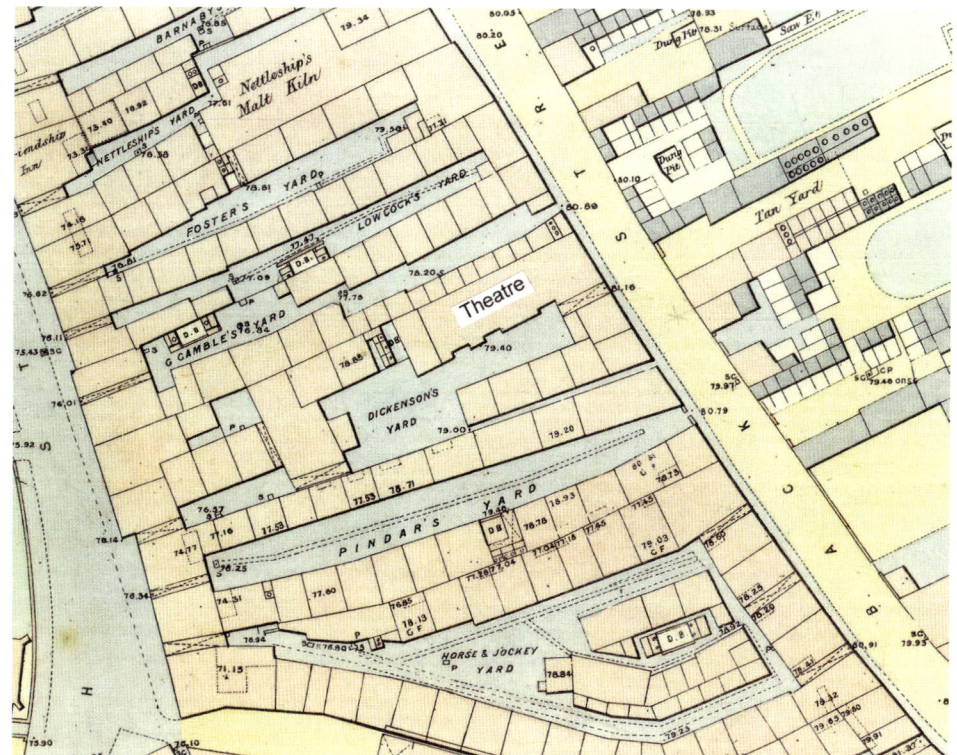

The first theatre in Dickenson's Yard is shown in detail in this extract from the 1853 Plan of the town, drawn by D.J.H. Ibbetson for the Local Board, 1853.
Gainsborough Library

he already had a James Robertson in his company he referred to the newcomer as Shaftoe Robertson. Wilkinson said that James 'had a good understanding, but he did not possess Lord Chesterfield's graces; quite the reverse, for he walked like a crab'. It was later said that 'his performance of the principal characters of Foote's dramas was highly esteemed'.[44] His three children were Thomas Shaftoe (1765-1831), who succeeded his father as manager at Lincoln, James (1773-1831), who became a manager on the Stamford circuit, and George (1774-1843), who became a printer and stationer in Peterborough.[45] Young James was christened on 30 June 1773 in St Mary Whitechapel in Stepney, London, and George on 16 July 1774 at St John's in Stamford. 'Master Shaftoe' (Thomas, aged 4½) appeared on the York stage on 17 April 1770. The 'Shaftoe' family performed for Wilkinson at Leeds in October 1771 before James moved to Lincoln as Whitley's representative.[46]

Robertson's first recorded appearance with the Lincoln company was in February 1772 at the old Newark theatre in Guildhall Street.[47] When the new partnership of Whitley and Nat Herbert performed at Stamford in 1773 it still used the name of 'Mr Whitley's company' while at other venues from July 1772

---

[44] Hemingway, *op. cit.*, pp.2, 3; Wilkinson, Tate, *Memoirs of his own life by Tate Wilkinson, patentee of the Theatre Royal, York and Hull*, Vol.2, York (1790), p.55; Stark, Adam, The History and Antiquities of Gainsborough, Gainsborough (2nd edn 1843), p.353.
[45] Warwick, Lou, *Theatre Unroyal*, p.26.
[46] Hemingway, *op. cit.*, pp.3, 4.
[47] Hemingway, *op. cit.*, p.4; Gresswell's Nottingham and Newark Journal, 1 February 1772, 23 March 1772.

until August 1775, such as the Leicester theatre in December 1772, it went by the name of 'Whitley and Herbert's company'.[48] In January, March, June and July of 1775 they performed at Stamford under the joint names, not just Whitley's company as before, but the joint company was last referred to in September 1775 for performances at Lincoln.[49] They apparently split up soon after that, as in October 1775 'Mr Whitley's company' performed at Stamford, while in January 1776 'Mr Herbert's company' were performing in Grantham and about to move to Boston.[50] So it would seem to be in late 1775 that Whitley withdrew after some three years and James Robertson, now aged over 50, purchased Whitley's share of the Lincoln company.

More theatres built

The emergence of James Robertson from the shadows happily coincided with a phase of theatre-building in the Lincolnshire area. The erection of a purpose-built theatre, either by a town corporation, a wealthy merchant or the manager of a company of comedians, was a big investment in the future. The owner of a theatre would want to have a good company of comedians committed to visit for a season every year and the manager of a company would like exclusive use of a theatre to keep other companies out of that town. So by the time a town got a proper theatre it would already be on a circuit, and after that it was, in the late eighteenth century, unlikely to be dropped from the circuit. Towns that only had temporary theatres, on the other hand, were in a rather fluid position in the developing circuit system.

Gainsborough's first theatre closed c.1790 and was demolished for road widening c.1938. The above photograph is from Eddie Sissons and the Delvers, That's Entertainment *(2001).*
Opposite page:
Watercolour painted by Karl Wood in the 1930s showing Dickenson's Yard. On the left of the picture is the rear of Gainsborough's first theatre.
Usher Art Gallery, Lincoln, reference LCNUG: 1977/350

It appears that after Lincoln and Stamford, the next theatre built in Lincolnshire was in Gainsborough. That was a port on the Trent and probably the third largest town in the county with an estimated population of about 3,200 in 1775. The theatre was erected about 1772 by Mr Dickenson, Mr Parker and others on the west side of North Street, then called Back Street, on a site that in 2015 is opposite the Co-operative Funeral Service. The most direct route from the rest of the town was via Church Street and a narrow alley leading into Dickenson's yard at the side of the theatre. It was a 'low but neat and somewhat tasty brick building' with a front in an Egyptian style with two pilasters on each side.[51] The proscenium arch was at the west end of the building, adjoining which were two dressing rooms in a separate low building. The gallery could hold about two hundred and sixty people; the pit extended a further twenty feet in front of the gallery but the theatre did not have any boxes.[52] Gainsborough theatre was used from its earliest days by

---

[48] *SM*, 9 July 1772, 18 March 1773, 8 April 1773, 3 June 1773, 14 July 1774, Leacroft, *op.cit.*, p.33; Warwick, Lou, *Drama that Smelled*, p.160.
[49] *SM*, 16 March 1775, 8 June 1775; Playbill, Lincoln, 6 September 1775.
[50] *SM*, 12 October 1775, 25 January 1776, 14 March 1776, 19 June 1777.
[51] Stark, Adam, op. cit., p.352.
[52] *Op. cit.* p.353.

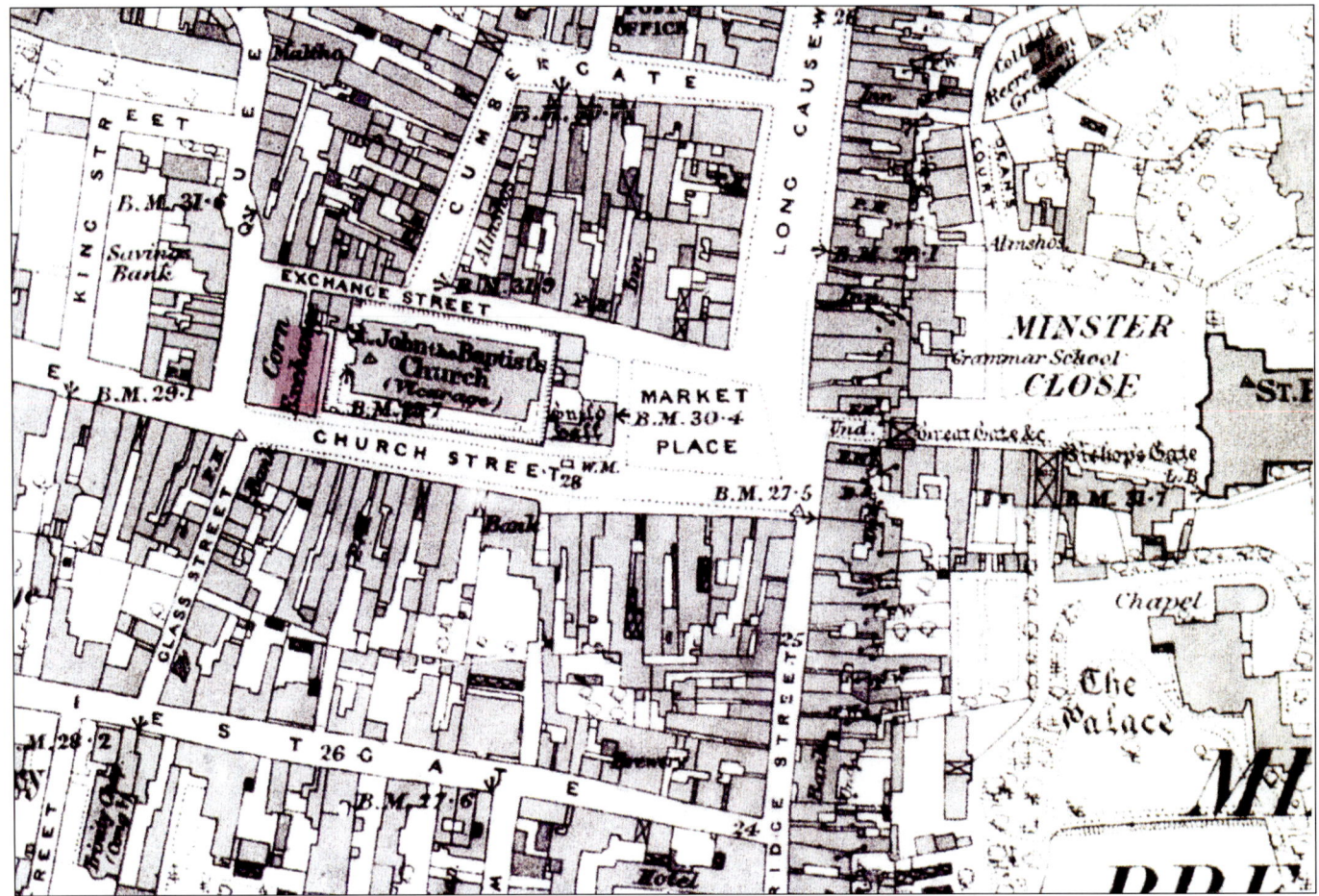

Peterborough's Georgian theatre, marked in red, was west of the parish church. Extract from Ordnance Survey 25in Plan, 1888.
Courtesy Vivacity Peterborough Archives

Nat Herbert's Lincoln company and was attended by 'the magnates of the town, who were at that time zealous supporters of the drama'.[53] A rival company opened a second theatre in Gainsborough's medieval Old Hall in 1787 and in the face of competition the Lincoln company dropped the town from their circuit about 1790 and the old theatre closed.[54] This is the only instance in the long eighteenth century of a Lincolnshire theatre closing due to the opening of a competing playhouse. Towns in this county were too small to support more than one theatre and nowhere else were there rival purpose built theatres in Georgian times.

Peterborough, then in Northamptonshire, was a small cathedral city with a population of about 3,500 in 1801, but it had a theatre with a pit and gallery on the Lincoln circuit by 1772, owned by a group of local men led by the Revd William Freeman.[55] In 1774 the 3rd Earl of Orford sailed a holiday fleet of three vessels across the fens from his home in Norfolk and arrived in Peterborough in June. They stayed in the city for several weeks, and one of the party went to the theatre 'and saw *She Stoops to Conquer* performed in a manner much beyond my expectations'.[56]

---

[53] *Ibid*
[54] *Op. cit.* p.354
[55] *SM*, 9 July 1772; Tebbs, H.F., *Peterborough – A History*, Cambridge (1979), p.174; Warwick, Lou, *Theatre Unroyal*, p.30.
[56] Tebbs, *op. cit.*, pp.174, 176.

Newark is an ancient town on the Great North Road through Nottinghamshire and it had a population of 6,730 in 1801. In November 1772 work started on building a new theatre for John Brough in Middlegate to replace a temporary one in Baldertongate that had only pit and gallery. It has been suggested that the first temporary theatre may have been in the old Guildhall in Guildhall Street, just off Baldertongate. The new theatre cost £360 3s 2d including the cost of demolishing the previous building on the site. The new theatre had front boxes and when filled to capacity it produced between £60 and £70.[57]

A sale advertisement of June 1818 described Newark theatre as:

> *neatly fitted up with Front Boxes and Lobby behind the same, two Tiers of Side Boxes, a good Pit, capacious Front and Side Galleries; and Stage 33' 6" wide and 20' 6" deep, situate in Middlegate. – convenient Dressing Rooms and Apartments are attached to the Stage, and excellent cellars underneath the whole Building. The theatre is capable of holding 890 persons.*

The first recorded play there was staged by Whitley and Herbert's company in June 1773, who performed for six nights on their way to Nottingham races before the

---

[57] Warner, Tim, 'Curtain rises on the town's first theatre', *Newark Civic Trust Magazine*, issue 68, Newark (February 2013), pp.13, 14; Hemingway, *op. cit.*, p.66; Warwick, Lou, *Theatre Unroyal*, p.30.

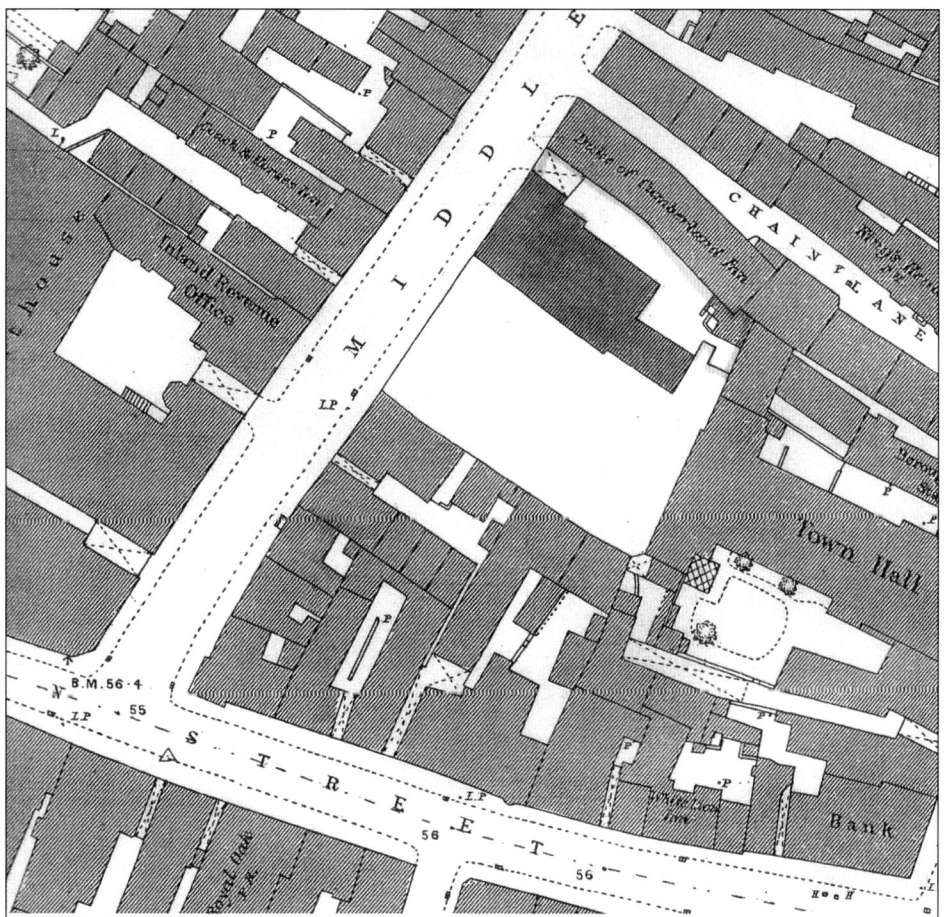

Newark theatre and its yard were in Middlegate, west of the Town Hall. Extract from Ordnance Survey 1:500 Plan, 1885.

Theatre in Boston Market Place, built in 1777 and closed in 1806. In 2016 it is part of a pub called The Folly.
Photograph by Neil Wright, 4 February 2012

final touches had been made to the new building.[58] In May 1779 Whitley also made a visit to Wisbech and opened a 'very neat and compact New Temporary theatre' near the High Street there. He said he would return to Wisbech again the following year and erect an 'elegant and extensive one' on which he would 'spare neither cost nor art', but 1779 was perhaps his only visit to that town.[59] He sometimes visited Northampton, but he gave up all three of those places and Newark and Wisbeach became part of the Lincoln circuit. It was also about this time, in 1774, that Whitley was driven out of Wakefield by Tate Wilkinson just before that town got its first purpose-built theatre.

The playhouses in Gainsborough, Peterborough and Newark were followed in 1777 by new theatres in Boston and Grantham. Boston was a port experiencing

---

[58] Hemingway, *op. cit.*, pp.66, 72; Warner, *op. cit.*, p.14.
[59] *SM*, 6 May 1779.

great growth in commerce and prosperity and its population rose from 3,470 in 1767 to 6,465 in 1801. Boston's temporary theatre had been in a granary where the Market Place turned into South Street and it had only a pit and gallery. Despite its lack of boxes it still attracted a quality audience from a wide area. In the summer of 1766 a lady from London visited Boston for six weeks, going to the theatre on three evenings, on two occasions not arriving until the first play was nearly over. On 4 July for *All in the Wrong* (1761) and *The Citizen* (1761) the house was very full, for *The Clandestine Marriage* (1766) and *The Mayor of Garratt* on 11 July the audience included 'the famous Miss Hunter, several other Fine Ladies from Spilsby, Mrs Mary Craddock', wife of the Anglican Bishop of Kilmore in Ireland, and her daughter Miss St George. The plays for her third visit were *The School for Lovers* (1762) and *The Reprisal* (1757). The latter evening was 'by desire of Mr Kerchever Thompson' and for the benefit of Mr Williams. The audience included the Rector of Wyberton and his family, Mr Massingberd and daughters, and the Miss Fydells of the town's leading family.

In 1769 Boston Corporation decided to build a new Fish Market on the west side of the Market Place, combined with houses to form the magnificent terrace known as the Corporation Building. Some members proposed combining the houses with a playhouse instead of a fish market, and when that was rejected they suggested that 'Rooms for Entertainment' be built over the market, but that had no more success. The idea did not go away and in 1775 the Corporation did decide to build a theatre, that could be a granary out of season, and combined it with two more houses.[60] The new theatre was in the Market Place, just three doors north of the previous one, and the architect was Thomas Lumby of Lincoln who had also designed the Corporation Building.

The new Boston theatre was very neatly fitted up, including front boxes, and was considered handsome. Lumby's instructions to the carpenter, Thomas Hunstan, specified a raking stage 13in higher at the back than at the front, a tongue and groove floor both to pit and boxes, and framed and panelled dressing rooms with 'shelves and wood pins for cloaths'. The theatre opened in 1777 and the outer walls still survive in 2016 as part of The Folly pub. That theatre, 'when filled to inconvenience', would produce about £40, and it served the town for nearly thirty years. The Lincoln company performed there for about six weeks every year, and the takings for the theatre during the 1777 season amounted to £372 8s 0d. The old temporary theatre remained as a warehouse until Sunday, 5 March 1820 when it burnt down.

Grantham, like Stamford and Newark, was a staging post on the Great North Road and its population rose from about 2,500 in 1750 to 4,288 in 1801. It is said that Grantham was being visited by Herbert's Lincoln company by 1757, and they used a rough structure in Westgate that had only a pit and gallery. Following the example of

---

[60] Minutes of Boston Corporation, 24 July 1769, 8 August 1769, 1 May 1770, 21 March 1775.

other towns, that first theatre may have been behind the George inn, as that inn did have a back entrance from Westgate. In 1777 Grantham's 'rude temporary building' was replaced by a more convenient one in the Market Place, though that lacked boxes until they were added in 1797. In 1753 the Spalding theatre was said to be in Crackpole, now called Broad Street, and was actually behind the White Hart, which fronted onto the Market Place.[61] It remained on that site throughout the Georgian period. The theatrical scene improved so much in the next quarter century that the theatres in both Grantham and Boston were replaced by new ones, in 1800 and 1806 respectively. After the spurt of theatre building in the mid 1770s there was a pause and it appears that only three new theatres were built in greater Lincolnshire during the next twenty years or so, a second one in Gainsborough and new ones in Retford and Louth. Overall the 1760s and '70s had seen theatre go forth and multiply, competing managers doing battle in towns without a purpose-built theatre, and getting a firm foothold in several main towns once a proper theatre was erected. The next decade was to see more managers but less progress.

---

[61] Honeybone, *op. cit.*, pp.187-88.

5

MANAGERS GALORE

THEATRE IN Lincolnshire suffered a double blow in 1781. Jemmy Whitley of Stamford died that year, and his protégé James Shaftoe Robertson of Lincoln died about the same time. These two men had provided the dynamic leadership that spread drama through Lincolnshire and adjacent parts. The 1770s had seen several purpose built theatres being erected, but in the next fifteen years there was less activity as the county had lost those two energetic leaders. The Lincoln and Stamford companies each had a number of successive managers in the 1780s and early 1790s, and suffered from poor or weak direction. At times the partners did not work well together. For much of this time the only Robertson involved was Mrs Ann Robertson, the widow of James, as her sons Thomas and James (Jnr) were still too young to take a leading part in theatrical affairs. There was no increase in the number of theatres in the county but there are more surviving playbills and newspaper advertisements than for previous years. From this time onwards the *Stamford Mercury* gave good coverage of the whole of Lincolnshire and parts of adjacent counties. The period of weak theatrical management came to an end in the mid 1790s when Tom Robertson entered a positive relationship to manage the Lincoln company, and his brother James became involved in running the Stamford troupe.

Lincoln

Since 1772 the Lincoln company of comedians had been run jointly by Nat Herbert and James Robertson, the latter as deputy for Whitley for the first few years. In the late 1770s they joined with Messrs Younger and Mattocks as partners in the management of the Manchester, Sheffield and old Birmingham theatres, while still keeping the Lincoln circuit. That was not a success so they soon dissolved the new partnership and confined themselves to greater Lincolnshire once more. About 1780 Herbert and Robertson took in a third partner, a Mr Green who paid £300 for his share. Green had been an army officer promoted from the ranks and apparently wanted to be an actor, though it was said that he knew little of acting or theatrical matters. Some twelve months after Green joined, James Robertson died in Sheffield probably early in 1781 and ownership of his share of the Lincoln company passed to his widow, Ann.[1] Robertson had been the active manager, 'with great ability both on and off the stage', and after his death the reputation of the company soon declined, together with its significance, success and income.[2]

---

[1] Gilliland, Thomas, *The Dramatic Mirror, containing the History of the Stage*, London (1808), pp.213, 214; Hemingway, G., *The Robertson Family and the Lincoln and Nottingham Theatrical Circuits* (1976), thesis in Lincoln Central Library, ref.UP 7467, p.6.
[2] Winston, James, *The Theatric Tourist*, London (1805 facsimile 2008), pp.36, 37.

About 1784 Nat Herbert was 'a little embarrassed in his private affairs [meaning he was short of money], and tired of a failing scheme' and retired from the theatre business. On the advice of his brother Dennis he sold his share in the Lincoln company to John Whitfield (1752-1814) for £300. Nat Herbert then became landlord of the White Horse Inn at Baldock in Hertfordshire, on the Great North Road, but did not enjoy his retirement for long and died there in 1787. Whitfield was an actor who had been with Herbert and Whitley's company in Leicester and Stamford in the early 1770s and had then gone on to work at Covent Garden theatre. He was also the brother-in-law of Mr Green.[3] The outcome of these changes was that for about three years in the mid 1780s the Lincoln circuit was jointly owned by the widow Ann Robertson, the actor John Whitfield, and Mr Green. Whitfield's existing contract kept him in London and he made Green his deputy 'to attend to his share of the concern', but given Green's lack of knowledge and experience the company declined even further.[4] It was not until late in 1786 that Whitfield and his wife came to Lincoln to start performing. Even then he still had an engagement in Liverpool in September to play five nights with the famous Royal mistress Dorothy Jordan. The *Stamford Mercury* praised the performance of Mrs Whitfield at Lincoln, and hoped that when her husband arrived he would help greatly to improve the reputation of the company. However the Lincoln company was not Whitfield's main interest; it continued to falter and he did not stay long.

Green and Whitfield, like Nat Herbert, both saw it as a losing business and left. On 31 August 1787 James Edward Miller, an actor who had been with the company since at least 1783, announced that he had purchased their shares and the company was called 'Miller and Robertson's' for the next nine years or so.[5] Miller had previously been with the Norwich circuit and on 1 August 1783 at Spalding theatre, in the course of a 'Speaking Pantomime', he performed the feat of a 'Leap thro' an Hogshead of Real Water', as he had performed it at Norwich, Yarmouth, Ipswich, Bury and elsewhere on that circuit 'to the general satisfaction of the public'.[6] It was said that Miller paid only £150 for Green's share and less than £100 for Whitfield's. On 7 September, a week after Miller had announced his acquisition, Mrs Ann Robertson advertised that her eldest son Thomas Shaftoe Robertson had returned from the Theatre Royal, Norwich, and she had assigned her management to him, to work jointly with Miller. She had not passed her share of the management to Tom when he became 21, but it was perhaps Miller's rise to joint manager that at last led her to summon her son to Lincoln. By September 1788 15-year-old James Robertson had also joined the cast of the Lincoln company, but perhaps he did not like being under the direction of his

---

[3] Gilliland, *ibid.*; Warwick, Lou, *Drama that Smelled; Or, Early Drama in Northampton and Hereabouts*, Northampton (1975), p.166; *Stamford Mercury*, 15 September 1786.
[4] Gilliland, *op. cit.*, p.214.
[5] Playbill, Lincoln, 27 August 1778; Lincolnshire County Archives, Misc. Don. 94/1/3 Hemingway, *op. cit.*, p.38; *SM*, 31 August 1787.
[6] Playbill, Lincoln, 1 August 1783, Lincolnshire County Archives, Misc. Don. 94/3.

elder brother and by March 1790, perhaps even by late 1788, he had left Lincoln and joined the Stamford company, where he stayed about thirty years.[7]

Tom Robertson was born at Alford on 2 August 1765 and at six or eight weeks old, being remarkably small, was put into a hand-basket and carried by his mother behind her husband on a double-horse from Alford to Boston where he made his first public appearance on stage. That was some seven years before his father became manager of the Lincoln company. It was also said that on one occasion baby Tom Robertson fell asleep in a chariot in the roof of King's Lynn theatre and was forgotten there![8] As a 13-year-old Tom played the part of *Quashaba*, a black girl, in *The Romp* (1767) by Bickerstaffe in Spalding on 7 August 1778 and ten days later played *Marianna*, another black girl, in *The Cozeners* (1774) by Samuel Foote. Only four days after that he ventured a more demanding role and 'attempted (for that night only)' the role of Dr Last in Foote's comedy of *The Devil upon two Sticks*. On 24 August Tom and his little brother James (aged 5) played the two princes in *Edward and Eleanora* (1739) by James Thomson.[9]

Tom ran the company until his death in 1831, an extraordinary total of 44 years. In later years the actor Francis Courtney Wemyss said of his friend:

> *Mr Robertson was regarded more like the father of a family than the director of a theatre: and were I asked, to point out a strict and justly honest man, Mr Thomas Robertson, the Lincoln manager, would be that man.*[10]

In a tribute in the *Lincoln Date Book* forty years after his death, Tom Robertson was said to have managed the company with 'the strictest integrity of purpose, and an esteemed and honourable name. His manners were humble, conciliating and obliging; his habits temperate' and his goodness of heart showed itself in all he did. All companies of comedians imposed fees on their actors for offences such as wearing stage costume out of the theatre or letting their dog be on the stage during rehearsals. Wemyss said that Tom Robertson put such fines into a fund, rather than into his own pocket, and that fund could provide help to actors in distress and also pay for an annual supper for the company. If the fund was insufficient Tom dipped into his own pocket.[11]

The Lincoln circuit was now in the hands of two men who were actors and were present on site, in contrast to the previous managers who were either absent or inexperienced. Robertson and Miller were to have quarrels over the years but at the start they made strenuous efforts to improve the company and renovate their main theatre. In September 1788 they reported that Lincoln theatre had been

John Whitfield (1752–1814). Actor and part owner of the Lincoln company of comedians c.1784–1787. Portrait in 1795.
From John Bell, Bell's British Theatre, *1795.*

---

[7] *SM*, 12 September 1788, 9 July 1790; Hemingway, *op. cit.*, p.21; Warwick, Lou, *Drama that Smelled*, p.187.
[8] Winston, *op. cit.*, p.38.
[9] Playbills, Lincoln, 7, 17, 21 and 24 August 1778; Lincolnshire County Archives, Misc.Don.94/1/3.
[10] Warwick, Lou, *Drama that Smelled*, p.190.
[11] Warwick, Lou, *Theatre Unroyal, Or, They called them Comedians*, Northampton (1974), p.27.

entirely newly painted, with new scenery and new props. They had also added many new plays to the repertoire, including Colman and Arnold's *Inkle and Yarico* (1787) and O'Keefe and Shield's *The Farmer, or, The Macaroni Staymaker* (1787).[12]

On 8 September 1793, while the company was at Spalding, Tom Robertson married Miss Frances Mary Ross (1768-1855), daughter of a celebrated actress Mrs Brown who, like Miller, had been in the Norwich company until lured away to Covent Garden in 1786. Mrs Brown's style of acting was said to have set the pattern for Dorothy Jordan.[13] Mrs Frances Robertson (or Fanny as she was called) was a great asset to the Lincoln company and it was said that she could have been on the London stage if her ambition had been so inclined. She preferred to remain in the provinces rather than act in London because she would rather 'reign in Hell than serve in Heaven'. Fanny was the star performer of the Lincoln company for nearly 50 years and was flatteringly described as a fine actress in the style of Sarah Siddons. Robertson wrote with great affection of his wife:

> It has been observed that a superior genius for the stage is hereditary in the family of Mrs Brown. Mrs T. Robertson is well-known to possess that genius in an extraordinary degree and being the wife of the manager of the circuit is the only tie that occasions her continuance in a provincial theatre. The Lincoln Circuit never had such an actress and [due] to her talents and exertions the Circuit has arisen to a fame it never before possessed.[14]

In October 1805 it was said that Fanny Robertson at Lincoln 'was particularly impressive and truly great' in *The Venetian Outlaw* (1805) and the *Stamford Mercury* added 'We hope the report of this lady's being positively engaged in London is not true, as the Theatre would not only lose a great attraction, but sustain an irrepairable loss'. She was appreciated by her local audience and never left the Lincoln company. On 29 November 1808 Fanny Robertson was so well received when she came onto the stage at Newark that 'she temporarily forgot her dramatic character'! The receipts of her benefit at Peterborough on 30 July 1813 were said to be the largest ever taken there.[15] She also wrote two plays that were performed by the Lincoln company, *The Nun* in 1833 and *Louis XIII* in 1836, and when her husband delivered speeches at the opening of new theatres the handbills declared that 'Mrs T. Robertson' had written them for him.

Fanny occasionally suffered from severe ill-health that stopped her performing though the details of her illness are not known. In September 1804 she was

---

[12] *SM*, 5 September 1788.
[13] Gilliland, *op. cit.*, p.688; Warwick, Lou, *Drama that Smelled*, 188, 189, 193; Grice, Elizabeth, *Rogues and Vagabonds*, Lavenham, Suffolk (1977), p.56.
[14] Gilliland, *op. cit.*, p.215; Warwick, Lou, *op. cit.*, p.188; Warwick, Lou, *Theatre Unroyal*, p.27.
[15] *SM*, 11 October 1805, 9 December 1808, 6 August 1813.

convalescing from a sudden severe indisposition and a year later, on 4 November 1805, she...

> ...appeared for the first time since her indisposition and was warmly greeted on her entree. Her benefit was, as usual, an overflow, and though we regretted to see the languor of illness, yet, if possible, it gave an additional interest to her performance.

Then again in November 1809 'the only subject of regret was the absence of Mrs T. Robertson, who, we are sorry to hear, is but slowly recovering from a very severe illness. – This lady's nice discrimination of character, joined to a correctly classical and elegant pronunciation, renders her absence in any of Shakespeare's plays particularly to be regretted.'[16] In May 1816 a 'painful complaint' prevented her acting for a while. The only child of Tom and Fanny who has been traced was John, who was baptised at Newark on 21 October 1796, but nothing more is known of him and he must have died young.[17] Was this lack of children related to her recurring illnesses?

The partnership of Tom Robertson and James Miller 'lasted a stormy ten or twelve years' recalled Robertson in a letter on 1 December 1803, 'during which time such frequent dissentions arose that it became necessary to separate'.[18] It actually lasted less than nine years but perhaps it seemed like twelve! Robertson purchased Miller's shares with effect from 2 May 1796, reportedly for the large sum of £1,200, and immediately sold half of them for £900 to a new partner, young Robert Henry Franklin (1770-1802).[19] Robertson and Franklin made a much happier team. Miller continued to work for the Lincoln company for some months, and with his wife he had a benefit on 5 August 1796 at Spalding. By October he had become the landlord of the Peacock inn in Boston Market Place, directly opposite the theatre, and called on his old fans to support his new venture. He only stayed there for four years and left at the end of 1800.[20]

Playbill, from Spalding theatre, 31 August 1796. The cast list shows that James Miller was still performing in Robertson and Franklin's company.
Lincolnshire Archives

---

[16] *SM*, 3 November 1809.
[17] Hemingway, *op. cit.*, p.11.
[18] Warwick, Lou, *Theatre Unroyal*, p.25.
[19] Warwick, Lou, *Drama that Smelled*, p.191; *SM*, 18 March 1796.
[20] *SM*, 21 October 1796, 9 January 1801.

Stamford

Stamford theatre had also lost its dynamic leader in 1781. Jemmy Whitley is buried in Wolverhampton where he died on 13 September. He was wealthy and left his theatres to Andrew Gosli (1746-1815) of Stamford and Elizabeth Gosli (*née* Whitley) his wife; an annuity to his other daughter Judith Whitley, and to John Anderson O'Brien (c1740-1810) rights of employment 'so long as my Nottingham circuit shall be continued'. Whitley also bequeathed to his veteran performers who survived him, a weekly salary for life.[21]

Andrew Joseph Gosli Carrighan was born in 1746 in Lisle (now Lille) the capital of French Flanders.[22] He had been christened Andrew Joseph Carrighan Carrighan but said he had acquired the name of Gosli because of 'being involved in an affair of honour in Lisle'. This suggests that he changed his name and left France because of a serious scandal in his home town. His mother's name, Marianne Veuteuat, has a Flemish ring but his father, Terentius Carrighan, sounds Irish, and Gosli's son the Revd Arthur Judd Carrighan (formerly Gosli) (1780-1845) later hinted that the family had some connection with Ireland, referring to his father as a 'Sligo Man'. Andrew Gosli migrated to Britain and as a young man became a dancer at Covent Garden theatre. On 11 January 1768 he married Whitley's daughter Elizabeth in Manchester and towards the end of his life, in 1810, became a naturalised British subject by private Act of Parliament. For several years he ran a dancing school in Stamford and, as dancing masters often pretended to be Italian, he used his name of Gosli. Dancing masters gave lessons to young men and women in the cotillion and the minuet which were vital skills for courtship, but they were often looked on askance as too foreign, fashionable and effeminate. Gosli held an annual ball in Stamford in June, and in 1779 tickets cost the high price of 5s 3d, tea included. In March 1780 he asked his pupils who intended to dance at the ball 'to return to Stamford, as soon as convenient, in order to practice for the same'.[23]

Mr and Mrs Gosli owned the Stamford company, with the theatres that Whitley had owned or leased, but did not want to manage it themselves. In March 1782 they informed the public that they had appointed John O'Brien, who had joined the company about 1768, as their manager. For the next twelve months advertisements referred to 'the Theatre in Stamford' rather than to the name of the company, but from April 1783 it was billed as the 'Nottingham, Derby, Leicester and Stamford Company'. They also visited Kettering, Northampton and Huntingdon but only at intervals of two years or more. In Stamford Whitley had rented the theatre from Lord Exeter but in Nottingham, Derby, Wolverhampton and Worcester he had built and owned the theatres and they were inherited by the Goslis. The rent of his theatres produced an income of nearly £500 a year which was on the border

---

[21] Warwick, Lou, *Drama that Smelled*, pp.166, 167.
[22] Information on Gosli is given in a private Act of Parliament, 50 Geo. III, ch.92, conferring British nationality, and on his will.
[23] *SM*, 10 June 1779, 30 March 1780.

between middle class and rich; in 1810 a labourer would earn about £15 to £20 a year and a gentleman could live comfortably on £300 a year. O'Brien was only manager for the Goslis until the second half of 1783 but he stayed on after that as an actor for another 25 years or so and a final benefit for him and his wife was given on 4 July 1808, after some 40 years service. It was said that they were only retiring from the stage due to his 'long and severe illness', and as they lacked the 'necessary means' to support themselves the managers, then Robertson and Manly, gave them a free benefit 'as an assistance in their declining years'. The O'Briens were then staying at Mr Porter's in St Paul's Street.[24] When O'Brien died in December 1810 it was said that he 'was much respected by an extensive and respectable circle of acquaintance'.[25]

The successor to O'Brien as manager, in post by March 1784, was William Pero (d.1803) who was another actor in the company and was said to be related by marriage to the Goslis. Pero came from Ireland and had married Miss Villars, an actress, on 24 March 1778 in Belfast where she was appearing. They performed in Belfast and Kilkenny in 1779 before moving to England. Pero was manager and then owner of the Stamford circuit for eleven years and for much of that time seems to have been a positive leader, spending money to bring Stamford up to the highest standard. He appeared on stage at Stamford in 1786, 1787 and 1790. In March 1784 he hired several new performers in addition to the existing company and obtained, at great expense, 'several pieces for their entertainment, which the managers in London have thought of too much consequence to publish'. He also obtained scenery painted by the celebrated De Loutherbourg.[26] He intended to give Stamford the latest and best London plays with the same fine scenery and he perhaps wanted to get his actors up to the best London standards. He used transparencies to show current events with dramatic effects. At Stamford on 9 July 1785 the evening's amusements concluded with 'a View of The City of Naples and Mount Vesuvius, or the Burning Mountain. Also a Grand Exhibition of the tremendous Eruption, with the progressive Motion and Resemblance of the Lava flowing down the Sides of the Mount from the Volcano, which forms a Current of Liquid Flame. As seen and described by Sir Richard Hamilton, our Ambassador at that Court.'[27]

In October 1785 Pero took the company to Sheffield and in May 1787 he advertised that the theatre in King Street, Melton Mowbray, had been 'considerably enlarged' and for a couple of years it was referred to as the New Theatre. That town had 2,106 inhabitants in 1801. As soon as he became manager in 1784 William Pero was spending money to improve the company and about four years later he parted from the Goslis, buying the company off them though they continued to own their theatres. Perhaps they thought he was spending too much of their money?

---

[24] Playbill, Stamford, 4 July 1808; Warwick, Lou, *Theatre Unroyal*, pp.166, 167, 169.
[25] *SM*, 14 December 1810.
[26] *SM*, 19 March 1784.
[27] *SM*, 8 July 1785

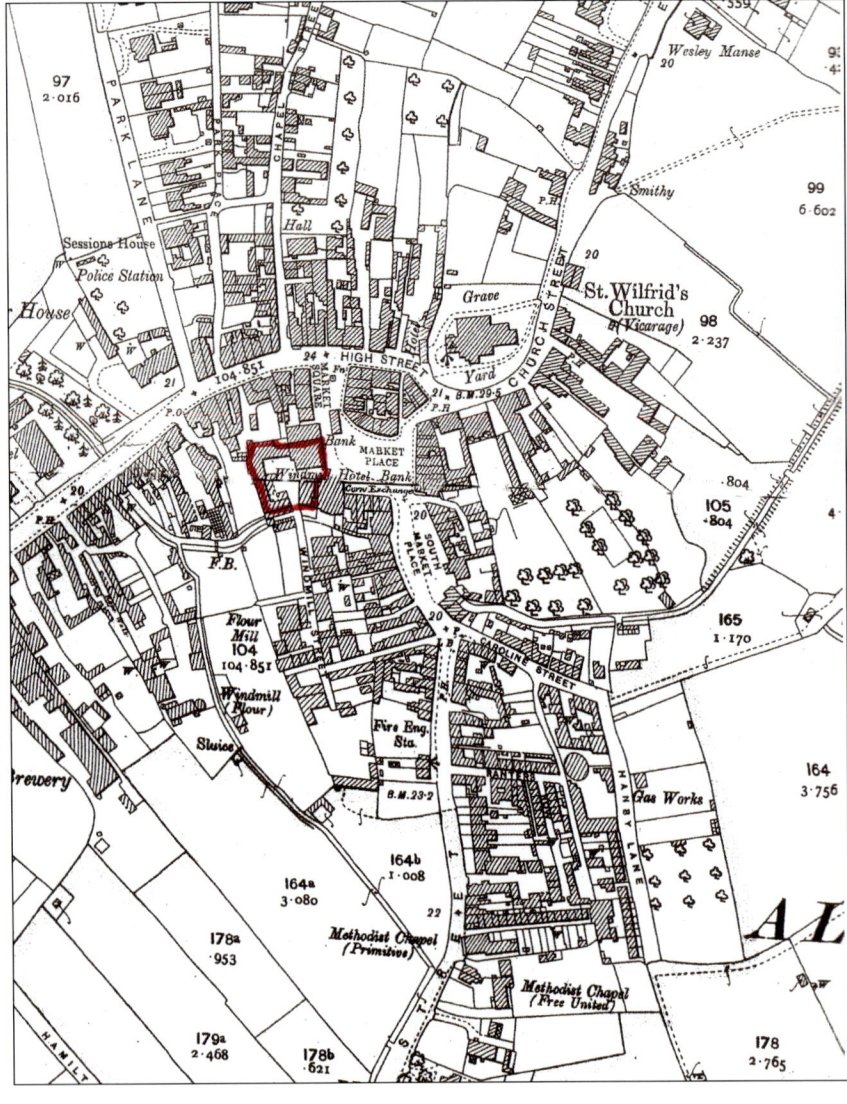

A map of Alford, showing the Windmill Hotel, which included a theatre.
Extract from Ordnance Survey 25in Plan, 1906

Pero also encountered problems with his actors and some leading members of the company left to form companies of their own. He probably purchased the Stamford company with effect from 1 July 1788 as in June of that year it was called the 'Stamford, Nottingham and Derby company' but on 1 July its title was 'Mr Pero's Co.'[28] Pero's circuit also included Melton Mowbray, Halifax, Sheffield, Northampton and Retford. From March 1789 his advertisements were headed 'His Majesty's Servants', a prestigious title suggesting a link to the crown even if Stamford theatre could not be called a Theatre Royal. His relations with the Goslis seem to have deteriorated further as a short time later he lost the Nottingham and Derby theatres, which they owned, as well as Northampton and Huntingdon theatres. About this time Pero also changed his Stamford lodgings, perhaps seeking somewhere cheaper; from 1784 to 1789 he lodged at Mr Redmile's in St Mary's Street but by June 1789 he had moved to Mr Hopson's, near the George hotel in St Martins. On 24 March 1789 his daughter Mary appeared on the Stamford stage as *Juliet*. Her forte was dancing and the advertisement for the show announced that she would dance a minuet with Mr Bell, as *Romeo*, in the first act, and on 24 July she also danced a minuet with Mr Bell in *As You Like It* (1599).

Pero had already spent money on new actors, plays and scenery and after becoming owner he had ideas to further develop the circuit. In 1788/89 he built a theatre at Retford, Nottinghamshire, in the centre of Carhillgate on land purchased from Sir Thomas Wollaston White, Bart. This was another town on the Great North Road and its population in 1801 was about 2,000. The external appearance of the theatre was plain and it was not large but the interior was attractive; its capacity was £40 to £50.[29] In 1789 a new theatre was built by subscription in the Yorkshire town of Halifax (population 8,886 in 1801), the foundation stone being laid on 12 September, and Pero added that to his circuit by 1795. It remained in the Stamford

---

[28] *SM*, 20 June 1788; Playbill, Stamford, 1 July 1788.
[29] Piercy, John S., *History of Retford*, Retford (1828), pp.146, 147.

The Windmill Hotel, in Alford Market Place. There was a theatre on the site in 1786.
David N. Robinson collection

circuit for about fifty years. Pero also made structural alterations to Stamford theatre and in July 1793 told James Winston that it was a 'wonderfully grand theatre. Lately we have much improved it by taking away the heavy pillars and putting in their place small cast iron ones.'[30] *The Clandestine Marriage* was performed on 20 August 1789 at Northampton by Pero's company together with a celebrated farce *Hunt the Slipper* (1784) by the Revd Henry Ryder Knapp of Stamford that had won 'the most universal applause' when performed at the Theatre Royal, Haymarket. Mr Knapp (1756-1817), who married Elizabeth Hartopp of Little Dalby Hall in Leicestershire in 1781 and was Vicar of Little Dalby from 1783 to 1788, had given Mr Pero a copy of the original manuscript.

On 30 June 1790 John Byng, later Lord Torrington, attended an evening at Stamford theatre and took one of the side boxes, 'being *too genteel* for the front'. The performance began at 7 o'clock and he said it was too long by half 'but every performer must add more, and more, to tempt the half price comers'. Three acts were enough for him and he left at 9 o'clock. The first play was *Which is the Man* (1782) by Hannah Cowley, which he thought a 'modern, unintelligible, walking novel' and he would have preferred a 'good old fashion'd, easy going comedy, as the *Stratagem* [*Beaux Stratagem* (1707)?], *Recruiting Officer* (1770), &c, &c' but the play put on may perhaps 'better suit the affected elegance of the country'.[31] Leaving as early as

---

[30] Warwick, Lou, *Drama that Smelled*, p.177.
[31] Andrews, C. Bruyn (ed), *The Torrington Diaries, containing the tours through England and Wales of the Hon. John Byng (later Fifth Lord Torrington) between the years 1781 and 1794*, Vol.2, London (1935), p.215.

he did Mr Byng missed a comic song and a humorous tale by James Robertson, a Pantomimical Interlude *Harlequin Rambler* and the farce *The Anatomist* (1696). Perhaps the 'affected elegance' that John Byng observed was exactly what William Pero was trying to achieve.

Breakaway companies

It would seem that some of the Stamford company were not happy after Pero became owner and they left to form new troupes of their own. Mr Beynon had joined Whitley's company with his wife by July 1778 and they and their daughter stayed with Pero until at least 1786. Beynon had worked at Glasgow theatre in 1775 and briefly for Tate Wilkinson in 1776 before joining Whitley; Wilkinson said that Beynon 'had a great share of spirit and did not want his own good opinion'.[32] Beynon formed his own company sometime between 1786 and 1788 when they were performing in Loughborough and by January 1790 Pero had lost Leicester theatre where Beynon engaged John Philip Kemble and his wife for three nights. In December 1790 Beynon said he had fitted up the Leicester theatre 'in a stile (sic) of elegance never yet attempted' there.[33] In June 1793 it was referred to as the Nottingham and Derby Company, suggesting that the Goslis, as owners of those theatres, had transferred them to him from Pero's Stamford company. Northampton theatre also changed its company, Pero visiting it for the last time in 1790. From then until 1797 Beynon appeared at Daventry, Northampton and Stratford on Avon.[34] It was also about this time that Huntingdon, previously part of Whitley's circuit, was taken by Robertson and Miller of Lincoln. It almost looks as if Pero was giving up his circuit to concentrate on building Stamford theatre to a very high standard.

Another breakaway from Pero was closer to home. On 12 April 1790 his daughter Mary had married William King, an actor who was with the Stamford company between 1788 and 1793. In October 1794 a Mr King, probably the same person, was putting on plays at Gainsborough theatre and a couple of years later this company was referred to as Butler and King.[35] More will be said about them in a later chapter.

Beynon's company was certainly a breakaway from the Stamford company and King's troupe looks to be another, so it seems that only four or five years after Pero became owner the Stamford company was starting to fall apart. Two other actors decided to save it. On 13 March 1795 William Perkins Taylor (d.1800) and James Robertson announced that 'at very considerable expense' they had purchased the company from Willliam Pero, and that the Earl of Exeter had transferred the lease of Stamford theatre to them. Pero then left the scene. On 4 March 1796 the Stamford Company was billed as 'Taylor and Robertson (late Pero's)'. Both of the new managers were actors with the company and were also related by marriage, as James had married Elizabeth Robinson, the daughter of Mrs Taylor by a previous husband.

---

[32] Warwick, Lou, *Drama that Smelled*, p.177.
[33] *Leicester Journal*, 10 December 1790.
[34] Warwick, Lou, *Drama that Smelled*, p.179; Warwick, Lou, *Theatre Unroyal*, pp.22, 57, 85.
[35] *SM*, 17 October 1794, 22 May 1795, 21 October 1796.

Gainsborough Old Hall. A theatre was created in 1787 in the central section shown here, with the main entrance on the left and the external stairs to the Gallery above that door.
From an original drawing by I. C. Nattes; Gainsborough Old Hall, Lincolnshire County Council

New theatres

Between 1781 and 1795 there were only four new theatres built in or near Lincolnshire, most in 1787-92, and in 1793 boxes were added to the theatre in Spalding. Retford theatre was built by William Pero, Gainsborough by James West the manager, Wisbech may have been built by Robertson of Lincoln, and Louth was erected by a local merchant. There was also a theatre in Alford (population 1,040 in 1801), but we do not know when that was built. There are only a few references to it and the first was in 1786 when 'that well known and well accustom'd inn called the Windmill', in the Market Place at Alford, was advertised to be let, 'together with the Theatre, Ball Room, &c with 49 acres of land, as also the tolls of the Market, if desired'.[36] It was probably a purpose built theatre on the inn site, much like the first theatre in Stamford, Lincoln's second theatre, or the Spalding theatre in the yard of the White Hart. Alford theatre was referred to again in 1797 and 1807 when Collier and Huggins company put on plays there and it was visited by Joseph Smedley's company in 1810, 1815, 1834, 1839 and 1842.[37] The visit in 1842, and possibly also in 1839, would have used a temporary theatre as the old one had become a 'temple of justice' by 1840.[38]

Gainsborough was a flourishing port on the river Trent at that time and its first purpose built theatre had been erected about 1772 as part of the Lincoln circuit. Its success proved its undoing. The medieval Old Hall in Gainsborough had been leased to Joseph Hornby, a local merchant, since about 1760 and after his plan to use it as a coarse linen factory had failed he turned it into a number of separate dwellings. A Mr West saw the success of the Gainsborough theatre and in 1787 rented the great hall, at the heart of the Old Hall, from Hornby for £50 per year to convert

---

[36] *SM*, 10 November 1786.
[37] *SM*, 10 March 1797, 13 March 1807, 8 October 1833, 4 January 1839, 28 October 1842.
[38] *SM*, 28 August 1840.

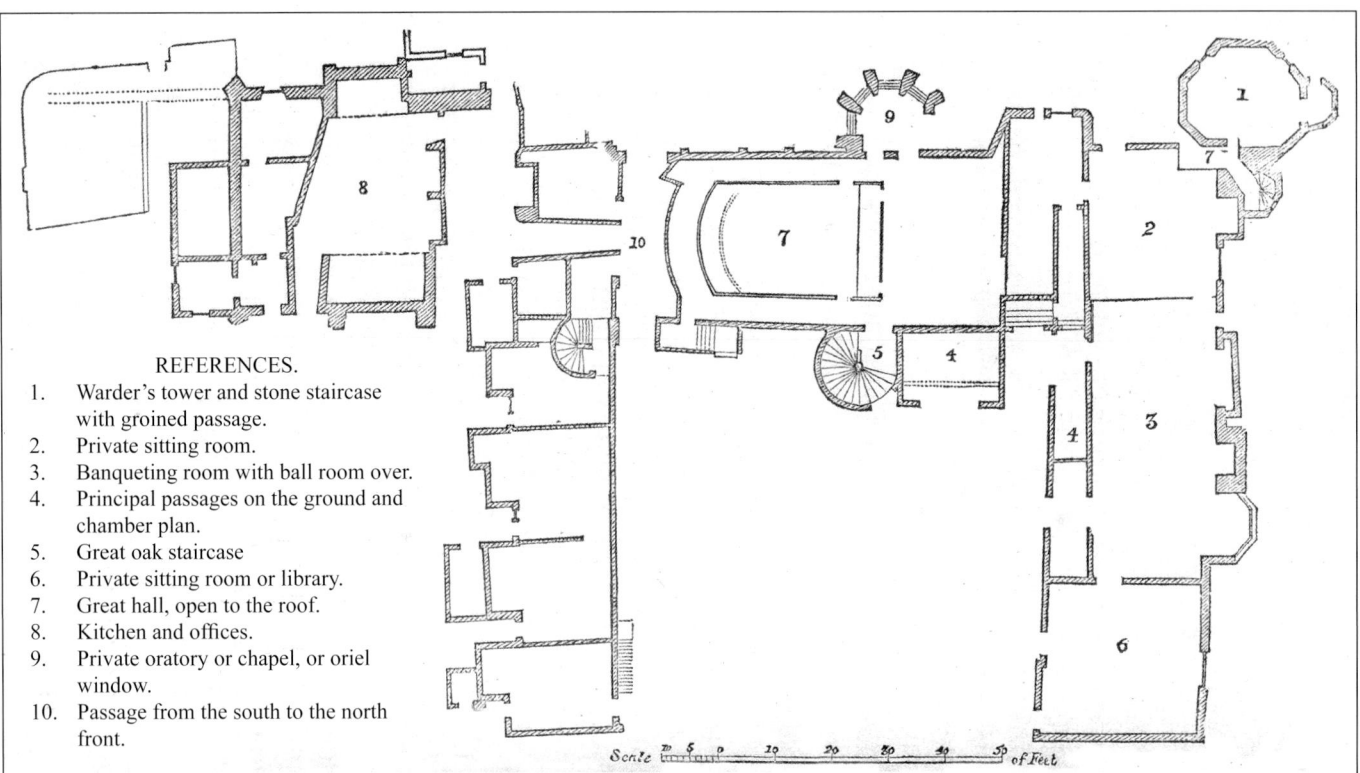

This plan of Gainsborough Old Hall, published in 1843, outlines the external stairs and the stage, Pit and Gallery in the Great Hall (7 on the plan).
From Adam Stark, The History and Antiquities of Gainsborough, 1843

it into the town's second theatre. This was James West (c1763-1805) who was the son of actor Mr D. West. James West was described as 'the manager of a theatre in the neighbourhood' but it is not known which theatre that was.[39] His father was a minor performer at Drury Lane and had visited Edinburgh and York in 1779 and 1780 with his talented theatrical family including his daughters Louisa and Miss D., and another son William, who were all dancers on the London stage. There was an actor called West, with his wife and daughter, who were leading players in the Stamford company in 1778-82 and this again was probably Mr D. West.[40] In March 1782 the Mr West at Stamford 'prepared and conducted' an elaborate and expensive pantomime called *Oriental Magic, or, Harlequin Sorcerer* (1782) and also starred as the Clown; the pantomime was repeated in 1783.[41]

The theatre in Gainsborough Old Hall was fitted up in a more showy style than the town's old theatre, with boxes, pit and gallery, and James West succeeded in drawing the pubic away from the old playhouse. The alterations to insert a theatre caused considerable damage to the medieval structure, and a number of oak arches and other carved devices were either taken away or destroyed. The new Gainsborough theatre was the same size as the one in Richmond, Yorkshire, and a plan of the Old Hall published in 1843 roughly shows how it fitted in the building.[42] The stage

---

[39] Stark, Adam, *The History and Antiquities of Gainsborough*, Gainsborough (2nd edn. 1843), p.419.
[40] Playbills, Stamford, August 1778, July 1780; Lincolnshire County Archives, Misc.Don.94/1, 94/2; *SM*, 5 April 1781, 7 March 1782; Highfill, Philip H., et al, *Biographical Dictionary of Actors etc*, Vol.16, Carbondale, Illinois (1993), p.372
[41] *SM*, 7 and 14 March 1782, 6 and 13 June 1782, 11 July 1782, 3 April 1783.

was at the east end and apparently extended into the space that in 2016 is a kitchen. The large stone bay at the north side of the hall may have been either a dressing room or the green room, and the fine tracery of the windows was walled up on the inside with rough brickwork.[43] The entrance to the gallery was by an external stair at the south-west corner of the theatre as shown in contemporary drawings. The south and north walls each had a ground floor door at the west end to give access to the boxes and pit. James West gave Joseph Hornby and his wife free admission to the centre box on each night of performance. A playbill for 28 September 1787 for the 'New Theatre, Gainsborough', perhaps the opening night, lists just one play, Hannah Cowley's *A Bold Stroke for a Husband* (1783) with acrobats forming the rest of the programme. In 1787 James West's company included his wife and daughter as well as a Mr Wetherall from the Theatre Royal, Windsor, a Mr Butler and a Mr Hamilton. None of these latter three actors were listed in 1788 and in that year West himself appeared on stage.

On 23 October 1788 the afterpiece at Gainsborough new theatre was *Rosina, Or, Love in a Cottage* by Mrs Frances Brooke (1724-89). Mrs Brooke was born in Claypole, Lincolnshire, the daughter of a clergyman. In the late 1740s she moved to London and started a career as a novelist, playwright and translator. By 1763 she was in the literary circle around Dr Johnson. Frances married the Revd. Dr. John Brooke in 1756 and in 1763 when it was safe to do so she followed him to Quebec where he was a military chaplain. She returned to London in 1768 to continue her career and the following year published *The History of Emily Montague*, which she had written in Canada, the first novel written in that country. About 1773 she became, with her close friend the tragedian Mary Ann Yates, joint manager of the Haymarket Opera House and though that venture lasted several years it was not a financial success.[44] Frances Brooke wrote her play *Rosina* in 1782, with music by William Shield. It was performed in greater Lincolnshire many

Playbill, Gainsborough, 23 October 1788. A rare illegal use of 'Theatre Royal' by James West, who later went to the United States.
Gainsborough Library, Lincolnshire County Council

---

[42] Stark, Adam, *op.cit.*, p.413.
[43] Stark, Adam, *The History and Antiquities of Gainsborough*, Gainsborough (1st edn.1817), p.xi.
[44] McMullen, Lorraine, Moore, Frances, *Dictionary of Canadian Biography*, Vol.IV, Toronto (2003)

Top:
Mrs Frances Brooke (née Moore) (1724–89), the Lincolnshire-born author of the first Canadian novel and also writer of the successful play Rosina.
Library and Archives Canada. Access no.1981-88-1, item no.C-117373.

Bottom:
No.2, Northgate, Sleaford, where Mrs Brooke died on 23 January 1789.
Photograph by Neil Wright, 27 August 2014

times between 1784 and 1805, with revivals in 1811, 1812, 1820 and 1834. The first performance in this county was on 22 March 1784 at Stamford when it was described as 'a new Musical Entertainment as performed 50 Nights at the Theatre Royal Covent Garden with universal applause, with new scenery adapted to the piece, designed by that celebrated Artist Mr Lowtherburg' (sic).[45] *Rosina* is still in print in 2016. Mrs Brooke's sister Sarah lived in Lincolnshire and Frances spent much time with her in the 1780s, being at their cousin's home at 2 Northgate, Sleaford, when she died on 23 January 1789.[46]

It is said that West made a success of the Gainsborough theatre but in 1792 he went to the United States and joined the Old American Company of comedians.[47] He made his American debut at the Southwark theatre in Philadelphia in September 1792 and specialised in comic opera roles. In late 1794 he joined a company in the southern states managed by Thomas Wade West (1725-99), no relation to James. T.W. West was a London actor who had formed a touring company with his son-in-law John Bignell (d.1794) in August 1790 in Richmond, Virginia. In 1792 T. W. West had built a theatre in Charleston, South Carolina and by 1798 the company was touring six venues in Virginia with seasons of about eight weeks each. James West had a narrow escape when their theatre in Richmond burnt down on 23 January 1798.[48] In 1795 he had married the widow of John Bignell, and died in Charleston on 8 July 1805.

For three years or so Gainsborough had two competing theatres, the only instance of this in Lincolnshire in the Georgian period, but about 1790 the Lincoln company gave the town up and the theatre in North Street closed after some 18 years. The old theatre was later used for over 100 years as an oil-cake and cattlefood warehouse before being demolished by the Urban District Council for road widening about 1938.[49] The theatre in Gainsborough Old Hall was used by many small companies of comedians over the next 60 years until its dismantling in 1849.

Louth was the main town in north-east Lincolnshire, with a population of 4,236 in 1801, and it got a purpose built theatre a few years after Gainsborough. On 8 December 1789 Edward Blyth of Louth, describing himself as a gentleman, purchased a site in the north-east corner of the Butcher Market, now known as the Cornmarket, on which he built a theatre. There is no known picture of the Louth theatre but the roof of the building, indicating its size, is shown in a preliminary sketch panel of 1844 for William Brown's Louth Panorama.[50] In 1796 this theatre was also leased by Butler and King, and they sold the leases of all their theatres to Collier and Huggins who had other playhouses elsewhere as will be described in a following chapter.

---

[45] SM, 19 March 1784.
[46] Atkin, Wendy J., 'A most ingenious Authress: Frances Brooke (1724-1789) and her Lincolnshire connections', *Lincolnshire History and Archaeology*, Vol.32, Lincoln (1997), p.17.
[47] Durham, Weldon B. (ed), *American Theatre Companies 1749-1887*, New York (1986), pp.19, 226, 548, 550.
[48] Stark, Adam, *op.cit*. (2nd edn), p.419.
[49] Sissons, Eddie, and the Delvers, *That's Entertainment* (Part 1), Gainsborough (2001), p.1.
[50] Lincolnshire County Archives, Goulding Papers 4/A/1/1/39; SM, 10 March 1797.

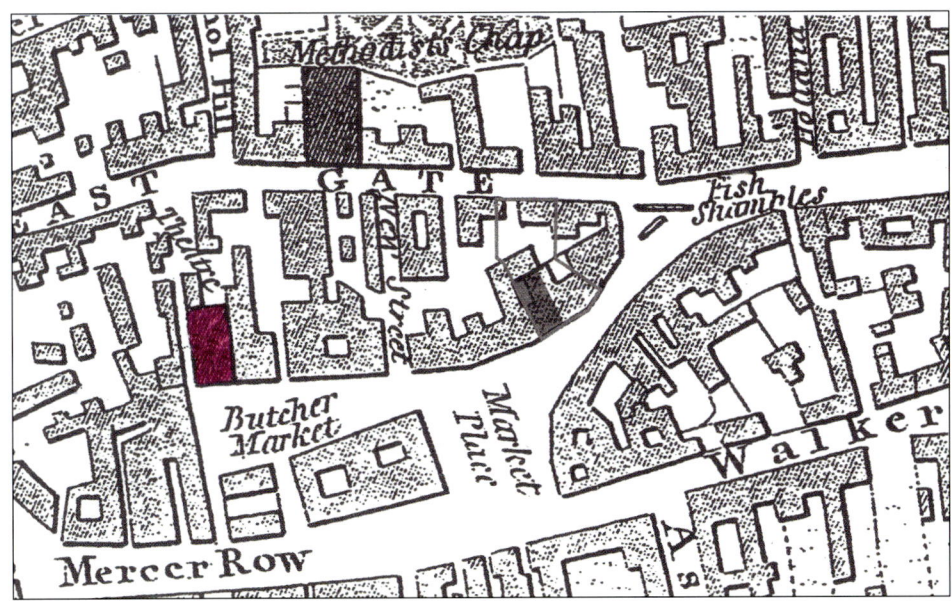

Thomas Espin's Plan of Louth in 1808, showing the site of the theatre in the Butcher Market, now Cornmarket.
David N Robinson collection

A preliminary sketch panel of about 1844 for William Brown's Louth Panorama. The long grey roof of the theatre is highlighted and shown enlarged below.
Louth Museum

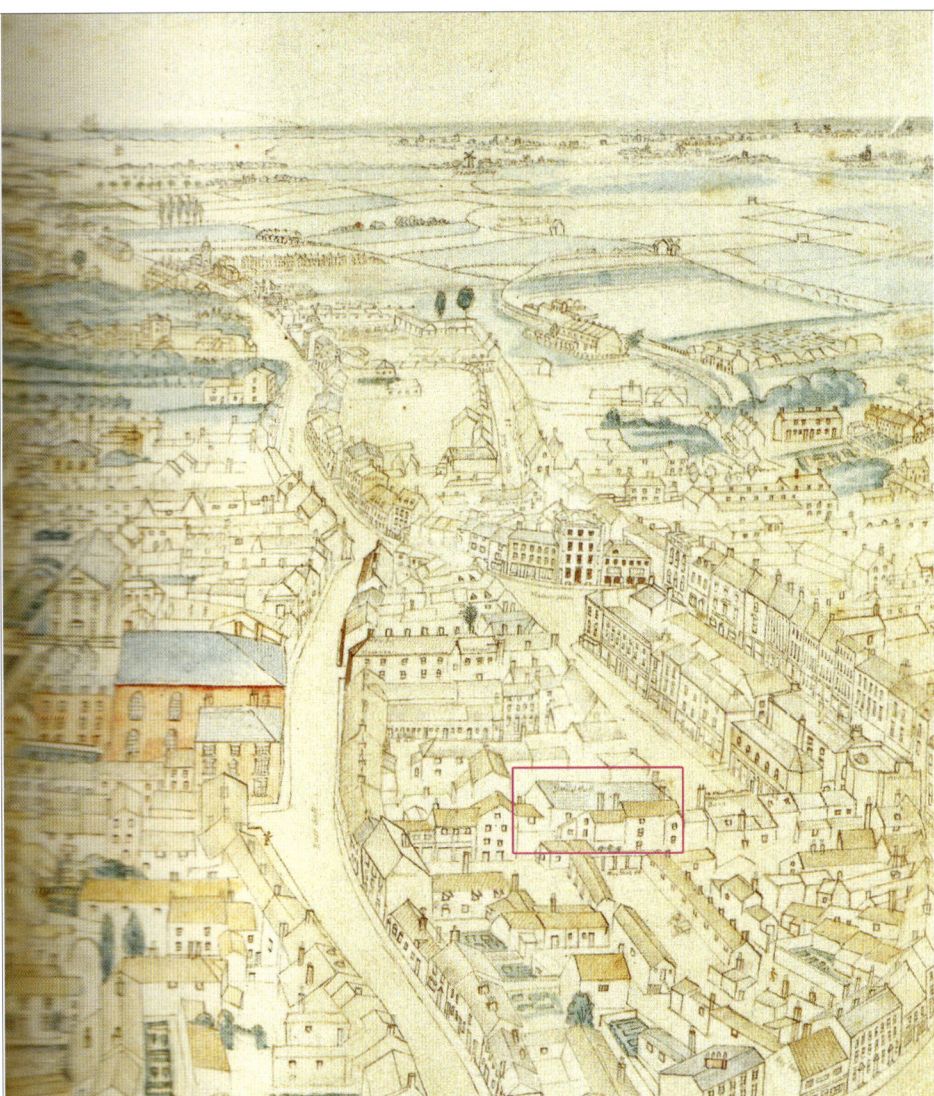

TREADING THE BOARDS

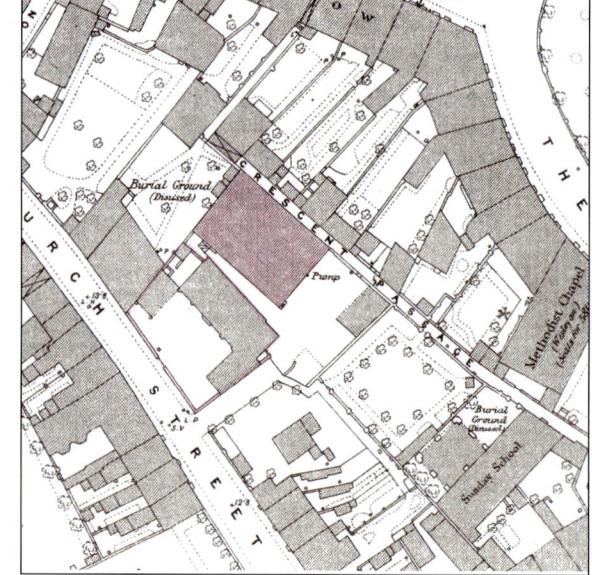

Above:
Wisbech theatre was in Great Church Street, south of The Crescent. The house where Fanny Robertson died in 1855 was at the north end of Norfolk Street (near Boulton's Hill), south of the parish church.
Extract from Ordnance Survey 25in Plan, 1889

Right:
Site plan of Wisbech theatre.
Extract from Ordnance Survey 1:500 Plan, 1887

The fourth new theatre to be erected at this time was in Wisbech on the river Nene, just south of Lincolnshire. Wisbech had a population of about 4,700 in 1801. For several years there had been a theatre at the west end of the town on the road to Spalding. Shakespeare's *As You Like It* (1599) and the musical farce of *No Song, No Supper* (1760) were put on at this 'very elegant theatre', said to be fitted up in the completest style, on 3 March 1792. When the lease ran out about 1793 a new theatre was built in a more convenient location in the centre of Wisbech in Great Church Street (at the back of York Row), now Alexandra Road. It was said that when full it held 'upwards of £40'. It may have been built by Tom Robertson, who certainly owned it by 1803.[51] The building still survives, set back from the road and hidden behind a later building of 1837; together they are now a theatre called the Angles Centre. Spalding theatre had been in Broad Street, to the rear of the White Hart, since at least 1753 and may have become a properly equipped theatre on that site by 1793 when boxes were added.[52]

Bespeaks

The leaders of Lincolnshire society in the long eighteenth century were the nobility and gentry, and some of them supported the theatre. The gentry who bespoke plays to be performed on nights when they visited the local theatre, included the Chaplin family in Louth, Lincoln and Stamford, Lady Welby and Lady Thorold at Grantham in 1802/3, Samuel Allenby of Maidenwell at Louth theatre in 1807, 1809, 1811 and 1813, members of the Sibthorp family at Lincoln in 1817, 1818, 1822, 1823, 1832, 1845 and 1849, and Mrs Theophilus Johnson of Spalding in September 1838. On a number of occasions the pairs of gentlemen who served as Stewards of the Races at either Lincoln or Stamford would also have a bespeak during the race week and in September 1806 the Stewards of the Stuff Ball bespoke a play at Lincoln theatre.

Not many peers lived in Lincolnshire, and of those who did it was often their wives who took an interest in drama and chose bespoke plays at the theatres. They did not do so as often as the gentry and social organisations but there were occasional instances of noble patronage. In June and July 1782 the Earl of Exeter and the Countess of Westmoreland patronised two nights at Stamford theatre, and Lord Exeter and Lord Eardley had bespeaks there in 1799. Lady Brownlow patronised Grantham theatre one night in each season in 1802/3, 1803/4, 1804/5 and 1806/7, and Lord Brownlow had a bespeak in 1809/10. Lady Monson patronised Lincoln theatre in September 1816 and, then as Countess of Warwick, again in 1817. Other noble patrons included Lady Cholmeley at Grantham in January 1807 and Lord Worsley in 1842. The Duke and Duchess of St Albans, who resided at Redbourn Hall, are recorded several times as visiting the theatre, including one night at Brigg as late as May 1844. The Duke's first wife, who died in 1837, had been an actress called Harriet Mellon. As it was often the wives of peers rather than their husbands who supported the theatre, that example of female support for the drama perhaps

---

[51] Warwick, Lou, *Theatre Unroyal*, p.30; *SM*, 24 February 1792.
[52] Warwick, Lou, *Theatre Unroyal*, p.10.

made it easier for the wives of the gentry to attend with their husbands. When noblemen did attend it was sometimes in an official context, such as Lord Tweedale with the Belvoir Hunt at Grantham in 1822 or the Earl of Yarborough as Colonel Commandant of the Lincolnshire Yeomanry at Lincoln in 1842.

When Lincolnshire companies were performing at towns outside the county they did get some patronage from nobles living nearby, such as Countess Fitzwilliam and her son Viscount Milton at Peterborough in 1805, the Duchess of Newcastle at Newark in 1806, 1815, 1816 and 1819, the Countess of Sandwich at Huntingdon in 1816, Earl Fitzwilliam at Peterborough in 1817 and 1821, the Ladies Fitzpatrick at Oundle in 1833, the Earl and Countess of Lincoln at Newark in 1835, and Lord Milton at Peterborough again in 1836. Earl Fitzwilliam was also part of the consortium that owned Peterborough Theatre in the early nineteenth century.[53]

The Grimsthorpe connection

At the top of the social ladder in Lincolnshire were the family of Peregrine, 3rd Duke of Ancaster and Kesteven (1714-78), and some of that family supported the stage in more unusual ways in the final quarter of the eighteenth century. The Duke himself invited the musician Thomas Linley (1756-78) and his sister to visit Grimsthorpe Castle in 1778. Linley has been referred to as 'the English Mozart' and was one of the most prodigiously talented musicians ever to have been seen in England, writing music for the stage as well as for concerts. The first known concert in which he performed was in 1763 at the age of seven, singing and playing the violin, and in 1770 whilst in Italy he met and became a close friend of Mozart. The teenage Linley was regularly leader of the orchestra at Bath from 1772 to 1776 and at Drury Lane theatre from 1773 to 1778. He was also a composer of great talent and his first large-scale work was performed in 1773. Had he lived longer and his talent continued to develop he might have become one of our greatest composers. But on 5 August 1778 during his stay at Grimsthorpe Castle Linley went boating on the lake with two friends and during a storm the boat overturned. Linley tragically drowned whilst attempting to swim ashore and he is buried in Edenham church.

In 1784 Mozart himself said that Linley had been a true genius. Works by Linley occasionally appeared in the theatres of Lincolnshire and adjacent counties; on 9 June 1783 at Stamford these included Ramsey's ballad opera *Patie and Roger, Or, The Gentle Shepherd* (1725) for which Linley had arranged the music. Also performed in the 1770s and 1780s at Nottingham was the song *No Flower that Blows* from Linley's *Selina and Azor*. In the 1790s they performed *The Camp* (1778) by Linley which featured military music that appealed to the prevailing patriotic spirit.[54] In the 1830s there was a further connection between Grimsthorpe Castle

---

53 Bull, June and Vernon, *Peterborough Then and Now*, Stroud (2013), p.8.
54 Evans, Rosemary, 'Theatre Music in Nottingham, 1760-1800', *Transactions of the Thoroton Society*, Vol.LXXVIII, Nottingham (1984), pp.50-52.

and the theatre when the Revd John Genest, M.A. (1764-1839), one time private chaplain to the 5th and last Duke of Ancaster (1729-1809) wrote 'Some Account of the English Stage from 1660 to 1830' that was published in 1832.[55]

The 3rd Duke's sister, Lady Mary Bertie (c1727-74), played a small part in the early life of Sarah Siddons. Lady Mary had married Samuel Greatheed in 1748 and moved to Guy's Cliffe House, one mile north of Warwick. In the early 1770s Roger Kemble, father of the future Mrs Siddons, was manager of the Warwickshire company of comedians and even as a small child Sarah worked as an actress in his theatres. In 1771 the teenage Sarah was becoming attracted to William Siddons, an actor, and to keep them apart a position was found for her as lady's maid to Lady Mary Greatheed. Sarah Kemble still yearned for the stage and when she accompanied Lady Mary on a visit to her mother the Dowager Duchess of Ancaster, Sarah recited to the servants in their hall. After two years at Guy's Cliffe House, Sarah persuaded her parents to let her marry William Siddons and return to the stage. The company were then at Coventry, and she married William at Holy Trinity Church on 26 November 1773. Her first appearance in London two years later was a flop and she spent more than six years in the provinces, but in 1782 she was offered another chance at Drury Lane and this time her success was phenomenal, leading to twenty years as a star of that theatre.

Sarah Siddons (née Kemble) (1755–1831). The leading actress of her day. Courtesy of the Rare Book & Manuscript Library, University of Illinois at Urbana-Champaign.

This connection with Sarah Siddons may have inspired Lady Mary's son Bertie Greatheed (1759-1826), who was four years younger than Sarah, to take an interest in drama. He wrote *The Regent* (1788), a tragedy in blank verse, which was staged at Drury Lane in 1788 with his friend Sarah Siddons and her brother John Kemble in the lead roles, but the play failed and was withdrawn after only nine nights. It was revived by the Lincoln company on at least two occasions. They performed it at Boston on 1 March 1797 for the benefit of Mr and Mrs Robertson when it was called 'a new historical play'. Then on 1 February 1813 they put it on at Grantham, the part of *The Duke* being played by Mr Musson of Barrowby. Bertie remained a life long friend of Sarah Siddons and she was a frequent guest of his at Guy's Cliffe.

Bertie Greatheed belonged to a group of expatriate poets based in Italy who in 1785 had published an anthology called *The Florentine Miscellany*. Their leader, Robert Merry, called himself 'Della Crusca' and in the late 1780s the 'Della Cruscan' style, flowery, effusive, artificial, was quite the rage. These poets were unashamedly concerned with style more than substance.

> *Like theatrical dresses if tinsel'd enough,*
> *The tinsel one stares at, nor thinks of the stuff'*

So say the dedicatory lines to the *Florentine Miscellany*. The Della Cruscans were mocked by the critics for their ornamental excess but were admired by readers for their fertility of invention.[56] Robert Merry himself later had an indirect connection

---

[55] *SM*, 27 December 1839.
[56] Byrne, Paula, *Perdita, the Life of Mary Robinson*, London (2004), p.263.

to the Lincolnshire theatre through his wife, Anne, whose younger brother John Brunton married Anna Ross, the sister of Fanny Robertson. John and Anna Brunton later performed with the Lincoln company in the first decade of the nineteenth century.

Albinia Bertie (1738-1816), love-child of Lord Vere Bertie and cousin of the 3rd Duke of Ancaster, had married George Hobart on 16 May 1757 and her husband became the 3rd Earl of Buckinghamshire in 1793. Mrs Hobart was notorious for her enthusiasm for amateur theatricals and gambling in high society and as Lady Buckinghamshire was frequently portrayed as a plump lady in cartoons by James Gillray. In 1775 she had the long gallery at their Lincolnshire home, Nocton Hall, fitted up as a theatre during the Christmas holidays. It was very exclusive with an invited audience of about sixty.

> None but people of fashion are admitted to any part of the performance on or off the stage.[57]

Many years later Lady Buckinghamshire bespoke performances at Lincoln theatre on 27 October 1798 and 26 September 1803.

The large lady with the feather headdress in this cartoon of 1803 is Lady Albinia, Countess of Buckinghamshire, who enjoyed gambling and amateur theatricals. She had a Lincolnshire home at Nocton Hall.

James Gilray, Dilletanti-theatricals: – or – a peep at the green room, © National Portrait Gallery, London

---

[57] Hill, Sir Francis, *Georgian Lincoln*, Cambridge (1966), p.10.

God Save the King

The theatres of the Georgian period were not only sources of entertainment but were also, in a small but perhaps powerful way, an alternative to churches and chapels as a medium for people to receive information and social values. The recovery of King George III from his first serious illness led to great relief among his loyal subjects, and a performance at Stamford on 27 March 1789 included a transparency of his Majesty, 'painted for the glorious occasion of celebrating the restoration of our beloved sovereign (whom God long preserve) to his pristine health and mental faculties'. While this was shown the actors Bell and King sang the patriotic songs *God Save the King* (not yet the national anthem) and *Rule Britannia*, the verses chorused by every loyal subject in the audience. Dr Willis, who had helped to treat the King's illness and lived not far from Stamford, had a bespeak performance on 17 July 1789. That provided an opportunity for his local friends to show their respect for his successful help to the King.

The French Revolution made a powerful impression on the propertied classes in Lincolnshire, as elsewhere. When it began on 14 July 1789 there were many people in Britain who at first supported its humanitarian ideals, and hoped that France would become a constitutional monarchy like the United Kingdom. William Wordsworth wrote:

> *Bliss was it in that dawn to be alive,*
> *But to be young was very heaven.*

This mood was reflected in the production of a 'new pantomimical piece founded on the subject of the late French Revolution' called *The Triumph of Liberty; Or, The Destruction of the Bastille* (1790) performed at Stamford on 19 March 1790 and repeated on 26 March.[58] However three years later the September massacres and the execution

This cartoon of 1802 depicts the horrified professional actors attacking the Countess of Buckinghamshire and her amateur performers. Kemble is dressed in black, Sheridan is Harlequin, and Mrs Siddons is between them. Even Garrick is rising from the grave.
James Gilray, Blowing up the Pic Nic's: – or – Harlequin Quixote attacking the puppets, © *National Portrait Gallery, London*

---
[58] *SM*, 26 February and 19 March 1790.

of King Louis XVI on 21 January 1793 spread an exaggerated terror in Britain. On 1 December 1792 the British government had called out the militia and a fortnight later Parliament reopened with a King's speech which warned of 'a spirit of insubordination, tumult and disorder' and 'some fixed design against the Constitution'. Relations between the two countries deteriorated until France declared war on Britain on 31 January 1793, and on other European countries shortly thereafter.

In reaction to the French Revolution, the King in Britain came to symbolise the nation to a degree that had not been seen since the reign of Queen Elizabeth. On Monday 3 December 1792 the audience at Gainsborough theatre demanded that the actors sing *God Save the King* before going on with the play. The whole audience, box, pit and gallery, stood up to join in the chorus. At this time some things said by Tom Robertson seem to have cast doubt on his loyalty to king and country. On 5 January 1793 he had to address the audience at Grantham, saying that 'for a little time he has laboured under the prejudice of public opinion', so he felt he had to declare his firm attachment to the King and the Constitution. This was reported in the *Stamford Mercury*, and the reporter assured the readers that Mr Robertson should be supported as he was 'respectable, peaceable and inoffensive'.[59]

Playbill, Lincoln, 27 October 1798. Lady Buckinghamshire bespeaking The Castle Spectre *by 'Monk' Lewis, the predecessor to melodrama.*
Lincolnshire County Archives

The execution of King Louis XVI was followed by that of Queen Marie Antoinette on 16 October 1793. On 31 March 1794 a play *Democratic Rage, Or, Louis the Unfortunate*, that had been performed at Dublin 'with unbounded applause' was put on at Stamford and it was repeated on 4 April and 27 June. Then on 4 July 1794 the new play at Stamford was *The Maid of Normandy, Or, The Death of the Queen of France* (1794) that dramatised the death of Marie Antoinette and the assassination of the revolutionary leader Marat by Charlotte Corday. That play was repeated on 11 July when admission was by ticket only. On both of these July dates the programme at Stamford included an item on the besieging and storming of the outer defences of the French town of Valenciennes on 23 May 1793 by British troops led by the

---

[59] *SM*, 11 January 1793.

Duke of York. The programme at Peterborough on 27 June 1795 included the farce *Arrived at Portsmouth* (1794) with transparencies to celebrate Lord Howe's great naval victory of the Glorious First of June 1794.

The showing of a patriotic transparency entitled *Loyalty Triumphant* and the singing of *God Save the King* took place in the theatres at Lincoln on 4 October 1793, at Newark on 18 December 1793 and at Spalding on 6 June 1794 and was reported in the county newspaper.[60] In Britain there was much rebellious sentiment around at this time, some due to the unpopularity of the war with France and some due to rising bread prices. Some leaders of society were concerned that the theatre was encouraging instability and topsy-turvy in rank and status. Class confusion was a central motif of eighteenth century comedy, and the basis of many a plot twist in plays such as Oliver Goldsmith's classic comedy *She Stoops to Conquer*, in which the gentleman-hero Marlow, who is terrified of high-born ladies, only falls in love with Kate Hardcastle because she dresses like a barmaid. In 1794 the government had suspended *habeas corpus* and in 1795 Tom Paine's *Rights of Man* was the best selling pamphlet in the country, but in the theatres of Lincolnshire patriotism was to the fore. On 21 December 1798 the first performance of a drama called *True Patriotism; Or, Poverty Ennobled by Virtue* (1798) by local author Thomas Robinson, a native of Bigby, was given at Louth theatre. The performance was said to have met with 'universal applause' and expressed the reactionary view that the humblest slave at the bottom of society, lacking wealth, food or political power, would nevertheless accept that the class divisions of society were a 'Heav'n-form'd Chain', and gladly die to defend the current Constitution once his soul had been lit by a blessed beam from heaven.[61]

Sometimes *God Save the King* led to trouble. When Robertson was in Northampton in 1807 an officer of a regiment stationed in the town refused to take his hat off while it was sung and members of the Household Cavalry who were also in the theatre attacked him with drawn swords.[62] In 1812 Nottingham theatre had to be closed temporarily as the officers from the barracks would go to the theatre and call for *God Save the King* to be played, and then assault those members of the audience who did not uncover their heads.[63] Both of these events took place outside Lincolnshire.

The people of Lincolnshire could hear announcements of victories and defeats in church or read about them in the papers, but in the theatres they could be presented with dramatic and pictorial representations of these great events. The stage was doing its part to arouse enthusiasm and engender patriotism during these wars that, with hardly a break, were to continue for twenty years and to make Britain the major

---

[60] *SM*, 27 September and 13 December 1793, 30 May 1794.
[61] *SM*, 4 January 1799.
[62] Warwick, Lou, *Theatre Unroyal*, p.45.
[63] Walker, J. Holland, 'An Itinerary of Nottingham', *Transactions of the Thoroton Society*, Vol.XXXII, Nottingham (1928), p.40.

world power during the nineteenth century. In 1794 the country was embarking on two decades of almost continuous war and though the actor-managers might not yet have realised it, theatres in Lincolnshire were just entering what was to be their most successful period, combining financial prosperity with popular acclaim.

6

WARTIME PROSPERITY

ON A COLD winter's night in November 1810 the great and the good of the cathedral city pushed through the yard of the Kings' Arms and crowded into the brightly lit Lincoln theatre. The space dazzled and light flashed off the glittering jewellery of the elegant ladies in the boxes. It was a benefit for Fanny Robertson, the highly talented star of the company, and so many of her admirers were present that she received 'the greatest receipts ever known' for such a night in the city. The years 1796 to 1810 were a great time to be an actor in Lincolnshire. This was the most popular and prosperous period for drama in the county, when new theatres were built and new companies of comedians were born. Britain had been at war with France since 31 January 1793 and in such times the theatre was a valuable place of escape and comfort. Every week the *Stamford Mercury* contained long and detailed advertisements for coming performances in those local theatres that were in season. Seven years earlier, on 4 November 1803, the house had been numerously and elegantly attended for Fanny Robertson's benefit at Lincoln and it 'overflowed at an early hour and many elegantes were deprived of places'. Later years were even more successful, many times the theatres were full to overflowing and in September 1808 during Lincoln race week, takings were greater than in any previous year. That final night of the 1810 season was one of the best.

Younger actors were flourishing but members of the previous generation were taking the final curtain. Mrs Pero died at Retford on 15 September 1801, aged 65, and her husband, William, passed away in Ireland after a lingering illness in December 1803.[1] Then the *Mercury* reported that 'Mr John Anderson O'Brien, lately of the Stamford,

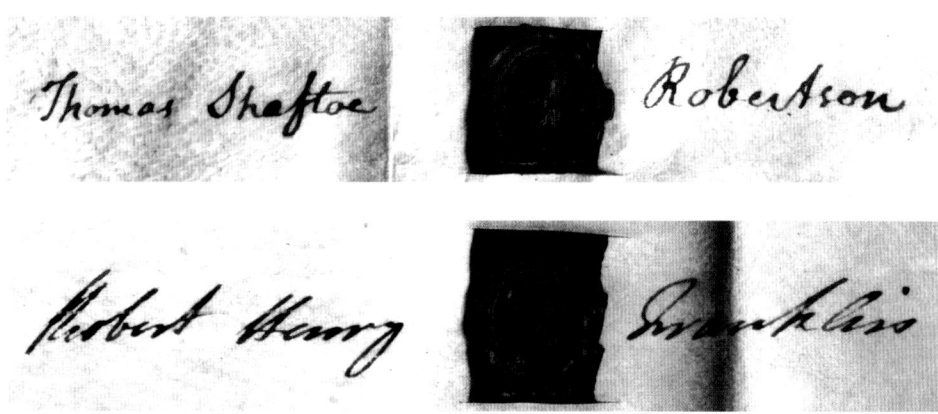

Signature of Thomas Shaftoe Robertson (1765–1831). Manager of Lincoln Company of Comedians for forty-four years (1787–1831).

Signature of Robert Henry Franklin. (1770–1802). Joint manager of the Lincoln Company 1796–1802.

Lincolnshire County Archives, ref:3-GM/4/4

---

[1] Stamford Mercury, 18 September 1801, 9 December 1803.

Nottingham and Derby company of comedians' had died aged 70 on 2 December 1810, 'at his lodgings in Greyhound-yard, Nottingham, after a long series of bodily afflictions'.[2] The next generation was taking over. In 1796 Tom Robertson entered into a new and successful partnership to run the Lincoln company of comedians and within five years his brother James got a firmer hold on the Stamford company. For the next fifty years the Robertson family, through Tom, then his widow, Fanny, and finally his nephew William, were to run the Lincoln circuit.

New Managers

Tom Robertson confirmed his control of the Lincoln company in 1796 by buying out James Miller and bringing in Robert Henry Franklin as his new co-manager. At the time Franklin was working as an actor with the Stamford company, having moved there from the Theatre Royal, Edinburgh in March 1792, and his commitments in Stamford delayed his first appearance at Lincoln. Franklin was the son of a landed Irish family, his father being a sheriff of County Limerick, and he had studied at Trinity College, Dublin, before going on the stage. He was said to have 'a natural turn for the muses' and wrote many good little pieces but his merit as an actor was mainly in the lower comic Irish characters.[3] Robertson and Franklin worked well together, in contrast to Robertson's previous partnership. In October 1796 their company finished the Lincoln season and had 'experienced greater success than ever before' in the city. Although Lincoln was the nominal base of the company, they always got good support from Grantham and, to show his gratitude for their liberal patronage of the theatre, Franklin presented Grantham Corporation with some gilt ironwork, which was fixed in front of the chief magistrate's seat in St Wulfram's parish church.

Unfortunately this amicable partnership lasted only six years, as Franklin died at Peterborough on 26 June 1802 at the age of 32. He had married Miss Elizabeth Forster, the daughter of a Stamford attorney, on 3 August 1793, but she died on 13 May 1799 after a long illness. Franklin's share of the company was left in the care of a trust, Robertson and two other gentlemen, until his son came of age, and for the first time Robertson was in effect the sole manager. Peterborough proved to be a sad place for Tom as his mother, Ann, died there just a few months later, on 18 April 1803, aged 62.

Tom's brother James Robertson, and James' father-in-law William Taylor, had replaced Pero as managers of the Stamford circuit in March 1795. James was then the junior partner but ten years later he was in the lead. Mrs Hannah Henrietta Taylor (c1757-1837), the co-manager's wife, was a fine actress and her daughters by a previous marriage were also on the stage. James Robertson had married one of those daughters, Elizabeth Robinson, on 6 October 1791 in Retford when

[2] *SM*, 14 December 1810.
[3] Warwick, Lou, *Drama that Smelled: Or, Early Drama in Northampton and Hereabouts*, Northampton (1975), p.188.

both were aged 18 and actors with the Stamford troupe. James and Elizabeth had several children: Georgianna (known by her second name of Caroline) was born in 1793, Henry c.1795, William (who later managed the Lincoln company) c.1796, Fanny 1799, Maria and Eliza. In 1791 Mrs Taylor was performing at the Theatre Royal, Bath, but within a few years she and her husband had joined the Stamford company. On 8 August 1801 at All Saints' church, Stamford, another of her daughters, Mary Henrietta Robinson, married Thomas Hill Wilson Manly (c1772-1840) whose real name was Wilson. Thomas Manly, like his wife Mary, was also an actor with the Stamford company and had been a favourite since his arrival from Bath in 1794.[4]

It was said that James Robertson, who had joined the Stamford company by March 1790, was a rough diamond, but a man of many talents. Not only did he become a great favourite as a low comedian but he wrote plays, painted scenery and danced the hornpipe.[5] He wrote comic songs, which he sang between the plays at his theatres, and in July 1805 he invited subscriptions for a book of twenty of his songs, with engraved caricatures, entitled *Broad Grins*, which would be published by Newcomb of Stamford and sold for five shillings 'to be paid on delivery'. Copies could also be bought from his brother George in Peterborough, and Burbage and Stretton of Nottingham. All of their children, except Henry, went on the stage. Georgianna first performed in 1800 and from 1802 to 1812 she regularly appeared as an actor and a dancer but then started to teach the pianoforte to young ladies in Halifax, and then in Nottingham from 1814, and left the stage.[6] When James and his wife, Eliza, had a benefit at Stamford theatre in July 1805, two of their children, Caroline and William, appeared as dancers on the same stage. Eliza died on 2 April 1806, and on 1 October 1810 James married a new bride in Chesterfield, Maria Lynam of Nottingham.

The initial Taylor-Robertson partnership ended five years later when William Taylor died at Derby on 18 May 1800 after a long illness, and his share of the company passed to his widow, Hannah, James' mother-in-law. By 1801 a young Benjamin Wrench (1778-1843) had joined the Stamford company at the start of his theatrical career and was being coached by Hannah Taylor. Their relationship changed from student-mentor to man and wife on 9 August 1802 at All Saints church, Stamford, when Hannah took him as her third husband. There was a story at the time that Manly and Wrench became engaged respectively to Mrs Taylor and her daughter, but changed partners before wedding vows were exchanged.[7]

Hannah's marriage to a husband 21 years her junior was to prove a disaster and they later pursued separate careers, but for the time being Wrench was James Robertson's

Benjamin Wrench (1778–1843). Comedian in the Stamford and Nottingham company.
Courtesey of the Rare Book & Manuscript Library, University of Illinois at Urbana-Champaign.

---

[4] Rosenfeld, Sybil, 'The Theatrical Notebooks of T.H. Wilson Manly', *Theatre Notebook*, Vol.7, No.1, London (October, December 1952), p.2.
[5] *Ibid.*
[6] Hemingway, G., *The Robertson Family and the Lincoln and Nottingham Theatrical Circuits*, thesis (1976), Lincoln Central Library ref:UP 7467, p.30.
[7] Rosenfeld, Sybil, *ibid.*

father-in-law. There must have been some unusual tensions in a company where James had one of his actors as his brother-in-law and another, as the young husband of James' mother-in-law, was now joint manager of the company. The new partnership lasted just two and a half years and in March 1805 James Robertson announced that Mr Adcock, an actor from the Lincoln company, had purchased Mrs Wrench's 'theatrical property'. Robertson and Adcock were now the joint managers of the Stamford company. From this time Adcock was a regular performer at Stamford, with a benefit in August 1806. It was significant that in a newspaper advertisement on 28 June 1805 the managers were listed as 'Messrs Robertson and Adcock', putting Robertson first, whereas in previous advertisements the other managers' names had priority: Mr Taylor (1799), Mrs Taylor (1801) and Mr Wrench (1803, 1804).[8]

Benjamin and Hannah Wrench both moved to the Hull and York company and later to other provincial theatres. Benjamin was a good comedian of considerable reputation and was introduced to London theatre-goers at the Lyceum in October 1809 in *The West Indian*, but he never reached the first rank. He had a drink problem and later left his wife in financial difficulties, though as a former owner of the Stamford company she was paid an annuity of £54 12s 0d per annum and was still receiving that in 1828. She lived a long life and died in Melton Mowbray in May 1837 at the age of 80.

The partnership with Adcock was even shorter than the one with Wrench, and by late 1806 the joint managers were James Robertson and Thomas Manly, his brother-in-law, listed as 'Robertson and Manly'.[9] Manly was to spend the rest of his life with the Stamford, Nottingham and Derby company, the latter two theatres having been returned to the Stamford circuit after being served by Beynon in 1793. By 1806 their circuit comprised Nottingham, Derby, Chesterfield, Halifax and Retford as well as Stamford, most of which were visited several times a year, and the circuit was still the same over twenty years later. Compared with the days of Whitley, Stamford was now in a smaller but more united circuit. Robertson took comic parts and Manly the more tragic ones as well as Irish roles. This partnership worked well for a dozen years until 1818 when James 'retired due to ill health', and Manly continued as sole manager of the Stamford company until his death in 1840. The early years were a good time for them, as they were for the Lincoln company. At Stamford on 4 August 1809 Manly's benefit yielded £54, and the season in total was 'the most productive ever known by the company at Stamford'.[10]

Manly's origin was obscure but his accent was Irish and he excelled in such roles as *Sir Lucius O'Trigger* in Sheridan's *The Rivals* (1775) and *Major Dennis O'Flaherty* in *The West Indian*. He was an admirable actor and it was said that his *Shylock* was superior to all but Kean's and 'his *O'Flaherty* more brilliant than Johnstone's'.[11] It

---

[8] *SM*, 15 March 1799, 19 June 1801, 29 April 1803, 9 March 1805.
[9] Warwick, Lou, *Theatre Unroyal, Or, They called them Comedians*, Northampton (1974), p.196; *SM*, 6 February 1807.
[10] *SM*, 11 August 1809.
[11] Donaldson, Walter, *Recollections of an Actor*, London (1865), p.19

is recorded that when Manly was in Halifax every night he would send to Mrs Murfitts, near the Piece Hall, for two veal pies – one for himself and one for his dog. He was highly educated and interested in history and politics; a proficient swearer and a little lame.[12] Throughout the 1820s Manly was plagued with gout, a malady then suffered by many men. That condition detained him at Retford when the company moved on in 1827 but he had some relief after a fortnight at Ashley Baths. In 1830 he recorded in his books: 'Gout gone. Huzza!'.[13]

This health problem may have contributed to his sour attitude. His relationship with his actors does not seem to have been good, and his comments when any left were usually sharp: 'a grave coxcomb', 'a drunken sot', 'a sleeping idiot', 'a heavy light comedian' 'a snuffling hero'. One dancer was 'sent off to a condemned regiment in India' in 1826 for stealing a joint of mutton from his employer. When the Vicar of Halifax died in 1827 Manly closed the theatre as a mark of respect but the actors took exception to having no pay for the night and went on strike, led by Mr Allen 'a factious pedagogue who noodled the rest into rebellion'.[14]

Manly's appearance at the end of his career was later described by John Coleman who as a child had seen him at Derby. The manager was

> ...a tall, stately man of seventy, with quick, piercing eyes, high cheekbones, aquiline nose, iron-grey hair, and distinctly Hibernian cast of features. He always carried a brown hazel-stick in his hand, wore a low crowned hat, a long coat of dead green, almost the shade of an autumn leaf when the colour is fading out of it. A red bandana silk handkerchief, with a stock inside it, was tied round his neck. His nether limbs (in excellent preservation) were clad in drab breeches to match the vest, and tied with drab ribbons at the knee. Grey worsted stockings, with high-tied shoes, completed this eccentric costume.[15]

Manly had a large family and managed to educate them, and to defray the debts of his wayward son Tom. He was anxious to keep his children from the stage and articled one son to a lawyer, Tom to a doctor, and apprenticed Hill to a draper, whilst his daughters taught dancing. The scapegrace Tom went on the stage in 1826 against his father's will, as later did Charles. Both were in the company and Charles was acting manager in 1837. Tom died in 1834, aged 37, and is buried in St Mary's Church, Nottingham, by the side of James Robertson. Ellen married a Mr Milner in Derby in December 1827 and received £100 'as a fortune from her Papa' and an additional £50 as a present. Maria married Freer, an actor in

---

[12] Rosenfeld, Sybil, ibid.
[13] Golland, Jim, 'A Dramatic Discovery or, A Manly Enterprise', *Local History Magazine*, No.42, Nottingham (1994), p.15.
[14] Golland, Jim, *ibid*.
[15] Rosenfeld, Sybil, *ibid*., quoting from Coleman, John, *Fifty Years of an Actor's Life*, London (1904), 1, p.25.

Mr. BRUNTON & MISS SMITH.
AS ALTAMONT & CALISTA.
Alt. *What means thy frantic rage?*
Cal. *Off! let me go.*

Pub.d as the Act directs by J. Roach, Russel Court, Drury Lane. Ap. 7. 1806.

John Brunton, here performing with a Miss Smith in 1806, was married to Fanny Robertson's sister Anna and was at times a member of the Lincoln company.
Courtesy of the Rare Book & Manuscript Library, University of Illinois at Urbana-Champaign.

the company, on 12 October 1828, much to her father's disgust. Another daughter, Clara, died in September 1822.[16]

When Andrew Gosli wrote his will on 26 October 1814 he still owned four theatres that had belonged to Jemmy Whitley – Derby, Nottingham, Wolverhampton and Worcester. He told his executors to sell them, and also the rest of his real estate and personal estate, but to continue to receive the income from them until they were sold. By 1814 Gosli had moved to London and was living the life of a gentleman on the rents of his theatres. When he died on 15 March 1815 his home was in Henrietta Street, off Brunswick Square in north London, close to the Foundling Hospital. His personal bequests included three rings, two with diamonds, portraits of himself and his late wife who had died on 7 February 1813, and the advowson of Stamford to his 'excellent friend' Samuel Coddington (1739-1830), a gunsmith and Mayor of Stamford in 1810. Gosli's son John Thomas was Lieutenant Colonel of the 2nd Durham Local Militia and had married a prosperous wife, Elizabeth Leaton of Whickham House, County Durham. Another son, Arthur Judd Gosli, or Carrighan, was an Anglican clergyman, Rector of Barrow in Suffolk, and a traveller. His papers are deposited in the library of St John's College, Cambridge, and the National Archives. The Executors did not sell the theatres immediately as the Carrighan family were still receiving the rent for Nottingham theatre as late as 1828.

Performers

In Tom Robertson's Lincoln company there were many people related by marriage including, at times between 1802 and 1815, Fanny Robertson's mother Mrs Elizabeth Brown (d.1823), stepfather John Brown, and their children.[17] On 23 January 1815 in Halifax Mary Brown (c1791-1816) married John Henry Clarke of the Stamford company and she moved to Stamford. Their married life came to a sudden tragic end on 29 November 1816 when Mary suffered a dreadful death in Stamford. While she was decorating

---
[16] Rosenfeld, Sybil, op. cit., p.45.
[17] Fanny's step-brothers and sisters included Mary Brown (c1791-1816), John Brown jnr (b.1787) and Master Brown, the eldest son.

a muslin dress a candle fell onto her and her clothes caught fire. She rushed into the street 'but the flames caught new vigour from the air and in a few moments the unhappy woman was one terrible blaze, from the ground to a considerable height above her head. She lingered for a few hours in great agony but then died'.[18] This dreadful end was not unusual as deaths by fire were being reported nearly every week in the *Stamford Mercury*. One of James Robertson's own children had been burnt to death in Sheffield in January 1799. On 30 December 1817 Mary's widowed husband married the daughter of a Derby grocer and corn-dealer.

Other family members performing with Robertson by 1802, if not earlier, were Fanny Robertson's sister Mrs Anna Brunton and Anna's husband John.[19] It is not clear how long they stayed but in 1806 Mrs Brunton was at the opening of the new Boston theatre and was engaged for the season in 1810. Her husband was hired for three nights in 1814 and another few nights in 1815.[20] By 1800 theatres in Lincolnshire were long established and the companies might include not only the family of the manager but also other actors who had been with them for many years, such as Mr O'Brien. At this time the Stamford company could afford a pension for some of its retired performers, such as Mrs Dunn who died on 17 January 1804 aged 78, having been 'for several years past a pensioner on their fund'[21].

An occasional member of the Stamford company was E H Seymour who 'had the manners of a gentleman and the dignity of a scholar'.[22] It was said that 'his forcible and chaste elocution' had made him a favourite with the Stamford audience. He wrote a book 'Remarks, Critical, Conjectural, and Explanatory, on the Works of Shakespeare', and was said to be 'well informed on most subjects, and gentlemanly and amiable in private life'.[23] His book was published in 1805, in two volumes, based on notes derived from his work as an actor in Norwich and Cambridge. In 1804 Seymour was left a very large legacy of £1,000 by Baron Chedworth (1754-1804), with permission to select fifty books from the Baron's valuable library. Lord Chedworth was a reclusive peer who had taken a great interest in racing and the theatre, latterly studying Shakespeare and regularly visiting the Green Room at Norwich theatre, which is where he may have met Seymour.

Throughout the first half of the nineteenth century London stars came to perform with local actors for a few days at a time. In the first decade of the nineteenth century William Henry West Betty 'the Infant Roscius' was a sensational success in London and got the same amazing reaction when he came to Lincolnshire. From the age of eleven to sixteen he played the leading roles in serious plays with such success that the House of Commons adjourned one day in 1805 in order to see his *Hamlet*. When

---

[18] *SM*, 6 December 1816.
[19] *SM*, 4 June 1802.
[20] *SM*, 30 September 1814, 13 January 1815.
[21] *SM*, 20 January 1804.
[22] *SM*, 22 and 29 June 1804.
[23] *SM*, 21 January 1819.

John Quick (1748–1831), in 1793. He was a comic actor who performed in Peterborough and Spalding in 1809.
Courtesy of the Rare Book & Manuscript Library, University of Illinois at Urbana-Champaign.

Master Betty visited Lincolnshire in 1807 the theatres doubled their prices, which at Boston were Boxes 6/- (six shillings), Pit 4/- and Gallery 2/- with the notice that 'No half prices can be taken'. When he came again in 1808 the prices were not so high, but still more than usual – at Huntingdon and Wisbech they were: Boxes 5/-, Upper Boxes (only at Huntingdon) 4/-, Pit 3/- and Gallery 2/-.

At Stamford in 1807 Master Betty was paid the huge sum of £800 for five weeks. Takings at the theatre for his last nine days were published in the *Stamford Mercury*.[24] Those for 9 to 14 March inclusive totalled £466, of which £120 was taken on 11 March alone. The last three days from 16 to 18 March were at reduced prices, as those people prepared to pay the higher prices had probably already seen him perform, and the takings totalled £101. He then went direct to Boston for three nights, where a recent benefit for the popular Fanny Robertson had produced takings of £81. The exceptional takings for Master Betty's nights at Boston on 19 to 21 March came to £365 17s 0d. Master Betty received half of those takings, amounting to £182 18s 6d.

Other visiting stars included the 'celebrated Comic Actor' John Quick (1748-1831) who came from Covent Garden theatre in August 1809 to perform for three nights at Peterborough and then three more at Spalding. Animal stars could also appear. In October 1815 the Stamford company was at Sheffield and 'the theatre has been crowded every night' of performances by the famous dog 'Tiger' in the *Forest of Bondy* (1814), in a role he had performed in London, Bath, Dublin and elsewhere. In November 'Tiger' appeared in Lincoln theatre, where he was equally successful.

London stars would only appear in Lincolnshire theatres for a few days a year and at other times it was often the spectacle that was stressed as the attraction of the stage. The introduction of melodrama was followed by a developing taste for spectacular pieces and grand processions in sumptuous robes, sometimes with animals. It is said that the first elephant appeared on the London stage in 1812 but 'an elephant as large as life' had appeared as part of a procession at Bourne theatre on 8 and 15 November 1806 in the 'grand dramatic romance' of *Blue Beard,* and the elephant was at Alford in March 1807. When the play was performed at Wisbech on 18 April 1817 *Blue Beard* was again seated on an elephant.[25]

---

[24] *SM*, 20 March 1807.
[25] Brewer, John, *The Pleasures of the Imagination: English Culture in the Eighteenth Century*, Abingdon (2013), p.336; *SM*, 7 November 1806, 27 March 1807, 11 April 1817.

Advertisements

In the early 1800s managers could afford to publish long, expensive advertisements describing the action and scenery of their new plays. The 'new Romantic drama' *Adelmorn the Outlaw* (1801) by 'Monk' Lewis was put on at Grantham on Saturday 5 January 1805 for the benefit of Tom Robertson himself, and the advertisement vividly described some scenes and the dramatic action:

> *View of a Forest and adjacent Country, with a German Cottage and natural Cavern. The inside of the Outlaw's Cottage, with a secret Recess. Interior of the Castle, by which scene is displayed the Vision of Adelmorn! The walls of the Castle are seen to open! The Outlaw's murdered Uncle appears, holding an uplifted Dagger, surrounded by brilliant Clouds! He then points to his Wounds – The Scene changes to the colour of Blood! – The real Murderer appears surrounded by Demons, who descend with him to the Abyss of Guilt!! The Castle Dungeon, in which Scene the Wall struck by Lightning falls, and discovers the secret Cell in which Father Cyprian is confined!*

The final scene is: 'The Chapel – Procession of Nuns, Friars, Guards etc conducting the unfortunate Adelmorn to the Scaffold'.[26] Only when Georgian theatre was at its most prosperous could managers afford such long dramatic word pictures in the papers.

A few months later in July 1805 the melodrama *The Lady of the Rock* (1805) was put on in Stamford with 'new scenery, dresses and decorations in the Highland costume'. Once again the newspaper advertisement described the exciting action:

> *View of the Rock, surrounded by the sea; Night – Dreadful Storm; Through the Darkness of which, by the Flashes of Lightning and the Concussion of the Waves, is uncovered THE LADY OF THE ROCK. The Storm increases, and the Waves are seen to gain upon the Rock. The Fisherman with his Son then enter – they unloose the Boat, and put to Sea, hopeless – are seen to labour with the Waves – they at last gain the Rock, and succeed in rescuing her from her approaching dreadful Fate! In the Last Scene – The Gathering of the Clan of Maclean, in Order of Procession to The Mock Funeral. The Rites are interrupted by the Arrival of the Clan of Campbell.*

The marches and gathering of the clans would be aided by 'the Gentlemen of the Volunteer Band'.

Charity

During the long war with France theatre was so popular that charitable performances were an enjoyable way of raising money to aid good causes and help the victims of natural and manmade disasters. Tom Robertson was keen to show his support for

---

[26] *SM*, 28, December 1805.

Spalding theatre was said to be on the site of the later Spalding Club in Broad Street, behind the White Hart inn.
Extract from Ordnance Survey 25in Plan, 1904/1932

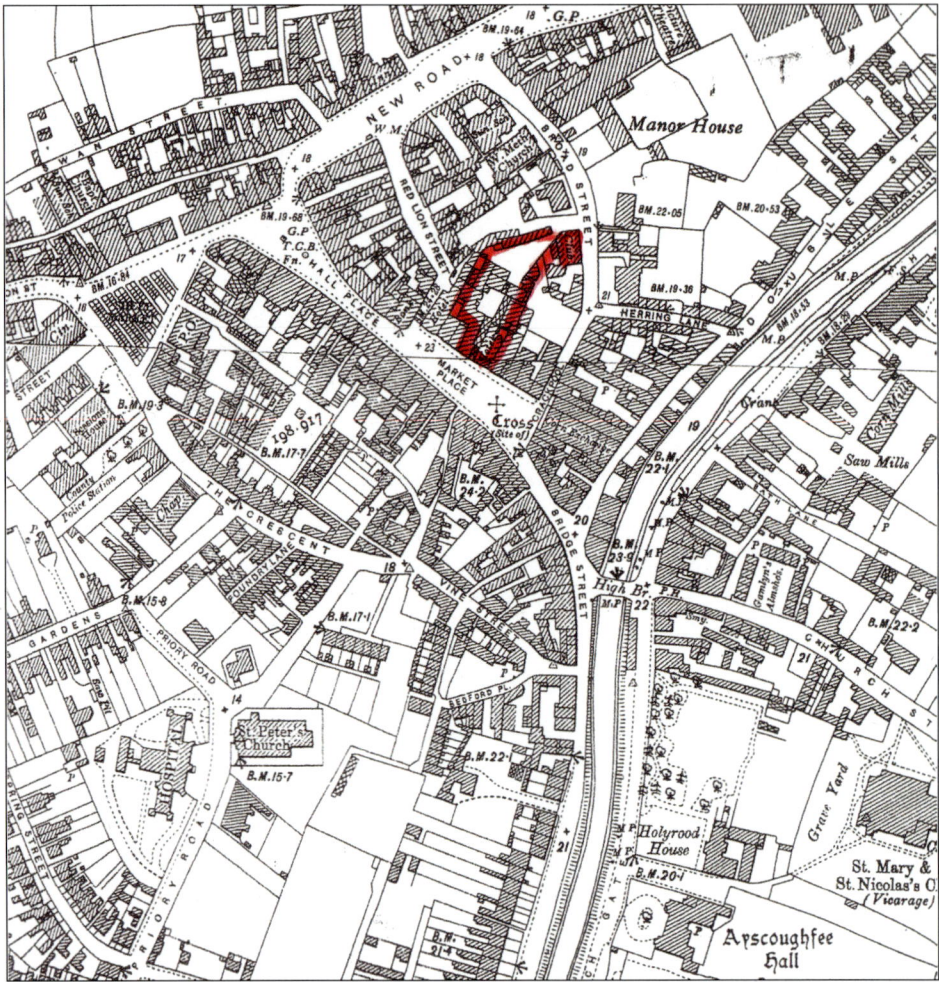

local communities by raising funds and helping amateur actors to do the same. For several years in the early 1800s he gave an annual benefit for the Sunday schools in Lincoln and the war produced more serious causes needing charitable help. On 16 November 1797 Robertson and Franklin gave a benefit at Lincoln for 'the widows and families of our gallant countrymen who fell in the late glorious victory over the Dutch fleet' at the battle of Camperdown on 17 October. On 14 March 1808 a benefit at Boston theatre raised £68 19s 6d towards 'the relief of the seamen of the port of Boston now prisoners in France', and Robertson had another benefit for that cause in February 1809.[27] Help was still needed in December 1812 when amateurs at Boston performed 'for the benefit of their fellow townsmen confined in French prisons'.[28] They repeated it on 14 January 1813 when, still charging only the normal admission prices, they raised the grand total of £105 6s 0d and further donations on later days increased the fund still further.

On 10 November 1810 the Boston area suffered the serious flooding that inspired Jean Ingelow to write the poem *High Tide on the Coast of Lincolnshire*, and on

---

[27] *SM*, 18 March 1808, 10 February 1809.
[28] *SM*, 27 November 1812.

Spalding Market Place, published 1 January 1822. The stage coach is standing in front of the White Hart inn. In the distance is the Town Hall, which was used as a temporary theatre until 1745.
Spalding Gentlemen's Society

13 February 1811 Tom Robertson gave that night's receipts of Boston theatre to the fund to help those who had suffered. In a number of years, when the winter weather was severely cold, amateur gentlemen in some towns put on productions to raise funds 'for the relief of the poor'. On 15 and 16 March 1813 there were amateur performances at Spalding 'for the relief of the Russian sufferers' after Napoleon's invasion of that country. The final wartime effort was on 10 August 1815 at Stamford when gentlemen amateurs performed *The Earl of Warwick* (1766) and Kenney's popular farce *Raising the Wind* (1803) 'for the benefit of the sufferers of the Battle of Waterloo'.[29] Although the male roles were taken by gentlemen, respectable ladies could not appear on a public stage (in contrast to one in a private house) so the female roles in *The Earl of Warwick* were played by Mrs Green, Miss Stannard and Miss R. Stannard of Tom Robertson's Lincoln company. Mrs Norris, described as being 'of the Huntingdon theatre', played Miss Laura Durable in *Raising the Wind*. On a patriotic note, though not a fund-raising effort, for three nights in early May 1807 Signor Belzoni had presented at Boston theatre 'an entire new Spectacle' representing:

> (in a Panoramic View), by Moving Figures, .. the Funeral Honours, Ceremonies, and magnificent Procession, both by Land and Water, observed to commemorate our late gallant Hero, LORD VISCOUNT NELSON, as represented at Covent Garden Theatre with unbounded applause.[30]

New theatres

The population of Lincolnshire's main towns was growing greatly by 1800, and in particular the middle class was becoming larger and more prosperous. Bigger

[29] *SM*, 26 July 1815.
[30] *SM*, 1 May 1807.

St John's church, Huntingdon, on the site of the town's Georgian theatre. To the right is the rear of the George Hotel.
Extract from Ordnance Survey 1:500 Plan, 1885

playhouses were needed for the increasing numbers in the audience. Very few theatres had been built in or near Lincolnshire since 1780, but then nine appeared between 1799 and 1811. Most of those on the Lincoln circuit were rebuilt, exceptions being Wisbech, which was still new, and Spalding. The theatre at the back of the White Hart yard, fronting Broad Street, Spalding, had been built before 1753 and boxes were added in 1793. In 1803 it produced over £40 when full but it is not known when a temporary theatre on that site was replaced by a permanent one. In 1836 it was called 'a small but neat edifice' and was later said to be on the site where the Spalding Club was erected in Victorian times.[31]

In 1799 the owners of the Leicestershire Hotel and Assembly Rooms decided to build a theatre on land next to the hotel, south of the Market Place, Leicester. The town was no longer part of the Stamford circuit and the theatre was opened on 18 March 1800 by a company of comedians from Cheltenham. From then until 1815 it was managed by Mr M'Cready an Irish actor who had previously played for ten years at Covent Garden. He also ran companies at Birmingham, Sheffield, Newcastle and Manchester and his son became the leading actor Charles Macready.

---

[31] John Saunders, Jnr, *Lincolnshire in 1836*, Lincoln (1836), p.121; Gould, Mervyn, *Boston and Spalding Entertainment and the Aspland Howdens*, Wakefield (2005), p.19.

Huntingdon theatre in George Street, 1805, with doors marked 'Gallery Upper' and 'Box'. St John's Street is to the right.
Houghton Library, Harvard University

Huntingdon, 17 miles south of Peterborough, was a small town with a population of 2,035 in 1801 and it had only been added to the Lincoln circuit in the 1790s. For many years the company used a barn as a theatre. About 1799 new premises were built to the rear of the George inn, designed by Mr Rowles, nephew of Henry Holland, architect of the Theatre Royal, Drury Lane. The new theatre was in George Street, at the north-west corner of the junction with St John's Street. In London's Drury Lane theatre cast iron columns had replaced bulky timber ones and it had been possible to include several tiers of boxes. The same may have been done at Huntingdon where the new theatre had two tiers of boxes. It was not one of the Lincoln company's most profitable venues and in 1803 it was said that they only visited Huntingdon every second year for the Race Week.[32]

A little later a new 'handsome and commodious' theatre was built in Peterborough, on a central site west of the parish church. It was within a few yards of the old theatre of 1772 or earlier, which had only a pit and gallery and was 'noted for being dirty and inconvenient'. The new theatre was opened on 10 June 1800 by the

---

[32] Warwick, Lou, *Drama that Smelled*, p.195.

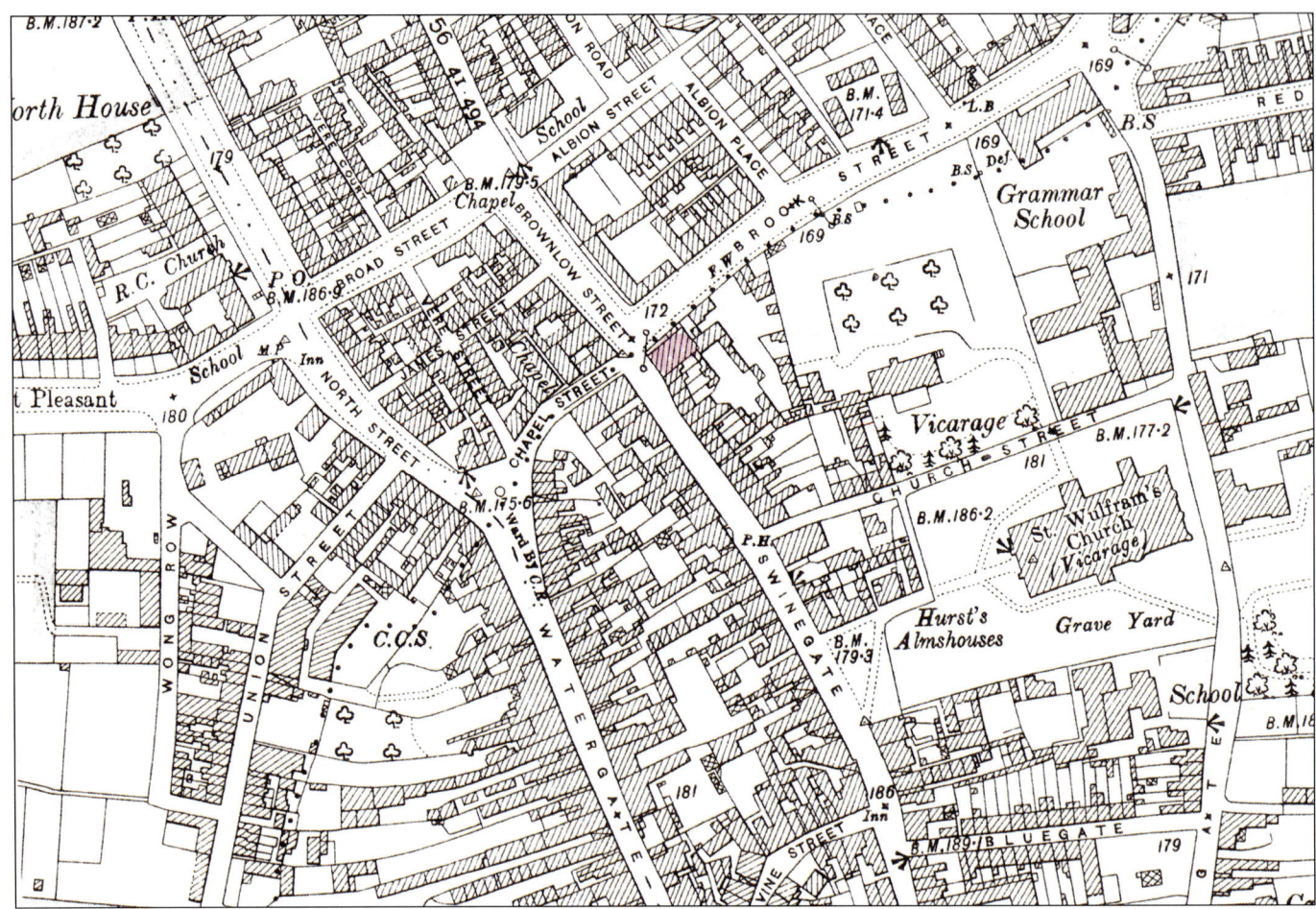

The first theatre in Grantham was in Westgate and the second in the Market Place, actual locations unknown. The third (highlighted) was at the junction of Swinegate and Brook Street.
Extract from Ordnance Survey 25in Plan, 1904

Lincoln company with a speech by Robert Franklin and performances of *Speed the Plough* (1800) and *Ways and Means* (1788). That was the start of an annual season of seven weeks around the time of Peterborough races. In 1803 the theatres in Peterborough and Huntingdon were both said to contain 'about £50' when full. Peterborough theatre, like Huntingdon, was built by subscription, which meant there were a number of local people with an interest in seeing it a success. By 1811 the proprietors included Earl Fitzwilliam, the Revd Henry Freeman of Alwalton, the Revd Robert Roberts of Stoke Doyle, and William Squire and Wright Thomas Squire who were merchants and the founders of Squires Bank.[33] The Races ended in 1816 when the Common was enclosed but the local theatre season continued to be held in June right until the end in the 1840s.

George Fowler Robertson (1774-1843), the younger brother of Tom and James, set up as a printer in Peterborough by 1800. He married in Peterborough in 1799 and had a son and daughter baptised there (as 'Robinson') in 1802 and 1803. As well as printing playbills for the theatre he also sold tickets and was their box-keeper until 1811 at least. The exact location of his business is uncertain, as in 1802 and 1811 it was said to be 'opposite the church', but in 1803, 1810, another 1811 entry and 1830

---

[33] Bull, June and Vernon, *Peterborough Then and Now*, Stroud (2013), p.8.

Grantham theatre in Swinegate in 1805.

Houghton Library, Harvard University

it was in the Market Place.³⁴ In 1817 tickets were to be obtained 'from Mr Robertson at Mrs Pridgeon's, Swanspool', and in 1818 places for the boxes were to be registered at Mr Sharpe's, hair dresser. There is a suggestion that George's premises were later taken over by J.S. Clarke which would place them just to the right of the Cathedral Gateway, in front of the present NatWest Bank as that side of the street was widened in the 1930s.³⁵ George's wife died in Peterborough in 1838 and George may then have retired, as he died at Little Gonerby, Grantham, on 6 November 1843.

Grantham had a new theatre built about 1777 in the Market Place and at first it consisted of pit and gallery, like the earlier building, but in 1797 boxes were added.³⁶ The lease of that theatre expired in 1800 and in May Grantham Corporation 'resolved that a theatre be erected on St Peter's Hill' but that proposal was controversial and was dropped.³⁷ Then Joseph Lawrence, a local merchant and banker, built a theatre at the junction of Swinegate and Brook Street (then part of Manthorpe Road) a little north of the parish church. That 'new and handsome theatre' on the Lincoln

---

³⁴ *SM*, 4 June 1802, 10 June 1803, 22 June 1810, 21 June 1811. *Claims on Peterborough Inclosure 1811. Pigot's Northamptonshire Directory*, 1830.
³⁵ Personal communication from Richard Hillier of Peterborough Archives, 24 May 2015.
³⁶ Warwick, Lou, *Theatre Unroyal*, p.30.
³⁷ Honeybone, Michael, *The Book of Grantham*, Buckingham (1980), p.125.

Grantham theatre, front elevation, in 1952 just before its demolition. Surveyed and drawn by Lawrence H Bond, architect.
Grantham Library

circuit had the auditorium on the first floor with two tiers of circular boxes, like Huntingdon, as well as the pit and gallery and was said to contain £50 when full.[38] The description 'circular boxes' meant that the junction between the front and side boxes, sometimes referred to as the 'rural angle', was a curve rather than a right angle. In 1836 Grantham theatre was described as 'a neat, brick building, comfortably fitted up'.[39] The opening night on Thursday 18 December 1800, like the recent one at Peterborough, had a special speech by Robert Franklin and then performances of *Speed the Plough* and *Ways and Means*. In December 1802 Tom Robertson reported that 'it having been suggested to him last year that the boxes admitted too great a current of air, so as to occasion it to be extremely cold', he had boarded up the Box Lobby at Grantham theatre and erected a fire-place within it, which he hoped would make it more comfortable and convenient.[40]

Grantham was on the Great North Road, and Huntingdon and Peterborough not far off it, and these new theatres were followed by the rebuilding of Newark theatre further along that major national route. The Newark theatre of about 1773 had received several improvements in later years. Then in 1803 it underwent a total alteration and enlargement including, like those that had just preceded it, two tiers of circular boxes. The new playhouse was said to contain between £60 and £70, so it was larger than the three recent ones. 'The design and execution of the theatre cannot be too highly spoken of' said the *Nottingham Journal*. 'It is truly elegant and Newark may now boast one of the handsomest provincial theatres in the kingdom'.[41] This improved theatre was opened by the Lincoln company on 8 November 1803 with a special speech at the start of its regular six week season.

During the reign of George III Boston was the fastest growing and wealthiest town in Lincolnshire, with a population of 6,465 in 1801. Its leading burgesses were not only aware of the new theatres in the west of the county but also of a new one at Ipswich, passed by shipping sailing between Boston and London. In May 1803 there was agitation to erect a new theatre in Boston, 'on the plan of the

---

[38] Title deeds, Lincolnshire County Archives, LCL/5626; Survey by Lawrence Bond, 1952, at Grantham Library; Gilliland, Thomas, *The Dramatic Mirror; containing the History of the Stage*, London (1805), p.216; Warwick, Lou, *Theatre Unroyal*, p.30.
[39] John Saunders, *op. cit.*, p.99.
[40] *SM*, 10 December 1802.
[41] Warner, Tim, 'Curtain rises on the town's first theatre', *Newark Civic Trust Magazine* issue 68, Newark (February 2013), p.14.

Newark theatre in Middlegate, 1805. The small door left of the lamp led into the yard north of the theatre.
Houghton Library, Harvard University

elegant and commodious one nearly finished at Ipswich, a model of which has been procured for the purpose'. The architect of Ipswich theatre was William Wilkins who later designed the National Gallery and the theatre at Bury St Edmunds. He was a classicist and Ipswich theatre had an imposing colonnade along the front wall.[42] Boston's existing theatre had been built in 1777 and twenty-six years later it was too small for the expanding and prosperous town. Boston Corporation had decided in March 1803 to sell the existing playhouse and twelve months later Tom Robertson asked for their help as he had been unable to find a site for a new one. The Corporation responded by offering part of the Mart Yard in front of the Grammar School. The headmaster objected and told the Corporation of the problems it could cause the school, and his particular concern at the loss of a site for a future house for himself and boarding pupils.[43] The Mart Yard idea was dropped and instead a site was found in Red Lion Square, a new area of development north of the Market Place, and funds were raised by subscription to build the theatre.

---

[42] Grice, Elizabeth, *Rogues and Vagabonds*, Lavenham, Suffolk (1977), p.87.
[43] Bagley, George S., *Floreat Bostona*, Boston (1985), pp.71, 72.

TREADING THE BOARDS

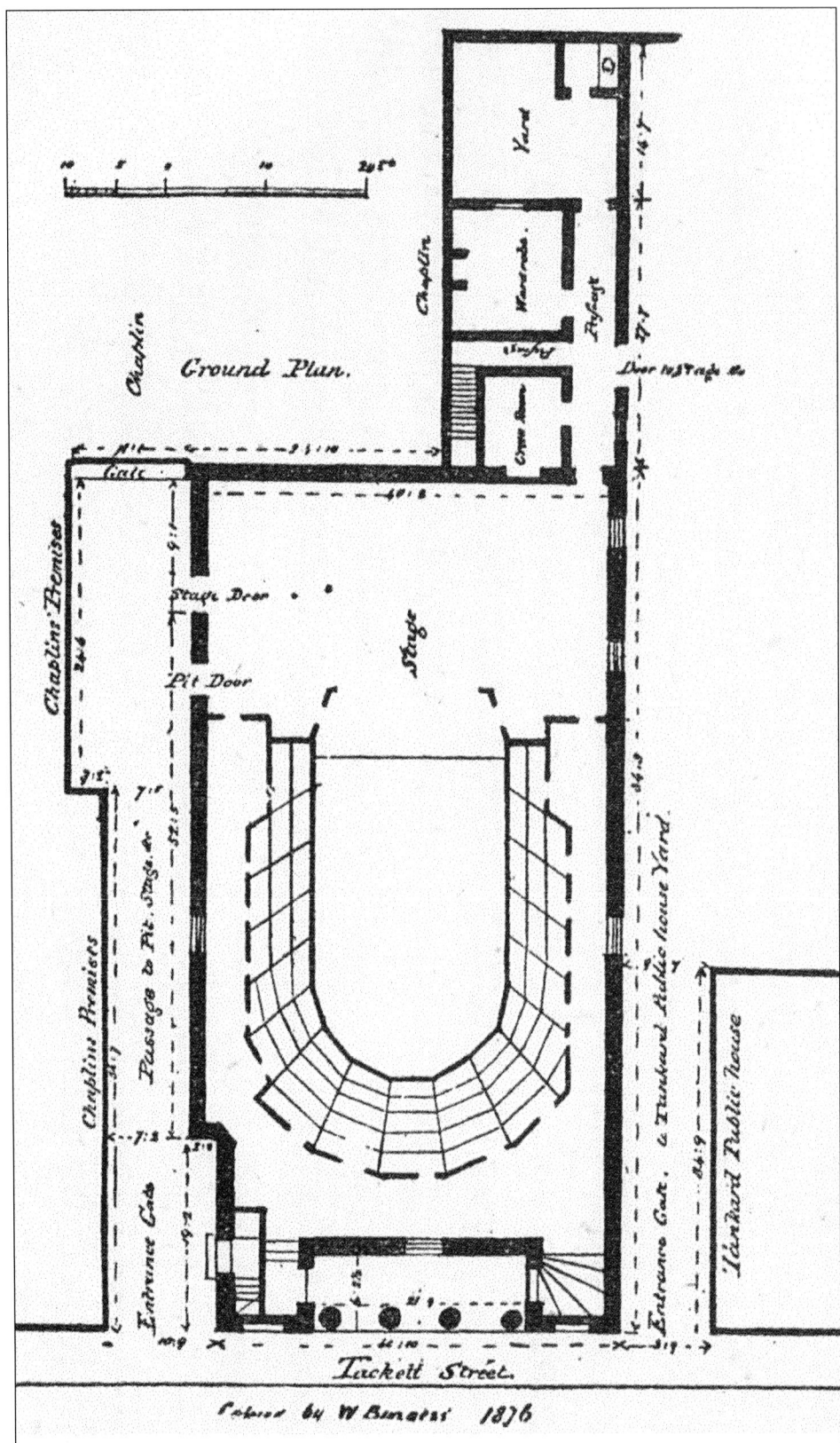

Plan of Ipswich theatre showing its arrangement in 1810. When the Boston 1806 theatre was being planned Ipswich was suggested as a model.
From Richard Southern, The Georgian Playhouse *(1948)*

A model of the new Boston theatre, made under the direction of local architect and builder John Watson, was 'highly approved of', and was said to reflect great credit on his judgement and taste. The building cost was estimated to be about £1,000 and the takings for a full house were expected to be £100. During Boston's 1805 season the first stone of the new theatre was laid on the morning of 4 March by Fanny Robertson, after which the ladies and gentlemen of the theatre were invited to a 'handsome cold collation' at the Red Lion inn next door. On the last night of that season, 14 March 1805, Tom Robertson told his audience that 'he would have the honour of opening a new theatre next season, which in point of elegance and accommodation would be equal to any theatre out of London'.[44] He said he was an old servant of the public and as his father had opened the old theatre 30 years before so he now had the honour of closing it.

By November 1805 the new Boston theatre was nearly complete. It was a plain substantial building 80ft by 45ft with a slate roof and a yard on the north side but the interior was elegant and well adapted for the use of scenery. It was said to be

> in the greatest degree comfortable, and the disposition of the various apartments highly convenient. The interior decorations from the masterly pencil of Mr Immanuel, are in great forwardness, and evince a taste and genius which adds to the reputation he has already acquired as an architect.[45]

It had 'a commodious Pit and Gallery, a tier of boxes surrounding the former, and upper boxes at each extremity of the Gallery'.[46] The best description we have of the theatre is in an advertisement when it was put up for sale in 1839, the owner having 'removed to a distant part of the Kingdom':

> The building is lofty, and very substantially built, with a Portico at the principal entrance and private stage door; the Dressing-rooms are extensive, affording accommodation for a large company; the Stage is very large, the proscenium handsome, and the wings roomy; there are two tiers of Boxes, a capacious Pit, and large Gallery capable together of containing upwards of £100 at the ordinary prices of admission. The theatre is brilliantly illuminated with gas, the whole of the fittings for which are nearly new, and of the best manufacture. The building was designed, and erected by an experienced architect by whom particular attention was paid for the conveyance of sound from the stage to the body of the house.[47]

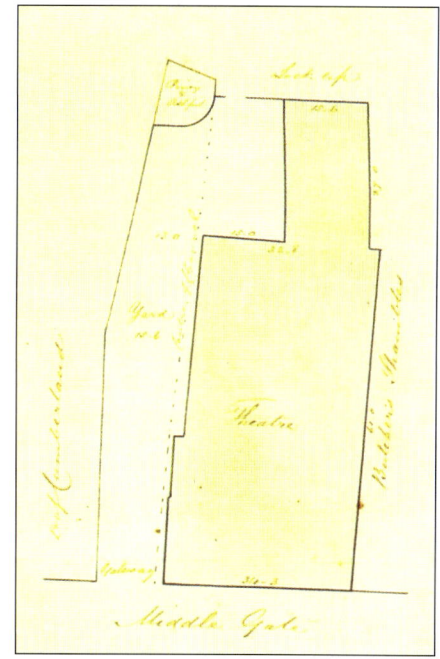

Interior of Ipswich theatre in 1885. Boston theatre of 1806 may have looked like this.
Richard Southern, The Georgian Playhouse, 1948

Site plan of the Newark theatre in Middlegate, date unknown. Perhaps early 19th century.
From Newark Civic Trust magazine, issue 68, February 2013.

---

[44] *SM*, 22 March 1805.
[45] *SM*, 15 November 1805.
[46] Porter, Herbert, *Boston 1800-1835*, Vol.II, Boston (1942), p.115.
[47] Gould, Mervyn, *Boston and Spalding Entertainment and the Aspland Howdens*, Wakefield (2005), p.13.

Sites of successive Georgian theatres in Boston.
1 *Temporary theatre in warehouse, used until 1772.*
2 *Theatre 1772–1806.*
3 *Theatre 1806–1849.*
Extract from Ordnance Survey 25in Plan, 1905

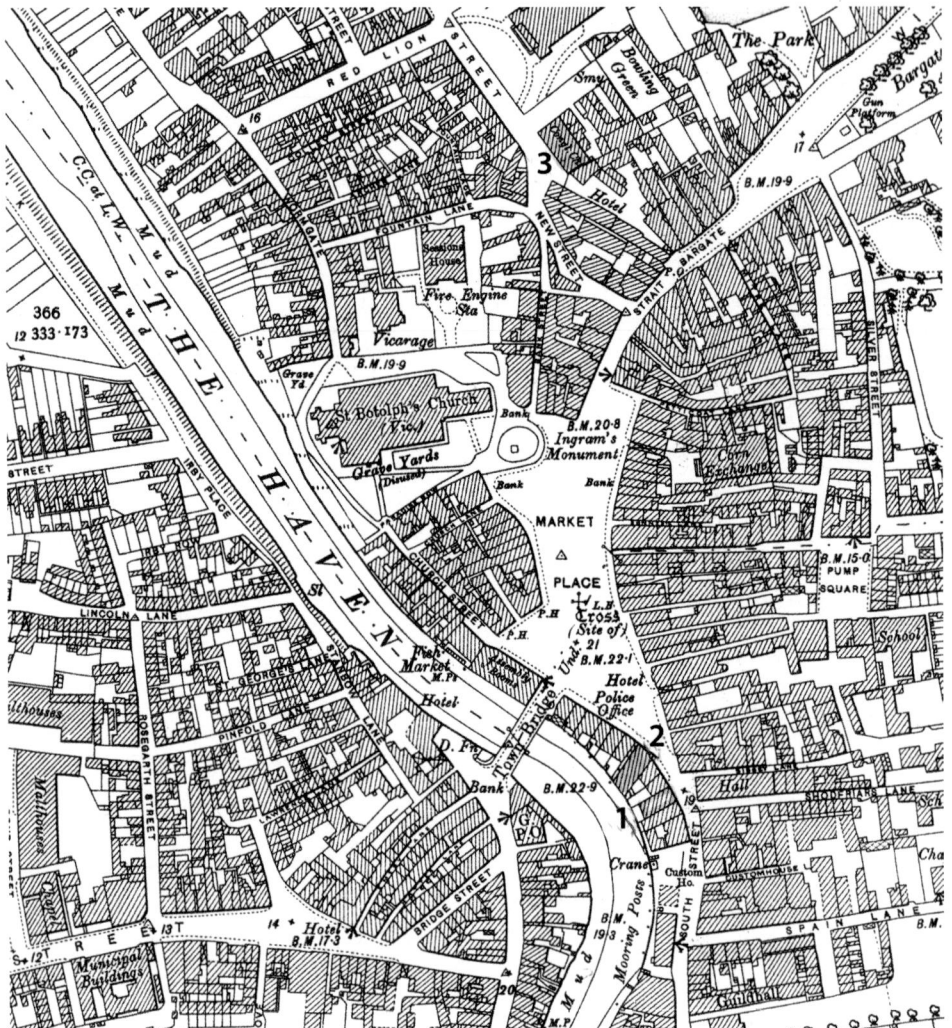

It sounds as if the theatre was actually on the first floor, like Grantham and Southwell, because the 1839 description also says that the ground floor had a separate entrance giving access to space beneath the theatre.

In 1803 it had been said that the old Boston theatre could hold 550 to produce about £40 'when filled to inconvenience' but the new theatre could hold 1,079 people and the maximum takings for a full house amounted to £106 4s 6d. It was opened on 29 January 1806, when Tom Robertson gave a speech written for the occasion. The plays on the first night were *The Castle Spectre*, and the new popular farce *The Weathercock* (1805). The entire receipts for the 1806 season were over £1,100. Robertson leased the theatre for 30 years from 1806 at a rent of £176 a year, 'with liberty reserved to the lessors of letting or occupying the premises, except during the season of dramatic performances'.[48] John Watson the builder owned the theatre until his death on 24 August 1811 when it passed to his widow, Hannah, and two years later it was listed as the first lot in a sale of Hannah's property.[49]

[48] *SM*, 3 September 1813.
[49] *Ibid.*

Interior of Lincoln 1806 theatre after the fire of 1892, showing two tiers of boxes and their decoration. Ross Challis, the owner, surveys the damage.
Lincolnshire Archives

Tom Robertson also opened new theatres in Lincoln and Northampton in 1806. The one at Northampton (population 7,020 in 1801) was, like Huntingdon, the first permanent theatre in a town recently added to the Lincoln circuit. The old theatre was a temporary one in St Giles Street, said by Robertson to be 'very bad', and when full it only contained £30. The new one was also built by subscription and was opened on 5 May 1806 with *The Castle Spectre*. There were two tiers of boxes, a pit and a gallery, the pit containing twelve rows of benches covered with matting.[50]

There was some 'regret' in Lincoln that Boston was getting its new theatre before the one in the county town was rebuilt, particularly as their theatre had seen little improvement since it was erected in 1768. On 2 November 1804, at the close of the Lincoln season, Tom Robertson announced that he had taken a lease of the old theatre, with an additional piece of ground, ,for the purpose of erecting a spacious theatre in the first style of elegance and accommodation'. There was delay in building the theatre as there were 'several public works' under construction in Lincoln and not only workmen but also materials were difficult to obtain. Plays in 1805 were still held in the old theatre 'as the workmen were not engaged to start until after the close of the season'.[51] It is not known whether Robertson attempted to look for a different site for the new theatre, as had happened in Boston and elsewhere.

---

[50] Warwick, Lou, *Theatre Unroyal*, p.41.
[51] *SM*, 6 September 1805.

Southwell theatre was on the upper floor of this building, viewed from Queen Street.
Photograph by Neil Wright, February 2012

Like the Boston theatre it was a plain brick building outside but elegant inside. A couple of weeks before its opening the *Stamford Mercury* described the interior. Reflecting the contemporary interest in the art of Egypt, they reported that

> *the centre of the costume (sic) is a l'Egyptienne. The ceiling is particularly spoken of, as being a very masterly piece of painting, representing a full length figure of Nature. The boxes over the stage are fitted up with Italian lattice-work of gold, with drapery of crimson satin, and will have a most beautiful and brilliant effect. The stage-boxes are in the style of Drury-lane, with chairs, &c.*[52]

A photograph taken after the fire of 1892 gives some idea of its internal appearance. The new theatre at Lincoln was opened in Race Week on 10 September 1806 with, as usual, a special speech written by Fanny Robertson for her husband, Tom. The plays on the first night were the comedy *The Honey Moon* (1804) and *The Weathercock*. Higher prices were charged as this was Race Week, but the cast included some new actors and for the whole week the theatre was 'lighted up with WAX' candles.[53] Having the entrance through the yard of the King's Arms could bring problems and in September 1811 Tom Robertson reported:

> *The encroachment of the building in the Theatre-yard is now so far removed, that a good and sufficient carriage-road is restored, and the convenience and safety of the public Mr R. hopes he has perfectly secured.*[54]

One of the last local places to get a permanent theatre was Southwell (population 2,674 in 1811) in Nottinghamshire, and parts of the internal structure of that

---

[52] *SM*, 29 August 1806.
[53] Playbill, Lincoln, 10 September 1806, in Lincoln Central Library.
[54] *SM*, 13 September 1811.

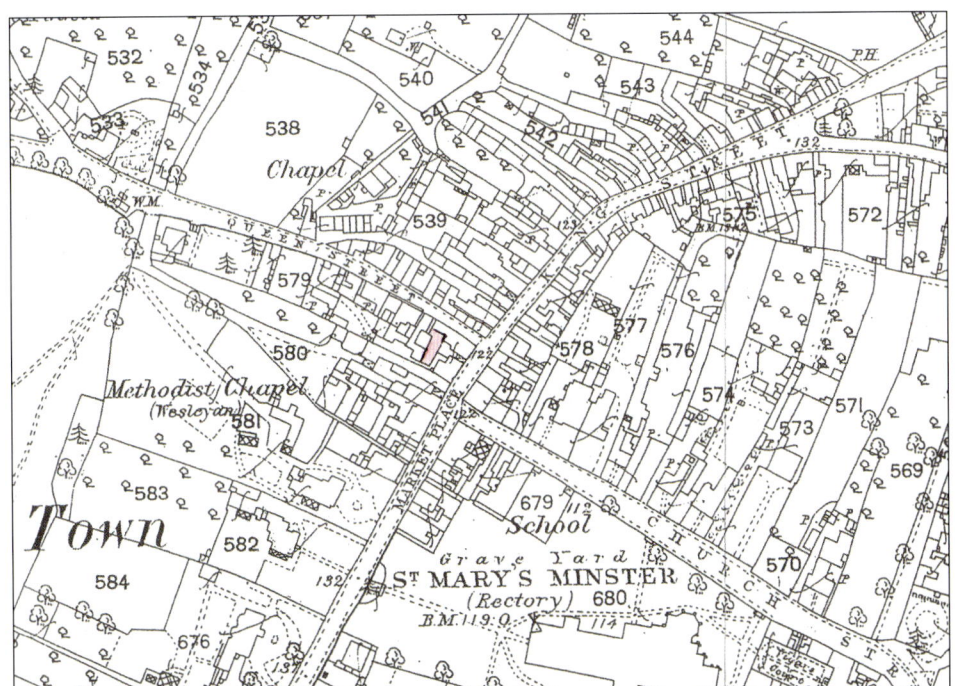

Southwell theatre was created in 1816 in a building behind the Cross Keys inn. The building between the theatre and Queen Street has since been demolished.
Extract from Ordnance Survey 25in Plan, 1885

playhouse still remain in 2016. For some years temporary theatres were set up in 'old prebends and dilapidated barns' until the summer of 1816 when two large rooms on the first floor of the premises of James Adams, whitesmith, close to the centre of town, were converted to a theatre. The rooms had previously been used as a depot for the weapons of the Southwell regiment of local militia. The building was in the yard of the former Cross Keys inn that was later demolished to widen the street. In May 1816 the magistrates of Southwell gave Joseph Smedley permission for his company to perform in the new theatre for 40 days from 7 July and a local commentator said that 'the public are wisely restricted to a visit once in two years'![55] More will be said about Smedley and other new companies in a later chapter.

There were also developments in Louth and Horncastle, though the details are not so clear, and in July 1813 the first stone of a new theatre in King's Lynn was laid by the mayor of that town, but that was no longer in the Lincoln circuit. The first lessee of the new Lynn theatre was John Brunton, Jnr., who opened it on 7 February 1815.[56] On 11 February 1806 Edward Blyth sold Louth theatre to Boston bankers Abraham and Challis Sheath, who then used the front part of the building for their local banking office. Sheath's bank failed in 1815 and on 18 December 1817 their assignees sold the theatre to Louth Corporation who converted it into a 'Guildhall' at a cost of £1,461.[57] The new Guildhall replaced the old Town Hall in the Market Place which had been demolished in 1815. The main room could be used as a theatre for the company of comedians' annual visit to the town, and the building was referred

---

[55] Shilton, Richard Phillips, *The History of Southwell*, Newark (1816 reprinted 2011), p.172.
[56] Grice, *op. cit.*, p.61.
[57] Title deeds in Goulding papers, 4/A/1/1/39 in Lincolnshire County Archives.

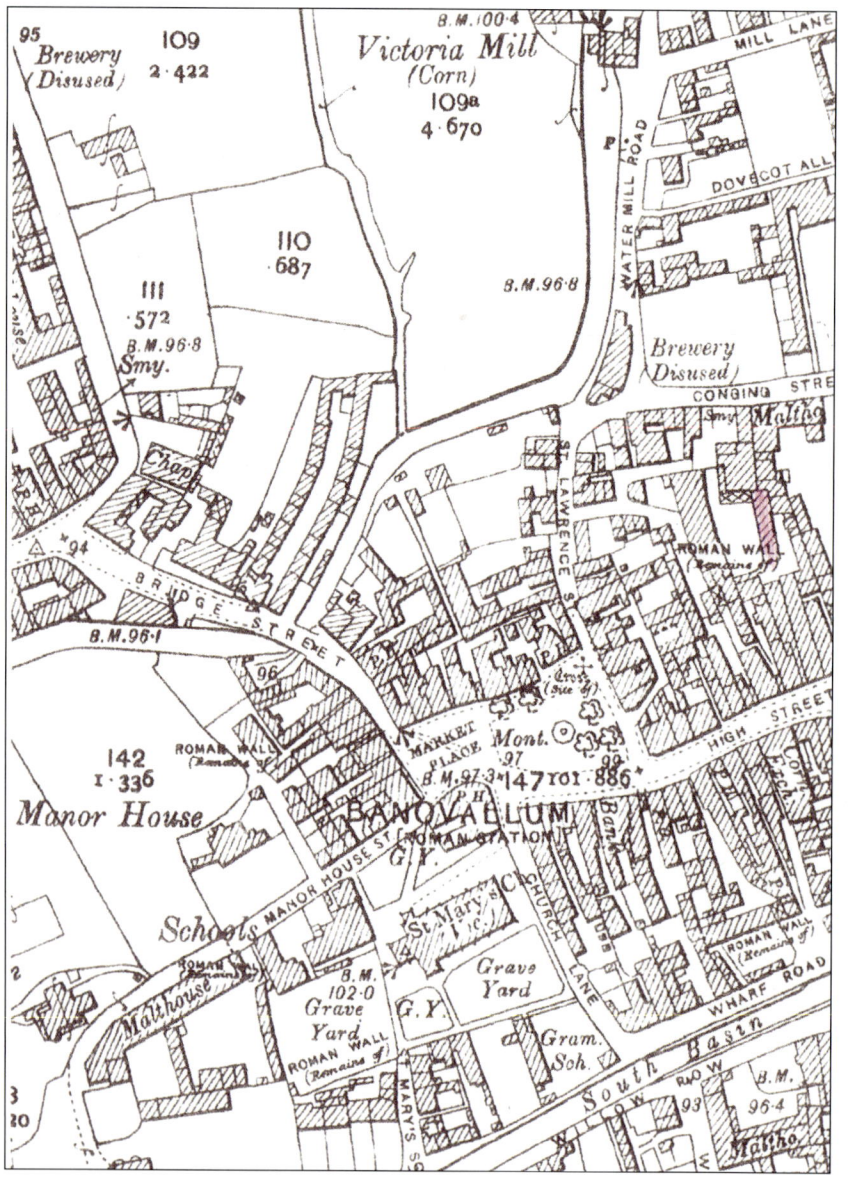

Horncastle's Georgian theatre was in Dog Kennel Yard off St Lawrence Street.

Extract from Ordnance Survey 25in Plan, 1906

to in 1826 as 'The Theatre and Town Hall'.[58] As late as February 1829 Louth Theatre still had only a Pit and Gallery, but boxes were added later that year or in 1830 as prices for 23 February 1831 were Boxes 3s (three shillings), Pit 2s and Gallery 1s.[59] When Charles Macready performed in Louth in 1834 he said that the theatre 'answers also the double purpose of a Sessions House; it is not the *worst* I have seen.'[60]

Horncastle, in the southern Wolds, was a growing town and its population rose from 2,015 in 1801 to 2,622 in 1811. A temporary theatre existed there by February 1796 when Collier and Huggins' company performed Shakespeare's *As You Like It* to raise funds for the benefit of the poor.[61] It was in a threshing barn, later used as a warehouse, in Dog Kennel Yard off St Lawrence Street just to the northeast of the Market Place, and it had a pit and gallery.[62] That building was converted into a proper theatre and in February 1811 was referred to as the 'New Theatre, Horncastle' where Huggins' company performed between 21 February and 9 March. It continued in use until 1836 and the appearance of the building clearly showed it was the conversion of a warehouse into a theatre; the structure survived until the 1970s.

Lincoln circuit

In 1803 James Winston was collecting information for a book on theatres of Britain. Tom Robertson sent him details of those in the Lincoln circuit and this showed just one significant change from 1796.[63] There had previously been a break in May and June but by 1803 Robertson was visiting Huntingdon or Northampton

---

[58] White, William, 1826 *Directory of Lincolnshire*, Sheffield (1826), p.154.
[59] Playbills 22 February 1829, 23 February 1831.
[60] Gould, Mervyn, 'Boston Entertainment', unpublished ms, 1978, Boston Library L.BOST.792.
[61] *SM*, 12 February 1796.
[62] Robinson, David N., *The Book of Horncastle and Woodhall Spa*, Buckingham (1983), p.160.
[63] The information supplied to Winston is reproduced in Appendix 5 to this volume.

Former Horncastle theatre as it was in October 1979. Note the elaborate windows.
Photograph by Neil Wright, 6 October 1979

in May of alternate years. The two week Huntingdon season had originally been in August, between Peterborough and Spalding, but now the Peterborough season was extended into August. The sequence of seasons in 1803 was Lincoln (September/October), Newark (November for six weeks), Grantham (December for five weeks), Boston (late January for six weeks), Wisbech (March for six weeks), Huntingdon or Northampton (May for six weeks), Peterborough (June into August for seven weeks) and Spalding (August for one month). At some time in the eighteenth century Newark had been part of Whitley's circuit, and again in 1804 it was said to be visited by James Robertson's Stamford company, but most of the time it was in the Lincoln circuit. In 1804 Tom Robertson offered to send exterior views of his theatres to James Winston and said that 'I have written to the different towns to painters, who paint for me as I keep no regular painter to make the sketches'.[64] In Boston Mr Brand, 'a Gentleman of Fortune & of great taste and ability as a draftsman', had promised to draw that theatre but a year later it had still not reached Robertson and may never have been produced. The Stamford circuit changed over the years, though Nottingham and Derby were with it most of the time. In 1804 their circuit also included Halifax and Sheffield, which they were still visiting in 1815.[65]

The Lincoln company had started their first season at Northampton on 25 April 1799 and stayed until 6 June. They returned in 1800 but after that only went in alternate years, 1802, 1804 and 1806. Robertson changed his itinerary to visit

---

[64] Richards, John, 'Thomas Shaftoe Robertson and The Theatric Tourist', *Theatre Notebook*, Vol. XXIX, No.1, London (1975), p.7.
[65] *SM*, 16 November 1804, 27 February 1807, 3 February 1815, 3 November 1815.

Part of a playbill for the opening night of the new Lincoln theatre on 10 September 1806.
Lincoln Central Library

Northampton annually, going there again in 1807, but then abruptly dropped it from his circuit altogether. The Lincoln company did return in 1812, for a season from 9 May to 19 June, but that was their final visit.[66] Robertson may have looked for other towns to visit at that time of the year, and in 1811 his company was at Whittlesey for five weeks in June. Whittlesey is only six miles east of Peterborough but was of similar size to that city, with a population of 3,841 in 1801, and was still being visited by the Lincoln company in the early 1840s. Its theatre was in Scaldgate. It does seem that May and June remained free months for most years and when Oundle was added to the circuit in 1828 their season was slotted into that period.

Tom Robertson said that his wife, Fanny, had the talent to succeed in London, and in 1809 it did look as if they were being tempted to sell the Lincoln company and move elsewhere. But it did not happen. On 12 May the *Stamford Mercury* reported that Robertson had sold his share of the company to George Robson (d.1814), who until recently had been an actor in the company, and that Mr and Mrs Robertson would only continue the circuit for one season more. 'The admirers of theatrical performances in the different towns which the company visit, will lament the loss of so valuable an actress as Mrs Robertson', said the paper, 'and the public in general will also regret being deprived of so worthy a character as Mr R. who has at all times been studious of their amusement and convenience.' Was Mrs Robertson contemplating a move to London? Three months later there was one reference to Mr Robson as 'proprietor of the Lincoln theatre', but after that there was no other mention of that proposed change. Even when Robson was called the 'proprietor' it was Tom Robertson's name in the advertisement where the manager was usually listed. Whatever change they had planned, it was not carried through. According to the *Stamford Mercury*, in November 1809 there was some criticism of Tom and Fanny Robertson in the new *Lincolnshire Chronicle* newspaper, but that did not stop people attending Fanny Robertson's benefit; the details are not now known as copies of the *Chronicle* of that date are not extant.[67]

During the wars with France there had been political repression in Britain but theatre had flourished. The early Romantic poets had challenged orthodoxy, and new ideas had been explored in literature, dress, furnishings and architecture. With peace in 1815 came economic difficulties and female fashion symbolised the loss of freedom as soft, white, muslin dresses gave way to tight corsets, heavier dresses and poke-bonnets. In the theatres the companies of comedians that had flourished in the war years were to see their moral opponents grow ever stronger in the years ahead, and theatres started on a slow road to oblivion.

---

[66] Warwick, Lou, *Theatre Unroyal*, pp.26, 28, 45, 61, 63.
[67] *SM*, 24 November 1809.

7

TWILIGHT IS COMING

Debtors Prison

A bombshell dropped on the Lincoln company of comedians in May 1816 and their survival was put in serious doubt. The manager Tom Robertson was imprisoned for debt in Lincoln Castle and his actors had to disperse to find work elsewhere. The *Stamford Mercury* expressed great sympathy with Robertson's situation, saying that 'the various causes that have combined to produce the present deplorable effects are too well known to need any statement or comment'. The causes may have been well known in 1816 but that is not the case 200 years later, though it was said that 'Mr Robertson's misfortunes have been the result of circumstances no human prudence could foresee or prevent'.[1]

The *Mercury* gives clues as to two of the factors that led to this deplorable situation. On 8 January 1816 the Boston magistrates refused Tom Robertson's

The Debtors' Prison in Lincoln Castle, where Tom Robertson was incarcerated in 1816.
Photograph by Neil Wright, 13 April, 2015

---

[1] *Stamford Mercury*, 24 May 1816, 7 June 1816.

annual application for permission to open Boston theatre, saying they did so 'in consideration of the depressed state of the times'.[2] This refusal would be a serious loss for him, as he usually spent six weeks at Boston, followed by a further six weeks in Wisbech, and then a spring break. The Grantham season finished on 17 February, and then for six weeks the company had no income. A second factor is referred to in May, as his wife, Fanny, the star of his company, was once more struck down with 'a painful complaint, which at present prevents the exertion of her professional talents, and adds to the embarrassment which she and her husband experience'.[3] The sympathetic *Mercury* was

> sorry to find the situation of our old friend, and the public's old servant, Mr T. Robertson, the comedian, is such as calls now for the commiseration and benevolence of those whom he has long studied to amuse. We heartily wish that the benefit projected for him at Boston may yield him something proportional to his necessities, and worthy of the character which he has through all the vicissitudes of life successfully maintained – that of an honest man.[4]

The Boston benefit referred to was an effort by his public to help him in his predicament, and is an indication of the high regard in which he and his company were held. As soon as they heard of his problems several of his friends in Boston rushed forward and volunteered to perform a play, 'the receipts of which will be applied to his immediate relief'. The performance at Boston theatre on 29 May 1816 was announced as being 'by permission of the Worshipful the Mayor and of the Magistrates of this borough', the people who had contributed to this crisis. The plays were *Venice Preserved* (1682) and the new farce of *How to Die for Love*. Tickets were available not only from the usual box-keeper, Mr Clarke, but also from six booksellers in the town and Mr Carleton of the Ship Tavern in Custom House Lane.

The response was great and demand for tickets exceeded the capacity of Boston theatre. The sum raised was £86 4s 6d, and it was announced from the stage that, at the request of a number of ladies and gentlemen, and of people unable to get a place in the theatre, the performance would shortly be repeated to raise more funds. Tom Robertson was overwhelmed when he heard of this show of support and through the *Stamford Mercury* he told them that their efforts had 'converted the hours of imprisonment and distress into those of hope and resignation', and thanked them 'for the bountiful means of comfort they have bestowed in the pressing hour of my calamity'.[5]

Several of his friends in Grantham put on an amateur play on 29 June to raise more money. This was under the patronage of the Alderman, showing the respect for him at the highest level in the town. The programme included *Venice Preserved*, as at

---

[2] *SM*, 5 and 12 January 1816.
[3] *SM*, 24 May 1816.
[4] *Ibid*.
[5] *SM*, 7 June 1816.

Boston, followed by Dibdin's *The Jew and the Doctor* (1798) as well as a new dance, and songs by the amateurs. The playhouse was filled 'with the most numerous and respectable audience ever witnessed at Grantham theatre'.[6] Performers wrote and delivered an opening and a concluding speech. By late June Fanny Robertson had recovered from her illness and took charge of the Grantham event:

> *The great talents of Mrs. T. Robertson were displayed upon the occasion, the whole being under the immediate direction of that lady.*[7]

Tom's brother James of the Stamford company, together with his joint manager Thomas Manly, also came forward to help. The actors of the Lincoln company had dispersed to find work where they could, so the Stamford troupe put on three days of plays during Peterborough fair in July and three days of plays at Huntingdon on 9, 10 and 12 August, which were places in the Lincoln circuit fairly close to Stamford. On 9 August the first play was *The Provoked Husband* (1782), with Thomas Manly as *Lord Townley* and Fanny Robertson as *Lady Townley*, perhaps the only time these two leading local actors ever performed together. The financial arrangements were probably the same as when James put on a season at Lincoln in September 1816, when all profits went to re-establish his brother's circuit.

Amateur actors in other towns also organised plays to help Tom Robertson, with performances in Spalding on 16 and 19 July, in Newark on 14 and 15 August, and in Wisbech on 24 and 31 August. At Newark the advertisement said that

> *the profits of the performances [would be] appropriated to the Relief of Mr Robertson by a Committee formed for the purpose of promoting his re-establishment in the circuit, after liberation from his present unhappy confinement. As Mr Robertson's distresses have arisen from a series of untoward circumstances, over which he has no control, it is hoped that he will have the sympathy of a feeling and generous public, and that these performances will merit their liberal support.*

They were not only raising funds to get him out of prison, but also to get his circuit going again and a 'Committee' had been formed to achieve that. The Grantham gentlemen then repeated *Venice Preserved* and *The Jew and the Doctor* on 28 August. So far Lincoln gentlemen had done nothing to help, and soon they did not need to. Instead the gentlemen of Grantham came to Lincoln theatre, 'in aid of the Fund making by a Committee for the purpose of re-establishing Mr Robertson in his theatrical circuit' on 30 August 1816.[8] Again they performed *Venice Preserved* and *The Jew and the Doctor*. Tom's brother James attended to sing comic songs.

In August 1816 an auction was advertised, under a distress warrant for arrears of rent for Grantham theatre, for the sale of Tom Robertson's belongings, including

Joseph Leathley Cowell (1792–1863). A member of the Lincoln company from 1816 to 1818, he later had a successful career in the United States. Print published in Philadelphia in 1826.
Courtesy of the Rare Book & Manuscript Library, University of Illinois at Urbana-Champaign

---

[6] *SM*, 21 June 1816.
[7] *SM*, 5 July 1816.
[8] *SM*, 23 August 1816.

not only 'all the Scenery, Machinery, Theatrical Dresses and Decorations' but also 'Mr and Mrs Robertson's theatrical and private Wardrobes'.⁹ The Committee purchased the 'travelling theatrical property' that was sold there, and perhaps elsewhere. In September the efforts of the Committee started to bear fruit. James Robertson became temporary manager of a new troupe that he formed with the financial support of the Committee. The members of the new Lincoln company included Mr Collier and Joseph Leathley Cowell (1792-1863) and his wife from the York company, Mrs Brooke from the English Opera company described as 'a great acquisition as a singer', with her daughter and John Springfield Hallam. From the old company there was still Fanny Robertson, and a Mr Armstrong and Mrs Norris both came back. Mr Armstrong, 'always a respectable performer', was said to have been greatly improved by the opportunities that his temporary absence had afforded him, and his acting now displayed 'a nice discernment of his author, and smoothness and ease and self-possession'.¹⁰

James announced on 13 September that:

> *to prevent his Brother's unfortunate situation from causing an interruption in the accustomed amusements of the season, it is his intention to open the* [Lincoln] *Theatre on Wednesday in the Race Week, for the usual period, and to appropriate any profits which may arise from the performances towards the promotion of his Brother's re-establishment in his Theatrical circuit.*

On the opening night, 18 September, the play was Morton's *Speed the Plough* followed by comic songs sung by Mr Collier, Joe Cowell and James Robertson himself. In the words of the *Stamford Mercury*'s reviewer, the new company was

> *one of the most respectable provincial companies we ever saw, and we heartily wish them that success which may reward their exertions, and heal the wounds of their worthy but unfortunate leader.*¹¹

The Lincoln season continued through September, October and November as usual and ended triumphantly with Tom Robertson's release. On 24 September it was reported that Robertson had filed a list of his creditors and the Lindsey magistrates would consider his case at the Quarter Sessions on 16 October.¹² Tom was released by the end of October and was free at last, after several awful months confined in the bleak debtors prison of Lincoln Castle. On 1 November he announced that the last night of the season, 8 November, would be for his benefit and he would play the part of *Heartly* in Leigh's new comedy *Where to Find a Friend* (1815). This title so expressed his own feelings and gratitude that he performed in this play at

---

9 Gould, Mervyn, *Boston and Spalding Entertainment and the Aspland Howdens,* Wakefield (2005), p.11; Hemingway, G., *The Robertson Family and the Lincoln and Nottingham Theatrical Circuits,* thesis, (1976), in Lincoln Central Library, ref.UP 7467, p.13
10 *SM*, 13 and 27 September 1816.
11 *SM*, 27 September 1816.
12 *London Gazette* 17176, 24 September 1816, p.16.

Grantham on 18 January 1817, Wisbech on 18 April and Peterborough on 28 June. The play was also performed at Newark on 18 November 1818 and at Grantham, which worked so hard for his release, again on 23 January 1819. The disaster had arisen from his not being allowed to open Boston theatre in 1816 and the reaction the following year during the Boston season 'exceeded the manager's expectations. Mr and Mrs Robertson's benefits were very productive, particularly Tom's, at which there was the fullest house that has been known at Boston for some years'.[13]

Decline

Tom Robertson's friends and supporters around Lincolnshire had made great money-raising efforts to get him out and create a new company of comedians to replace his actors who had dispersed. But any euphoria about the future of theatre in Lincolnshire was misplaced. Theatres had provided solace and diversion during the war years, but when peace came in 1815 playhouses in Lincolnshire, as elsewhere in the provinces, started on a long and slow decline that was only occasionally interrupted by some nights with deceptively good attendances. The middle class had been the financial mainstay of local theatres and their steady withdrawal as society expected more 'moral' behaviour drove the companies of comedians into penury and eventual extinction, and nearly all Lincolnshire theatres into oblivion.

Some signs of this decline appeared early in the new century but were at first dismissed as temporary problems that could be overcome by redecorating theatres, putting on moral plays and bringing more stars from London. Companies still had the occasional exhilaration of a full house, long and loud applause and good reviews but such events became ever rarer and were worth celebrating when they did happen. The size and frequency of theatre advertisements in the *Stamford Mercury* declined but from about 1809 the paper started to publish reviews of performances and comments on the abilities of local actors. The financial position of theatres teetered on a knife-edge; they needed full houses, but attendance could be affected by hot or cold weather, competing attractions, and good or bad reviews by those who attended.

Robertson's circuit

James Robertson had been joint manager of the Stamford company with Thomas Manly since 1806 but the amount of time he gave to saving his brother's Lincoln company in 1816 may have strained their partnership. In July 1818 James announced that, 'in consequence of his declining state of health', he had agreed that Manly should take his share of the company and, in a few months, he would retire to private life in Nottingham. The *Mercury* understood that James would get 'a moderate annuity' from the Stamford company on his retirement.[14] Ten years later he was still receiving an annual annuity of £109 4s 0d (104 guineas) from the

---

[13] *SM*, 4 April 1817.
[14] *SM*, 10 July 1818.

Stamford company, and was also allowed an annual benefit, from which he received half the takings.[15] His last benefit at Stamford before retiring was on 17 July 1818 when he thanked his audience for the support he had received for 30 years. 'The old comic favourite of the Stamford and Nottingham company of comedians' sang two new comic songs he had written, and introduced Little Shock, his dancing dog. An excessively crowded house complimented the mock hero of the buskin on this his leave-taking – which was managed in his usual way, at the end of a comic song, but not without visible emotion.[16]

James Robertson's share of the company was purchased by his sister-in-law, Mrs Manly, and the Manlys ran the Stamford company for 21 more years. It was said that Robertson opened a general shop in Nottingham, over the door of which he inscribed:

Everything made here except a fortune.[17]

Whatever may have been the real reason for his 'retirement', within eighteen months James Robertson was back working on the stage, but instead of returning to Stamford he had joined his brother's company. In December 1819 James played the part of *Lazarillo* in Jephson's *Two Strings to your Bow, Or, The Servant of Two Masters* (1791) at Newark theatre. Carlo Goldoni's 1743 version of this play was successfully revived in 2012 as *One Man, Two Guvnors*. In August 1820 another side of James Robertson's talent reappeared, when he painted the new scenery for *Aladdin, Or, The Wonderful Lamp* being performed at Spalding. Tom must have been pleased with the result, for he used James to paint new scenery for Planche's *The Vampyre* that was the highlight of the last night of the Lincoln season on 3 November 1820. James' arrival was most timely as William Hilton, 'an artist of considerable celebrity' who for many years had painted scenery for the Lincoln company, died on 7 September 1822 'at an advanced age'.[18] James did similar work for Manly, because in 1824 the scenery at Nottingham theatre included 'a new scene by Mr Robertson showing the Market Place as seen from the Bell. Prints of the scene were sold for half a guinea.[19]

Another member of the Robertson family had joined the Lincoln company by January 1820. This was Frederick, the teenage son of Tom's brother, George, the Peterborough printer. The first mention of Frederick in the *Stamford Mercury* is damning with faint praise: 'Mr F. Robertson should not be forgotten: he is a young man whose talents are far from being below mediocrity'. Nearly three years later, in November 1822, the *Mercury* reported that 'Mr F. Robertson is particularly improved, and promises

---

[15] *Manly Notebook*, March 1828, in British Library; Rosenfeld, Sybil, 'The Theatrical Notebooks of T. H. Wilson Manly', *Theatre Notebook*, Vol.7, No.1, London (October, December 1952, p.4.
[16] *SM*, 10 July, 1818.
[17] Rosenfeld, Sybil, *op. cit.*, p.2.
[18] *SM*, 13 September 1822.
[19] Golland, Jim, 'A Dramatic Discovery or, A Manly Enterprise', *Local History Magazine*, No.42, Nottingham (1994), p.14; Wood, A.C., 'Nottingham 1836-1865: 1.The Borough 1835-1865', *Transactions of the Thoroton Society*, Vol.LIX, Nottingham (1955), pp.33,34.

to become a shining actor'.[20] His next mention in the paper was about his love life. In February 1824 he eloped with Miss Anne Tindall, the only child of Grantham businessman Josh Tindall, and they married at Gretna Green. Frederick had been 'attached' to her for seven years but her father had not agreed to their marriage and had then found a more 'suitable' suitor for his daughter, which precipitated the elopement. It seems that all was forgiven, as after the first wedding in Scotland, they returned to Grantham and had a second marriage ceremony in St Wulfram's church on the next Sunday. Frederick then entered his father-in-law's business as a tanner and 25 years later was sufficiently prosperous to be elected a director of the local Ambergate, Nottingham and Boston and Eastern Junction Railway.[21]

In September 1825 another nephew joined Tom's company. William Shaftoe Robertson (1796-1872), the son of James, had been born in Stamford and was on the stage as a child aged 9 to 11 before being sent to school for a few years. Then he was articled to Mr Whitsed, a solicitor in Derby, but he chose instead to become an actor.[22] A talented Danish-born actress, Miss Margharetta Elisabetta Marinus, came from the Theatre Royal, Brighton, to join the Lincoln company in the summer of 1824 and played the leading role of *Mrs Haller* in Kotzebue's *The Stranger*.[23] That was a sentimental play, with a mildly sensational plot dealing with adultery and reconciliation, that was a runaway success from the start and remained popular throughout the first half of the nineteenth century. Many critics saw Kotzebue's work as immoral but he wrote over 200 plays and was one of the most popular writers of his time. William Robertson's working relationship with Miss Marinus blossomed into something stronger and in 1828 they were married in Lambeth, London. Over the next nineteen years they had 22 children and it was said that 'they always had a juvenile stock company ready for any emergency'.[24] Fanny Robertson had for long been the star of the Lincoln company and Miss Marinus, or Mrs W S Robertson as she now was, became the leading young actress and in 1836 was referred to as 'the gem of the company', anglicising her name to Margaret Elizabeth Robertson.[25]

In 1816 the actors in Tom Robertson's Lincoln company of comedians had dispersed and James had to create a new Lincoln company of comedians, including the best of the old company and some good new actors. Ironically the disaster had led to an improved company, which made it easier to attract good actors though in turn they were of a quality that could move on to bigger and better theatres. Joseph Cowell (1792-1863) had joined them as a low comedian at that time, but in September 1818 he suddenly left the company and had a 'successful debut' at Drury

---

[20] *SM*, 28 January 1820, 1 November 1822.
[21] Hemingway, *op. cit.*, p.25.
[22] Hemingway, *op. cit.*, p.26; Robertson, Thomas William, Jnr., *The Principal Dramatic Works of Thomas William Robertson*, Vol.1, London (1889), p.xviii.
[23] *SM*, 27 August 1824.
[24] Donaldson, Walter, *Recollections of an Actor*, London (1865), p.27.
[25] *SM*, 28 October 1836.

Above left: Playbill, Wisbech, 14 May 1819. The members of the Lincoln company include Mr Wemyss and Mr Hallam who both later went to the United States. Miss Stannard may be the actress who later married Hallam.
Wisbech Museum

Above right: Playbill Grantham, 17 May 1828. An amateur performance to raise funds for the widow Chesterton, with professional actresses from Lincoln giving their services for free.
Grantham Library

Lane. In 1821 Cowell sailed to New York and from then on had a long career as a comedian and theatre manager in the chief cities of the United States including Boston, Philadelphia and Charleston. Cowell's place as the low comedian in the Lincoln company was taken by Mr Rayner who had been at Stamford in 1813-14. Mr Rayner was said to be 'a great prize' gained by the company, and he 'possesses naturally so much of the genuine *vis comica* [comic face] that he cannot fail to establish himself as a favourite throughout the circuit'.[26]

Mrs Norris was a leading member of the Lincoln company for nearly twenty years, from 1804 to 1821, and was said to have 'very excellent comic talents'. In October 1818 it was thought that she must soon retire from the theatre owing to age and infirmities, and three amateur plays were put on in Spalding for her benefit as she would have no income after retirement. In fact she did not leave until the end of 1821 and then some of her admirers started a subscription so she could 'enjoy a

---
[26] *SM*, 5 November 1819.

few of the comforts of life in the evening of her days'.[27] A Mr Chesterton had joined the Lincoln company by January 1820, and was said to be 'as useful and excellent a comedian as we ever saw in a provincial corps. He undertakes nothing in which he does not acquit himself with extreme correctness and propriety'.[28] In early 1828 he was afflicted with 'a serious illness that prevented him speaking'. An amateur play was arranged in Grantham to raise funds to help him during his illness, Miss Marinus and Miss H. Noel offering their services for free, but he died before it was put on and the funds were then raised for his widow and six children. Other fundraising events for Mrs Chesterton included a lecture in Spalding in April and an amateur performance at Newark on 3 September, in which Mr Chesterton's eldest son filled one role.

Other actors who joined the Lincoln company included Mr Raymond in January 1819 'who in genteel comedy and in the younger characters of tragedy, such as *Romeo, Jaffier*, &c., would be an acquisition and an ornament to any stage'.[29] Francis Courtney Wemyss (1797-1859) was an actor in the Lincoln company in 1818-19 and he also went to America. After making his debut on the stage in New York in 1824 he later became manager of theatres in Washington, New York, Philadelphia, Baltimore and Pittsburgh, some simultaneously. In 1822 Mr J. Gann played the tragic hero with the Lincoln company, 'a very respectable and improving performer – perhaps as good a one as the limited patronage of a country theatre affords us any right to expect. On the whole we think him most happy in genteel comedy'.[30] Another favourite in 1822 was Mr Gurner who

> *continues to delight us with his natural and unobtrusive humour in low comedy. He is a very clever young man, and has the rare talent of stirring our risibility without stooping to buffoonery, or playing exclusively to the galleries*[31]

Several members of the Stannard family were active in the theatre world of Lincolnshire between 1797 and 1838. Some were with the Lincoln company from 1797 and others with Huggins' Louth company. They might perhaps be related to a Mr Stannard who had been in William Herbert's company way back in 1755 to 1757, and 1762.[32] One Mr Stannard was Leader of the Orchestra with the Lincoln company in 1804, and died at Newark on 22 December 1809. In September 1806 young Miss Stannard played the *Duke of York* in Shakespeare's *Richard III* (1592) and Mrs Stannard played a gypsey in *Blind Bargain* (1804). Miss Stannard was listed as a dancer with the Lincoln company in 1811, 1817, 1820 and 1826. In 1820 it was

---

[27] *SM*, 25 January 1822.
[28] *SM*, 1 November 1822.
[29] *SM*, 5 November 1819.
[30] *SM*, 1 November 1822.
[31] *SM*, 1 November 1822.
[32] Hemingway, *op. cit.*, pp.36, 38.

said that she 'plays gracefully, her dancing never fails to elicit peals of applause'.[33] On 23 April 1818 and 16 May 1820 there were benefits for 'Mrs and Miss Stannard' at Wisbech. On 30 April 1827 Stannard's daughter Frances was married in St Botolph's church, Boston, to John Springfield Hallam, a Sheffield-born actor who had worked in the Lincoln company between 1816 and 1820 before emigrating to the United States. After the wedding John Hallam took his wife back with him to America but he died in Boston, Massachusetts in March 1829.[34] Miss Stannard is not referred to after 1826, but in 1827 and 1838 Mrs Stannard was still listed as an actress with the company. By November 1838 the Lincoln company was in dire straits and Mr Stannard had left to become Leader of the Orchestra at the Leicester theatre.

On 11 November 1828 'gentlemen amateurs' in Grantham opened a new 'Minor Theatre' with the musical entertainment of *The Purse, or The Benevolent Tar* (1794) 'to a very crowded house'. It is not known which building was being used as a 'Minor Theatre' and it did not last. A young lady sang *the Oyster Girl* 'in a very pleasing manner' and got cheers of applause. It was said that the tragedy of *Cato* was being prepared for performance early in December. The *Stamford Mercury* disapproved of this activity and chillingly declared 'we leave the matter to those parents and masters whom it immediately concerns'.[35]

Stars from the London stage continued to visit the provinces and appear with local companies. Edmund Kean came to Lincoln in April 1824 to play six parts in six nights. In two of the plays Fanny Robertson had the wonderful opportunity to perform with him, playing *Portia* to his *Shylock* in *The Merchant of Venice* and *Desdemona* to his *Othello*. At the same time the other great actor of the period, William Charles Macready (1793-1873) was also playing *Othello* in Stamford on 6 and 7 April 1824.

Manly's accounts

In the British Library are two volumes of account books kept by Thomas Manly for the periods December 1820 to 11 July 1823 and 24 July 1826 to 28 May 1830. They contain notes about the Stamford circuit and actors as well as his accounts at a time when theatre was everywhere in decline.[36] The Stamford circuit had always been flexible and in the 1820s it consisted of Stamford, Nottingham, Derby, Retford, Chesterfield, Halifax and, in 1821 only, Rochdale. The Sheffield theatre had been leased by James Robertson and Manly until June 1817 but it was then taken by Mr Fitzgerald of the York and Hull theatres. The longest time spent in any one town in the 1820s was twelve weeks (in Halifax in 1828 and 1829), which exceeded the legally permitted sixty nights; frequently the stay was as short as four nights. There was not just one season in each town as before but the company went backwards and

---

[33] *SM*, 28 January 1820.
[34] *SM*, 4 May 1827, 14 April 1829.
[35] *SM*, 14 November 1828.
[36] Rosenfeld, Sybil, *op. cit.*, pp.2, 3; SM, 20 January 1826.

forwards between them to attend during Marts and Race meetings: Stamford races in June or July, Nottingham and Derby races in July and August, Chesterfield races in September, and Nottingham Goose Fair in October. Only once did Manly meet with opposition when in December 1821 'A Mr Bickerton offered a higher rent for the Halifax house which threw this co. out the regular season (from Christmas to about the end of Feb.) he forgot to pay so I had it after at £80 – instead of £100'. Manly gave a season at Retford instead and returned to Halifax by 23 January after Bickerton had run off owing everyone. The Chesterfield theatre visited by Manly in the 1820s and '30s was externally a plain brick building, with a 'neat' interior, in a yard or court at the bottom of the Market Place, and was owned by Chesterfield Corporation.[37]

Manly was a devotee of the legitimate drama and disliked spectacle. His repertoire was a mixture of stock plays and the latest London successes. The famous *Maria Marten, or, The Murder in the Red Barn* (1828), based on a real murder in 1827, had to be cancelled at Stamford in April 1829 as the Mayor had been told it was a horrid thing, and at his request Manly changed it for *The Bee Hive* (1811). It was, however, played elsewhere in the circuit. An analysis of the Stamford circuit in 1821 shows that 63 plays and 72 afterpieces were performed by the company. Knowles' *Virginius* (1820) had nine performances which was the most and eighteen plays were given only one performance. Of the afterpieces *The Actress of All Work* (1822?) was the most popular with twelve because it was a vehicle for the young star Clara Fisher (1811-98), and twenty-three afterpieces were presented only once.

Miss Clara Fisher (1811–1898). Infant prodigy who performed in Lincolnshire.
Courtesy of the Rare Book & Manuscript Library, University of Illinois at Urbana-Champaign.

On two occasions in the 1820s Manly divided his company. In October 1827 Chesterfield races overlapped with Nottingham Goose Fair and 'The change of time in the races made it necessary to have two companies, great expence and little satisfaction to the audience here [Chesterfield]: company very bad and thinly numbered. This remark applies only to the week of the Chesterfield races. Nottingham goosefair fared better in the way of talent and Novelty'. The population of Chesterfield in 1831 was 5,775. When the same thing happened the following year the results were good: receipts of £73 15s 0d a week at Chesterfield and £70 18s 0d at Nottingham amounted to an unusually high total of £144 13s 0d. The notebooks show that Manly's Stamford circuit sometimes made a profit but many weeks made a loss. In 1820 the total income for the year was £3,065 13s 5d but his expenditure was £61 17s 4d higher. In 1822 total income was £2,664 0s 7d but expenditure was still greater and the deficit on that year was £217 11s 10d. Manly sometimes borrowed money to cover his losses. The first notebook starts with a stock of £31 18s 5d in December 1820 but after some ups and downs at the end of the first notebook in July 1823 there was a deficit of £126 3s 7d. When the second surviving notebook opens in July 1826 there was a stock of £155 8s 3d which rose to £349 19s 9d by October 1827. By mid-September 1828 all had been lost and in March 1830 the deficit had risen to £363 10s 7d and Manly wrote 'bankrupt' in his book. Despite the financial difficulties, he managed to keep going for another nine years.

---

[37] Hall, George, *The History of Chesterfield*, Chesterfield (1839), p.281.

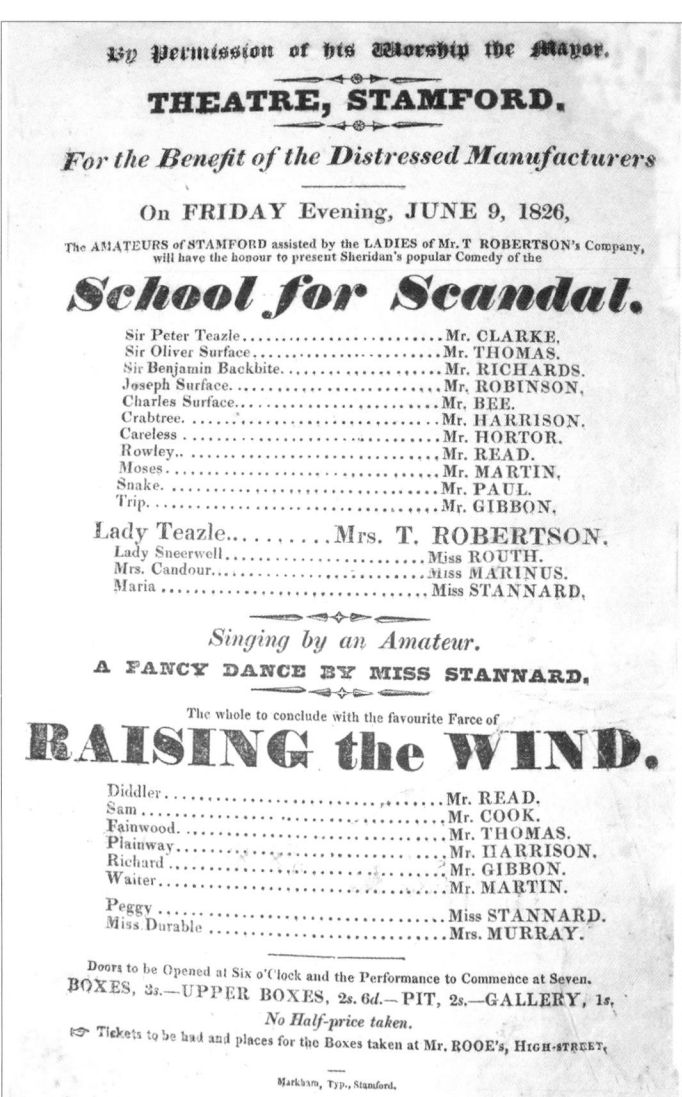

Playbill, Stamford, 9 June 1826. An amateur production with Fanny Robertson, Margaret Marinus, Miss Routh and Miss Stannard of the Lincoln company in the female roles.
Stamford Town Council

One difference between Tom Robertson and Tom Manly may be that one was of a generous nature and the other less so. In June 1826 amateur actors put on a performance in Stamford theatre 'in aid of the distressed manufacturers' but it was the ladies of Tom Robertson's Lincoln company who 'generously offered their services on the occasion' and declined any payment except travelling expenses. The *Stamford Mercury* caustically reported that 'Mr Manly charged 6 guineas for the use of the theatre, but we understand contributed something to the charitable fund'.[38] If Manly had given more than he charged, the paper might have been more specific. Four years later, on 1 March 1830, amateurs put on another play at Stamford theatre, this time for the town's new Infirmary, and once again the female roles were taken by ladies of Robertson's company. His ladies also performed with amateurs for charity in Lincoln as in March 1831 when they appeared to raise funds for the Widow Leafe and her ten children. Even more surprising is that when Mr W P Roberts, Stage Manager to Tom Manly, died in April 1834 and amateurs put on a performance in Stamford theatre for his widow, the female parts were once more taken by actresses from the Lincoln company.

Theatres redecorated

Most Lincolnshire theatres had been built in the eighteenth century or the early years of the nineteenth and by the 1820s they were showing their age and needing renovation. In June 1824 Thomas Manly announced that Stamford theatre had been 'painted, decorated and improved throughout'.[39] Tom Robertson followed suit in several of his theatres, starting with the little theatre in Spalding in August 1824. The next year he spent a lot to employ a Mr Fraser, 'an artist of acknowledged ability', in painting and embellishing the ornamental parts of the theatres in Lincoln, Newark, Grantham and Peterborough. On 4 November 1825 Mr Fraser was actually called 'Artist of the Theatre'.[40]

Robertson said he was redecorating Lincoln theatre because he was anxious to 'make his establishment meet the general improvement of this extensive and opulent county'. A new chandelier, made especially for the purpose, would occupy the

---

[38] *SM*, 16 June 1826.
[39] *SM*, 25 June 1824.
[40] *SM*, 16 September and 4 November 1825.

centre of the theatre and would diffuse a soft, clear and beautiful light throughout. A 'Drop Curtain, on the newest London models, will be introduced', with other tasty decorations.[41] Fraser was decorating Newark theatre in November 1825 and Grantham in December. By July of the following year the one at Peterborough had been entirely repainted and it also had a large glass chandelier, containing six Grecian lamps, 'which light the whole house, and give it a most brilliant appearance'.[42] In 1826 and 1827 the spending continued; in Wisbech Robertson announced that 'in addition to the late expensive improvements, the theatre has been entirely new painted', and that theatre, as well as Lincoln and Grantham, would have a variety of new and appropriate picturesque scenery. Manly then employed Fraser to improve and redecorate Retford theatre in his circuit so that it was entitled 'to rank in the second class of country theatres'.[43]

Spalding theatre had been improved first and the work was perhaps not up to the standard adopted in the larger towns. In September 1833 it was 'being fresh painted, and was undergoing considerable improvements by an artist from Edinburgh'. Just two years later further changes were made to that 'pretty little Thespian temple' in Spalding; 'side-boxes had been added, and the rustic angle both in pit and gallery had been removed or turned', giving it a circular appearance. An artist with good taste had been employed for some time in decorating it; both pit and gallery were hung round with beautiful landscapes in gilt frames, which 'had a most splendid appearance'.[44] In October 1836 it was said that Peterborough theatre had been repainted by Messrs Beaumont and Reeve, 'artists of the theatre'.[45] They were probably members of the company as it is known that a Mr Reeve joined in 1834.

Lincoln circuit

For over fifty years there were very few changes to the Lincoln company's circuit. Between 1816 and 1831 Oundle in Northamptonshire was the only town added to the circuit and Robertson took a long time to agree to that change. In October 1825 he was said to be 'very desirous' that his company should visit that town annually (population 2,308 in 1831), thirteen miles from Peterborough, and if no single individual would erect a theatre there it might be done by subscription, in shares of £50 or £100 each. The hope that Robertson would visit Oundle was repeated in July 1826 and in December 1827 it was suggested that the town hall could be converted into a temporary theatre.[46] Those pressing for the opening of a theatre in the town probably included the Reverend Robert Roberts (d.1829), Rector of Stoke Doyle, just outside Oundle, who in 1811 had been one of the shareholders in Peterborough theatre. This pressure eventually paid off and in February 1828

---

[41] *SM*, 23 September 1825.
[42] *SM*, 7 July 1826.
[43] Piercy, John S., *History of Retford*, Retford (1828),pp.146, 147.
[44] *SM*, 30 March 1833, 11 September 1835.
[45] Playbill, Peterborough, October 1836, in Peterborough Library.
[46] *SM*, 21 October 1825, 28 July 1826, 14 December 1827.

Robertson announced that he 'will commence his first theatrical campaign at Oundle the latter end of next May'.[47] So that year, having finished the Wisbech season on 16 May, he opened a temporary theatre in Oundle on 22 May, for a period of one month. The pit and gallery were filled every night but towards the end of the season the boxes were 'almost deserted'. This was said to be due to their 'inconvenient situation' and that Robertson was thinking about fitting up 'a more commodious theatre in another season'.[48] He did not go there in 1829 and his next visit to Oundle was in May 1830.

In greater Lincolnshire, as in other parts of provincial Britain, all theatres saw declining attendance and income in the years after 1815. The local press blamed this on poor weather, the absence of leading families and similar causes. Only in the 1830s and '40s was it suggested that audiences were staying away for moral or religious reasons. The entire receipts for the 1806 season for Boston theatre had exceeded £1,100 but by 1819 its fortunes had greatly declined and they continued in that state until its closure thirty years later. Lincoln also did badly in 1819:

> *A variety of circumstances have, we fear, concurred to blight the harvest which the manager always anticipates in this, the principal town of the circuit.*[49]

This poor showing was repeated at Grantham in January 1820 when the newspaper said that 'the unfavourableness of the weather has undoubtedly been the only cause'.[50] It was not a continuous decline, and some years did better, which encouraged companies to believe that good days would return. When the Lincoln company performed at Newark in December 1822, for Mr Robertson's benefit, 'the boxes were brilliant, and crowded to excess'.[51] In August 1824 the *Stamford Mercury* was

> *happy to hear that at Huntingdon he has just closed the most successful season he has known for a long time. Under the patronage of the Countess of Sandwich, and all the considerable families of the neighbourhood, the company have played to good houses, and met with the applause to which their respective merits and general excellence entitle them.*[52]

Tom Robertson kept spending money to attract audiences. In November 1824 the *Stamford Mercury* referred to *Ivanhoe*, for Fanny Robertson's benefit, which was

> *...got up with new dresses and scenery, and must have cost the manager a considerable sum: the costume was highly admired and applauded. Mrs T. Robertson's dress was only exceeded by her acting in the character of Rebecca.*[53]

---

[47] *SM*, 8 February 1828.
[48] *SM*, 30 May and 20 June 1826,
[49] *SM*, 5 November 1819.
[50] *SM*, 28 January 1820.
[51] *SM*, 6 December 1822.
[52] *SM*, 27 August 1824.
[53] *SM*, 26 November 1824.

In November 1827 the Lincoln theatre had good support, said to be due to the kindness of the leading families. The presence of nobility and gentry would encourage the middle class to attend. In December 1829

> *His Grace the Duke of Newcastle honoured the Newark theatre with his presence on Friday evening last. The house was brilliantly filled, and the amusements went off with great éclat.*[54]

There were some nights when Lincoln and Grantham theatres were well-filled, but generally 1829 was a year of financial difficulties. Robertson cut the length and frequency of advertisements in the *Stamford Mercury*. In the first three decades of the nineteenth century the *Mercury* had carried many advertisements for plays at local theatres. The advertisements had been most numerous between 1803 and 1813 and then were reduced to about half as many column inches each year until 1828. From 1830 onwards the advertisements were even fewer and shorter and the column inches each year were about a tenth of what they had been in the first quarter of the century.

An exciting night at Stamford theatre occurred on Monday 13 September 1830. Lord Thomas Cecil and Colonel Chaplin had been elected as Members of Parliament for the town and their supporters decided to celebrate with an exclusive evening in the theatre. They tried to keep other people out of the theatre and, under orders from Alderman Thomas Mills, the constables took into custody the first person (a young man named Buck) who had paid his money at the door as, not being a member of Alderman Mills' political party, he had been unable to get a ticket in advance. He was quietly seated in the theatre when he was seized by a constable and dragged out. This started a riot amongst the large crowd waiting at the entrance, and caused great agitation inside the theatre. The crowd outside tore down the large folding doors at the main entrance (leading to the boxes and the pit), carried them to the town bridge and threw them into the river Welland. The gallery door was also forced open, and many people got into the gallery without paying. Thomas Manly, from the stage, said he was unable to preserve order, and even hinted at danger to the ladies in the house, some of whom, at his suggestion, climbed out of the boxes and took to the stage for safety. That proved to be an unnecessary alarm as, the papers said, 'No personal violence was offered by the intruders'. However, due to conflicting party cries, much of the play and farce could only be seen and not heard, so the 'celebration' was a bit of a failure. At the end, the ladies were safely escorted out, and the popular excitement passed off in loud condemnation of the bad judgment and the arrogant idea that an exclusive group could take over a licensed public theatre.[55]

---

[54] *SM*, 25 December 1829
[55] *SM*, 17 September 1830.

The end of an era

Just when theatres in Lincolnshire were facing great challenges, an era came to an end in 1831 with the deaths of the two Robertson brothers, James and Thomas, though the effect of their deaths was not as great as it might have been if theatre in Lincolnshire had been in a more flourishing state. James had finally retired to Nottingham, as he had announced many years before, and he died there on 1 January 1831, aged 57.[56] He had retired from management of the Stamford circuit in July 1818 but then worked for the Lincoln company for several years and his death was a reminder of the past rather than a precursor of future change.

Eight months later his brother Thomas gently slipped away on 31 August 1831, aged 66, and that was not in Lincoln but at Huntingdon, the small southern outlier of his circuit. It was said that he endured, with fortitude and resignation, a severe and protracted illness of great suffering and towards the end of 1830 his nephew William, who had been with the company since 1825, had temporarily taken over as manager. Tom's widow, Fanny, recorded in her diary that he died 'without one struggle or even a sigh', much as he had lived.

> *He was a man much respected in the towns of his circuit for the suavity of his manners, and his upright conduct.*[57]

In contrast to the violently passionate Jemmy Whitley, Tom Robertson was sometimes referred to as humble and inoffensive though others said that he was honourable, suave, honest, upright, good-hearted and well respected. Although Tom was called the Mogul, Wemyss said he was more like the father of a family than the director of a theatre. His widow managed the company for some time after his death but then passed it on to her nephew William Shaftoe Robertson, the son of James.

In 1831 the state of the theatre in Lincolnshire was bad compared with the years before the Battle of Waterloo, and things were to get even worse not only for the two major circuits but also for the numerous smaller companies that had emerged since the turn of the century. Tragedy is the story of men and women facing overwhelming forces, and showing strength of character in the process, and that was what the next two decades held.

---

[56] Wood, A.C., *op. cit.*, p.34; *SM*, 14 January 1831.
[57] *Lincoln Date Book*, Lincoln (c1870), p.330; Hemingway, *op.cit.*, p.46; Warwick. Lou, *Theatre Unroyal*, p.167; *SM*, 2 September 1831.

8

THEATRE RURAL

WILLIAM HUGGINS was lucky in love. When the 23-year-old married the talented 19-year-old Sarah Richardson in Boston in 1787 she had already inherited a theatre in Durham from her father. William added more theatres in northeast England, and then five more in Lincolnshire and Nottinghamshire in 1796, and toured them with his own troupe. His was just one of a number of new companies of comedians who were spawned as a result of the popularity and profitability of theatre during the Napoleonic wars, and who took the drama to other towns in Lincolnshire. Theatre was flourishing in this county and it spread beyond the main towns that were served by the Lincoln and Stamford companies. Stamford was linked to places outside Lincolnshire and the Lincoln circuit was inflexible so other towns had little chance of getting onto it. Some actors recognised a gap in the market and set up new companies of their own to tour the smaller towns. The newcomers did not challenge the established companies as there were plenty of other places for them to visit. This chapter will consider the new companies that toured Lincolnshire and adjacent parts and their key personnel.

Two companies, formed by William Huggins and Joseph Smedley respectively, had high standards that were comparable with those of the Lincoln and Stamford companies, and they toured for many years. Other troupes were more ephemeral and short-lived, and might be facetiously referred to as 'Theatre Rural' in contrast with the quality expected from Theatres Royal outside Lincolnshire. Later small companies from elsewhere made brief forays into the county. The first new troupes were formed by actors leaving the Stamford company. The Beynon family went in the late 1780s and their company visited theatres in the Midlands as described in Chapter 5. Other actors left Stamford in the mid 1790s and then Robertson and Taylor bought the management of the Stamford company from William Pero in March 1795, all of which does suggest dissatisfaction with the way Pero was running it.

Butler and King – operated 1794–96

An actor called William King had joined the Stamford company by 1788 and, on 12 April 1790, married Mary Pero, daughter of the manager. The Kings were still in Stamford in 1793 but by October 1794 William had moved to Gainsborough theatre as a manager, perhaps in succession to James West. King announced that he had engaged two other leading actors from Stamford, Mr Grist and Mrs Mason, the latter being aunt to his wife. Mrs Mason was a leading member of the Stamford company from 1785 to 1793 and performed in the higher walks of tragedy and comedy while Mr Grist played characters such as *Falstaff* and 'characteristic

Irishman'.¹ Mrs Mason married a Mr Rawling at Stamford on 15 May 1795 and her 'bride maid' was her niece Mrs King.

On 16 December 1794 King's company were at Brigg (population 1,327 in 1801), and within two years he was in partnership with a Mr Butler and they had five theatres under their control, at Mansfield and Worksop in Nottinghamshire and Louth in Lincolnshire as well as Gainsborough and Brigg.² Those five theatres might have been West's circuit. In February 1796 King's company also performed in a barn theatre in Horncastle. Louth was the main town of this circuit until 1830; they were sometimes referred to as the Louth company and at other times as the Gainsborough company. There had been an actor called Butler in West's Gainsborough company in 1787 and another in the Stamford company in 1789 but it is not known if they were the same person or if either was King's partner in 1796.³ Butler and King's company only lasted about two years and on 21 October 1796 they sold the leases of their five theatres to another new company, led by William Huggins, that had also started to tour Lincolnshire.

The Huggins family – operated 1796-1830

William Huggins (1764-1821) was born in Market Deeping. He became an actor and on 23 April 1787 married Sarah Maria Richardson (c1768-1835) in St Botolph's church, Boston. Couples usually married in the bride's home parish, and as neither William nor Sarah was born in Boston the use of this church suggests that they were both members of the Lincoln company which would be in Boston at that time. Their first son Frederick was christened in Boston on 20 January 1788 but they left Lincolnshire and in 1790 Sarah Huggins appeared at the Theatre, Leeds when she was described as being 'from the theatre, Worcester'. Their second son was christened in March 1793 at Walsall in Staffordshire. William and Sarah Huggins later joined the Stamford company and they appeared together in *Louis the Unfortunate* on 31 March 1794, when Sarah was described as being 'from the Theatre Royal, Bath'.⁴

Sarah Huggins' father, John Richardson, had owned the Sadler Street theatre in the city of Durham since 1754 and replaced it with a new one he built in Drury Lane, Durham, in 1771. That was used by Mr Bates' company of comedians who also visited theatres at Scarborough, Whitby, Stockton, Darlington, Sunderland and North Shields, in northern Yorkshire and County Durham. In 1782 a young relative of Bates, James Cawdell (1750-1800), became a partner in his company and took full control after Bates' retirement in 1787. When Richardson died in 1785 the Durham theatre was inherited by his young daughter Sarah who refused to renew the lease

---

1. *Stamford Mercury*, 17 October 1794.
2. *SM*, 12 December 1794, 21 October 1796.
3. Stark, Adam, *The History and Antiquities of Gainsborough*, Gainsborough (2nd edn 1843), p.419; *SM* 19 June, 17 and 24 July 1789.
4. *SM*, 28 March 1794.

to Bates and Cawdell. A bitter dispute ensued.[5] It is not clear what use Sarah made of the Durham theatre over the next eleven years while herself performing at Boston, Worcester, Leeds, Walsall, Bath and Stamford. On her marriage in 1787 ownership of her theatre passed to her husband, William Huggins, who by 21 October 1796 was in partnership with a Mr Collier and they had theatres at Scarborough, Shields and Sunderland as well as Durham. So William had built on his wife's inheritance. In addition they had 'at considerable expense' recently purchased Butler and King's leases of five theatres. Huggins and Collier said they would open at Gainsborough on 25 October 1796.[6]

Some time after 1796 Huggins and Collier disposed of their northern theatres. Stephen Kemble, the brother of Sarah Siddons, had become manager of the Newcastle theatre in 1791 and took over many others in the north including those at Sheffield, Edinburgh and Glasgow. From 1799 he also ran the Durham circuit, which then included the theatres in North Shields, Sunderland, South Shields, Stockton and Scarborough, so it was perhaps at that date that Collier and Huggins sold their interest to Kemble. Winston said that Kemble purchased those theatres from Cawdell in 1799, which suggests that Collier and Huggins had sold them to Cawdell first, or that Winston was mistaken. After losing the lease of Richardson's theatre in Durham, Cawdell built a new one of his own in the city and that opened in March 1792; Kemble purchased that on Cawdell's death in 1800.

Huggins and Collier were performing in Lincolnshire even before taking over Butler and King's theatres. On 9 February 1796 they put on Shakespeare's *As You Like it* at Horncastle to raise funds for the benefit of the poor. Very little is known of Mr Collier, and it was clearly William Huggins who was running the company and his wife Sarah who was the star. In February 1807 the *Stamford Mercury* said that 'whilst Mrs Huggins (who stands unrivalled) continues to greet us with her presence, we have no doubt of being well-entertained'.[7] It was said of William that 'in the line of character that he took, few were superior to him, and in that of *Diggery* for true and entire delineation he will never be excelled'.

On 15 March 1797 a benefit was put on at Louth theatre for Mr and Mrs Collier with a new historical play called *England Preserv'd* (1797) and the company then opened Alford theatre on 18 March. That may have been the only benefit for the Colliers, and after 1801 the company changed its name to Huggins and Clarke. Mr and Mrs Clarke were actors with the company by 1798, so they were perhaps there from the beginning, and they stayed until it closed in 1830, but the Huggins family were always the managers of the Louth company. There had been a Mr J. Clarke with the Stamford company in 1793 but it is not known if that was the same person.[8]

---

[5] *Northern Echo*, Durham theatre history website.
[6] *SM*, 12 February and 21 October 1796.
[7] *SM*, 20 February 1807.
[8] *SM*, 21 June 1793.

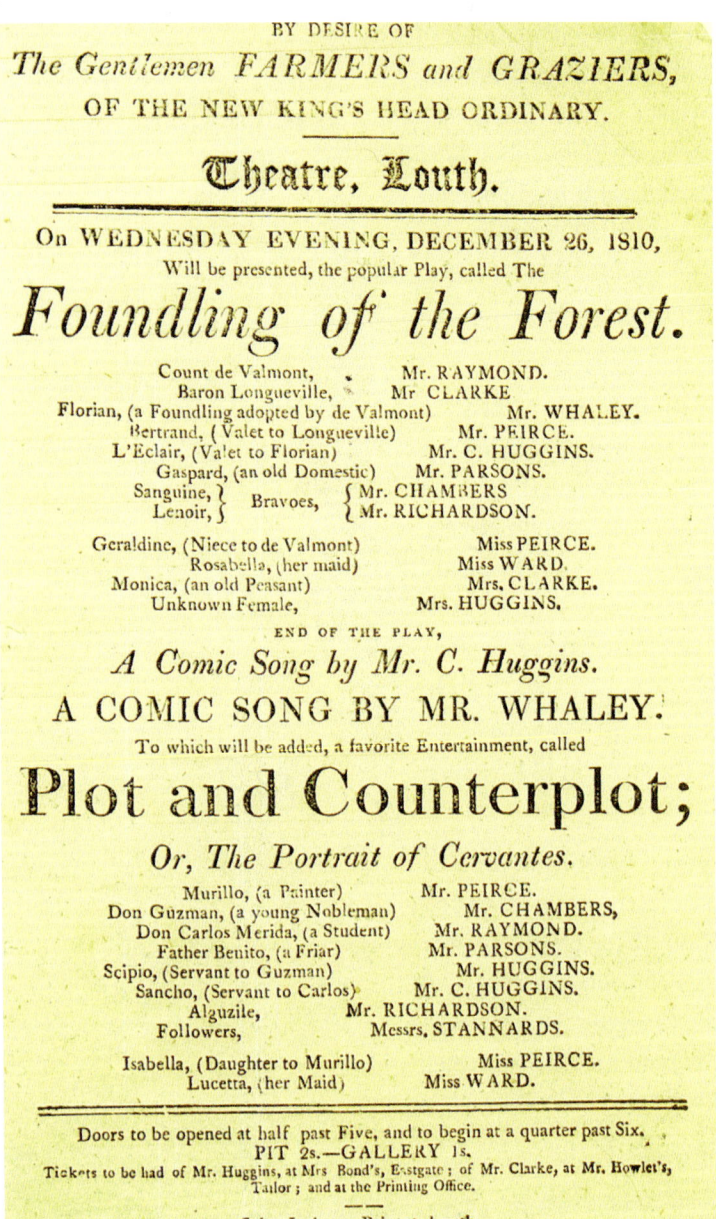

Playbill, Louth, 26 December 1810. Notice the Huggins, Clarke and Stannard families, and Miss Frances Pierce who later married Edwin Huggins.
Louth Museum

William and Sarah Huggins had seven children. As well as Frederick (born 1788) and William Charles (1793) they were Benjamin Edwin (1798), John Ebeneza (1801), Aaron (1803), Frances Frederica (1806) and Ellen Maria (1812). They all went on the stage from an early age and in February 1825 the cast included Mr C. Huggins, Miss Huggins [Frances] and Miss E. Huggins as well as Mr and Mrs Edwin Huggins. William Charles was known as Charles to distinguish him from his father, and Ellen also went by her second name of Maria. Charles had a benefit at Louth on 4 March 1803 when he was only ten years old. Benjamin called himself Edwin Huggins and when he later made an independent career with his wife he went even further and reversed his names, calling himself Mr Huggins Edwin. Edwin married Miss Frances Pierce in Sheffield Cathedral on 16 March 1818 and both she and her father Thomas were actors in Huggins' company. Edwin and his wife appeared at Liverpool in 1819 and then went on to Bath and Bristol before returning to the family company in 1825.

William Huggins ran the company for twenty-five years until he died on 15 November 1821 in Gainsborough. His son Charles was then 28 and had performed with the company all his life, and he took over as sole manager of the company for the next nine years, even though it continued to be referred to as Huggins and Clarke's company right up to the end. Charles' older brother Frederick died on 14 November 1823, aged 34, also at Gainsborough. Then the *Stamford Mercury* reported in January 1822 that 19-year-old John Huggins 'of the theatres Gainsborough, Mansfield, etc.' had also died, but the paper was wrong as John lived until 1865, latterly described as a 'labourer'.

The Huggins circuit included theatres in the smaller towns of mid-Lincolnshire, Nottinghamshire and southwest Yorkshire. When the company closed in 1830 it was said that they were visiting Pontefract and Barnsley as well as the original Gainsborough, Louth, Horncastle, Mansfield and Worksop theatres.[9] That was not much different to their circuit some thirty-five years earlier. Louth and Horncastle 'were considered the best in Messrs Huggins and Clarke's circuit' and in 1829

---

[9] *SM*, 15 October 1830.

their season at Horncastle lasted six weeks.[10] The Louth theatre had been built about 1790 and in 1807 it was 'understood' that Huggins intended to enlarge and improve the theatre. It was hoped that the visits of the company would be annual, which suggests that some of Huggins' theatres were not visited every year. On 21 February 1811 Huggins' company put on a performance at the 'New Theatre, Horncastle', which was the improved playhouse in Dog Kennel Yard. In March 1826 when Madame Tussaud exhibited waxworks in Gainsborough theatre, she commented that it had been 'entirely re-decorated and embellished' and in this Huggins was perhaps following the example of the Lincoln company that redecorated its theatres at that time.[11] Huggins' company occasionally visited some other small towns. In 1796 the theatre leases they purchased included Brigg, but there are very few other references to a theatre in that town – one in 1806 when the 'Young Roscius' performed there and others in 1835, 1839 and 1844 after Huggins' company had closed.[12] In 1797 and 1807 they visited Alford[13] and it is said that at one time they also performed in Spalding but that would be a rare event as the town was part of the Lincoln circuit.

Some members of the Stannard family were active in Huggins' company, as others were in the Lincoln company. As early as 1798 a Mr Stannard had a benefit at Louth, and in 1810 there were benefits for a Mr Stannard, Mrs Stannard, and Mr J. Stannard. In January 1811 it was specifically stated that Mr J. Stannard was a musician, and Mr I. Stannard was the 'Stage-Keeper' at Louth but in May of that year both of them appeared in plays in Worksop. One or other of these Mr Stannards had further benefits in 1815, 1817, 1819 and 1823. Then from 1831 to 1834, after Louth had become part of the Lincoln circuit, there were benefits each year at Louth for Mrs Stannard and Mr A. Stannard who was Leader of the Orchestra. By November 1838 Mr Stannard had left to become Leader of the Orchestra at the Leicester theatre.

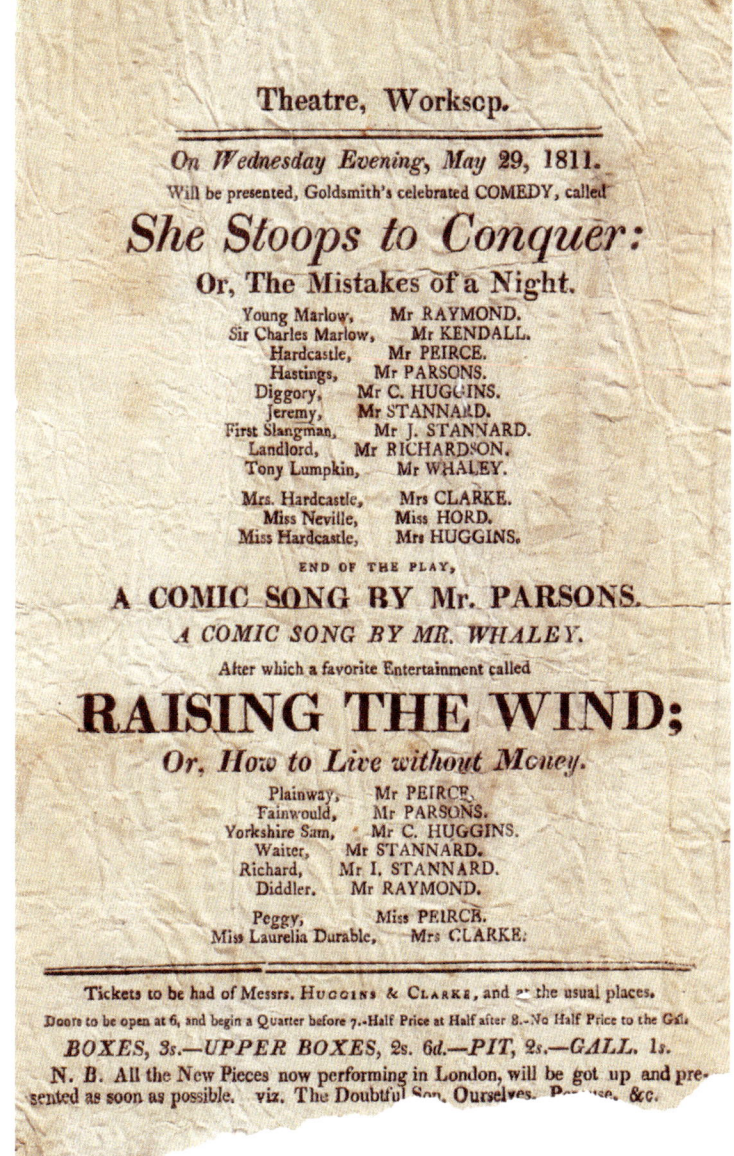

Playbill, Worksop, 29 May 1811. The Huggins and Clarke company performing in Nottinghamshire.
In author's collection

---

[10] *SM*, 28 October 1842, 1 January 1830.
[11] *SM*, 17 March 1826.
[12] *SM*, 12 December 1806, 10 April 1835, 4 January 1839. 31 May 1844; Playbill, Brigg, 19 February 1839.
[13] *SM*, 10 March 1797, 13 March 1807.

On the evening of Monday 27 October 1828 'the Gainsborough Theatrical Company under the management of Messrs Huggins and Clarke' performed before the Duke and Duchess of St Albans and guests at Redbourn Hall. In July of that year the noble couple had attended Peterborough theatre, on their way home to Redbourn, and in 1829 they visited Lincoln theatre when the Duke was one of the Stewards of Lincoln Races. A rumour that they might attend Gainsborough theatre in January 1839 helped to fill the 'long deserted' theatre there and then in May 1844 they went to Brigg theatre to see plays by Mr Bullen's company.

The steady decline in support for the theatre affected Huggins as much as it did the Lincoln and Stamford companies, and in 1830 Charles decided to call an end after nearly thirty-five years. In October he announced that 'Messrs Huggins and Clarke' had 'deemed it expedient to break up their establishment for the present, in consequence of the ill support they have met with on their circuit'.[14] He still kept open the chance of starting again if public demand should return but that did not happen. Joseph Smedley's company succeeded Huggins in Gainsborough and Horncastle, and proposed opening the former theatre early in the spring instead of the autumn as had usually been the practice.

Sarah Huggins, mother of Charles, was in the company from beginning to end. After the closure in October 1830 people in different towns of the circuit considered raising a subscription to provide an annuity for her. 'Such of her friends as remember the talented performances of her earlier days, and all who feel for the vicissitudes of a player's life, will no doubt have much satisfaction in thus contributing to the support of a highly respectable and deserving old servant of the public.'[15] Sarah did not live long to enjoy what might have been raised as she died on 14 February 1835 at Louth.[16]

Huggins Edwin left Lincolnshire and with his wife pursued a theatrical career around England but it did not bring in enough to support him and at various times he listed his occupation as bookseller, professor of education, teacher of elocution and, curiously, 'medical, not practising'! In the end these expediencies did not save him and when he died on 31 March 1873 he was a pauper in the Union Workhouse at Warwick. Less is known about Charles Huggins' later life, with just two references in the late 1830s. On 25 November 1836 'Mr Charles Huggins, formerly manager of the Gainsborough company' was the main attraction at Lincoln theatre and in June 1838 he was referred to 'as of this city' [Lincoln] so perhaps he was still a member of the Lincoln company, though he is not listed in the detailed reviews of the period.[17]

Joseph Smedley – operated 1807–40

Even after William Huggins had acquired the Louth and Gainsborough circuit there were still other Lincolnshire towns that had no regular visits by companies

---

[14] *SM*, 15 October 1830.
[15] *SM*, 19 November 1830.
[16] *SM*, 20 February 1835.
[17] *SM*, 25 November 1836, 8 June 1838.

of comedians. In 1807 Joseph Close Smedley (1784-1863), with a partner called Mr Clarke, formed a company that served theatres scattered over Lincolnshire and adjacent counties for nearly thirty-five years.

Joseph Smedley was born at Catterick in the North Riding of Yorkshire, where his father was land agent and steward to the Dundas family who in 1838 became Earls of Zetland. Joseph was sent to study law at the Temple in London to become a barrister but he chose the theatre instead.[18] On 20 May 1803 at the age of 19, he married an actress, 22-year-old Melinda Bullen, in the actors church of St Peter Mancroft in Norwich. Both of them were in the Lincoln company, Melinda since at least April 1800 when she performed with them at Northampton, and Joseph by 21 October 1803 when during their benefit he and his wife appeared in *Speed the Plough* and Joseph sang the popular song *Paddy O'Blarney*.[19]

His granddaughter later said that Joseph 'was a man of fine intellect, clever, well read, honourable in principle but stern and one who would never brook to servitude'.[20] In a letter written on 10 July 1837, near the end of his theatrical career, he said he was proud to have fulfilled his early pledge 'that the Stage by me should not be perverted from its original purpose – that it should be made a School of morality'. He might unconsciously employ actors who failed to follow that precept but when it did so happen and he knew it, he 'never yet hesitated to cast them off as worthless'. He declared that he lived for the purity of his profession.[21] When the Southwell magistrates gave Smedley a licence to perform in their new theatre in 1816, his lawyer told him that his 'uniform regularity and good conduct' had been powerful inducements for them to grant the licence. In 1824 newspaper reports of his appearances in Market Deeping, Holbeach and Barton-on-Humber referred to the praiseworthy private character of the manager, his superior talents, great exertion to produce novelty, the honest and peaceable demeanour of his 'respectable company' and his 'regard for the legitimate drama'. His company was often said to be 'numerous and attractive' and to constitute 'as respectable a provincial dramatic corps as it has ever been our fortune to see'.[22] At Southwell on 22 July 1828 he put on the highly moral play of *George Barnwell* and for the opening night, 'according to the usual custom' as he said, he charged half the regular prices 'to enable children, servants and apprentices to witness' the dreadful fate of an apprentice who fell into bad ways and ended on the gallows.[23]

---

[18] Smedley papers, Biographical note, LLHS/38/5/9, Lincolnshire County Archives.
[19] Warwick, Lou, *Theatre Unroyal; Or, They called them Comedians*, Northampton (1974), pp.28, 29; Warwick, Lou, *Drama that Smelled; Or, Early Drama in Northampton and Hereabouts*, Northampton (1975), p.190; SM, 14 October 1803.
[20] Smedley papers, Biographical note, LLHS/38/5/9, Lincolnshire County Archives.
[21] Smedley papers, Letter 10 July 1837, LLHS/38/5/3/30, Lincolnshire County Archives.
[22] Shilton, Richard Phillips, *The History of Southwell*, Newark (1816 reprinted 2011), p.172; SM, 8 October 1824, 14 February and 1 July 1825, 3 April 1829.
[23] Playbill, Southwell, 22 July 1828.

Joseph's wife, Melinda Bullen, was born on 25 January 1781 in Norwich and claimed to be descended from the noble Boleyn family, her parents being Joseph Bullen and Susannah Melinda. Joseph and Melinda Smedley had at least nine children of whom six lived to maturity, two sons and four daughters, and some joined them on the stage. When the Smedleys were performing in Grimsby in April 1808 one of their children died of a fever. Their eldest daughter was given the middle name of Brunton so it is likely that Melinda Bullen had started her theatrical career with Brunton's company in Norwich. Of Smedley's two daughters who went on the stage, the younger, Annette (b.1810), had the greater liking for it and played more important roles than her sister. *Ophelia, Belvidera, Rebecca* in *Ivanhoe* and *Lady Teazle* were amongst the parts she played. Annette eloped and married Mr Fawcett, an artist, and her father never spoke to her again; she is buried in Belfast. Miss Melinda Smedley, the elder sister, played boys' parts, such as the *Prince of Wales* in *Richard III*, and *Paul* in *The Wandering Boys* (1814), or girls masquerading as boys, such as *Viola* in *Twelfth Night*.[24] In Sleaford on 22 April 1834 Melinda married Joseph Tinsdale Young, a highly respectable farmer. Their daughter said that 'in her youth and even in her old age' Melinda 'was considered a handsome woman'. She had 'the most even temperament, but she could give a most telling reproach when necessary'.[25] Joseph Smedley, junior, also went on the stage and one evening in Wakefield 'tripled' *Osric, Rosencrantz* and *the first Gravedigger* and at other times, if not wanted on the stage, played second violin in the orchestra.[26]

Joseph Smedley left the Lincoln company and set up his own troupe in partnership with a Mr Clarke about whom practically nothing is known. As Joseph was only 23 or 24 years of age perhaps Mr Clarke provided the necessary starting capital. William Huggins also had a partner called Clarke but no evidence has been seen to suggest they were the same person. The first reference to Smedley and Clarke's company of comedians, said to be recruited 'from the Theatres Lincoln, Boston, etc', was in the summer of 1807 when they 'fitted up a commodious theatre' at Market Rasen (population 964 in 1811). That may have been in a barn behind the Greyhound inn just off the Market Place, which is the recorded venue for a theatre company in 1830 during the celebrations for the coronation of King William IV, or a 'spacious room' at the inn used in 1843.[27] From 20 June 1807 they performed there on Tuesdays, Thursdays and Saturdays and gave a programme of plays first performed in the previous ten years.[28] Smedley avoided taking his company to any towns that were served by the Lincoln or Louth companies and to do this he ranged much further over Lincolnshire and adjacent counties in search of venues. Smedley

---

[24] Senior, William, *The Old Wakefield Theatre*, Wakefield (1894), p.56.
[25] Biographical note, LLHS/38/5/9, Lincolnshire County Archives
[26] Senior, William, *ibid*.
[27] Ward, Brian, 'A History of the Public Houses of Market Rasen', *Lincolnshire Past and Present*, No.86, Lincoln (January 2012), p.7.
[28] *SM*, 12 June 1807.

only rarely advertised performances in the local newspapers and few playbills survive for the theatres he used, so information about his venues is sparse, except for the period 1810 to 1815 for which some notebooks survive.

Smedley's circuit sometimes included Holbeach, Sleaford and Alford where his children were christened between 1807 and 1823 and notebooks give his itineraries for 1810, 1812, 1814 and, in less detail, for 1815.[29] In each of these early years he followed a completely different circuit and few towns were visited more than once. The exceptions were Grimsby, which was visited in each of the four years, and Alford, Caistor, Folkingham, Howden and Southwell which were each visited twice in four years. Grimsby, then a small town on the coast with borough status, was their main base and was visited each winter for about two months.[30] It usually produced a profit for the company, unlike some other venues. When they visited Alford they also stayed there about two months but in most other towns the season was only four, five or six weeks. Though Smedley avoided towns served by the older companies, some of his venues were small villages perhaps chosen for their proximity to larger towns. So Upwell was close to Wisbech, Southwell to Newark, Bingham to Nottingham, Hedon to Hull, and Mildenhall in Suffolk was accessible from Ely, Newmarket, Thetford and Bury St Edmunds. In June 1807, at about the time that Smedley was setting up his own company, there was a reference to a theatre at Market Deeping but there was no indication as to whether it was Smedley who visited it at that time.[31]

In 1810 Smedley's tour started in Grimsby and then went south as far as Suffolk before returning to Lincolnshire. They went to Alford, Holbeach, Upwell, Brandon, Mildenhall, Stoke, Crowland and Folkingham. In 1812 he again started in Grimsby and then went west via 'Castor' [Caistor?], Southwell, Belper, Ripley, Alfreton, Wirksworth, Castle Donington, Aston, Bingham and Oakham. The following year they perhaps visited Grimsby in the back end of the year as in January 1814 they were at Sleaford and went in a circle through Folkingham, Bourne, Bingham, Melton Mowbray, Southwell, Bawtry, Howden, Great Driffield and finished at Grimsby. In 1815 Smedley performed in a much smaller circuit, going from Grimsby to Alford, Castor (sic), Barton-on-Humber and then across the Humber to visit Bridlington, Howden and Hedon before returning to Grimsby. All these different itineraries were in the first nine years of Smedley's company and show him searching for profitable venues, with Grimsby as his main base.

In 1810 Smedley spent six weeks at Mildenhall and the profit of £18 1s 0d was more than from any other venue that year. He then went to 'Stoke' for four weeks, which could be any of six 'Stokes' between Suffolk and Northamptonshire. The

---

[29] Smedley papers, Biographical note, LLHS/38/5/9, Account Book 1, LLHS/38/5/1, Lincolnshire County Archives
[30] *SM*, 15 and 22 April 1808.
[31] *SM*, 12 June 1807.

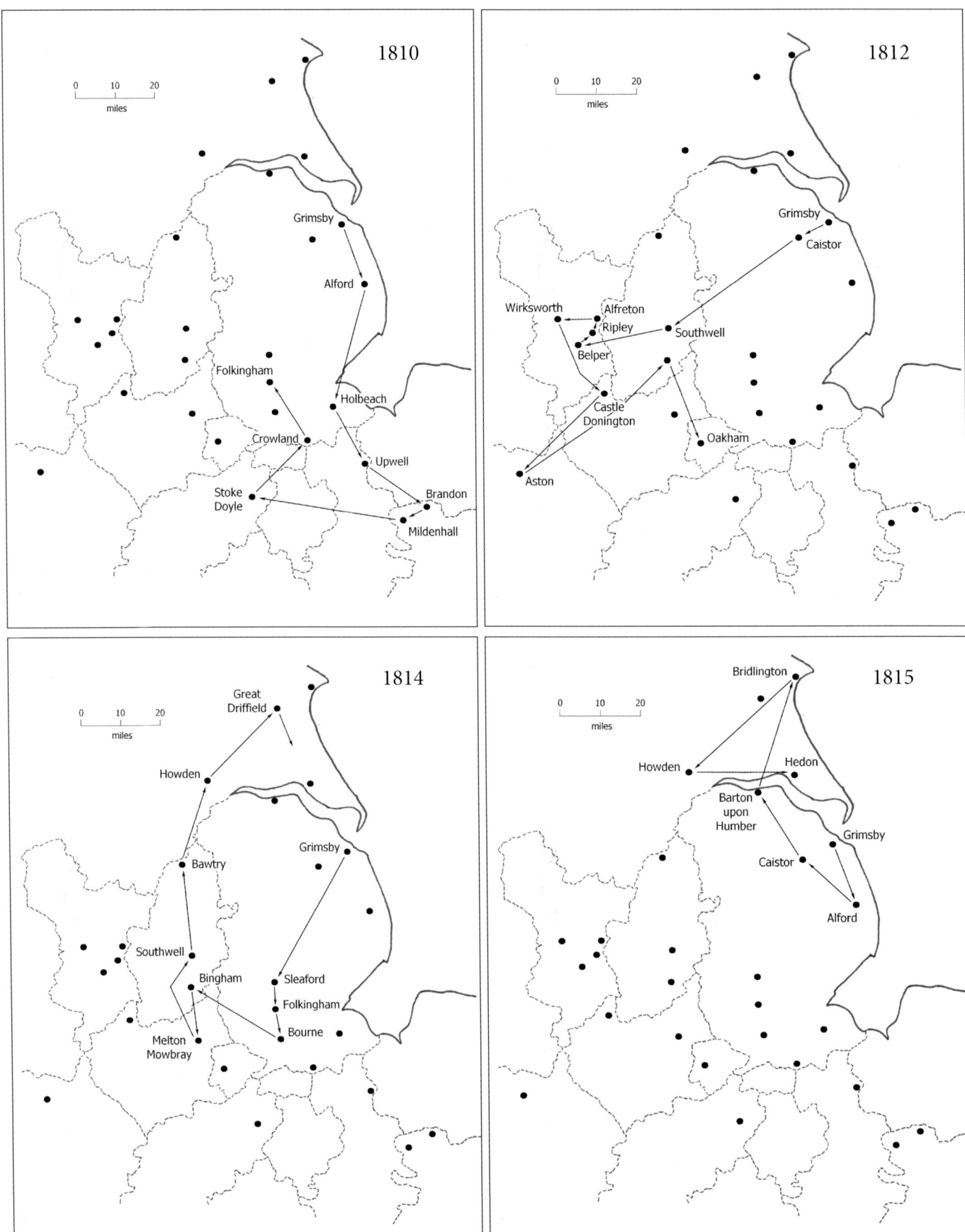

most likely place is probably Stoke Doyle, one mile outside Oundle, as in 1811 the Reverend Robert Roberts of that parish had a share in Peterborough theatre, indicating his strong support for the stage.[32] Stoke was such a small venue that the rent was only 10s 6d, but in addition Smedley had to pay £1 2s 0d for 'insurance of barn at Stoke' so perhaps the barn he used for his theatre was not a very safe structure. The rent at Brandon had been £5 5s 0d and at Mildenhall just £2.

In 1801 the population of Grimsby was just 1,524 and by 1841 it was still only 4,048 though it grew tremendously after the railway arrived in 1848 and built new docks. Grimsby did not have a purpose-built theatre until Smedley came in 1807, when his company performed *Pizarro* (1799) at the 'New Theatre' in Burgess Street, behind the Golden Fleece public house that fronted onto Loft Street, now Victoria Street.[33] There were springs in the area and on 19 November 1818 Smedley's agent in Grimsby wrote that he had 'left open the door under the stage that communicates with the yard, in consequence of a spring of water running through the theatre, lest the passage should by any means get stopped and inundate the place'.[34]

Grimsby had a modest theatre and as late as 1827 it still had no boxes.[35] In 1818 Smedley paid a rent of £5 per half year to Mr E. Goodrick, owner of the theatre.[36] At Smedley's suggestion, Goodrick rented it out to others when Joseph was not there, but there seem to have been few takers. In the first half of 1818 Goodrick got £1 11s 6d from a Mr Matthews and 12s from some jugglers so only £2 16s 6d was needed to make the £5. We know that Smedley visited Grimsby each year between 1810 and 1815 and in 1812 his company performed a piece written by George Oliver, the local schoolmaster.[37] Although Grimsby would appear to be his most regular venue, there are not many other early references to theatre in the town. Smedley visited again in January 1826, June 1827 and the winter of 1833/34, after Gainsborough and before Alford. In 1835/36 he visited Grimsby after Gainsborough, Wakefield and Beverley

Above: The Grimsby theatre used by Smedley in the early 19th century was in Upper Burgess Street behind the Golden Fleece Inn in Loft Street, later Victoria Street.
Extract from Ordnance Survey 25in Plan, 1885

Opposite page: Maps showing four annual tours by Smedley, in 1810, 1812, 1814, 1815. Grimsby is the only town that was visited each year.
Drawn by Ken Redmore

---

[32] Bull, June and Vernon, *Peterborough Then and Now*, Stroud (2013), p.8.
[33] Gillett, Edward, *A History of Grimsby*, London (1970), p.185.
[34] Smedley papers, LLHS/38/5/3/5, Lincolnshire County Archives.
[35] Playbill, 11 June 1827, Grimsby Library.
[36] Smedley papers, Letter, LLHS/38/5/3/4, Lincolnshire County Archives.
[37] Smedley papers, Account book, LLHS/38/5/1, Lincolnshire County Archives; Gillett, Edward, *A History of Grimsby*, London (1970), pp.184, 185.

Top: Part of a Grimsby playbill, 13 January 1826. Joseph Smedley quotes the Archbishop of Canterbury on the moral value of the theatre.
Grimsby Library

Bottom: Site Plan of the Golden Fleece inn, Grimsby, with the theatre to the rear.
Extract from Ordnance Survey 1:500 Plan, 1883

and before 'the rest of his Lincolnshire circuit'.[38] In most theatres half-price only applied to the boxes, but Grimsby lacked boxes and in January 1826 half-price applied to all seats. Prices were 'Pit 2s, Second-price 1s; Gallery 1s, Second-price 6d'. Performances then only took place on Mondays, Wednesdays and Fridays so demand for drama was evidently not as great as in the larger towns of the Lincoln circuit.[39]

Whatever difficulties might have confronted Huggins and other theatre companies in the second quarter of the nineteenth century, there are signs that for Joseph Smedley the period from 1824 to 1835 was in many ways a successful one. His company may have continued to attract regular audiences as he set high moral standards and abided by them. In February 1830 he had a route of his 'seats' planned for the next two years, all of which he said he had 'sat for' for over twenty-one years, which would mean since 1809 at least. Unfortunately we do not have the list to which he referred.[40]

Smedley never did establish a regular annual pattern, though he did apparently reduce the number of places he visited and concentrated on small towns in Lincolnshire and a few towns in Yorkshire plus Melton Mowbray. Some places might only be visited once in two years, and the dates could vary by a month or two each year. For example Holbeach was visited in April 1823, February 1825, April 1829 and January 1835, and perhaps other times in other years. His applications to Quarter Sessions and some advertisements in the 1830s show how the theatre season could change each year. In January 1831 he was granted permission to perform in Gainsborough for 21 days in February to April, in January 1833 he got permission to perform in Barton on Humber and in January 1836 his authority related to Spilsby, Alford and Market Rasen.[41] From late October 1833 Smedley was at Gainsborough, then Grimsby, and in early 1834

---

[38] *SM*, 16 October 1835.
[39] Playbill, 4 January 1826, Grimsby Library.
[40] Smedley papers, LLHS/38/5/3/14, Lincolnshire County Archives
[41] Quarter Sessions Records – Lindsey – 8 January 1831, 5 January 1833, 11 January 1836. Supplied by Chris Padley.

moved to Alford, Spilsby, Horncastle, Sleaford and Bourne; it seems that he stayed about a month at each place.[42] In contrast a year later, from January to May 1835, he was at Holbeach, Melton Mowbray, Gainsborough and Brigg.[43] In January 1839 Smedley's company was at Gainsborough and would then proceed to Grimsby, Alford, Spilsby, Horncastle, Brigg and Barton, a similar itinerary to 1833 but different dates.[44]

Caistor in north Lincolnshire (population 1,051 in 1811), like Stoke Doyle, had a parson who was keen on theatre. The Reverend Samuel Turner (c1756-1835) was a pluralist with several church livings, and with an income of about £900 a year he led a comfortable, worldly and hedonistic lifestyle. Whenever there were players in Caistor he would buy several tickets and give them to his friends. Sometimes the company used a barn in Caistor's High Street, now the site of an antique shop near the later Town Hall, and at least once, in 1833, they used the Assembly Room of the Talbot inn.[45] Turner's sister was the grandmother of Alfred Tennyson the poet, and Samuel was a keen supporter of his great-nephews; he left his wealth to Alfred's brother Charles on condition he changed his last name to Turner.

Sleaford theatre in 2014. Built by Joseph Smedley in 1824 and opened in 1826.
Photograph by Neil Wright, August 2014

Smedley's first visit to Sleaford (population 1,904 in 1811) was about the year 1814 and that town eventually became his home after he retired from the theatrical life in 1841. When Huggins' company was disbanded in 1830 Smedley added Gainsborough, Horncastle and Brigg to his itinerary, and in 1835 he took in at least four towns in south-west Yorkshire.[46] He sometimes visited other places including Belper in Derbyshire in 1811 and 1812, where Mr Strutt may have been prepared to provide a theatre in later years, Ely in 1828 and March in Cambridgeshire where he built a theatre in 1826. After a proper theatre was set up in Southwell in 1816 Smedley planned to visit it once every two years.[47]

---

[42] *SM*, 18 October 1833.
[43] *SM*, 2 January, 13 February, 13 March, 10 April 1835.
[44] *SM*, 4 January 1839.
[45] Playbill, 2 April 1833, Caistor. Supplied by David Saunders. See p.201.
[46] *SM*, 3 March 1833, 10 April 1835.
[47] Shilton, Richard Phillips, *op. cit.*, p.172.

Sleaford's Georgian theatre was in Westgate, next to Playhouse Yard.
Extract from Ordnance Survey 25in Plan, 1882

In some places Smedley had to provide temporary theatres. In 1825 the inhabitants of Barton-on-Humber (population 1,305 in 1821) were well pleased with the superiority of their small theatre, which Smedley had fitted up in a 'remarkably neat manner' and they 'no longer envy the immense and ridiculous size of the theatres in the metropolis and some provincial towns, from which the audience cannot see the expression of countenance, nor hear the different modulations of voice in the performer'. They were also pleased that the gods in the gallery were not at such a dizzy height that 'the men that walk upon the stage appear like mice'.[48]

In 1828 a new Cock-pit was built in Melton Mowbray and in May Smedley rented the old one to fit it up as a theatre for his season in the town.[49] Melton was in the heart of Leicestershire hunting country and the theatre had many noble and gentry sponsors, including, in 1833, the Earl of Wilton, the Russian Ambassador Count Matouschevitz, the Hungarian nobleman Count Batthyany (1803-83) who bred horses in England, and Lords Gardner and Rokeby.[50] In May 1837 a building in Melton was put up for sale and was advertised as

> ...a large and commodious building which for several years past has been used as a THEATRE AND COCKPIT, it has been erected within the last ten years, is substantially built, and may, at a moderate expense, be converted into warehouses or dwelling houses.[51]

---

[48] *SM*, 1 July 1825.
[49] *SM*, 16 May 1828.
[50] *SM*, 8 March 1833.
[51] *Leicester Journal*, 5 May 1837, quoted in Leacroft, Helen and Richard, *The Theatre in Leicestershire*, Leicester (1986), p.14.

This indicates that after the 1828 season it was the new cock-pit that was used as a theatre. By September 1838 the theatre/cockpit had been converted into a Mechanics Institute.[52]

In 1829 and 1830 Smedley took his company to theatres in the small Yorkshire towns of Selby, Howden, Great Driffield and Bridlington. He had been there two or three times before but it is not clear how frequently he visited them.[53] Smedley preferred to get other people to build theatres, which he then leased. This system committed local people to support the theatre for their own financial benefit, but in the Cambridgeshire town of March (population 3,850 in 1821), and in Sleaford, Smedley himself owned two theatres that had been erected in 1824-26. In 1830 in Selby (4,600 in 1831), the steward of local landowner Mr Petrie offered a site for a theatre and Smedley drew a plan and sent it to Mr Galpine, who was arranging the matter. In February Smedley told Galpine that a new theatre was being built at Howden (4,531 in 1831) and there 'the money is already raised in shares of £10 each'. He had '5 shares in the one at Howden, and would have 5 in the Selby, or 10 rather than it should stop for want of them'.[54]

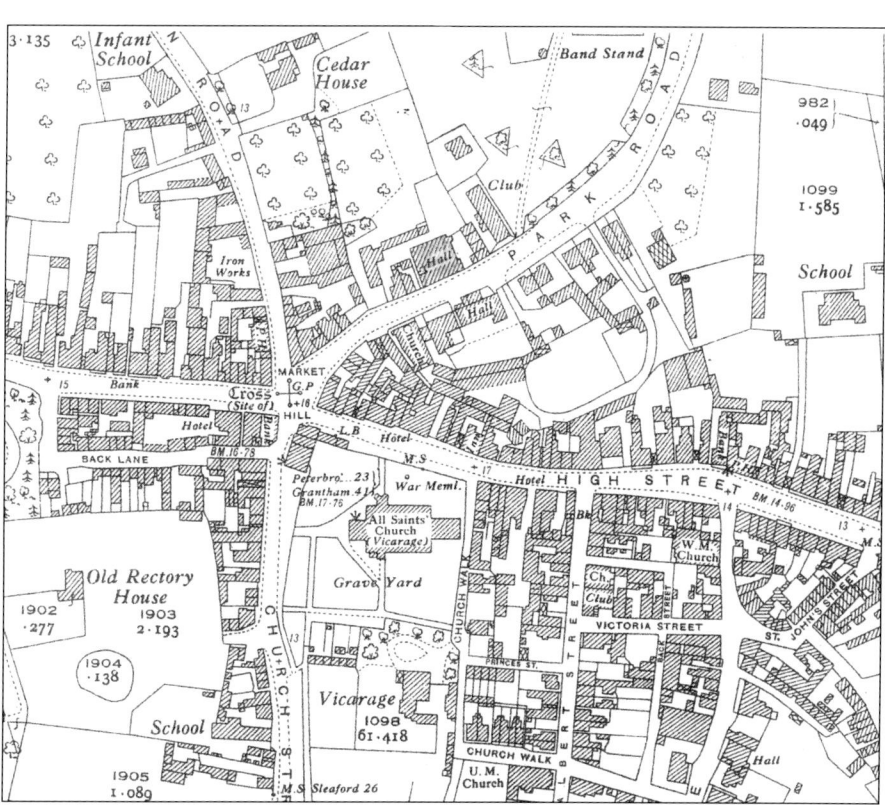

Holbeach's Georgian theatre was built in 1829 for Joseph Smedley as the 'Public Rooms' in Park Road.
Extract from Ordnance Survey 25in Plan, 1902

The theatre at Howden was to the same size and plan as those at Sleaford and March, and Smedley suggested the same for Selby. If Mr Petrie accepted his steward's proposal and the site at Selby was obtained at a nominal value then Smedley was sure that the theatre could be built for £500. His theatre at March, of brick and slate, was built in 1826 and had cost £611 and 'Materials and Workmanship are at all times cheaper at Selby, but more so now'. His Sleaford theatre in Westgate, which was built of stone procured within a mile of its site, had cost just £478. It was said to be built in 1824 but was not opened until 27 March 1826.[55] Smedley said of the Selby theatre that he would 'have no objections to take it when erected on a Lease and will allow the Subscribers 2½ per cent

---

[52] Smedley papers, LLHS/38/5/3/31, Lincolnshire County Archives.
[53] *SM*, 25 September 1829.
[54] Smedley papers, LLHS/38/5/3/14, Lincolnshire County Archives.
[55] Smedley papers, LLHS/38/5/3/14, LLHS/38/5/3/2, Lincolnshire County Archives; White, William, *Directory of Lincolnshire 1856*, Sheffield (1856), p.433.

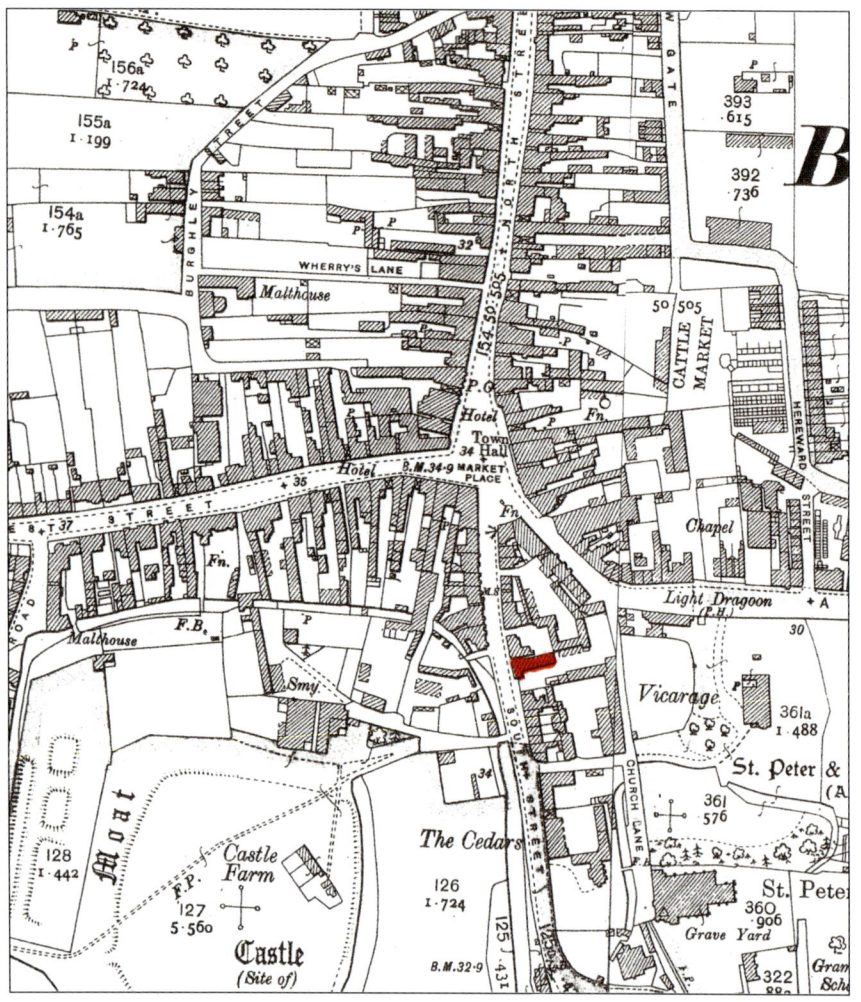

Map of Bourne, showing the site of the Red Lion inn, Southgate. The site offered for a theatre was said to be opposite the Red Lion.
Extract from Ordnance Survey 25in Plan, 1904

per Annum for my occupation of it, say Two months once in Two Years – or 5 weeks Yearly, as may be most desirable to the inhabitants, or convenient to myself and if it does not produce 2½ per cent or more, during my absence as Tenements, Billiard Rooms, and other amusements (not Theatrical ones) I will make up the deficiency – That is it *shall* pay 5 per cent at *least* – but if it produces more the Subscribers of course to be entitled to it.'[56]

The form of funding that Smedley suggested at Selby had already been mentioned in 1811 in Bingham, Nottinghamshire, when John Stafford and two or three others had formed a Committee to provide a theatre for Smedley if they could raise the funds by subscriptions of £5 or £10 a share.[57] In February 1825 Smedley finished a season at Holbeach (population 3,890 in 1831) where the public were so pleased with the manager and his company that they had decided to build him a theatre by subscription. One supporter had already promised £100 and several others £50 each; in 1833 each share was worth £40. Smedley opened that new theatre in Park Road in April 1829. The large building was called the Public Rooms and served as Assembly Rooms when not in use for theatricals.[58] When Smedley's company was performing in the theatre in Bridlington (population 5,673 in 1831) on the Yorkshire coast in September 1829 the audience included influential people and a subscription was started to erect a new theatre 'on a scale commensurate with that improving and fashionable bathing place'.[59] In June 1830 it was reported that a purpose built theatre was to be erected in Bourne (population 2,569 in 1831) for Smedley's company. The Marquess of Exeter had promised the site, opposite the Red Lion inn in Southgate, on a 99-year lease and as usual the cost of the building would be borne by shares.[60] A site opposite the

---

[56] Smedley papers, LLHS/38/5/3/14, Lincolnshire County Archives
[57] Smedley papers, LLHS/38/5/3/2, Lincolnshire County Archives
[58] *SM*, 11 February 1825, 3 April 1829; Satherley, Jeremy, *A neat little town – the history of Holbeach*, Holbeach (2004), p.32; Saunders, John Jnr., *Lincolnshire in 1836*, Lincoln (1836), p.90.
[59] *SM*, 25 September 1829.
[60] *SM*, 18 June 1830.

Red Lion would be beyond the last building on the west side of Southgate, behind the northern branch of the Bourne Eau. Smedley later took his company to other theatres in Yorkshire, and in September 1836 it was said that he was so appreciated at Bradford, where he had just completed a season, that nearly £5,000 had been subscribed to build a new theatre.[61] In November 1837 Smedley also owned a theatre at Malton, Yorkshire.

We know the names of only a few actors in Smedley's company, other than the members of his own family. A notebook lists the names of actors in the company just three years after he started, families like the Smedleys, Tannetts and Kellys each being listed as one item. In addition to those three families only four other individual actors were named in January 1810 and of those Goldfinch was the best paid, receiving £1 18s 0d for one week which was not much less than the whole Smedley family who were regularly paid £2 2s 0d a week, amounting to £109 4s 0d a year. The other three actors listed that week were Hodgson (18s), Spragg (16s) and Smith (12s).[62] If there were two or three actors in each of the three families then the total performers in the company would be between ten and thirteen. Later in 1810 the Kellys left, and Tuthills and Wards joined, Wards only briefly, as well as an individual actor called Neville who was paid £1 1s 0d a week from the start. In later years the notebooks do not name any actors individually, but there were two brief references in 1814 and 1815 to 'Northouse', which may refer to George Northouse who was born in 1798 and later performed with the Huggins and Lincoln companies.

One of Smedley's longest serving actors was William Major, who was with the company in 1822

---

[61] *SM*, 30 September 1836.
[62] Accounts for week ending 18 January 1810, in Smedley papers, Account book, LLHS/38/5/1, Lincolnshire County Archives.

Playbill, Brigg, 19 February 1839. Visited by Smedley 'for a very limited season'. Tickets for the performance of George Barnwell *are offered at half price to encourage children and servants to watch that moral play.*
Lincolnshire Archives

in Sleaford and also in 1834 when he was said to be of Deeping St James, and 'for many years a performer in Mr Smedley's company'. On 30 June 1834 he married Miss Mary Ann Wilson of Bourne, and it was in Bourne that he died on 17 April 1850, long after retiring. Other names that occur include a Mr Mantle and Miss Goldfinch in 1822, the latter may be the Goldfinch listed in 1810, a Mr Compton and William Thompson in 1833, and a Mr Young in 1840. Those listed in a playbill for 19 February 1839 at Brigg included Mr Horton, who had just arrived from the Margate theatre, Miss Palmer from the Victoria theatre, London, Miss Andrews from the Sadlers Wells theatre, Mr Mosley and six other actors and two more actresses, listing 12 in total.[63] Another was Robert Howell Hooper 'of the Grimsby theatre' who died on 14 February 1828 aged 25; it was said that 'his talents for low comedy were very superior'.[64] A Mr Neville of Smedley's company moved to Rogers and Mosley about 1836 when Smedley transferred some of his theatres to them. If this was the same Neville who joined Smedley in 1810 then he may have been with that company for over twenty-five years. A few playbills remain for 1839, towards the end of Smedley's theatrical life, and one listed the cast for a night's performance in Wakefield on 25 November 1839. Seventeen people were named, including three Smedleys (Joseph and his son and daughter), two Montagues, two Wiltons and two Woolgars. None of these actors are heard of again in Lincolnshire, except perhaps Mr Montague who was with the Lincoln company in 1846. At least once Smedley followed the example of the bigger companies and hired a London star for a few nights. In June 1827 the celebrated Miss Booth of the Covent Garden and Drury Lane theatres appeared at Sleaford. She pleased all who heard her, but 'We are only sorry to say this favourite actress did not meet with the encouragement her talents justly called for', so as she only got a small audience he probably did not repeat the experiment.[65]

In May 1834 at Bourne Smedley's company included 'a most astonishing child, only 8½ years old, called Reeve', who was the stepdaughter of one of his performers. Her talent had only been discovered a few months earlier, and she was said to surpass the well-known Miss Clara Fisher. Smedley failed to keep this new discovered talent and by November Miss Reeve had joined the Lincoln circuit. In November 1836 she was playing a number of different roles, from low comedy to deep feeling, and was still getting great praise. In October 1838 the *Stamford Mercury* said 'not a single performer on the boards, however, merits greater praise than Miss Reeve, her personation of *Ines* (in whom there are some of the most attractive traits of Shakespeare's *Ophelia*, we fancy), was a most

---

[63] Smedley papers, Playbill, Brigg, 19 February 1839, LLHS/38/5/4/2gii, Lincolnshire County Archives.
[64] *SM*, 22 February 1828.
[65] *SM*, 8 June 1827.

impressive and moving effort'. However, by September 1840 she had left Lincoln and joined a company managed by a Mr Battle at Leicester.[66]

Smedley continued to take more theatres and in 1835 he leased the one in Wakefield (population 12,232 in 1831) and set about rejuvenating it, opening a season there on 10 November. At the same time he added the adjacent large mill towns of Bradford, Huddersfield and Pontefract as well as Beverley (population 7,432 in 1831) near Hull.[67] A notice announcing a benefit for Smedley's daughters at Wakefield in January 1836 added that

> *Mr Smedley takes leave to say that having purchased* [the lease of] *the theatre (at a price which nothing but the increased, and still increasing kindness of his Friends and Patrons could justify) it must and will act as a stimulus and induce him to use every effort in his power to deserve their good opinion.*[68]

Adding these Yorkshire theatres to his existing circuit in late 1835 proved more than one man could manage. As Smedley had found 'the necessary attention in Towns so large and a Company so numerous to be more than he could himself do justice to, he is induced to retain his Eldest Son's assistance at least until his Second Son is old enough to be of the same service'. This implies that his eldest son (Joseph junior, age 19) was either not of much help or wanted to leave, and Smedley expected greater things of his second son (George, aged 12) in a few years' time. Smedley's granddaughter Annette Josephine Young later revealed that Joseph junior had shown promise but ended badly.

> [He] *was a man of most fascinating manners, full of talent (as all the Smedleys were), a good musician and singer and a mean amateur artist, a clever writer, in fact highly gifted. He started well in life, had his thousands, drew his landau, kept his hunters, his wife dressed in black velvet &c., but he spent his last days in a small cottage leading the life of a recluse and dependent on his sister Georgiana for support who also undertook a mortgage in his favour.*[69]

Even with the assistance of Joseph (junior), Smedley could still not manage all his theatres, so 'in the meantime', until George was old enough to help run the company, he 'has committed the Management of these theatres which have been in his possession so many years to Messrs Rogers and Mosley, whom he has selected for their talent, activity, probity and good conduct'. He confidently recommended them as being in every way worthy of patronage and support.[70] More will be said about Rogers and Mosley a little later in this chapter. The theatres transferred to them included Sleaford, Bourne, Melton Mowbray and Market Deeping. Joseph

---

[66] *SM*, 16 May, 7 November 1834, 11 and 25 November 1836, 26 October 1838, 25 September 1840.
[67] *SM*, 16 October 1835; Senior, William, *The Old Wakefield Theatre*, Wakefield (1894), p.53; Smedley papers, LLHS/38/5/3/30, Lincolnshire County Archives.
[68] Smedley papers, LLHS/38/5/3/30, Lincolnshire County Archives.
[69] Smedley papers, LLHS/39/5/9, Lincolnshire County Archives.
[70] Smedley papers, LLHS/38/5/3/30, Lincolnshire County Archives.

(senior) seems to have operated his Yorkshire theatres, with some of his actors, and let his son manage the remaining Lincolnshire theatres, as in March 1836 it was reported that 'Mr Smedley, jun., and a part of his father's talented company' were delighting the playgoers of Spilsby with theatrical performances. On Wednesday 9 March the play was bespoken by the Freemasons and attracted a very respectable audience.

Smedley's company survived until the late 1830s despite the general decline of theatre-going, but the end was near. Theatres were being used for drama less frequently and for shorter seasons. By 1839 Joseph (senior) was going round his Lincolnshire circuit, but for seasons 'unusually limited' in each place. He started in Gainsborough on 9 January 1839, and on 11 January performed *Nicholas Nickleby* (1839), based on Charles Dickens' new novel, for the benefit of himself and his wife. Mr H B Hickman of Thonock, owner of the Old Hall, which included the theatre, bespoke the Smedley's benefit night, and a report that the Duke and Duchess of St Albans would be present ensured that the theatre was filled to overflowing. The theatre was described as 'long deserted' as Smedley had last been there in October 1835.[71] Hickman's niece, Mrs Hutton of Gate Burton Hall, patronised the theatre on 29 January and that night was also well filled. He moved to Brigg in late February and Horncastle theatre was also visited at the start of 1839, but in November of that year the *Stamford Mercury* reported:

> ...dramatic taste appears to have become quite extinct at Horncastle. The theatre at that place, after remaining closed for three years, is at length abandoned by the proprietor, and the materials employed in fitting up the interior have been consigned to the hammer of Mr Weir [an auctioneer].[72]

By April 1839 some of Smedley's theatres had been sublet to a Mr Knight, but that month a disagreement between Smedley and Knight resulted in the Gainsborough theatre being closed for a week. The season ended two weeks later and Knight declared that he would never open that theatre again, having lost £150 in six weeks. The arrangement with Rogers and Mosley also seems to have ended before February 1839 and in April 1840 Smedley himself opened his Sleaford theatre 'for a very limited season'.[73] Smedley struggled against declining audiences during the last half of the 1830s, but kept going until the end of the decade. In October 1840 he opened Gainsborough theatre 'for the first time in two years' and acted Shakespeare to empty benches. The *Stamford Mercury* correctly predicted that this would be the last time Smedley would appear in that theatre. On Monday 26 October 'after a brief and not very propitious season' Joseph Smedley announced 'his intention to resign the stage, in consequence of the falling off of dramatic patronage'.[74] He was not just abandoning Gainsborough, but disbanding his whole company.

---

[71] *SM*, 16 October 1835, 4 January 1839.
[72] *SM*, 1 November 1839.
[73] *SM*, 17 April 1840.
[74] *SM*, 30 October 1840.

One of the last things Joseph Smedley did in the theatrical line was to buy Wakefield theatre, a brick and slate building in Westgate that had opened in September 1776. It was built by James Banks, passed to his widow and when Mrs Banks died her heirs sold it to Smedley on 23 January 1839. The theatre later passed to Joseph's widow Melinda and daughter Georgiana and on 30 June 1865 they sold it to Nathaniel Webster of Wakefield, comedian. It was by then a music hall, and it was demolished in March 1894. Only two years after buying Wakefield theatre, in November or December 1840, Smedley announced that his seven Yorkshire theatres were to let. He described them as:

> The theatre at Wakefield, together with Six others in the immediate neighbourhood, forming one of the most compact Circuits in the Kingdom, and with them will be let the Use of all the Scenery, Machinery and Properties, as well as the Wardrobes, Books and Music. Each theatre is amply stocked with Scenery, the Wardrobe is one of the most complete in the Kingdom, and the Library of Books and Music such as few can boast of.

He said that 'the company has been under the present management for Thirty-Six Years and offers a rare opportunity of embarking in a large concern with a comparatively small capital'. He added that if an 'eligible' tenant did not come forward then from 1 January next the company would be carried on by 'Mr Smedley, junior'.[75]

After retiring from the theatrical life, Smedley set up in Northgate, Sleaford, as a printer, stationer and bookseller and lived for another quarter century as a local businessman. He sold the Sleaford theatre on 6 July 1840 but owned Wakefield theatre for the rest of his life. He did print posters, sell tickets and book the boxes whenever Sleaford theatre was used in later years. His devoted granddaughter Annette kept mementoes of Joseph's theatrical life and these are now in the Lincolnshire Archives. Smedley was well regarded by his friends and in 1845 joined with some other small businessmen to lease Sleaford gas works which they held until 1850. Joseph's son George was employed in the works by 1849 and later became manager until about 1863 when he moved to Buxton gas works and managed that for many years. Joseph Smedley died in Sleaford in March 1863, aged 79.

Other Companies

As well as the Stamford and Lincoln companies, and those of Huggins and Smedley, there were a few other actor-managers with small companies in Lincolnshire in the early nineteenth century, but they were all short-lived and very little is known about them. For some we only know the name of the manager. It appears that several were attempts to fill the gap left by the dissolution of Smedley's company.

---

[75] Smedley papers, LLHS/38/5/6/2, Lincolnshire County Archives

John Mosley and partners

Among this minor league the actor-manager who gets the most mention is John Mosley, who was active in Lincolnshire and adjacent parts from the mid-1830s to the mid-1840s and during that time was with three different partners: Mr Rogers, Mr Abbott and Charles Rice.

The first reference to Rogers and Mosley was in the undated note issued by Joseph Smedley, probably in late 1835 or early 1836, indicating that he had transferred some of his theatres to this partnership, whom he had selected because of their 'talent, activity, probity and good conduct'. The first mention of them in the *Stamford Mercury* refers to the opening of the theatre at Melton Mowbray on 15 February 1837 by 'a talented company' under their management.[76] That season closed on 6 April but it had not been successful. The *Mercury* said

> It is no easy task to ensure success in following so respected and talented a man as Mr Smedley, but we have no doubt that our new friends, when better known, will meet with the encouragement they so highly deserve.

The reporter considered Mr Rogers the better actor of the two. 'The acting of Mr Rogers is of a decidedly superior cast – clear and distinct enunciation, a high and manly bearing, with a correct conception of the meaning of his authors' whereas Mr Mosley was 'an actor of considerable promise, especially in genteel comedy'.[77]

After Melton the company went on to Sleaford and then to Bourne for a short season from late May 1837 until 21 June. 'The company is not so numerous as when under Mr Smedley's management. There is, however, no deficiency of talent, and the parts are better cast.'[78] Every night the theatre was thinly attended and the *Mercury* thought that was because they were strangers 'with an entirely strange company, with the exception of the respected and respectable Neville'.[79] From Bourne they went to Market Deeping, but after June 1837 no more is heard of this partnership. Rogers and Mosley split up and both managers became actors in other local companies for a while.

In February 1839 John Mosley was performing with Smedley's company at Gainsborough and Brigg but by November 1839 he was apparently at Long Sutton in a company managed by Messrs Abbott and Harper. There is some ambiguity about this, as a Mr Mosley was also listed in the cast of Smedley's company performing at Wakefield on 25 November 1839. His former partner Mr Rogers is referred to in April 1839 when Messrs Knight and Rogers are recorded as opening Gainsborough theatre but, as mentioned above, Knight lost money on

---

[76] *SM*, 17 February 1837.
[77] *SM*, 7 April 1837.
[78] *SM*, 26 May 1837.
[79] *SM*, 9 and 23 June 1837.

that venture and we hear no more of him after that.[80] On 3 November 1841 a Mr Rogers had a benefit as a member of Mrs Robertson's company performing at Stamford but he then also disappeared.[81]

The Abbott and Harper company of 1839 was perhaps the successor to one that first appeared in 1834 in Rutland and Northamptonshire when Mr Abbott was the sole manager. Abbott's company performed in the Rutland town of Uppingham (population 1,754 in 1831) in February 1834, then went to Oakham (1,558 in 1831) in April for a short season ending on 16 May 1834 that was 'successful and gave great satisfaction'.[82] On 13 June it was said that Abbott's company had enjoyed the patronage of Lord Sondes in the previous week, and were about to open a theatrical season at Kettering.[83] They are not mentioned in the Lincolnshire area until five years later, in November 1839, when as 'a company of very respectable comedians, under the management of Messrs Abbott and Harper' they arrived in Long Sutton (population 5,845 in 1841) with John Mosley as a member of the cast.[84]

By August 1840 Mosley had taken Harper's place as joint manager. The *Stamford Mercury* reported that 'Messrs Abbott and Mosley, with their select and efficient company of comedians' were about to close a pretty successful season at Uppingham before going on to Oakham. In October 1840 they were still at Oakham 'where they continue to delight the lovers of the drama'. They then went to Bourne for about a month.[85] By November 1840 the troupe was called 'Mosley and Abbott's company'; they were then 'winning golden opinions in Bourne' and on 11 November the Oddfellows bespoke a play which attracted a very full house.[86] On 12 December 1840 they moved from Bourne to Sleaford. Joseph Smedley had sold the Sleaford theatre by then but it continued in use as a playhouse and in 1845, when it was again offered for

---

[80] *Hull Advertiser and Exchange Gazette*, 12 April 1839.
[81] SM, 26 October 1841.
[82] SM, 7 February, 11 April, 16 May 1834.
[83] SM, 13 June 1834.
[84] SM, 22 November 1839.
[85] SM, 23 October 1840.
[86] SM, 13 November 1840.

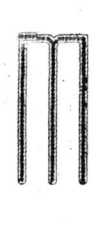

Playbill, Sleaford, 17 January 1844. Patronised by the Cricket Club and starring 'Monsr. Gouffe, the celebrated Man-Monkey', John Mosley's company includes Mr Rice, perhaps his future partner.
Lincolnshire Archives

sale, it was said to be still 'in constant request for theatrical performances, for concerts, and other amusements of that character' and to be 'in an excellent state of repair'.[87]

Mosley's partnership with Abbott lasted longer than the one with Mr Rogers. In mid January 1842 they again opened the Sleaford theatre, having come from Gainsborough where 'they gave great satisfaction'.[88] In February they 'engaged Mr Barnardo Eagle, the Great Wizard of the South' for a few nights to perform his 'wonderful feats of magic' and got overflowing houses. In mid February they went from Sleaford to Oundle. Mosley and Abbott's company is next referred to in the *Mercury* at the start of December 1842, when they were due to leave Bourne. It was said that a benefit for Miss Thompson was held on 29 November 'when she received the compliment of a good house'. In January 1843 'Abbott and Mosley' opened the Sleaford theatre for a few nights, presenting a visiting star from London, Miss E. Land of the Theatres Royal Drury Lane and the Haymarket. Then from 6 February they were at Newark theatre with their 'numerous and talented company' and in July at Gainsborough. Miss Land performed for a few nights in both towns.[89] This partnership lasted about four years and they split up in August 1843, at the end of the Gainsborough season. They said that 'each gentleman will embark in a voyage single-handed', each taking about half the actors. Mr Mosley said he would visit the bathing places, and Mr Abbott would continue on his usual circuit. Abbott was asking his London agent for additional performers, 'and from the depression of the times, and the abundance of stock in the talent-market, some good actors may be expected'.[90]

For a while John Mosley was on his own again and in January 1844 his company had a 'very indifferent season' at the Sleaford theatre. The playbill for 17 January lists a Mr Rice as one of the company and also shows that Joseph Smedley, 'bookseller and stationer', was dealing with ticket sales and places for the boxes. However, just a little later, still early in 1844, Mosley had formed a third partnership, this time with Charles Rice (1820-80) who may be the actor in his troupe. They leased Wakefield theatre and were again described as the 'successors to Mr Smedley'.[91] The first reference to Charles Rice in Lincolnshire had been in December 1843 when 'Mr Rice' had a benefit in Gainsborough theatre. There was a furore because the Gainsborough Brass Band when attending free of charge to play music were usually allowed to sit in the boxes but on this occasion their box was locked and they were asked to sit in the orchestra pit to which they strongly objected.[92]

---

[87] *SM*, 25 July 1845.
[88] *SM*, 28 January 1842.
[89] *SM*, 2 December 1842, 6 and 20 January 1843, 3 February 1843, 28 July 1843.
[90] *SM*, 11 August 1843.
[91] Senior, William, *The Old Wakefield Theatre*, Wakefield (1894), pp.129, 130.
[92] *SM*, 8 and 15 December 1843.

In May 1845 Mosley and Rice opened Gainsborough theatre but they got only a poor audience. It was said that the managers were likely to be minus a considerable sum, as they had been at no little expense in repairing and decorating the interior of the theatre, though still more needed to be done to make it 'warmer and more comfortable'.[93] The season ended on 16 May when the presence of H B Hickman and his party from Thonock Hall ensured a full house. In a farewell address from the stage it was indicated that 'the theatre had been kept open at a considerable loss, but the company promised to renew their efforts to restore the taste for the drama at Gainsborough'. From Gainsborough they went to Worksop. Their hope of reviving the drama was not fulfilled and after this date nothing more is heard of John Mosley or Charles Rice in Lincolnshire. At a later date Rice leased the Theatre Royal, Bradford, for many years, where he and his wife, who succeeded him as manager when he died, were much respected. Rice was in those later years celebrated for the production of traditional pantomimes.[94]

Bruce and Bullen's company

During the first half of the 1840s Mosley faced competition from another small troupe called 'Bruce and Bullen's company', of which it seems that Mr Bullen was the leading partner. He may have been related to Mrs Smedley as she was a Bullen before her marriage and Bullen's company was first referred to just after Smedley had disbanded his own company. Few personal details about Mr Bullen have yet been found, not even the initial of his first name, though it is known that he had a daughter who was aged seven by the end of 1841.[95] It is also recorded that a 'Mr J. Bullen' was a steward at a Shakespeare dinner held in Lincoln in 1835, and if that is the same person he may have been an actor in Robertson's Lincoln company at that date.[96]

A little more is known about Bullen's partner, John Bruce. On 4 August 1843 a baby was born to Mrs Bruce 'of the Louth and Horncastle theatres' and he was christened Robert Frederick Bruce in Louth on 20 August, his parents being John and Louisa Bruce.[97] The 1841 census lists a Louisa Bullen in Stone in Staffordshire, then aged between fifteen and nineteen, and records show that John Bruce married Louisa Bullen on 7 July 1841 at St Mary's church, Stafford, so this would seem to be the couple in the Lincolnshire theatre company. This also suggests that the two partners were related by marriage, as Mr Bullen shared Louisa's maiden surname.

---

[93] *SM*, 16 May 1845; *Eastern Counties Herald*, 24 April 1845.
[94] Senior, *op. cit.*, p.59.
[95] *SM*, 31 December 1841.
[96] *SM*, 30 October and 6 November 1835.
[97] *SM*, 11 August 1843.

In December 1841 Bruce and Bullen's 'small company of comedians' visited Melton Mowbray and performed in the Auction-Rooms for a short season. At first they did not 'meet with the encouragement formerly enjoyed by Mr Smedley' but the pieces they put on for the Christmas holidays gave 'great satisfaction to crowded houses'. On New Year's Eve, in addition to the usual performances, they put on a ball and masquerade to usher in the New Year. Infant prodigies often attracted good audiences, and it was reported that Mr Bullen's seven-year-old daughter had 'called forth the highest praise'.[98] In January 1842 Mr Bullen, 'with a talented company of comedians' went from Melton to Uppingham 'for a short season' and then in April moved to Bourne. In mid-May 1842 they opened the theatre at Market Deeping (population 1,219 in 1841) where the Cricket Club bespoke Sheridan's *The Rivals* for one night.[99]

Then disaster struck on Monday, 30 May 1842. The Oddfellows of Market Deeping had patronised the night for Colman's *The Poor Gentleman* (1801) and 'the house was crowded to suffocation'. Whilst the epilogue was being delivered, the whole of the gallery came down with a fearful crash, burying everyone in the boxes beneath.

> *The scene was dreadful, and the screams were appalling until the extent of the injury was known. Ladies were dug out of the fallen timbers, with ribs broken, shoulders dislocated, severe contusions, and blood running in streams from hundreds, but providentially no life was lost.*

The blame was put on the carpenter who had erected the temporary building. The managers had lately spent a large amount to have the theatre newly painted and decorated by George Northouse of Boston, 'but the shocking accident of Monday night is likely to ruin their prospects at Deeping', which was putting it mildly![100]

In September 1842 their company was performing at Long Sutton with plays that had been 'chosen with taste, and are worthy of the best patronage' including Shakespeare, Colman, Garrick and others. 'Mrs Bullen's lady-like talents, and Mr Bruce's singing, are excellent, and the whole company deserves success for their abilities and respectable conduct.'[101] In October they were attracting full houses at Spilsby (population 1,457 in 1841). A Mr Melvin, from Liverpool, had joined their company to take the lead in *King Lear* and other Shakespearean plays. They then went to Alford, Louth and Horncastle. The contents of the theatre in Horncastle had been sold off some time before but the building stood until the middle of the twentieth century, so it would still be the most convenient venue for Bullen and Bruce in 1842. They were patronised by the leading families of the town and neighbourhood, and 'their exertions gained them esteem and respectable

---

[98] *SM*, 10 and 31 December 1841.
[99] *SM*, 21 January, 25 February, 15 April, 20 May 1842.
[100] *SM*, 3 June 1842.
[101] *SM*, 2 September 1842.

encouragement'. That season ended on 22 February 1843 with a benefit for Mrs Bullen. They then moved to Market Rasen where they set up a theatre in a spacious room attached to the Greyhound inn, and again they received 'the approbation and encouragement of some of the principal persons of the town and neighbourhood'.[102]

The reports in the *Stamford Mercury* painted a rosy picture but beneath the surface all was not well and in July 1843 the Bullen and Bruce partnership came to an end. For the previous three months their company had performed in a 'subscription theatre' in a large room in Louth belonging to 'Mr Thompson the broker' and concluded the season with four 'last nights'. The final 'last night' was on 12 July and at the end Mr Bullen announced that the partnership had been dissolved and he would be going alone to perform at Hull and Beverley.[103] At the end of September 1843 Mr Bruce, 'from Louth', opened a theatre in Wainfleet, 'with splendid scenery and dresses'. It was said that he had visited the town 'at the express desire of several influential parties here and at Skegness'.[104] Wainfleet was a small town with a population of 1,386 in 1841 and though Skegness had only 316 inhabitants that year it was starting to grow as a seaside resort. Bruce's company was probably still in Wainfleet a few weeks later as two of his actors got married in All Saints church there on 16 October 1843.[105]

John Bruce did not last long on his own and when Mr Bullen opened a theatre in Brigg in April 1844 for a short season his 'select and effective company' included Mr Bruce who had apparently returned after spending some time on the London stage.[106] By this date moral disapproval of the theatre was so common that the *Stamford Mercury* thought 'we can scarcely hope that he will meet with much support in a town where a church and two chapels have been built within the short space of two years'.[107] The Brigg season continued during May 1844 and Bullen met with more success than had been expected. The *Mercury* said

[102] *SM*, 17 and 24 February, 31 March 1843.
[103] *SM*, 16 June, 21 July 1843.
[104] *SM*, 1 September 1843.
[105] *SM*, 20 October 1843.
[106] *SM*, 31 May 1844.
[107] *SM*, 26 April 1844.

Top: *The Great Hall, Irnham Hall, near Grantham where, in a highly unusual arrangement, theatre manager Mr J. Simms was allowed to set up a commercial theatre in the stately home of Mr Arundell. Simms had no need to set up a gallery in his temporary theatre as one already existed.*
Illustrated London News, 26 November 1887, in the author's collection

Bottom: *Playbill, Irnham Hall, 8 October 1807*
The Bodleian Library, University of Oxford: John Johnson Collection; Provincial Playbills box Salisbury-Stratford (20)

that 'the company possess more ability than is generally found in the provinces'. The attendance of the Duke and Duchess of St Albans on one evening and Lord Worsley on another assured a respectable audience on those nights. The nobility could disregard middle class morality, and their presence gave encouragement to other lovers of the drama. The paper now thought that 'if Mr Bullen could procure a more eligible theatre, we doubt not his success in Brigg would be commensurate with his merits'.[108]

The split and then the return of John Bruce indicate yet again the uncertain state of the theatre at this time, notwithstanding good attendance on some nights due to elite patronage. In November 1844 the Bullens commenced a series of performances in Lincoln theatre, but the company was now described as 'Mrs Bullen and family'.[109] In January 1845 the *Stamford Mercury* said that several companies had tried their luck at Lincoln theatre but most had done badly, and some had 'been in a shocking state of destitution'.[110] In September 1845 Mr and Mrs Bullen 'from the Louth and Spilsby company of comedians' entertained Spalding with a variety of theatricals and had respectable houses at the 'New Assembly Rooms' in the former theatre. The next week it was again referred to as 'Mrs Bullen's theatrical company' implying that her husband was no longer capable of management.[111] This seems to be confirmed by a report on 28 November 1845 that

> *an itinerant manager of a theatrical company named Bullen was brought before the Mayor of Wisbech and J. R. Weatherhead, Esq., on Saturday last, charged with obtaining goods under false pretences. He had obtained goods from several parties, which it was stated he had not the slightest prospect of paying for.*

The magistrates were kind to him:

> *He was severely reprimanded and allowed to depart upon making a solemn promise to liquidate the demands upon him in a few days.*

This sounds like a man overwhelmed by the downturn of his fortunes, and unable to recognise the reality of his situation. Nothing more was heard of Bruce or Bullen after this date.

And finally, some others

There are a few other people who appear briefly in the sources and call themselves actor-managers in Lincolnshire, but of whom we have little or no record of any performances. There are also one or two references to theatres in small places with no players named. About the turn of the century, there was a performance at a 'theatre' in the village of Laceby outside Grimsby, and a report of a marriage

---

[108] *SM*, 31 May 1844.
[109] *SM*, 22 November 1844.
[110] *SM*, 17 January 1845.
[111] *SM*, 5 and 12 September 1845.

in the *Stamford Mercury* in February 1813 refers to a theatre at Tuxford, on the Great North Road in Nottinghamshire.[112] This was presumably a temporary theatre, perhaps in the yard of the Newcastle Arms coaching inn.

When Richard Jones (1784-1840) of the Albion Pavilion, Hull, died on 22 April 1840 he was said to be a theatrical manager working in the East Riding of Yorkshire and north Lincolnshire.[113] He started life as a travelling musician and when he married Sarah the daughter of Mr T. Jones of Louth on 21 February 1805 they were both actors in Huggins' company. Miss Jones' first appearance on a stage had been at Lincoln in October 1803. They tried their luck elsewhere and when they appeared at Louth theatre again in March 1809 it was their first appearance there for four years. Sarah Jones died in July 1823 aged 40 and Richard Jones was then with the Edinburgh company of comedians.[114]

There was a Mr J. Simms who managed theatres in the Midlands, particularly in Warwickshire and Northamptonshire, between 1809 and 1818. His only recorded appearances in Lincolnshire were in December 1806 and October 1807. On the first occasion he opened a theatre at Sleaford for a short season, with Cherry's new play *The Soldier's Daughter* (1804) and Colman's *The Wags of Windsor* (1800).[115] His second recorded visit to the county is very unusual. While barns were often adapted as theatres, and private theatricals were occasionally put on in big country houses, three posters record that a company of comedians actually set up a public theatre inside a stately home near Corby (now Corby Glen) in south Lincolnshire. At that date the Irnham estate belonged to Lady Arundell of Wardour and Irnham Hall was occupied by her nephew and son-in-law James Everard Arundell (1763-1817). Then, as the poster says:

> *J. E. Arundell, Esq., with his accustomed Liberality, has handsomely invited Mr Simms, and his Company of Comedians, to play the three following Nights at the Hall, during* Corby Races; *and in addition to this Favor* (sic) *has kindly allowed the Admittance of the Public in general, at Playhouse prices. – The Doors open at seven o'Clock, and to begin at half-past.*

The prices were Boxes 3s, Pit 2s, Gallery 1s, so a proper theatre was erected in the great hall of the house with boxes and a gallery and they charged commercial prices.[116]

Simms' first night was Tuesday 6 October 1807, when the plays were the comedy of *The Honey-Moon* followed by the entertainment called *Matrimony* (1804). On

---

[112] Lincolnshire Archives Committee, Archivist's Report for 1950/51.p.54; SM, 12 February 1813.
[113] *SM*, 1 May 1840.
[114] *SM*, 22 February 1805, 7 October 1803, 3 March 1809, 18 July 1823.
[115] Warwick, Lou, *Theatre Unroyal*, pp.52-64, 83; SM, 21 November 1806.
[116] The Bodleian Library, University of Oxford, John Johnson Collection, Provincial Playbills box, Salisbury-Stratford (20).

Wednesday they presented the favourite new comedy of *The School of Reform, Or, How to Rule a Husband* (1805), then a comic song, followed by the laughable farce 'never acted here', *Love Laughs at Locksmiths*. The last night was Thursday, and they performed the favourite comedy *The Soldier's Daughter* followed by a comic song and then the musical farce *Of Age To-Morrow* (1800). There were a dozen actors in the company, and at least six of them were in all six plays, as well as musicians, so this was a hectic exercise. There is a further link nearly seventeen years later when Mr Simms' daughter married a Mr Henderson at Bourne on 30 June 1824, by which date her father had passed away.[117] It is not known if they were actors, though they may have been as in February 1826 there were a Mr and Mrs Henderson performing in Huggins' company in Horncastle.[118]

There could have been other events in barns and inn yards for which no playbills survive and so we have no knowledge of them. Other landowners might allow barns or other buildings to be used as theatres, but it is extremely rare to hear of a private house like Irnham Hall, however large, being used for the setting up of a commercial theatre. Georgian theatre was at its most popular and profitable in the opening years of the nineteenth century so this was perhaps the most likely period for a landowner to open his house in this way, at least until the late twentieth century.

Simms visited the area only a couple of times, but Myrton Hamilton (c1745-1818) is unusual in that he had his greatest theatrical successes elsewhere and spent the twilight of his career in Lincolnshire and Leicestershire. When Hamilton died on 17 December 1818 at the age of 73, after a protracted illness, it was said that 'he was formerly manager of a small company of comedians in this [Lincolnshire] and adjoining counties'.[119] On Sunday 2 December 1804 two of his daughters got married at St Mary's church, Hinckley in Leicestershire, Sophia married William Turner, a bookseller of Hull, and lately of Nottingham, and Catherine married James Morton Dodds (listed as Mr Morton Dodds), lately of the Stamford theatre.[120] Hamilton's youngest daughter Leydell had got married at Holbeach in July 1802.[121]

Their father was the youngest of a celebrated acting family and had a relatively distinguished career on the Irish stage in the last third of the eighteenth century. He performed in Belfast and Newry from 1768 and for a short time from 1778 was manager of the Belfast theatre and moved the company to the new Ann Street theatre. Then in 1780 he went to Dublin's Smock Alley theatre where he played lesser roles. In 1781 he formed a company that toured the northern part of Ireland until 1783, then returned to Dublin in 1784 before apparently

---

[117] *SM*, 2 July 1824.
[118] Robinson, David N., *The Book of Horncastle and Woodhall Spa*, Buckingham (1983), p.164.
[119] *SM*, 25 December 1818.
[120] *SM*, 14 December 1804.
[121] *SM*, 16 July 1802.

leaving the country. It is not clear where he then went. His brother William performed in London at some time, but Myrton never did.[122] Some ten years after leaving Ireland he was in Leicestershire and evidently spent most of his last years there and in Lincolnshire. In 1787 there was a Mr Hamilton with James West's Gainsborough company and that might have been Myrton Hamilton.[123] In November 1795 Hamilton opened a temporary theatre in the Coal Hill Assembly Rooms in Leicester, and his company performed there until February 1796.[124] The only specific reference to him performing in Lincolnshire was in May 1803 when he had a benefit at the Bourne theatre in Colman's popular new comedy *John Bull, Or, the Englishman's Fireside* (1803).[125] Perhaps Holbeach and Hinckley, where his daughters got married, were also places where they performed.

One gentry family, the Hartopps, put on amateur theatricals at their country house, Little Dalby Hall near Melton Mowbray, from 1777 until 1878 and in 1800 built their own theatre next door to the hall. That private theatre opened in July 1801 and the whole of Mr Hamilton's company, together with other actors from Stamford, Cheltenham and Drury Lane (London) theatres, helped the amateurs on that occasion.[126] All of Myrton's daughters were actresses and in January 1803 'the three Miss Hamiltons' filled the female parts in the amateur performances of *The Stranger* and *Three Weeks*

---

[122] Highfill, Philip H., et. al., *Biographical Dictionary of Actors, etc* Vol.7, Carbondale (1973-93), p.62.
[123] Parker, B.J., *The Theatre of Gainsborough. From 1772 until 1850*, thesis (1963), in Gainsborough Library.
[124] Leacroft, Helen and Richard, *The Theatre in Leicestershire*, Leicester (1986), pp.11,13; *Leicester Journal*, 2 October 1795, 26 February 1796.
[125] *SM*, 27 May 1803.
[126] Leacroft, *op. cit.*, pp.33, 34.

Playbill, Caistor, 2 April 1833. Mr Macarty setting up a temporary theatre, with pit and gallery only, in the Assembly Room of the Talbot Inn.
Grimsby Library, via David Saunders

after Marriage (1764) at Little Dalby Hall.[127] His eldest daughter, who 'has long been a favourite actress in most towns of the counties of Lincoln and Leicester', made her first appearance at the Theatre Royal, Bath, on 9 June 1804. The theatre was crowded and she got a very enthusiastic reception. She played *Angela* in *The Castle Spectre* and *Catherine* in *Catherine and Petrucio* (1803).[128] On 27 August 1804 an amateur performance was put on at Stamford theatre to raise funds for a widow Selby and Miss Hamilton of the Theatre Royal, Bath, appeared for free as *Belvidera* in *Venice Preserv'd*, this being her first appearance on the Stamford stage. The evening raised £65 12s 0d at the door and £50 was paid to Mrs Selby, who thanked Miss Hamilton in particular for her help.[129] Myrton Hamilton's last years were spent as a printer in Hull, perhaps in association with his son-in-law William Turner, and he died there in 1818.[130]

The Bradys were a small family touring company, consisting of two parents, their son Charles aged ten and their daughter. In October 1818 they appeared in the village of Wragby for their second season there and after that 'theatre' closed they were to move to equally small Bardney.[131] On 6 August 1819 Skegness was reported to abound with fashionable company and Mr Brady and his family opened a theatre there. It was said that the performances were 'numerously attended'.

A Mr Macarty brought a company to the area in 1833. On 2 and 3 April 1833 they performed in a 'theatre' in the Assembly Room of the Talbot inn in Caistor, and were said to be 'numerous and highly respectable, many of them from the principal Theatres Royal in the United Kingdom, and of great experience and talent'. That theatre had only a pit and gallery but the programme on 2 April included two plays and a 'Musical Melange' of at least seven songs and tunes. The first play was a melodrama *The Floating Beacon, Or, the Norwegian Wreckers* (1824) and included not only 'a terrific combat between Messrs Smith and Macarty' but also 'Dreadful Combat and total Destruction of the Beacon in Fire'.[132] The Talbot inn is now the site of the new Co-op store next to the Town Hall of 1887. That winter Macarty's company appeared at Melton Mowbray but that must have been the end of a losing streak and Macarty suddenly left there without paying the charges incurred during his short stay. The carpenter who furnished the boards for fitting up the temporary theatre had to pay the rent of the place before he was allowed to take away his own wood, and some of the performers were bilked of their salaries and left in a state of destitution. In July 1834 Mr McCarty was heard to be in Hull, at a minor theatre called the Adelphi.[133]

---

[127] *SM*, 7 August 1801, 21 January 1803.
[128] *SM*, 15 June 1804.
[129] *SM*, 24 and 31 August 1804.
[130] *SM*, 25 December 1818.
[131] *SM*, 23 October 1818.
[132] Playbill, Caistor, 2 April 1833, supplied by David Saunders.
[133] *SM*, 18 July 1834.

In November 1834 a David Grose opened 'a very neat and comfortable' theatre in Market Rasen.[134] In November 1837 he asked permission to use Smedley's theatre at Malton in Yorkshire but was refused. Grose said that 'former bickering took place between us' and in September 1838 published a letter criticising Smedley for not letting him use the theatre.[135]

In June 1843 Messrs Henderson and Melvin opened a theatre at Barton on Humber 'with a most excellent company'. These may have been the Mr Henderson who came from Northampton and joined the Lincoln company in late 1842 and the Mr Melvin from Liverpool who had joined Bullen and Bruce in October 1842.[136] The manager of Northampton theatre said, in January 1843:

> *Henderson has left us and gone into the Lincoln circuit but I think he is again on the look-out, the sooner he cuts the stage the better, he is a respectable good-natured fellow but he will never be an actor.*[137]

After the first week at Barton, Henderson and Melvin 'had not obtained the success that their anxiety to please had entitled them to expect', and nothing more was heard of them as a separate company.[138] It is possible that they both joined the Lincoln company, as in April 1844 a Mr Melvin was 'the vocalist in Mr Robertson's theatrical company' and a Mr Henderson was later a member of Mr Caple's company that performed in Lincoln and other local theatres.[139]

The Giffords were another theatrical family who toured the county twenty-five years after the Bradys, visiting Sleaford and Boston in June and July 1843. It was said that 'the precocious attainments of the children, the eldest being only 12 years of age, almost surpassed belief; and their performances upon the stage, to be admired, 'need but be seen'. In May 1844 they were performing at Market Rasen – 'They are certainly very talented children, especially Miss Rose Gifford, who is a prodigy' – and they were in Lincoln in January 1845, but put on performances in the City Assembly Rooms rather than the theatre.[140]

A small company managed by a Mr Clifford briefly visited the county in 1845. On 7 May 1845 he opened Grantham theatre, with a company from the London and provincial theatres, but audiences were thin. In June it was said that the company had improved, and it was a pity that the manager's efforts were beginning to be appreciated just as the company was about to leave. The performers included Mr Clifford, Mr Melville, Mrs Simeon and young Miss Clifford. In August 1845

---

[134] *SM*, 14 November 1834.
[135] Smedley papers, LLHS/38/5/31, Lincolnshire County Archives
[136] Warwick, Lou, *Theatre Unroyal*, p.155.
[137] *Ibid.*
[138] *SM*, 2 and 9 June 1843.
[139] *SM*, 12 April 1844.
[140] *SM*, 14 July 1843, 17 May 1844, 17 January 1845.

Mr Clifford's company were in Bourne where they were said to be having a good season, and they planned to go on to Chesterfield.[141]

In November 1846 a company managed by a Mr Thompson visited Gainsborough about the mart time, and left the town in mid-November. Some of the performers had not paid for their lodgings, and were locked up by the landlord while he went for the police. Before he returned, they kicked down the door and took their departure.[142]

William Scraggs (c.1748-1808) ran a company of comedians that toured the smaller towns of East Anglia, including King's Lynn, from 1784, with David Fisher as partner and senior manager from April 1792. When Scraggs died in Beccles, Suffolk, on 5 February 1808 the *Stamford Mercury* referred to him as 'a joint actor manager in this county' but nothing else is known about that suggested connection with Lincolnshire. His widow inherited his share of the company but she died four years later and it passed to their son Robert Beeston Scraggs who then left Fisher and started his own company.[143]

However difficult their finances became the Lincolnshire companies always seem to have done their best to pay their debts and not abscond like Macarty. The minor companies of comedians in Lincolnshire failed to survive the challenging times of the 1830s and '40s, so how was the flagship Lincoln company coping in these stormy waters?

---

[141] *SM*, 9 May, 27 June, 15 August 1845.
[142] *SM*, 20 November 1846; Parker, *op. cit.*, p.27.
[143] Grice, Elizabeth, *Rogues and Vagabonds*, Lavenham, Suffolk (1977), pp.90-91; Field, Moira, *The Lamplit Stage*, Norwich (1985), p.12; SM, 12 February 1808, 14 February 1812.

9

A SHOCKING STATE OF DESTITUTION

FOR FANNY ROBERTSON, leading actress of the Lincolnshire stage, it could truly be said that the 1830s were the worst of times, and the best of times. Her husband, Tom, manager of the Lincoln company, had died, audience numbers kept going down, income kept falling, her nephew William wanted to take over the running of the company and, perhaps what was worst for her, even if she did not like to admit it, William's talented Danish-born wife was challenging Fanny's position as the female star of the Lincolnshire stage. On the positive side were some benefits and opportunities. Since Tom had died Fanny was manager of the company, however much young William might want to take over, and she took the decisions. Her creative writing could be given full vent, and in the early 1830s she penned two plays that were performed by her own company. And her rival local actress, Sarah Huggins, about the same age as Fanny, had left the stage and retired following the demise of the Louth company. That demise had also allowed Fanny to take Louth theatre into her circuit. Although Fanny was now in her 60s, she still had the talent and energy to dominate the theatrical scene in Lincolnshire with its many challenges.

Theatre in London was flourishing in the 1830s and no fewer than fourteen new theatres were opened there in the decade, but in Lincolnshire the 1830s started badly and got worse.[1] Puritanical opposition to theatre had grown stronger during the eighteenth and nineteenth centuries as Christianity in Britain became more evangelical, the spiritual life of the Church of England was revived and Methodism arose to become in time a separate church. The changing moral atmosphere meant that sentimental Regency fops were no longer fashionable in the audience and masculinity was defined by a new austerity and emotional repression – although corsets were less popular, men were nevertheless more staid. Showing loud emotion or throwing objects at the stage was seen as morally objectionable – a bear pit.

Charles Huggins had dissolved his company in October 1830 and James and Thomas Robertson both died in 1831. For nearly twenty years there had been a slow but steady decline in support for theatres in greater Lincolnshire but in the 1830s the situation became dire and managers had to take drastic action. In response to

---

[1] Brewer, John, *The Pleasures of the Imagination: English Culture in the Eighteenth Century*, Abingdon (2013), p.312.

religious objections to the drama managers stressed its moral power to improve the character and behaviour of servants, apprentices and children. When that did not bring the audience back in droves, they made changes to cope with the lack of customers and cash. They shortened or abandoned seasons, put on shows where and when they hoped to attract an audience and brought in London stars, but even those big names did not always get a good audience.

In 1833 there was a phenomenon which gave the misleading impression that theatres could be profitable again. On 15 October the virtuoso Italian violinist Niccolo Paganini (1782-1840) performed for one night at Lincoln theatre, in the middle of the theatrical season. He proposed to charge 7/6, 5/- and 2/6 but when challenged he agreed that the Pit and Gallery should be 3/- and 1/6 which is what he had charged at York a few days earlier, though he stuck to the higher price of 7/6 for the boxes. The total receipts of the night were said to be about £100.[2] This national tour made him a very wealthy man, but it was in striking contrast to the decline in support for drama, comedy and everything else that theatres offered.

In 1830 William Cobbett wrote:

> *One of the great signs of the poverty of people in the middle rank of life is the falling off of the audiences at the playhouse. There is a playhouse in almost every country town where the players used to act occasionally, and in large towns almost always. In some places, they have of late abandoned acting altogether. In others, they have acted, very frequently, to no more than ten or twelve persons. I have heard of one manager who has become porter in a warehouse.*[3]

Some theatres had experimented with charging lower prices but that had not increased attendance, so Cobbett was wrong about middle class poverty being the cause. The young Queen Victoria came to the throne in 1837 and married Prince Albert in 1840. She and her husband enjoyed drama and had a stage built at Windsor Castle on which professional actors could perform for her family and close relatives. But her support failed to make the theatre fashionable again. During the 1820s the *Stamford Mercury* had started publishing reviews of theatrical performances in Lincolnshire, written by people who enjoyed theatre, but in the 1830s these were slowly being joined or replaced by reports that welcomed news of theatre closures as signs of the moral improvement of society.

After Tom Robertson died on 31 August 1831 the Lincoln company battled on for another sixteen years. Fanny was the manager, assisted by her nephew, William Robertson. He was sometimes referred to as acting manager, but Fanny kept effective control until 1843. That long established circuit saw changes from the early 1830s as they and other troupes stepped in to fill the gap left by Huggins' departure.

---

[2] *Stamford Mercury*, 11 and 18 October 1833.
[3] Chamberlin, Russell, *The National Trust. The English Country Town*, London (1983), p.194.

Gainsborough and Horncastle theatres were taken by Smedley, and Louth passed to the Lincoln company, but audiences were still declining. William and Fanny Robertson shortened the seasons in the towns of their circuit and added brief stops in other towns, trying to make even more use of gatherings for fairs, horse-races and similar crowd-pulling events. Fanny's play *The Nun* (1833), performed in Lincoln on 22 November 1833, was a tale of Napoleon's conquest of Italy in 1797, and Fanny took the title role herself. On 2 December 1836 her other new play entitled *Louis XIII* (1836) was performed for her benefit.[4]

In the early 1830s bad nights and seasons were interspersed with good nights and seasons. In July 1832 Robertson's company at Peterborough were said to have had 'a very unprofitable season'. Yet in contrast to that, at Grantham in February 1832, and again in February 1833, the season was said to have been 'very successful' and the same was said about Smedley's 1832 visit to Spilsby.[5] An entry in Fanny Robertson's frank diary during a season at Oundle gives a pessimistic view of the state of things: "The theatre has been open four nights and the business bad, I fear I shall again lose a heavy sum and if so I think I shall sing 'Oundle Farewell!' A few days later the picture was a little brighter:

> *The great excitement of the week is over and within a few pounds of last year. Bad enough 'tis true but I am grateful even as it is. I have sent £20 to Boston, £20 to Newark and £5 to Wisbech so there is £45 debt paid. God give me the means through his mercy to pay everyone and I will ask no more.*[6]

Dame Madge Kendal later recounted that on one thirty mile 'stroll' with the company in the 1832-35 period, her father, William Robertson, Mr Chippendale and Henry Compton were walking together but one of them had only one shoe.

> *Under these circumstances there was only one thing to be done and to the credit of the profession they did it. They stuck by each other, as they always do, always have done and I hope always will do – and took it in turns to walk with a single shoe.*[7]

Noble patronage could help fill the theatres when they were there, which was not every night. On 22 January 1834 the Duke of Newcastle attended Retford theatre with his Duchess, the Earl and Countess of Winchilsea and younger members of both families. As a result of this the theatre 'was crowded almost to suffocation'.[8] On 1 and 3 June 1842 performances at Lincoln theatre were patronised by the Earl of Yarborough and Lord Worsley respectively, the Earl letting the band of the Lindsey Yeomanry attend and play 'a variety of airs' on the night of his bespeak,

---

[4] *SM*, 15 November 1833, 2 December 1836.
[5] *SM*, 3 February, 2 March, 27 July 1832, 15 February 1833.
[6] Warwick, Lou, *Theatre Unroyal; Or, They called them Comedians*, Northampton (1974), p.167.
[7] *Op. cit.*, p.63.
[8] *SM*, 31 January 1834.

Mr. MACREADY as VIRGINIUS.

"Does no one Speak?"

Above Right: William Charles Macready (1793–1873), one of the leading actors of his age, who visited Lincolnshire several times.
Courtesy of the Rare Book & Manuscript Library, University of Illinois at Urbana-Champaign

Above Left: Playbill, Stamford, 9 April 1824. Macready performing Virginius, *one of his famous roles, with Manly's company.*
Stamford Town Council

which had a good house.[9] During the general election in November 1832 Colonel Sibthorp, one of the candidates for Lincoln, bespoke a night's performance to rally his supporters and the house was filled in every part. That was supposed to be the last night of the season, but not all of his supporters got in so the Colonel bespoke a repeat performance the following night. Friends of the opposing candidate then announced a third 'last night' performance as a muster for their party and Robertson got a bumper house for that as well. Gentry like the Hartopps could have performances in their own halls and in 1839 members of the Tennyson D'Eyncourt family performed *One Hour, or, the Carnival Ball* and *The Widow of Wicklow* at Bayons Manor in Tealby.[10]

---

[9] *SM*, 27 May, 1842.
[10] Lincolnshire County Archives, TDE/H.171.

The appearance of stars from the London theatres sometimes boosted attendances, but not every time. Fanny had performed with Edmund Kean when he visited Lincolnshire in 1824 and she was again *Portia* to his *Shylock* in *the Merchant of Venice* when he visited once more in March 1831.[11] In January and February 1834 Fanny engaged a London star, Miss Eliza Patton, 'a popular and accomplished vocalist' to perform for a few nights at the theatres in Louth, Boston, Lincoln, Grantham and Newark. Her engagement at Lincoln on Wednesday 29 January was to 'a full house of rapturous applause', but the season as a whole was not so successful as it could have been and 'the weather' was blamed.[12]

In November 1834 Fanny brought William Charles Macready, the great tragedian, to Louth theatre for three nights but the reception was not good. On the first night he appeared in the character of *Virginius*, one of his famous roles, but the takings were only £3 12s 0d! It was said that Macready wanted to return to London straight away, without playing the other nights, but at the earnest entreaty of William Robertson he agreed to appear. On Monday evening he played *Hamlet* and £14 was taken at the doors.[13] Macready recorded this incident in his own diary in terms more favourable to himself, though we don't know which is the correct version. He said that on the first night of his engagement he was ready to go on stage when William Robertson appeared with a face full of dismay. The diary of the tragedian recalls:

> *He began to apologise and I guessed the remainder, Bad House?*
> *Bad, sir! There's no one!*
> *What, nobody at all?*
> *Not a soul, sir, except the Warden's party in the boxes.*
> *What the devil? Not one person in the pit or gallery? – Oh yes, there are one or two.*
> *Are there five? – Oh yes, five.*
> *Then go on: we have no right to give ourselves airs if the people do not choose to come and see us: go on at once!*
> *Mr Robertson was evidently astonished at what he thought my philosophy, being accustomed, as he said, to being blown up by his stars when the houses were bad.*[14]

Macready was back in June 1836 and appeared for three consecutive nights with Robertson's company in Wisbech to perform *Hamlet*, *Virginius* and *Macbeth*.

Most evenings there were no nobles or London stars and the theatre depended on the attraction of the local company to bring in the audience. In October 1836 the *Stamford Mercury* commented on the leading players in the Lincoln company:

> *A Mr Cooper takes the principal characters in tragedy and melodrama: the best thing we have seen him do is the Stranger. It was certainly a*

---

[11] *SM*, 25 March 1831.
[12] *SM*, 31 January 1834.
[13] *SM*, 21 November, 5 December 1834.
[14] Warwick, Lou, *op. cit.*, p.168.

personification of great excellence: cold as marble in the first part of the drama, and full of intense feeling in the conclusion of the piece. Of Mrs W. Robertson we can only say that her representation of Mrs Haller *in the play of* Kotzebue *just named,* Mrs Lockwood *in the* Farmer's Story, *(a new play on Friday last), and of* Lydia Languish *in Sheriden's fine comedy of* The Rivals, *on Monday last, were all and equally excellent. Mrs R. is certainly the gem of the Lincoln company. Of Mr Euston we must also speak in commendation, his skill as a living artist in a double sense was admirably evinced in the character of* Bristles *in the* Farmer's Story, *and not less so as* Captain Absolute. *Mr Ray is a capital performer: his* Sir Anthony Absolute *was surpassing on Monday last – no rant or extravagance – but passion enough to choke a man, escaping through the safety valves of his trembling limbs and piping voice, till it convulses you with admiration. Mr R.'s* Alley Croaker, *in one of the afterpieces, was nearly as good: it was most rich as a piece of uproarious humour. Mr Davidson, we need scarcely say, is as moving as ever – quite the prime requisite with the lovers of fun.*[15]

Fanny Robertson must have had mixed feelings at seeing William's wife called the gem of the company.

One effort to increase support for the theatre in Lincoln was an annual Shakespeare Dinner held each November from 1832, if not earlier, for a few years. In 1835 they dined at the City Arms, 23 The Strait, and it was suggested that future dinners could be held in the theatre itself. The 1835 dinner was on the table at 4 o'clock; tickets were 3s 6d each and those present included the Mayor, Colonel Sibthorp, MP, and William Robertson with the whole *corps dramatique.* There was talk of perhaps setting up a Shakespeare Club in Lincoln that might hold weekly 'social and convivial' meetings and could lead to greater support for the drama. But they were whistling in the wind and there are no later references to this dinner or club.[16]

Another lure to potential audiences was to put on adaptations of popular new novels. So the works of Walter Scott, including *The Heart of Midlothian,* and *Ivanhoe,* were quickly put on the stage, as were Charles Dickens' *Pickwick Papers, Nicholas Nickleby* and *A Christmas Carol.* Even Victor Hugo's *The Hunchback of Notre Dame* became the play *Esmeralda* (1836) performed in Spalding in September 1838. Those plays were adapted for the stage by other writers and few novelists wrote plays. One of the few authors who did write successful plays was Edward Bulwer-Lytton (1803-73) a Member of Parliament for Lincoln 1832-41 and a successful novelist, journalist and poet. Three plays he wrote, *The Lady of Lyon* (1838), *Richelieu* (1839), which gave the world the immortal line 'the pen is mightier than the sword', and

---

[15] *SM*, 28 October 1836.
[16] *SM*, 30 October, 6 November 1835.

Money (1840) were all performed in greater Lincolnshire in the 1840s, as well as an adaptation of his novel *Eugene Aram* (1832). As an MP he brought in the Bill abolishing the monopoly in serious drama hitherto held by Drury Lane and Covent Garden, as well as introducing dramatic copyright and attempting, without success, to end theatrical censorship by the Lord Chamberlain. 'The true censor of the age', he told the House of Commons, 'is the spirit of the age'.[17] Lincolnshire-born Alfred Tennyson also tried writing plays but not with much success.

Declining attendances at all local theatres and the dispersal of other troupes led the Lincoln company to change its long-established circuit. New towns were added, seasons in existing towns shortened and changed so that the newer places could be visited at fair times or race meetings. In May 1837 they opened the Lincoln theatre for one week during the fair, whereas the usual Lincoln season was from September to November, but theatre was now so tainted that it could not out-do the other entertainments provided by the fair. The attendance on the first night of the week to see Shakespeare's *Richard III* 'was a small one'.[18] On Saturday evening the house was again a very thin one, and would have been still more so, 'had not the presence of a few red coats enlivened it'.[19] Robertson's company then went to Grantham, which they usually visited at Christmas or just after. They were back at Lincoln in September 1837, but after only a week they went to Peterborough before returning to Lincoln to complete the season there. The next year Lincoln theatre opened for one week during the fair at the end of April, then closed for a short time and reopened at the end of May. No longer was there a regular pattern to the theatrical seasons.

The Louth company of comedians had been dissolved in October 1830 and Huggins' actors had to look for work with Robertson, Manly, Smedley or other managers. George Northouse, Huggins' leading comic actor, got the job of 'low comedian' with Robertson's company in place of Mr J O Gurner who had gone to Plymouth after ten years with the Lincoln company.[20] On 2 November 1838 *The Pickwickians*, (1838), based on *Pickwick Papers*, was performed at Lincoln to uncontrollable laughter and Northouse as *Weller the Elder* "was incontestably the cleverest hit in the piece". This play was repeated for his benefit a few days later, and he 'had the best benefit of the season, and the performance gave unqualified satisfaction'.[21] By November 1831, soon after he joined the Lincoln company, Northouse painted three sets of scenery for them. When he had a benefit in Boston on 9 April 1832 he painted a 'view of Boston Market Place ... expressly for this occasion' and for his benefit at Grantham on 16 February 1833 he introduced a view

---

[17] Bence-Jones, Marc, *The National Trust. Ancestral Houses*, London (1984), p.138.
[18] *SM*, 19 May 1837.
[19] *SM*, 26 May 1837.
[20] *SM*, 11 November 1831.
[21] *SM*, 9 and 16 November 1838.

of Grantham Market Place and an interior view of Peterborough Cathedral.[22] Despite his popularity he had retired from the stage by 1841 and was then living in lodgings in Red Lion Street, Boston. He continued his interest in painting, and decorated the temporary theatre at Market Deeping in 1842.[23] He died on 16 February 1844 after painting a view of the Sheep Fair in Wide Bargate, Boston, prints of which were for sale three months later.[24] Copies of this print can still be bought in the twenty-first century and are one of the few indications we have of what scenery may have looked like in a Lincolnshire theatre in Georgian times.

Theatre in the provinces might have been dying but some actors who first appeared in the 1830s went on to have successful national careers. Hull-born performer William Wallett (1813-92) began his working life as a scenery painter, odd job man and 'jobbing actor' and when young was looked after by Ann Smith, *née* Obey, also known as Nancy, who was a member of one of the companies of comedians who performed at Caistor, perhaps Smedley's. Wallett was quick witted and intelligent and developed a personal act as a clown, performing in circuses as well as on the stage. He adopted the dress of a traditional jester and after appearing before Queen Victoria in 1844 he styled himself 'The Queen's Jester'. He had a successful career throughout the kingdom and also visited the United States. On 26 April 1839 Wallett married his first wife, Mary Orme. As her father disapproved of the alliance the couple eloped from Hull and married in Lincoln. Henry Compton (1805-77) (born Charles Mackenzie in Huntingdon) came from Jackman's Bedford company in 1832 and joined Robertson's company before going for a spell at York in 1835. Compton eventually made the grade in London as one of the most popular light comedians of the day and the best Shakespearian clown of his generation.[25]

The political power of the middle class increased in the 1830s as King George IV was succeeded by William IV, who would support reform. In March 1831 at a performance in Lincoln theatre

> God Save the King *was well sung by the amateur performers and chorused by the audience who all gave three times three cheers for the Reforming King with the utmost enthusiasm.*[26]

A portrait of Henry Compton (Charles Mackenzie) (1805–77). A member of the Lincoln company of comedians 1832–35.
© *National Portrait Gallery*

---

[22] Gould, Mervyn, *Boston and Spalding Entertainment and the Aspland Howdens,* Wakefield (2005), p.12; *SM*, 11 November 1831, 15 February 1833.
[23] *SM*, 3 June 1842.
[24] *SM*, 24 May 1844.
[25] Warwick, Lou, *The McKenzies called Compton*, Northampton (1977), p.148.
[26] *SM*, 1 April 1831.

Parliament was reformed in 1832 and it then modernised other institutions. After 1835 the first election of members of the corporations running towns led to changes in political control in many places, and in Louth that killed the theatre. At a meeting of the new Corporation on 15 November 1836 its members considered the annual application by Fanny Robertson to hire the Guildhall for dramatic performances. The members were non-conformists who believed that theatre was immoral and they turned her application down.[27] In July 1838 Mrs Robertson applied again to use the Guildhall and the Mayor took it to the full Council but he got no support and the previous decision to refuse was confirmed.[28] That was the end of regular theatre in Louth, though in later years some alternative venues were used on an occasional basis and the Guildhall was used at least once more before its demolition in 1853.

As the love of drama was dying actors sank into poverty and theatre buildings were demolished or converted to other uses. In July 1835 James Hill had bought Wisbech theatre and refitted it with a painted ceiling based on Rubens, and mythological figures on the front of the two tiers of boxes. In 1837 he built an infant school in front of the theatre, completely hiding it, though the theatre still continued in occasional use. In 1840 Hill went bankrupt and the theatre was sold and became an auction room but in 1843 it was sold anew and reverted to theatrical use. William Robertson's company of comedians was there in 1846, Mr Davenport's Norfolk company performed there in May 1847 and it was still being used for lectures in January 1848.[29] In Walker and Craddock's *History of Wisbech* of 1849 it was described as

> a wretched building, but so situated among back lanes and back yards that its wretchedness is in private, as such things ought to be. It is merely four bare walls and a roof, painted and boxed in the interior into a tolerable illusion. Still, wretched as it is, it is too pretending for the poor fallen amusement for which it is appropriated, and it is now oftener opened to the auctioneer than to the heroes of the buskin.[30]

Playbill, Louth, 25 November 1833. Fanny Robertson's company includes Henry Compton who will sing a comic song in the interval as well as act in both plays.
Louth Museum

---

[27] SM, 18 November 1836.
[28] SM, 27 July 1838.
[29] SM, 10 April and 5 June 1846, 21 May 1847, 7 January 1848.
[30] Walker, Neil and Craddock, Thomas, *The History of Wisbech, and the Fens*, Wisbech (1849), p.429.

Top: Wisbech theatre – reconstruction drawing of the interior in Georgian times. Notice the passage under the boxes to get into the pit, and three trap doors in the stage floor.
Angles Theatre, Wisbech

Bottom: This picture shows the few people there might be in an 1838 audience.
From Charles Dickens, Nicholas Nickleby, 1838–39

In the late twentieth century both buildings became a theatre once more, called the Angles Centre, joined by a short and narrow staircase, with the old school now forming the foyer to the theatre.

In September 1837 Fanny Robertson was still the lessee of the Newark theatre, as she gave permission for an amateur performance there, but after that date there are no references to her company in that town until William Robertson took the company there in December 1846 for the last time.[31] That theatre had been put up for sale by auction on 29 July 1818, but it would appear that no sale was completed at that time. In Shilton's *History of Newark* published in 1820 he said the theatre was 'now owned by the Rev. Dr Fynes and the Rev. Dr Staunton who had inherited it in right of their wives who were the daughters of Job Brough, the original owner'. However, it is possible that Shilton may have written that before the 1818 sale.

In 1841 it was advertised as:

To be Let and entered upon immediately, all those premises hitherto occupied as a Theatre, capable of being converted into extensive warehouse, having Cellars underneath and a Tenement adjoining.

Despite that, its use as a theatre continued for several years yet and Abbott and Moseley gave a season there in February 1843.[32] A year later it was again put up for sale, and at that time was still 'fitted-up with Front and Side-boxes, a large Pit and Gallery, with seats, all of which may be taken at a valuation, or the whole may be sold if taken by a Person in Trade'.[33] An unnamed company appeared in May 1847 but one night there were only six in the house so the performance was cancelled.

Spalding theatre was 'tastefully fitted up as an auction room' by Mr Pigot from London in April 1838 though that was said to be done 'without detracting from its use as a playhouse'. The side and front boxes were filled, and many people were in the pit, but the centre of the pit was reserved for

---

[31] *SM*, 22 September 1837; Hemingway, G., *The Robertson Family and the Lincoln and Nottingham Theatrical Circuits*, thesis (1976), Lincoln Central Library, ref:UP 7467, p.76.
[32] Hemingway, *op. cit.*, p.75.
[33] *Ibid.*

the furniture for sale.[34] It was used for a dinner for teetotallers on 28 June 1838 to celebrate the coronation of Queen Victoria but a theatrical season started in the building on 3 September 1838.[35]

In Melton Mowbray the theatre/cockpit used by Smedley was sold and converted into a Mechanics Institute by September 1838.[36] Alford also lost its theatre sometime before 1840, and the local correspondent of the *Stamford Mercury* regarded that as a moral improvement.

> In no town has a greater change taken place in a few years than in Alford. Formerly it was like a little Vanity-fair, now it contains four chapels, and two others (a Baptist and a Warrenite Methodist) are erecting; a room also is shortly to be opened as a place of worship for the Roman Catholics. The theatre has long since ceased to be such, and has been converted into a temple of Justice.[37]

In 1842 the magistrates held Petty Sessions in Alford once every three weeks and after a police station was built in 1844 the court was held there instead of in the former theatre.[38]

The situation of drama in Lincolnshire was so dire that in December 1838 William Robertson declared that he intended not to visit Lincoln for two years, missing the usual season in the main town of his circuit.[39] In 1839 the owner of Boston theatre moved 'to a distant part of the Kingdom' and put the theatre up for sale. The description of the theatre said:

> On the ground floor, and having a separate entrance, are large Vaults recently fitted up and occupied by a Wine and Spirit Merchant, the underletting of which will go far towards paying the rent of the theatre, which, in addition to theatrical performance, may be profitably used for Lectures, Public Meetings, &c

At the auction on 24 September there were no takers, even though it was said that it would be sold cheap, and it continued as a playhouse for a few years more.[40]

In total contrast to what was happening in Lincolnshire, the Leicester theatre was replaced with a new, larger and grander building in 1836. Demolition of the old theatre started on 17 March and the new one was built over part of the site, at right angles to the old one and with a very grand entrance on Horsefair-street. It could hold about 1,300 people and was opened on 12 September 1836. A succession of managers

---

[34] *SM*, 20 April 1838.
[35] *SM*, 15 June, 31 August 1838.
[36] Smedley papers, LLHS/38/5/3/31, Lincolnshire County Archives.
[37] *SM*, 28 August 1840.
[38] *White's Directory of Lincolnshire 1842*, p.311; *Kelly's Directory of Lincolnshire 1849*.
[39] *SM*, 7 December 1838.
[40] Gould, *op. cit.*, p.13.

leased the theatre, the first for three seasons but several for less than that. They all suffered from small support and empty boxes, and struggled to pay the rent.[41]

As theatre seasons grew shorter the owners of playhouses welcomed alternative uses for their buildings, and these included campaigners fighting the evil of drink. Boston theatre became a regular meeting place for the Boston Teetotal Society in the late 1830s, with a lecture by W. Mumford, and other uses in 1838 included a Conservative dinner. In May 1839 there were lectures in Peterborough theatre by a delegate from the Anti-Corn-Law Association. More teetotal lectures were given in Boston theatre in early October 1841, and temperance lectures in Wisbech theatre in February 1844. Lincoln theatre in 1845 was used for a teetotal tea meeting one evening, and a meeting to petition Parliament to prohibit the sale of intoxicating drinks on Sundays on another.

In March 1839 Manly announced that he would not open Stamford theatre for the Mid Lent fair, 'the company having a better engagement in the North'; this was perhaps the first time in almost eighty years that the theatre was not open during the fair.[42] The company's other engagement was believed to be in Halifax, and in May his company may have been in Leeds as the wife of Mr F. Wass, one of his actors, died there. After forty years with the Stamford company Manly was worn out by 'the advance of age and its infirmities' and 1839 was the end of his acting career; he never again performed at Stamford though he continued to lease the theatre.[43] His health had probably been deteriorating for some time as his son Charles Manly was called acting manager of the company in 1836 and 1837.[44]

Thomas Manly's abandonment of Stamford tempted Fanny Robertson to try her luck in the town and her company started a season there in July 1839. But the *Mercury* reported that if the season 'should finish as it has begun, she will be minus something considerable by her visit. It seems as if the citizens generally do not feel disposed to patronise the drama, however effective and respectable the company may be'.[45] Despite her experience in Stamford, and what William had said earlier, Fanny decided not to abandon Lincoln altogether and put on a very short season, of only four nights during the races, from 26 September 1839. This proved a successful tactic and they had good attendance on each night. That 'season' of four nights instead of eight weeks was a reflection on how far interest in drama had deteriorated in twenty years. The company was back in November 1839 and something, perhaps the risk of losing their theatre altogether, led to a temporary

---

[41] Leacroft, Helen and Richard, *The Theatre in Leicestershire*, Leicester (1986), pp.37, 51, 52.
[42] *SM*, 1 March 1839.
[43] Golland, Jim, 'A Dramatic Discovery or, A Manly Enterprise', *Local History Magazine*, No.42, Nottingham (1994), p.14.
[44] Playbill, 29 July 1836, Stamford Town Hall collection; Rosenfeld, Sybil, 'The Theatrical Notebooks of T.H. Wilson Manly', *Theatre Notebook*, Vol.7, No.1, London (October, December 1952), p.45.
[45] *SM*, 5 July 1839.

revival of support. The *Stamford Mercury* attributed this mainly to the 'fashionable' moral approach of William the manager:

> ...having resorted to the representation of the legitimate drama, instead of presenting the pantomimic balderdash for which none save persons of depraved taste had relish.[46]

On the last night, Friday 29 November, William Robertson thanked his audience for the increased patronage during the latter half of the season, and stated his intention to visit Lincoln again in the following spring, 'with some metropolitan actor of accredited merit'.[47] The temporary revival of Lincoln theatre did not last. In May 1840, with the exception of one evening when the Earl of Yarborough's bespeak attracted a full house, the company 'have been playing nightly to thinner audiences than the zeal and taste exercised by [Mrs Robertson] at this festive season ought to have drawn together'.[48]

After his retirement Manly sublet Stamford theatre to one of his actors, Mr Boddie, who had been with the company since at least 1830, but that did not work well.[49] In March 1840 a dispute between Boddie and Manly about rent and 'pecuniary matters' led to the theatre being again closed for the Midlent fair.[50] Those matters were sorted by July and John Braham, a nationally famous singer, appeared at the theatre. At first he had poor houses and one night there were only twenty people at full price in the boxes, one in the pit, and half a dozen children in the gallery, the whole sum taken at the door being only £4. The *Mercury* castigated the people of the town for such poor support and the next Friday the house was full to overflowing.

> So crowded was the theatre, in boxes, pit and gallery, that standing room was not to be had, the passages were filled, and we believe many went away, being unable to obtain admission. So great was the throng, that the lady of high caste was glad to squeeze in between the humble sempstress and the plodding tradesman, and several went begging for admission from door to door of the boxes, but were unsuccessful. The receipts of the night amounted to about £50.[51]

This turnabout encouraged Boddie and in August 1840 he was confident enough to put on a whole month of performances at Stamford.

Then on Friday 20 November 1840 the whole situation of Stamford theatre changed. Thomas Manly died in Nottingham, aged 68.[52] He had joined the Stamford and Nottingham circuit in 1799, had been a manager since 1806, and had kept the

---

[46] *SM*, 22 November 1839.
[47] *SM*, 29 November 1839, 6 December 1839.
[48] *SM*, 29 May 1840.
[49] Playbill, 31 July 1830, Stamford Town Hall collection.
[50] *SM*, 27 March 1840.
[51] *SM*, 24 and 31 July 1840.
[52] *SM*, 27 November 1840.

circuit intact. But with his death its theatres were dispersed and other companies took the playhouses in different towns. Boddie's reign at Stamford came to a premature end and in December 1840 it was announced that Fanny Robertson had taken the lease of Stamford theatre and would visit the town at the usual periods, in place of the Nottingham company. She would take the scenery etc at a valuation.[53] In November 1841 her performers in Stamford were called 'highly creditable' and it was said that she had tempted back some people who had not been to the theatre for several years, 'who will hail Mrs Robertson's future visits to the town with a friendly and pleasurable interest'.[54] Stamford theatre remained part of the Lincoln circuit for most of the 1840s.

A Mr Baker took over Nottingham theatre and by September 1841 had also leased Leicester theatre 'with the Adelphi company'.[55] However just a few months later, in January 1842, the *Stamford Mercury* reported that Fanny Robertson had leased Leicester theatre, and the Leicester and Lincoln companies would be united 'at Lincoln races in September, previously to the public weeks at Spalding, Peterborough, Stamford, etc'. In 1840 it had been said that the professional season at Leicester theatre was 'only' three months in a year, but in 1843 it was down to just five weeks. On 14 October 1842 the *Leicester Journal* announced that the owners intended to sell the building to pay off their outstanding liabilities as the rental income was not sufficient, but it was several years before they found a buyer. The building of a large theatre had been over ambitious for the time. On 13 September 1842 the Lincoln company opened Leicester theatre for the race week but in mid October the attendances were thin, 'considering the array of talent the manager has with him'.[56] They attended Leicester theatre in September and October, after Whittlesey, for five successive years but by March 1847 Robertson had stopped visiting and the theatre was finally sold by auction for less than half what it had cost to build.[57] From 1847 to 1853 the lessee was Charles Gill and when he left there was a rumour that it would become a Corn Exchange or chapel, but it continued to struggle bravely on as a theatre. By 1845 the Nottingham theatre was leased by John Faucit Saville in succession to a Mr Skerrett, and when it was sold in 1854 Saville bought it for £1,950. Skerrett, like Boddie, had been an actor in Leicester theatre in 1834.[58]

Taking on extra theatres led to changes in the dates when the Lincoln company visited some towns as they wanted to be there when fairs or horse races were held. In September 1841 Fanny Robertson said that Spalding theatre would open for the fair nights, and then Peterborough for its fair nights, but then she would make

---

[53] *SM*, 18 December 1840.
[54] *SM*, 12 November 1841.
[55] *SM*, 3 September 1841.
[56] *SM*, 9 September, 28 October 1842.
[57] *SM*, 19 March 1847,
[58] Leacroft, *op. cit.*, pp.24, 52; Wood, A.C., 'Nottingham 1836-1865; 1.The Borough 1836-1865', *Transactions of the Thoroton Society*, Vol.LIX, Nottingham (1955), p.34.

a second visit to Peterborough on the 2nd, 4th and 9th of October because of the interruption of Stamford races. She would start her season at Stamford on the first night of their races, on 5 October, and it would be limited to five weeks. It was difficult to juggle all her dates with the races at Lincoln, Leicester and Stamford all coming close to fair weeks in Spalding and Peterborough.

Theatricals in Lincolnshire experienced a step-change about 1840 as Thomas Manly retired in 1839, Joseph Smedley broke up his troupe in 1840 and Stamford joined the Lincoln circuit in 1841. In the 1840s the circuit system was dying; theatres were closing and either being demolished or converted to more morally acceptable uses. Even the best provincial actors were faced with real poverty, food was scarce and clothing became shabby. In 1842 the *Stamford Mercury* said of actors: 'There is perhaps no class of society driven to have recourse to such miserable shifts to obtain a supply of this life's essentials, as are the unfortunate followers of the sock and buskin'. While professional actors were getting little support, amateurs of the 'Elocution Class' in Lincoln put on a performance in aid of the depressed funds of the Dispensary and 'were the means of attracting what is too much of a novelty, an overflowing audience'.[59] The irony was that two of the roles were taken by professionals from the Lincoln company, Mrs Margaret Robertson and Mr Cooper.

Fanny Robertson could still captivate her audience. In November 1836, when she was aged 68, it had been said that 'notwithstanding her age and decay of voice, [she] enchained the attention of the crowded audience by her sensible and spirited action'.[60] However difficult things were getting, she still kept high standards for her company and in November 1840 the acting at Lincoln theatre was said to be good:

> *in the lighter departments, singing and dancing, the company never was better qualified to suit modern taste. In the scenic and other arrangements of the kind, upon which much of effect depends, there has been an expenditure of skill and money unmerited by the scanty patronage: talent and art, and zeal in the theatre line, seem wasted on a Lincoln public, quite as much as in other places.*[61]

In 1842 at Wisbech it was said that 'the company of performers is decidedly the best we have had the pleasure of meeting in this place for many years' and Fanny Robertson had gone to 'a very serious expense in beautifying the theatre'.[62] The company included several new faces. By this time Fanny's supremacy on the local stage was being challenged by Margaret Robertson, the wife of William. Even in the early 1840s Fanny was still popular and for her benefit at Wisbech on 13 May 1842 the house was well filled, though overall the visit to that town was very unsuccessful.

---

[59] *SM*, 30 October, 6 November 1840.
[60] *SM*, 25 November 1836.
[61] *SM*, 11 December 1840.
[62] *SM*, 20 May 1842.

William Robertson had occasionally been referred to as manager since 1831 but his aunt Fanny had kept control. Only in 1843, at the age of 74, did she finally retire with farewell performances in the main towns of the circuit. At her farewell benefit in Lincoln on 12 January she announced that she had 'resigned the management to her nephew, Mr William Robertson', after having been in the company for half a century, which was a very long time. Her Lincoln farewell was as *Lady Elinor Irwin* in Mrs Inchbald's comedy *Every One Has His Fault* (1793).[63] Her final appearance in Boston was on 22 February and the elderly Pishey Thompson wrote in his diary of attending 'Mrs Robertson's benefit, who this night took leave of the stage. Poor old woman: I remember her almost as long as I can remember anything, and of her performance this evening it may truly be said 'Still in her ashes lives her wonted fire'. The house was very crowded and filled with well dressed but not fine people.' Thompson got home about midnight, and went to bed after cocoa.[64] In retirement Fanny Robertson lived in Wisbech, in 1851 occupying a house at the north end of Norfolk Street, close to the church.[65] That town had been part of the Lincoln circuit for many years and she and her husband had received regular support from the local Freemasons whenever the company performed there.

When William Robertson finally got control of the company he was, like his uncle before him, married to the company's leading lady. William and Margaret had twenty-two children, the fourth generation of Robertsons to appear on the Lincolnshire stage. Their eldest, Newark-born Thomas William Robertson (1829–71), acted in juvenile parts from the age of five in *Rob Roy* (1818), *Pizarro* and *The Stranger*, 'French' parts and eccentric comedy. About 1836 he went to school in Spalding and acted during his holidays. When he was fourteen he was withdrawn from school in Whittlesey in order to save fees. He returned home to write plays for a cast composed of his brothers and sisters, paint scenery, prompt and act in his father's company.[66] Thomas William and his sister Margaret (1848–1935), the latter as Madge Kendal, both later achieved fame on the national stage.

William Robertson's period of full control started well but that was not to last and it ended with the death of the company. Their February 1843 season at Boston was 'decidedly the best the company has experienced for some years' and in an optimistic gesture he announced that he had arranged to add 'the improving town of March, in Cambridgeshire, to the Lincoln circuit'.[67] From Boston they went to Wisbech, where it was noted that the company included not only new actors from the Leicester company, but also Miss Land the popular singer. We do not have a

---

[63] *SM*, 20 January 1843.
[64] Bailey, Isabel (ed), *Transcript of Pishey Thompson's Boston Diary, 18 October 1842 to 8 April 1844*, Boston (1994), p.48.
[65] 1851 census, information from Maureen Nichols.
[66] *SM*, 15 May 1845; Warwick, Lou, *Theatre Unroyal*, pp.63, 167; Donaldson, Walter, *Recollections of an Actor*, London (1865), pp.27-28.
[67] *SM*, 10 February 1843.

list of all the theatres where they performed in the 1840s. The pattern changed each year, and some towns got more than one visit as the company attended for fairs and race meetings. In May 1843 Robertson told the *Mercury* that he intended to adopt the system of 'quick action' and 'short seasons', and to include more large towns in his round. With this 'railway principle', as he called it (like a railway train travelling fast and stopping briefly in each station it passed through), he hoped that patronage would also revive in Stamford and Lincoln where he had found that long seasons produced large losses.[68] Some years the company was in Lincoln in January and back again in March or April. They were in Peterborough or Stamford in July or August, and after Peterborough they usually went to the neighbouring town of Whittlesey. In 1843 their venues included Lincoln, Boston, Wisbech, Stamford, Peterborough and Oundle, and in 1844 also Sheffield, Whittlesey and Leicester. As well as adding March and Sheffield, Robertson took the lease of Doncaster theatre when that became available in July 1845; there had been seven or eight applicants but the Town Council gave the lease to William.[69] Robertson still had the lease of Grantham theatre in December 1846 when he announced an amateur performance there.

In 1843 there was said to be a revival of the taste for drama in London, but no such symptoms were visible in Lincolnshire. Many local companies could barely scrape together a subsistence. Adam Stark, writing in 1843, implied that the magnates of Gainsborough were no longer in the habit of attending the theatre and that was true of most of the middle class throughout greater Lincolnshire.[70] The *Mercury* feared that numbers of patrons were falling off so much that many companies would shortly be extinguished. On 23 February 1845 actor/manager Mr B. Shaw wrote to Joseph Smedley asking to hire Wakefield theatre. When he had previously hired that theatre he had lost money because of the high rent Smedley demanded so now Shaw asked him to take one fifth of the gross receipts for a few nights instead of rent. Shaw's troupe had worked on that basis in Halifax, Leeds, Rochdale, York and Hull theatres. He employed eight people and unless they took £5 per night they lost money. He reminded Smedley: 'You are well aware business in our way is now good for nothing to what it formerly was.'[71] We do not know Smedley's reply to this plea.

On 19 April 1843 Stamford tradesmen arranged a bespeak that produced £40 on the night, but with declining support and competition from other amusements Robertson's losses for the season at Stamford were very serious – for nine nights in four weeks the average takings were less than twenty shillings. The season was so bad that the next year Robertson went to Sheffield instead of Stamford – only the third

---

[68] *SM*, 2 June 1843.
[69] *SM*, 1 August 1845.
[70] Stark, Adam, *The History and Antiquities of Gainsborough*, Gainsborough (2nd edn 1843), p.353.
[71] Smedley papers, LLHS/38/5/3/35, Lincolnshire County Archives.

time in nearly eighty years that the theatre was closed during the Mid-lent fair.[72] In some cases bespeaks were contrived by groups of local businessmen or theatre-supporters on a one-off basis. In July 1843 Robertson had a 'very indifferent' season in Peterborough and then moved to Oundle for a few days at the start of August. There he got such a 'gratifying and profitable reception' that he proposed paying the town another short visit before he left the district.[73] In fact on 7 August he announced that arrangements had been completed for the erection of a purpose-built theatre in Oundle and that he intended to open that theatre annually for a limited season each August.[74] The short-lived pleasure generated by an enthusiastic audience had temporarily blinded him to the real bleakness of his situation.

The company's annual progress was now so flexible that in 1844 William Robertson dropped Lincoln as he had previously dropped Stamford. This was despite the fact that the May 1843 season in the city had been 'considerably better attended than could have been anticipated' as the North Lincolnshire Yeomanry Cavalry were in the city for their annual training week. One night had been patronised by the Earl of Yarborough as Colonel Commandant of the cavalry, and another night by the Non-Commissioned Officers and Privates.[75] In June 1844 during the annual training week Robertson was in Wisbech instead, but that was an unproductive season with few gentry present. The old pattern of seasons had gone, and in March 1845 William Robertson announced that 'the dramatic season in the City of Lincoln will in future commence the last week in April and will continue until the Cavalry meeting in May. The Races and every Public Week will be punctually attended, constituting a visit of six weeks in every year.'[76]

The birth of the negro minstrel show, white singers performing with blackened faces, was on 6 February 1843 when the Virginia Minstrels performed at the Bowery Amphitheatre in New York. In December 1843 there was the first reference to a group of 'American Southern Minstrels', in Stamford and from then on blacked-up touring 'Minstrels' appeared regularly in Lincolnshire theatres.[77] In September 1846 'Ethiopian Serenaders' visited Gainsborough theatre, performing on the accordion, banjos, tambourine etc and playing a variety of what they called 'Nigger' melodies. The audience was remarkably small every evening.[78] In October 1846 the 'British Dancers', a troupe of thirty-six girls who danced with precise movements, appeared in Robertson's Lincoln theatre, but due to competition from other amusements the theatre was not so well patronised as it had been the previous year. Robertson then

---

[72] *SM*, 5 and 12 May 1843, 8 March 1844.
[73] *SM*, 14 and 28 July 1843, 4 August 1843.
[74] *SM*, 4 August 1843.
[75] *SM*, 2 June 1843.
[76] *SM*, 21 March 1845.
[77] *SM*, 15 December 1843.
[78] *SM*, 25 September 1846.

opened Grantham theatre with the British Dancers but he did so badly that 'several respectable gentlemen' decided to give an amateur performance, assisted by the ladies of William's company, to raise money for the company's general fund! The amateurs got such a good reception that Robertson 'influenced' them to put on a second performance on 5 December 1846.[79]

During a recession in May 1844 Robertson tried reducing prices to attract audiences, following the example of a circus that successfully combined a short visit to Stamford with cheap admission. This idea had been discussed in Lincoln in November 1836 when it was suggested that lowering the prices would create a greater demand for the drama but other people said that depreciating the value of the theatre would not increase its worth.[80] It was tried in February 1842 when Ira Aldridge was performing at Lincoln, but to no avail, showing that the low attendance was not due to prices but to 'the taste of the people'.[81] It was no more effective in May 1844 for William Robertson's benefit in Stamford: 'the attendance of our gentry in the boxes was anything but numerous. The reduced price of admission does not appear to have increased the box and pit audiences.'[82] Respectable tradesmen enjoyed the performances 'but 'the gentry' (so called) have almost forsaken the theatre, the average number in the boxes each evening has been 10 or 12 persons'.[83] On 22 July 1844 there was not a single person in the boxes. Robertson had presented the notorious Captain Harvey Tucket, who had fought a duel with Lord Cardigan, in Stamford for three nights in July and had then taken him to Peterborough theatre, but this gamble to attract the curious did not pay off. It was said that from March to July the manager had lost a considerable sum every week.[84]

The theatrical situation in Lincoln was so bad that in November 1844, when the Bullen family were performing there, Robertson had let the licence of the theatre expire and it was rumoured 'that the theatre is about to be disposed of'.[85] In January 1845 it was noted that many groups of strolling players had visited Lincoln during the winter, and most had done very badly. Some of them were in a shocking state of destitution. It was said to be 'no rare occurrence' for takings on some nights to be only 5/-.[86] The *Mercury* reported:

> *Persons of real talent who have visited Lincoln very recently have literally starved on the 'bountiful' patronage, and the proprietor of the theatre has all but forsaken Lincoln.*

---

[79] *SM*, 6 November, 4 December 1846.
[80] *SM*, 18 November 1836.
[81] *SM*, 25 February 1842.
[82] *SM*, 17 and 24 May 1844.
[83] *SM*, 14 June 1844.
[84] *SM*, 2 August 1844.
[85] *SM*, 22 November 1844.
[86] *SM*, 17 January 1845.

Edward Stirling later recalled:

> At Sheffield in 1846 my benefit was to be half the receipts of an evening. Mrs Robertson kindly invited me one evening to tea in a family way. The repast over, Mr Robertson quitted the room with all his children, leaving the baby, Mrs R and myself. She could talk as will be seen. She painted a mournful picture of bad business, expenses of a home, difficulty in paying actors and winding up with many compliments on my kindness of heart.

Stirling never did get his money; asked to wait first one week and then another he finished up months later with an offer of knives and spoons in lieu![87]

A concept that proved popular, though not enough to save the theatres of greater Lincolnshire, was the introduction of season tickets for the boxes. The idea was not new. In January 1778 Jemmy Whitley had proposed a subscription of 14/- for fourteen plays at Leicester theatre, each subscriber to receive a transferable silver token and in the 1820s Thomas Manly also had a system of season subscription by silver ticket.[88] William Robertson tried this system in Lincoln in May 1845, and gentlemen took all forty tickets at £1 each. He tried it at Stamford the following month, when the forty tickets at £1 each were again all taken up and '20 performances during the year were guaranteed for that sum'.[89] It was expected that this would encourage a good box audience at the rising of the curtain, and dispel the worries of those reluctant to visit the theatre in case they met a depressing scene of empty benches.[90] In April 1846 Robertson pushed the season ticket much more aggressively in the smaller town of Wisbech. He said that the opening of the theatre in June was dependent on the inhabitants taking 30 season tickets at £1 each

> the subscription to extend over one year, for which Mr Robertson guarantees 20 separate performances. The arrangement to include the engagement of *all* stars *that may be introduced in the course of the year; the ticket not to be transferable except to the family of the party taking them*

The response was good and many tickets for Wisbech were already taken by 10 April.[91]

The appearance of London stars in Lincolnshire theatres could sometimes still attract good audiences. In May 1845 the *Stamford Mercury* was glad to learn that Mr Robertson 'has reappeared in the county with his company' due to the success of his bringing 'stars' into Lincolnshire.[92] In April 1845 he hired Mr and Mrs Charles Kean (the former the son of the famous actor) from London to perform

---

[87] Warwick, Lou, *Theatre Unroyal*, p.168.
[88] Leacroft, op. cit., pp.10, 11; Rosenfeld, Sybil, 'The Theatrical Notebooks of T.H. Wilson Manly', *Theatre Notebook*, Vol.7, No.1, London (October, December 1952), p.4.
[89] *SM*, 2 and 30 May 1845.
[90] *SM*, 13 June 1845.
[91] *SM*, 10 April, 5 June 1846.
[92] *SM*, 15 May 1845.

at Stamford, Peterborough, Wisbech, Boston and Lincoln theatres for one, two or three nights in each place. These performers had been paid £1,000 for twenty nights' performance in Dublin and £100 per night in Plymouth and Exeter so he hoped they would be well patronised in his theatres.[93] They appeared for two nights at Stamford and on Friday, the second night, they attracted one of the most profitable houses seen there for a long time, the boxes, pit and gallery all being filled by the time the curtain rose. Even "several of the clergy" were present.[94] After the Keans came Mrs Fitzwilliams who appeared with Robertson's company in Lincoln, Boston, Stamford and Peterborough, and the Mayors of Boston and Lincoln each bespoke an evening. When William Macready performed at Stamford for a few days at the end of August 1845 'temporary stalls' were erected in the pit to supplement the boxes for the quality audience.[95]

Full houses for London stars were the exception and were not enough to keep theatres alive. Greater Lincolnshire lost another two theatres, Spalding and March, in 1845. Robert Gray, the owner of Spalding theatre in Broad Street, behind the White Hart inn, made 'considerable improvements to the interior' to change it from a theatre into a space for 'public exhibitions' and to provide 'a suitable place of amusement'. These 'improvements' were achieved by turning what he now called the 'dress circle' into refreshment rooms, and boarding over the pit.[96] The 'New Rooms' were opened with a Ball and Card Assembly on 3 April 1845. Concerts could be held in the Rooms and when required it could still become a temporary theatre.[97] In May 1845 'the commodious and pretty theatre at March, which for many years flourished under the respectable management of Mr Smedley', and which William Robertson had taken on as recently as 1843, was 'being converted into a room for the use of the British School, the declining taste for theatrical amusements being as evident in the fen towns as in more populous places.'[98]

In early 1846 Robertson must have been feeling optimistic about his future in Lincoln (or desperate) because he repainted and redecorated the theatre and had several new scenes painted. When he had adopted the 'railway principle' of visiting more towns and having shorter seasons, he said it should enable him to provide 'superior and attractive talent' and in February 1846 he was reported to have 'an almost entirely fresh dramatic corps'.[99] The house was 'fairly' patronised, and it was said that the educated classes were coming to it for 'agreeable relaxation and moral lessons'. Robertson had done some self-censorship and 'Coarse wit and indelicate

---

[93] *SM*, 21 March 1845.
[94] *SM*, 25 April 1845.
[95] *SM*, 22 August 1845.
[96] *SM*, 3 January 1845.
[97] *SM*, 21 March, 5 September 1845.
[98] *SM*, 2 May 1845.
[99] *SM*, 2 June 1843, 6 and 27 February 1846.

allusions have now been banished from the stage'.[100] The gallery was crowded by the lower classes, and it was considered that this was good for moral reform as it drew them away 'from bad old habits' and 'may impel them to fasten upon literature for satisfaction'.[101]

The decline in attendance on moral grounds had been worsening for decades, but in the 1840s there were additional factors that gave the *coup de grace* to the Georgian theatre. Railways now covered much of the country, reaching Peterborough in 1845, Lincoln and Stamford in 1846 and the rest of Lincolnshire two years later. They made the prosperous audience more mobile, giving them access to theatres in London and large provincial cities. There they could see the highest standards of performance and so become more aware and less satisfied with the local comedians. They could also do so without their censorious neighbours back home knowing that they had visited a theatre. The railways gave other touring companies easier access to Lincolnshire, and the Theatre Regulation Act, 1843 relaxed the restrictions of the 1737 Act and allowed the development of music halls. There was a severe economic depression so even the numbers in the gods fell off as money was needed for food and other necessities. There were more ephemeral causes as well, such as hot weather in summer and competition from political meetings at general elections as in 1842. In 1844 it was even suggested that poor attendance in Lincoln was due to the lack of effort to 'secure the residence here of persons forming the retired class, and who lead and give a taste to amusements', and competition from the Mechanics Institute and concerts.[102]

Without the middle classes local theatres were no longer financially viable. Theatre was dying throughout provincial Britain, not just in Lincolnshire, and the Norwich company of comedians that served theatres in East Anglia disbanded in 1843 following the opening of railways there in 1840.[103] The 1846 season in Stamford was a disaster. It started well on the first night of the races when Lord Burghley attended but things then fell off and on three or four evenings they were playing to empty benches. During part of the season the manager did not receive enough to pay the charges for gas and printing. On one evening the first three acts of *Othello* were played to a one-shilling house, and after the half-price receipts there was only 10s in the treasury.[104] As the middle class withdrew from local theatres, so more raucous elements formed an increasing proportion of the remaining audience and the auditorium when occupied was the scene of much more coarseness, vulgarity and tumult.

---

[100] *SM*, 6 March 1846.
[101] *SM*, 10 April 1846.
[102] *SM*, 29 November 1844.
[103] Taylor, David, 'Discoveries and recoveries in the laboratory of Georgian Drama', *New Theatre Quarterly*, Vol.27, No.3 (2011), p.230.
[104] *SM*, 14 and 28 August 1846.

One consequence of abandoning the old regular season dates, necessary though that may have been, was to let other companies into the proper theatres in main towns. The theatre in Gainsborough Old Hall was one of the few playhouses in the county that was not part of Robertson's circuit. As described in chapter 8 it was regularly visited by Huggins and then Smedley. After 1840 it was one of the venues taken over by John Mosley and his successive partners until May 1845, though they did not have exclusive use of it. In November 1841 it was reported that the improvements made by the managers had attracted playgoers.

> *Instead of empty benches, which used to be seen, a respectable audience is in nightly attendance, effective means having been adopted to put a stop to those disgusting shouts which were indulged in by a set of bacchanalians visiting the gallery; also smoking in the theatre is disallowed, and a reduction of the price has been made.*[105]

By the 1840s other amusements were available at the time of horse races and fairs, and the theatres suffered. Competition even came from travelling troupes of actors, who set up temporary theatres in tents and could undercut the theatre prices to draw away working-class playgoers. At Gainsborough Mart in November 1842 there were 'two companies of the Shakespeare family' though neither was in the theatre, which was occupied by a boxing match. Later in November, after the Mart, one of these, 'Rickatson's' company, managed by a Mr Strutt, moved into the theatre.[106] They issued handbills for *Rob Roy* and other pieces but they failed to attract an audience despite reducing the prices. There was a mere sprinkling in the pit and very few gods in the gallery. As luck would have it, just in the nick of time, when Mr Strutt was meditating a flight, 'the celebrated Mr Green with a Parisian company of rope-dancers and jugglers' arrived and wanted the theatre. Mr Strutt held the key and 'possession is nine points of the law', so he set conditions including a free benefit for himself before handing over the theatre. However, on the night of the benefit 'everything was as still as the tomb' so the actors all absconded. Mr Green was not inclined to take on the theatre, and with it the bills left unpaid by the actors, so he put on his performance at the Cross Keys inn instead.[107]

There were performances in Gainsborough theatre in March 1847, the lessee and manager being a Mr Sankey. An amateur play was to be put on during the following week, but the lead actor was 'suddenly indisposed' and a professional actor, Edgar Newby, stepped in.[108] Sankey reopened the theatre in the middle of April and put on a season that was longer than Mosley's of two years before. It was said that there

---

[105] *SM*, 12 November 1841.
[106] *SM*, 4 and 18 November 1842, 2 December 1842.
[107] *SM*, 18 November 1842, 2 December 1842.
[108] *SM*, 2, 9 and 23 April 1847; Parker, B.J., *The Theatre of Gainsborough. From 1772 until 1850*, thesis (1963) held in Gainsborough Library, p.27.

had been good numbers in the gallery and a small circle in the boxes, but overall Gainsborough people did not support the theatre well. At the end of April 1847 the leading roles in two of Shakespeare's plays were taken by a visiting actor, George Owen. There was a small attendance for *Othello* and when he played *Hamlet* for his benefit a delay occurred at the end of the second act. It was said that an accident had happened to Mrs Newby, the leading lady, and the play resumed after a delay of an hour. There was then another pause, and in reality the delay was caused by Mr Hayes, one of the actors, who refused to go on until Owen had paid all the performers their share of the proceeds of the evening. Even when the play was proceeding it was difficult to follow because Owen's father was in a box and clapped, cheered and thumped his stick at the end of every piece spoken by his son, and his example was followed by the gods in the gallery.[109] The season at Gainsborough finally ended on 5 May 1847 when *Pizarro* was performed for Mr Newby's benefit.

> *As all the ladies had taken their departure except Mrs Edgar Newby, that talented actress had to double every part, which she accomplished with surprising ability. A similar feat has seldom, if ever, been performed in Gainsborough theatre.*[110]

By June 1846 Robertson had given up the lease of Boston theatre and it had been taken by London-born Thomas Fricker (1812-58). Fricker had arrived in Stamford by 1838 and edited the *Lincolnshire Chronicle* newspaper but also wrote plays in 1837, 1838 and 1839 of which the latter two were performed there. Fricker moved to Boston and bought the Tory *Lincolnshire Herald* as well as leasing the theatre, and was later also Borough Coroner.[111] His printing office was at 12 or 13 Red Lion Street, close to the theatre. The Boston magistrates disapproved of some of Fricker's attempts to make the theatre pay and imposed extra conditions on him. They stipulated that 'itinerant players in booths, discharged by the Mayor and Magistrates, shall not be permitted to take refuge in the theatre, there to enact plays and other performances', and 'that, as the theatre is licensed for *dramatic* performances only, no other use shall be made of the same, unless by permission of the Mayor and Magistrates'.[112]

On 15 January 1847 William Robertson opened the Lincoln theatre but week after week was a losing affair. Despite that, he gave a night's benefit for the Widows and Orphans Fund of the Manchester Unity of Oddfellows, and as he had lost money himself that was considered a very Christian gesture. He opened Stamford theatre on 17 March 1847, but the season was a very bad one and again at the end there was special patronage by leading families to try to attract a larger audience. He was back to Lincoln theatre at the start of April 1847 for a short season that continued

---

[109] *SM*, 7 May 1847.
[110] *SM*, 14 May 1847.
[111] Bagley, George S., *Boston, Its Story and People*, Boston (1986), p.270.
[112] *SM*, 19 June 1846.

during the fair. On 16 April 1847 a group of amateurs put on a performance to raise funds for the benefit of the manager and a good attendance was expected as the public seemed to think that a worthy cause. They raised £10 15s and as only 15s were claimed as expenses they handed over £10. It was a sign of theatre's near-fatal condition that professional actors were becoming dependent on charity raised by amateur players. By April 1847 Robertson had given up Wisbech theatre and Mr Davenport, lessee of King's Lynn and other theatres in Norfolk, obtained a licence to perform there. Davenport opened it on 17 May for a season of five or six weeks but got poor support.[113]

In July 1847 the *Stamford Mercury* complained:

> ...the abuse of the Stamford theatre is becoming a matter of notoriety, the place is now used by every set of vagabonds who happen to enter the town. It was said that Mr Robertson's licence for the theatre expires this week, and some doubt arises whether it will be renewed. We hear that the fees due to the magistrates' clerk for the present licence have not been paid although a year has elapsed since the licence was granted.[114]

Robertson announced his own benefit on 23 July 1847, and at the same time revealed 'that it is not his intention to apply for a renewal of his licence (which expired some days since) to open the theatre'. On 6 August 1847 there was a bespeak at Stamford theatre under the patronage of 'a Committee and Friends of the Marquis of Granby and Mr Herries' for which Mr Robertson's company came specially from Peterborough. The receipts amounted to little more than £23 and Robertson announced that it would be the last time the theatre would open under his management.[115] Performances by Robertson at Stamford came to an end, not with a bang but a whimper.

William Robertson had given up the Boston, Wisbech and Stamford theatres, and at the same time he also withdrew from the Lincoln theatre, where four generations of his family had performed for 75 years. He had virtually given up the battle, but did not leave Lincolnshire immediately, and during the next two years he still toured theatres in Boston and some smaller places. Perhaps it was because his family had been here for so long that it took him a while to sever his links with this county.

---

[113] *SM*, 2 April 1847, 21 and 28 May 1847.
[114] *SM*, 16 August 1847.
[115] *SM*, 23 August 1847; Hemingway, *op. cit.*, p.48.

Travelling actors at a turnpike toll gate, about 1825. From Pierce Egan, *The Life of an Actor* (1825).

10

LAST OF THE COMEDIANS

AFTER DEATH a body may twitch and show a few false signs of life. That was the state of theatre in Lincolnshire in the late 1840s, as the last companies of comedians toured the county.

Acording to the *Stamford Mercury* in 1850:

> *Almost every one is aware that the theatrical life is one of terrible privation and misery; some of the actors are now at their wit's end – absolutely starving. Anyone with common sense would rather break stones on the roads than take to the stage. One occupation gets bread, the other a mere sop to vanity.*[1]

In September 1850 the local paper in Newark said that 'it is quite evident that the Drama has had its day in this locality', and in 1853 that theatre was converted into a shop and dwelling.[2] By 1850 most theatres in and around the county were closed. Some had been demolished and others converted to schools, chapels, mechanics institutes or corn exchanges. Only four playhouses were left by mid century and two of those closed later. There were temporary theatres in use for a while, and later music halls arrived in some places.

Railways had reached many Lincolnshire towns by 1850 and that made it quicker and cheaper to travel to London and other major cities than it had ever been by stagecoach. Middle class professional people had for many years been able to visit London on business or pleasure, and see plays in Covent Garden or Drury Lane in the evening, as Matthew Flinders of Donington did in October 1796.[3] Railways now made this easier. As local theatres closed such travel became a necessity, not just an option, for those who still wanted to enjoy drama. In spring 1850 it was reported in Newark that 'during last winter the cheap trains to Nottingham have been more largely patronised than ever' as 'large sections of the Newark public' now had to travel away in search of theatrical performances.[4]

---

[1] *Stamford Mercury*, 12 July 1850.
[2] Hemingway, G., *The Robertson Family and the Lincoln and Nottingham Theatrical Circuits*, thesis (1976), Lincoln Central Library, ref.UP 7467, p.76.
[3] Beardsley, Martyn and Bennett, Nicholas (eds), *Grateful to Providence. The Diary and Accounts of Matthew Flinders, Surgeon, Apothecary and Man-Midwife 1775-1802*, Vol.2 1785-1802, Lincoln Record Society Vol.97, Lincoln (2009), pp.172-73.
[4] Warner, Tim, 'Curtain rises on the town's first theatre', *Newark Civic Trust Magazine* Issue 68, Newark (February 2013), p.16.

True lovers of drama found it hard to believe what was really happening. In 1849 Walker and Craddock of Wisbech wrote optimistically that their theatre was not likely to be wholly abandoned.

> The drama is no more dying, as many pretend, than the oak is dying when it sheds its leaves in autumn. It is based too firmly on the nature, and the senses, and the feelings of mankind ever to be overthrown either by commerce, art or prejudice. The noblest men that ever lived have consecrated it in a hundred immortal forms, and their detractors are to them only 'as the gourd compared with the cedar.' When France forgets Moliere, and Spain Calderon, and Germany Schiller, and England Shakespeare, and all of them forget Sophocles, the drama may perish – but not till then.[5]

They were right in the sense that theatres survived in London and major cities, but 1849 was the year when died the last Lincolnshire companies of professional actors. The demise of the Norwich company of comedians and closure of theatres in Yorkshire show that drama was dying not only in Lincolnshire but in other counties as well.

After William Robertson gave up Stamford and Lincoln theatres in 1847 his company continued, like a ghostly presence, to perform in other Lincolnshire towns for a couple more years. At the same time an energetic new incomer, John Caple, worked strenuously and valiantly for two and a half years to try to keep a circuit of playhouses open in the county. Many theatres, purpose built or temporary, were last used during the 1840s. Those at Market Deeping and Spilsby were not referred to after 1842, and Market Rasen, Barton, Louth and Oundle were last mentioned in 1843. In 1845 March theatre became a school while Spalding theatre was converted into the 'New Rooms'. Then Peterborough theatre was sold and demolished in 1847, Wisbech last mentioned in 1848, and Gainsborough removed from the Old Hall in June 1849. Grantham became a chapel in 1850, Boston was demolished and Melton Mowbray was last mentioned that year. Within Lincolnshire the few purpose-built theatres left by mid century were in Stamford, Lincoln, Sleaford and Grimsby. The theatre at Holbeach had been one use of the public rooms opened in 1829, and that building in Park Road continued as assembly rooms under the name of the Public Hall.[6] Newark theatre was finally sold on 15 December 1852, still with its seats and fittings, and in February 1853 was 'about to be converted into a dwelling-house and shop, and the back part of the premises into workshops and a warehouse'. The change was completed that autumn.[7]

For a while William Robertson still toured Lincolnshire. On 24 August 1847 his company started a season at Spalding with *Othello* played by 'an African', who was

---

[5] Walker, Neil and Craddock, Thomas, *The History of Wisbech, and the Fens*, Wisbech (1849), pp.429-30.
[6] Saunders, John, Jnr., *Lincolnshire in 1836*, Lincoln (1836), p.90.
[7] Hemingway, *op. cit.*, p.76.

probably Ira Aldridge once again.[8] On 2 December his company opened at Alford and there was a good house on the first night for *The Stranger*. Robertson brought other American actors to Lincolnshire in his company's twilight years. In June 1846 in Wisbech they included the sisters Fanny and Julia Wallack who had made their debut in December 1839 at the New Chatham Theatre in Bowery, New York.[9] Then in November and December 1848 a star of the company in Boston (Lincolnshire) was George Vandenhoff (1820-84), with his daughter. He was a British born actor who had gone to New York in 1842 and also performed in New Orleans and other southwestern cities.[10]

Two events in Peterborough illustrate the condition of the drama in this area by mid century. The first was the sale of the theatre on 9 October 1847 when it was described as a 'large and extensive stone, brick and slate building, formerly used as a theatre'.[11] Kelly's Directory for that year described the theatre as 'a small building in Church Street, but in a bad state of repair'.[12] It was purchased for £610 by Andrew Percival, Esq, a solicitor, on behalf of the clergy in the Minster-yard, who wanted to prevent its possible conversion into a Roman Catholic chapel. The clergy did not have any use for the building themselves and in December it was put up for sale again with restrictions that would prevent its use by comedians, Roman Catholics or other Dissenters.[13] Peterborough Corn Exchange Company was formed on 23 December 1847 and it purchased the site of the theatre for £525.[14] The financial loss to the clergy was a sacrifice they evidently thought worth paying to rid their city of an institution they considered undesirable. The Corn Exchange, where farmers and merchants could buy and sell corn, was quickly built on the site and was opened on 30 September 1848.[15] It closed in 1962 and was pulled down in June

Peterborough Corn Exchange was built in 1848 on the site of the former theatre, next door to the parish church.
Vivacity, Peterborough

---

[8] *SM*, 27 August 1847.
[9] *SM*, 5 June 1846.
[10] *SM*, 8 and 22 December 1848; Hughes, Glenn, *A History of the American Theatre 1700-1950*, New York (1950), pp.140, 141, 164.
[11] *SM*, 8 October 1847.
[12] Hemingway, *op. cit.*, p.60.
[13] *SM*, 22 and 29 October 1847, 10 December 1847.
[14] Bull, June and Vernon, *Peterborough Then and Now*, Stroud (2013), p.8.
[15] *SM*, 4 February, 3 March, 15 September 1848.

1964 to be replaced by an office block for the Norwich Union insurance company. That later became the Central Post office which was demolished in November 2009 to create the open space of St John's Square completed in 2011.

The second event came in March 1848, a few months after the theatre was first sold. Peterborough was thrown into excitement by the discovery of starving children in the house of two women called Green who were 'milliners and schoolmistresses' and lived at the back of the theatre. The children were Georgiana and Ellen Robertson, aged 11 and 5, daughters of William Robertson. As he had a large family, and it was inconvenient to take the younger ones with him on tour, he boarded them in the towns which he visited. The girls had been left in Peterborough for some time, but with the Greens for only the last six months. The 'very marked decline of the theatrical business throughout his circuit' left him short of cash and the payment of the children's board was neglected. The Greens could not afford to keep the children without payment so they applied to the Board of Guardians and received an allowance, but it was said that the money had not been spent on supporting the children. The occupation of the women as milliners, and the location of their house at the back of the theatre, suggests that they had been dress-makers employed by the theatre and had lost part of their livelihoods when the theatre closed. They were ably defended by Mr Percival and the magistrates released the women on bail, with two sureties each, to answer any charge that may be made against them at the Quarter Sessions. A crowd had gathered outside the court and the women, at their own request, stayed several hours in the building until the people had gone and it was safe for them to leave. No more is heard of this case, so evidently the authorities decided to take it no further.[16]

In April 1848 it was said that 'so completely has the taste for the drama declined in the provincial districts that [Robertson's] once respectable company has been entirely broken up, and its leaders reduced to the greatest poverty'.[17] Despite his almost penniless state, William still kept performing in his old stomping ground until early 1849. The last reference to Wisbech theatre being used was in January 1848 so for a week in August 1848 'a portable theatre' for 'William Robertson and his family' was erected in Pickard's Lane, Wisbech and they used that instead of the old theatre. It was said that the moveable theatre, made of wood, had been built by Mr Parlett of Wisbech, 'for Mr Mildenhal'.[18] Some groups still bespoke plays and one night was under the patronage of the Wisbech Cricket Club. Boston was no longer visited on a regular basis but in 1848 Robertson hired that theatre during the May fair and went back for a second season there in November 1848, when it was said that they 'have met with a little more support than usual'.[19] In December they

---

[16] *SM*, 31 March 1848.
[17] *SM*, 21 April 1848.
[18] *SM*, 4 August 1848.
[19] *SM*, 28 April, 24 November 1848.

had a bespeak by the Mayor, Meaburn Staniland, but when the season ended in January 1849 it was called 'a long and losing' campaign; the 'histrionic art seems to be ill appreciated in the town, and even the "Gods" have forsaken their wonted place in the theatre'.[20] On 26 February 1849 Robertson opened a theatre in Brigg, a town which had not seen theatricals for many years.[21] That seems to be the last reference to him in Lincolnshire, and he then moved to London, taking his family with him. So Lincolnshire lost the family that through four generations had provided drama, comedy, song and dance, and brought to the county some of the greatest stars of the London stage. The Robertsons joined Whitley, Manly, Huggins and Smedley as a distinguished part of the county's theatrical history.

After William Robertson gave up the permanent theatres in the county and became a stroller, an ambitious young manager appeared on the scene. As Dr Frankenstein stimulated a lifeless body in the novel of that name, so an energetic John Caple sought to bring the Georgian drama in Lincolnshire back to life, but with less success than Mary Shelley's literary creation. This young man, born in Herefordshire in the early nineteenth century, had positive ideas and set about leasing theatres in Lincolnshire and elsewhere. In July 1847 he took Lincoln theatre and refitted it, got new and excellent scenery, and engaged a 'well-selected' company.[22] In the lease Caple gave two addresses, one at 18 Butchers Street, Lincoln, close to the theatre, and the other at Great Russell Street, London. His season in Lincoln started on 22 September with *The Merchant of Venice*. His leading lady was Miss Eleanor Goddard and his leading man James Bennett. By offering Shakespeare and other serious drama Caple started to attract back former patrons. On 1 October 1847, during the races, the theatre was 'crowded to the roof ... and numbers could not gain admission', but during the following week the audience was rather scanty though several respectable houses were achieved in the week after that. The *Stamford Mercury* said that 'nothing could be sunk into more disrepute than the drama lately was in Lincoln' and 'the success of this first season of the "new series" is highly gratifying'.[23] By the end of October Caple's company included Mr Hazlewood, formerly in William Robertson's company, who was said to be 'a very clever comedian' who had briefly tried his own company at Newark and Grantham during September 1847.[24]

Following his success at Lincoln, John Caple sought to create a Lincoln circuit of his own, adding Grantham, Stamford and Gainsborough, and later looked beyond the county. In October 1847 he leased Grantham theatre 'and proposed thoroughly refitting it'.[25] His season there opened in late November and on the night of the

---

[20] *SM*, 19 January 1849.
[21] *SM*, 2 March 1849.
[22] *SM*, 23 July 1847.
[23] *SM*, 1, 8, 15 and 22 October, 19 November 1847.
[24] *SM*, 3 September, 29 October 1847.
[25] *SM*, 29 October 1847.

The neglected state of Stamford theatre in 1948.
From Richard Southern, The Georgian Playhouse *(1948).*

Mayor's bespeak the house was crowded everywhere except the upper boxes but when it closed on 21 December Caple had not done much better than Robertson. He had incurred great expense in refitting and refurnishing the theatre, and brought a very respectable and talented company, but it was feared that he had made a considerable loss. He had tried to revive the taste for the legitimate drama but 'if another season should pass as disregarded as this', said the *Mercury,* 'the Grantham theatre in all probability will finally close'.[26] From the beginning Caple was fighting pessimism as well as moral fundamentalism, and the expectation was that he would fail.

Caple opened Lincoln theatre on 27 March 1848 for another season of five nights during the races. New scenery had been painted by Mr Fisher from the Queen's Theatre, Manchester, 'in addition to which will be exhibited a new and magnificent Act Drop'. The company had been 'most carefully selected and improved', and consisted of 'established favourites from the principal provincial theatres'. The

---

[26] *SM,* 24 December 1847.

orchestra was conducted by Mr Rogers, from the Theatre Royal, Dublin. In his eagerness to promote his theatres in Lincoln and Stamford, Caple described them in the bills as 'Theatre Royal' but soon dropped that name as they had no right to use it. Lincoln theatre was not to become 'Royal' until the late nineteenth century.[27]

Caple then leased Stamford theatre and opened it at the beginning of April 1848 for the mid-Lent fair, but he had to compete with two separate dramatic troupes who each put on a tragedy and a pantomime in their temporary structures on the Sheep-Market and St Peter's Hill. A full list of his actors was printed in the playbill and these are listed in Appendix 6.[28] On 24 April Caple opened Lincoln theatre for the fair week only and he had also taken the Gainsborough theatre for a short season that would start at the end of the month. He started a second 1848 season at Stamford in mid-July, and reduced his prices to pit 1s, and gallery 6d. That season finished on 7 August, and it was said that his company was spoken of as 'being liberal and judicious, and that several members of his company (which is more extensive than Stamford audiences have been accustomed to) have made a favourable impression'. His company were said to 'elevate the legitimate drama, and discourage productions that do not convey instruction as well as amusement'.[29] Caple was also looking beyond Lincolnshire, and by July 1848 he had 'engaged and re-fitted Macclesfield theatre' in Cheshire. In October 1848 he closed a successful season at Dumfries in Scotland, then in November he was at Whitehaven in Cumberland and was said to have contributed very liberally to a fund for widows and orphans of colliers killed in a recent coal-mine explosion.[30]

In December 1848 very extensive alterations were made in the theatre at Stamford, at the joint expense of Caple and his landlord, Lord Exeter. A new stage was laid down, at a lower level than the old one, and the floor of the pit was also lowered 'thus effecting a greater separation between the pit and the boxes'. The entire house was redecorated, and it was to be made warm and comfortable.

> The decorations are exceedingly tasteful, the interior of the boxes is splendidly papered, the front panels of the lower tier are moulded and ornamented with landscapes, and those of the upper with scenes from the most popular of Shakespeare's plays. A new drop-scene, said to be a Sicilian view, adds to the novel appearance of the house.

There were two Private Boxes in the Dress Circle which cost patrons 4s or one guinea for six persons, compared with 3s and 2s for the lower and upper boxes. When the work was finished Stamford theatre was said to be 'one of the prettiest places of amusement outside London. The metamorphosis from sombre to gay is complete and an air of elegant comfort pervades the entire building.'[31]

---

[27] *SM*, 24 and 31 March 1848.
[28] *SM*, 7 April 1848; Playbill, 3 April 1848, Stamford Town Hall collection.
[29] *SM*, 14 July, 11 August 1848.
[30] *SM*, 7 July, 27 October, 24 November 1848.
[31] *SM*, 15 December 1848, 23 March 1849.

John Caple was leading the last ditch fight for drama in Lincolnshire and expending great energy and resources. He started a Lincoln season on 8 January 1849. In the first week it was quite promising and they had good audiences on several nights but when the season closed on 10 March it had been 'far from a profitable one'.[32] Ira Aldridge appeared as *Othello* and as *Mungo* in *The Padlock* (1768). As Caple was opening theatres in several parts of the country he left 'acting managers' or 'stage managers' in local control or sublet the playhouses to other actor-managers. In March 1849 there was a benefit for Mr Henderson, the stage-manager of Caple's theatres, who was said to be 'entitled to great praise for the excellent and consistent style in which he puts pieces upon the stage'.[33] He was said to have come from Birmingham and could be the Henderson who briefly had a company of his own in Lincolnshire in 1843 and may then have joined Robertson's company. In Stamford when the theatre opened in March 1849 during the mid-Lent fair the sub-lessee, or 'acting manager' as he styled himself, was John Faucit Saville who had previously performed in London in the Haymarket, St James' and Adelphi theatres.[34] He was also lessee of the Sheffield, Nottingham and Derby theatres having taken them after the break-up of the Stamford and Nottingham circuit.[35] Unfortunately Stamford was a sorry speculation for Saville and it was said that the visit resulted in a loss of £50 to the manager.[36]

Grantham theatre, like Stamford, was also sublet and in both cases this was said to be because Caple had leased the Queen's Theatre, Hull, which he thought would be a better speculation. His subtenant at Grantham in April 1849 was Mr W.H. Maddocks from Salisbury, but the magistrates objected to the change as they had given their licence to Caple, and Maddocks had to obtain a licence from them in his own name. They required him to close the theatre during the week before Easter, as was usual, and in fairness to him the Mayor also made some temporary theatres, that had been put up for the fair, to also close during Passion Week. Maddocks had perhaps been misled about the popularity of the theatre in Grantham, 'and the old repute of the town for theatrical success', and he expected to make a loss on his visit.

> *It would appear that the taste or fashion for theatrical amusements, which has been long on the wane, cannot be revived, and that no merit on the part of managers or actors can retrieve affairs. People will crowd*

---

[32] *SM*, 16 March 1849.
[33] *SM*, 12 January, 2 March 1849.
[34] Playbill, 26 March 1849, Stamford Town Hall collection.
[35] Warwick, Lou, *Theatre Unroyal; Or, They called them Comedians*, Northampton (1974), p.196.
[36] *SM*, 6 April 1849.

to the circus to see a horse gallop round a ring, but they will not sit and listen to Shakespeare, Knowles or Bulwer! declared the *Mercury*.[37]

After leaving Grantham Maddocks went to Lincoln theatre for the pleasure fair, and some tolerable houses were attracted in the first week, but later attendances were not good. The season was said to be a most unprofitable one due to 'the present financial state of Lincoln'.[38] Maddocks went back to Grantham after Easter and the season there ended on 17 May 1849. It was said to be disastrous for the manager so several gentlemen gave amateur assistance to the last night to try to boost his takings. However, it was once again thought 'probable that Grantham theatre will not be opened again for the purpose of drama'.[39]

In June 1849 Caple brought the principal members of 'the Drury-lane opera company' to put on grand concerts in Gainsborough, Lincoln, Boston and Stamford theatres. The boxes in Gainsborough theatre were crowded, but the attendance in the pit and gallery was not numerous. The concerts at Stamford, Lincoln and Boston were highly successful and filled the respective theatres.[40] In July he brought the famed singer Charles Braham, son of the veteran singer, to perform in Lincoln and Boston theatres. Attendance was low, and it was noted that 'a summer evening's walk is in many respects preferable to the atmosphere of a theatre' but it was still suggested that 'if the enterprising manager would visit Boston in the winter season, he would meet with a large share of support'.[41] However bad things were, there always seemed to be some encouragement, but throughout the year the *Stamford Mercury* kept reiterating that individual theatres were not expected to reopen.

John Saville having lost money on Stamford theatre during the mid-Lent fair a couple of months earlier, Caple brought his own company to the town in July 1849. However, his exertions were 'niggardly rewarded, and the probability is that, unless a change for the better should soon take place, the manager will be compelled to retire from the struggle he has energetically made to revive a taste for the rational recreation afforded by the stage'.[42] This season at Stamford was most unsuccessful and Caple lost money. He had spent a lot on stage decorations and appointments, but the poor attendance by the public was 'such as to render it doubtful whether

Part of a Stamford playbill, 3 August 1849. John Caple's last season there, with a benefit for his leading lady Miss Goddard.
Stamford Town Council

---

[37] *SM*, 20 April 1849.
[38] *SM*, 27 April, 4 and 11 May 1849.
[39] *SM*, 25 May 1849.
[40] *SM*, 8, 15 and 22 June 1849.
[41] *SM*, 6 and 13 July 1849.
[42] *SM*, 27 July 1849.

Right: The western facade of Grantham theatre during its demolition in September 1952.
John Pinchbeck

Below: The north side of Grantham theatre during its demolition, two openings showing the height of the ground floor beneath the auditorium.
John Pinchbeck

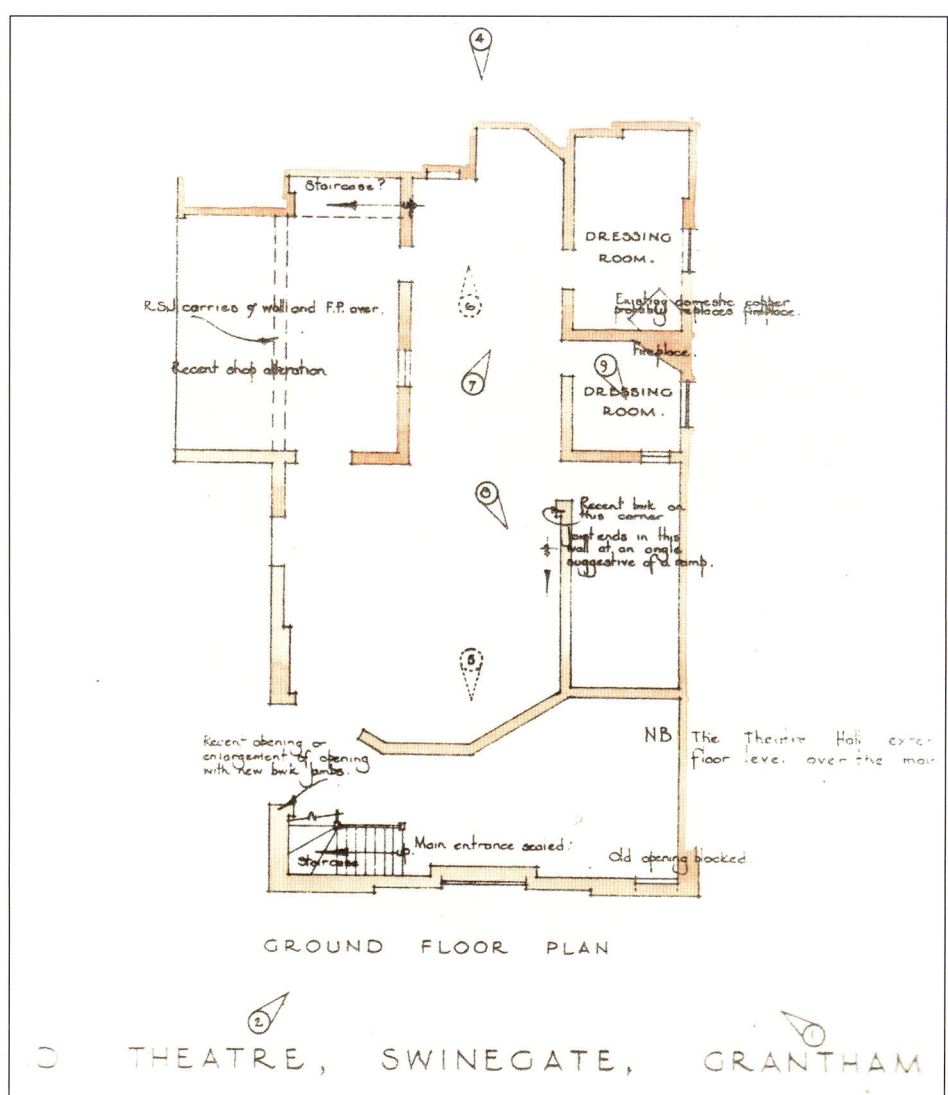

Ground floor of the former Grantham theatre, surveyed by Lawrence H. Bond in 1952. The auditorium on the floor above was reached by the stairs in the bottom left (northwest) corner. Bond identified two of the rooms as 'Dressing Rooms', and suggested the location of stairs to the stage in the top left (northeast) corner.
Grantham Library

the theatre will again be opened, at least for a lengthened period'.[43] In August Caple engaged Italian opera singers to perform at Hull, but he would not take them to Lincoln or Stamford.

At the end of 1849 Caple finally gave up his valiant attempts to save the theatrical life of Lincolnshire. He opened a short season at Lincoln on 30 October and the theatre had again been redecorated and made warm and comfortable so it was hoped that it would get better support than his previous season. But no, once again the support was poor, and anything but profitable. This was the end for Caple. His last appearance in the county was a farewell benefit at Lincoln on 7 December 1849 which was a bumper and all parts of the theatre were filled.[44] Some people still hoped local theatre might survive. It was suggested that Mr Henderson, late stage-manager to Caple, would take over the Lincoln theatre but nothing more was heard

[43] *SM*, 10 August 1849.
[44] *SM*, 26 October, 9 and 30 November, 14 December 1849.

of him or of a local company. It was also reported that fifty local citizens, determined if possible to prevent the extinction of the drama in Lincoln, had put their names down for season-tickets at a guinea each, but that gesture came too late. A farewell supper for Caple was held at the King's Arms on the evening before the final night on 7 December, and it was well attended with 'spirited conviviality'.[45] His company was disbanded and to help the actors there was a performance in Lincoln theatre on 21 December 1849, with some parts taken by amateurs and other parts by 'some of Mr Caple's late company', in order to raise funds for Caple's unemployed actors.[46]

John Caple still tried his luck elsewhere. In June 1850 it was reported that he had taken the lease of a theatre at Tenby in Pembrokeshire, and he also leased the Theatre Royal in York between 1850 and 1854.[47] Then in 1854-57 he undertook a tour of Australian and Californian goldfields with his wife, Eleanor Goddard. After their return his wife played *Hamlet* in the north of England, and again in Northampton in 1862. Caple died in 1863 in London. He had tried hard to revive theatre in Lincolnshire and beyond but in the end he failed, as the old form of theatrical culture was slowly moving to its end. He was only here for two and a half years but during that time had expended much time, energy and money on what proved to be a hopeless task. Perhaps it was the enthusiasm shown by Caple that encouraged William Robertson to keep trying his luck in other Lincolnshire towns for two years. The year 1849 saw William Robertson and John Caple both leave Lincolnshire. As the flame of Caple's enthusiasm burned out, so died the last attempt to save the Georgian theatre circuits of Lincolnshire. Henceforth each of the few remaining theatres was a besieged encampment on its own and one by one they fell down before the assault of Victorian morality until only Lincoln theatre remained. The years 1849 and 1850 saw the demise of several substantial theatres in and around Lincolnshire, despite the continuous existence of a tiny rump of dedicated theatregoers who could produce the occasional full house. There were too few of them, scattered about the county, and only four playhouses remained as the nineteenth century moved past its mid-point.

Grantham theatre survived only for a few weeks after Caple left the county. At the end of 1849 Samuel Rayner, whose company was performing at Loughborough, got a license to open Grantham theatre from a week before Christmas until 31 January 1850.[48] Nothing more is heard of this company. The next reference to Grantham theatre is six months later when it was reported that 'the theatre at this place, having been fitted up as a place of worship', was opened on Tuesday 30 July 1850 by one of several ministers expelled from the Wesleyan Methodist church. It was used as a chapel for Wesleyan Reformers for many years, then as a saleroom, a gymnasium,

---

[45] *SM*, 14 December 1849.
[46] *SM*, 21 and 28 December 1849.
[47] *SM*, 28 June 1850; York history website.
[48] *SM*, 23 November 1849.

a dining room and a billiard room, before demolition in 1952.[49] Local architect Lawrence H. Bond surveyed the building just before its demolition and produced a front elevation and ground floor plan as it was in 1952. The site became part of the Empire Garage and about 2000 was added to the grounds of the adjacent King's School, a new building being erected on the site by 2015.[50]

Gainsborough and Boston theatres both closed in 1849. Gainsborough's was in the Old Hall, owned by the Hickman family, lords of the manor, whose local representative was Henry Bacon Hickman, Esq (1789-1862) of Thonock Hall. That theatre had the strong support of two local baronets, Sir Charles Anderson of Lea and Sir Thomas Beckett of Somerby Park, even if the clergy and respectable middle classes of the town regarded theatre as immoral. Antiquarian as well as moral objections were raised to the use of the former great hall of the manor house as a theatre. On 17 December 1847 a correspondent to the *Stamford Mercury*, signing himself 'Monasticon', decried the state of the Old Hall 'which should be the pride of the place but which is fast falling into ruin'. He complained that its chapel, by which he meant the oriel window of the great hall,

> ...is desecrated by its transformation into a country theatre, subjecting it alike to the burlesque of the stage, the licentiousness of the green-room, and the vulgarity of the audience.[51]

'Topographicus' (perhaps local historian Adam Stark) wrote a week later and gave the history of the theatre in the Old Hall as well as saying that Henry Hickman had spent a considerable sum on repairs to the outside, the roof, passages and staircases.[52] On 31 December 'Gainsburgher' suggested that the area now used as a theatre should become a concert and lecture room; that would substitute 'an innocent recreation for one which has unfortunately become so debased as to be shunned by many right-thinking people'. In its next issue the *Mercury* itself said that the 'entire abolition [of theatrical performances] would be no detriment to the morals of the town'. The continuing antiquarian interest in the building was shown in August 1848 when 'members of the Archaeological Institution' visited the Old Hall.

Mr Hickman responded quickly and at first it looked as if the antiquarians and moralists had gained the day. John Wooldridge Bowden, bookseller of the Market Place, became the new lessee of the theatre, with Hickman's full support, and would make it available for lectures, public meetings, concerts or any other purpose for which it would be suitable. The *Mercury* reporter added: 'as regards theatricals, it will only be let to a respectable company, if at all', scarcely concealing his own

---

[49] *SM*, 9 August 1850; Honeybone, Michael, *The Book of Grantham*, Buckingham (1980), p.125.
[50] Pinchbeck, John, *Grantham in Focus*, Altrincham (2007), pp.26, 27.
[51] *SM*, 17 December 1847.
[52] *SM*, 24 December 1847.

distaste for the stage. Other rooms in the Old Hall would be converted for use by the Mechanics Institute and to provide assembly rooms.[53]

However the *Mercury* and the moralists had misjudged Hickman's response. What he was really doing at this time was quickly renovating his theatre to make it more attractive and so, perhaps, more profitable. The improvements were done by February 1848 and it was described as 'a complete metamorphosis'. To remedy the coldness of the theatre

> *the saloon has been entirely remodelled, a new door added at the top of the stairs, and others made to fit. A new stove had been placed in the saloon and another in the centre of the theatre.*

The whole interior had been redecorated by a Mr Foster who had also painted new scenery.[54] Hickman, as landlord, had done his bit by repairing the windows of the dressing and green rooms. The theatre was re-opened with a grand concert on Friday 18 February 1848 of which Hickman was patron.

A theatrical season started at Gainsborough on 9 November 1848, under Mr Stretton Sandon as acting manager for John Caple. It was said that:

> *the getting up of the pieces, the stage management altogether, and also the band, are in keeping with the company, which is by far the best that has been seen in Gainsborough since the time when Huggins' company was here, 25 years ago.*

Caple's new company apparently did well, and it was said that on 17 November 'the theatre was so crowded that several were refused tickets for want of room'. On that night it had been attended by 'the ladies from Thonock Hall [the Hickman family] and Lady and the Misses Becket' (sic).[55]

The real threat to Gainsborough theatre came not from the moralists and antiquarians but from a dispute between Hickman and the commercial men of the town. For some years there had been agitation for a Corn Exchange in Gainsborough, and on 8 May 1849 a public meeting was called to consider the issue. Mr Guy, as Hickman's agent, then revealed how precarious was the future of drama in the town as he proposed a plan to convert the theatre into a Corn Exchange. That was opposed by traders in the Market Place and Silver Street, who wanted a more central location, and the meeting appointed a 'Provisional Committee' of gentlemen to consider another plan. Hickman's supporters were confident that funds would not be found for the other scheme, so it would be a choice of the theatre or nothing.[56]

---

[53] *SM*, 14 and 21 January 1848.
[54] *Eastern Counties Herald* 17 February 1848; SM, 18 February 1848.
[55] *SM*, 17 and 24 November 1848; *Hull Advertiser*, 24 November 1848.
[56] *SM*, 11 May 1849.

The Provisional Committee soon realised that the money could not be raised, and by 22 June it was said that meetings of the Committee were 'becoming needless'. Hickman offered a further inducement for people to support his proposal, saying that 'he had consented to convert part of his property at the Town Hall into a butter market, provided the committee will offer no further opposition to his plan of making the theatre into a Corn Exchange'.[57]

With this threat to the theatre's existence no one would be interested in taking it as a subtenant, so on 14 May 1849 Caple opened it himself during the Mart. The company included Mr Henderson, Caple's 'stage manager' at Lincoln. Perhaps because of its danger Caple got an 'increased show of patronage' and as 'it continues to attract considerable numbers' it was suggested that the season might be extended beyond the three weeks originally planned. Sir Charles Anderson patronised one of the last nights at the theatre and he and Sir Thomas Beckett, both living just outside Gainsborough, appealed unsuccessfully to Hickman to keep the theatre for dramatic performances.[58] The *Stamford Mercury* reported that 'the last dramatic performance of a respectable character' would take place in the theatre on Friday, 8 June 1849,

> ...as the theatre, one of the most attractive in the provinces, and which has been recently restored and beautified at great expense, is doomed to destruction, the site being required for another purpose.

Although there would be no more drama, as a kind of encore, Caple brought the principal members of 'the Drury-lane opera company' to put on a grand concert in the theatre during the following week. The boxes were crowded but 'the trade of Gainsborough being in a depressed condition, prevents the middle and lower classes from spending much in luxuries' and the rest of the theatre was not numerously attended.[59]

The owner put a positive spin on the removal of Gainsborough theatre, which started on 26 June 1849. It was said that Hickman had 'determined on restoring to its original splendour this magnificent banqueting-hall of the olden time'. At that stage, probably to avoid antagonising those who had not yet given up hope of a town-centre Corn Exchange, it was said that the great hall would not be a corn-exchange. The demolition was complete by 13 July 1849 and the original minstrels gallery of the Old Hall, which had perhaps become part of the theatre gallery, was taken down at the same time.[60] After it was gone the *Mercury* displayed a little nostalgia, declaring that 'for more than 60 years' it was 'a splendid little theatre that would vie with any in England. The oriel window was

---

[57] *Eastern Counties Herald*, 21 June 1849.
[58] *SM*, 1 June 1849.
[59] *SM*, 8 and 15 June 1849.
[60] *SM*, 29 June, 13 July 1849; Parker, B.J., *The Theatre of Gainsborough. From 1772 until 1850*, thesis (1963), at Gainsborough Library, pp.16, 39.

so noble and large that it formerly was used as the manager's private room, where several eminent performers had attired themselves in theatrical costume.'[61] Then in August 1849 the gentlemen and farmers 'who usually dine at the White Hart' resolved to use the space of the former theatre as a Corn Exchange and on 9 November the *Mercury* reported that the corn market was indeed now held in the Old Hall on the site of the theatre.

Boston theatre continued to be used by small visiting companies of comedians for a few years after William Robertson had dropped it in 1846. Other uses included an annual masked ball held there in January 1846 and again in 1847. Dancers could hire costumes and dominoes, and other people took places in the boxes to watch.[62] In October 1848 when Boston celebrated the opening of railways through the town, the theatre was hired for a dinner attended by directors of the Great Northern and East Lincolnshire Railway companies and other dignitaries.[63] In February 1849 the owners of Boston theatre put it up 'to be let or for sale by private contract'. It was described as

> ...that spacious, well-built, and modern erection, the Theatre, situated in Red Lion-street, fitted up in a commodious style with Boxes, Pit and Gallery, a spacious Stage, Proscenium etc., with extent and capabilities qualified to meet all the demands of the Modern Drama. The extent of the building is 46 feet by 80 feet, and it is finished in every respect in a most substantial way. Beneath the Theatre are very Spacious and dry Cellars, admirably qualified for Ale and Porter stores, or the warehousing of goods. The extent and situation of this valuable property is such that it may easily be converted to any other purpose.[64]

Independent Congregational Chapel, Red Lion Street, Boston. Built in 1850 on the site of the theatre of 1806.
From Pishey Thompson, History and Antiquities of Boston *(1856).*

The market had no demand for local theatres, to be used as such, and it was not until late August 1849 that the *Mercury* announced

> Boston theatre has been purchased by the adherents of the Rev. Isaac Watts and is very shortly to be converted into a chapel for their use. We suppose this will cause the death of the drama in Boston, as no person will be found with such a plenty of money as to invest it in so ruinous a speculation as the late theatre has proved.[65]

A division in the Grove Street Independent congregation in Boston had occurred in May 1847 and the supporters of the Rev. Isaac Watts 'were anxious to build a chapel

---

[61] *SM*, 9 November 1849.
[62] *SM*, 8 January 1847.
[63] *SM*, 13 and 20 October 1848.
[64] *SM*, 9 February 1849.
[65] *SM*, 24 August, 7 September 1849.

for that gentleman'. It was said that the theatre would provide accommodation not only for a chapel but also a minister's house and school-rooms. Fundraising efforts to complete the purchase included a tea-meeting 'on a large scale', for between 600 and 700 people, held in the theatre on 4 September 1849. Speeches during the tea-meeting 'dwelt chiefly on the circumstances of the theatre's being about to be converted into a place of religious worship – contrasting the beneficial influence of religious teaching with the drama and its associations'.[66] Ownership of the theatre was signed over to the Independents on 18 December 1849; the theatre was demolished by May 1850 and the foundation stone of the new chapel was laid on 9 July. Some of the materials of the former theatre were used in the construction of the chapel, which was built quickly and opened on 21 November 1850, though it only survived until 1867 when a new chapel was built on the site.[67]

In February 1850 there were performances at Lincoln theatre during the races, and an amateur production in May for the benefit of the Lincoln Dispensary, but few other references to performances, though this and other theatres were occasionally used for lectures and public meetings. In May 1850 Lincoln theatre was opened under the management of Herr Teasdale, lessee of theatres in Oldham, Derby, Halifax and elsewhere, with a very talented and effective company.[68] The cast included Mr Rayner and his wife, perhaps the person who had taken Grantham theatre just five months before. The cast also included James Anderson who had performed before Queen Victoria at Windsor Castle but his name awakened no interest in Lincoln. Attendance during the first week or two was promising but after that 'the drama has had only a miserable share of patronage'. *Othello* was performed to a thin house and on 25 June *Hamlet* was to have been performed 'but the display of empty boxes and benches was more than usually beggarly, and the money taken (said to be 4s 6d) was returned' and no performance took place. Then by 12 July Herr Teasdale had disappeared, 'and with him have vanished all the hopes some tradesmen entertained of obtaining payment of their accounts'. The poverty of theatre was now so well known that the *Stamford Mercury* expressed incredulity that any tradesmen should extend credit 'with the settled truth in their minds that the drama is without hope in Lincoln'.[69]

The city of Lincoln started to grow into an industrial town in the 1840s and remained large even though overtaken in size by Grimsby during the nineteenth century. It was perhaps this growth that saved Lincoln theatre, which later adopted the name Theatre Royal. It might not have survived. In August 1850 some prospective purchasers approached the owner of the theatre, and it was thought that they wanted to convert it into a public hall for lectures, public meetings etc. The

---

[66] *SM*, 7 September 1849.
[67] *SM*, 24 August, 21 December 1849; 12 July, 29 November 1850.
[68] *SM*, 31 May, 14 and 28 June 1850.
[69] *SM*, 12 July 1850.

owner set his asking price at £800, which the purchasers thought too much, so the deal fell through and the theatre is still going in the twenty-first century.[70]

One of the last local theatres to close was in Sleaford. Joseph Smedley had sold it on 6 July 1840 and on 7 August 1845 the new owner, Mr John Hyde, silversmith, of Sleaford, put it up for sale again by auction. It was then described as:

> a large and substantial building of stone and slated, the lower part of which is occupied as four tenements, and the upper portion is fitted up and furnished as a Theatre, for which purpose it was originally erected by Mr Smedley, and it is now in constant request for theatrical performances, for concerts, and other amusements of that character. There is a yard adjoining, with suitable offices, piggeries, etc. The whole is in an excellent state of repair.[71]

This building was still in use as a theatre in 1848 and 1853 but in 1856 it was 'about to be converted to an infant school for two hundred children'.[72]

While theatres were dying in most of Lincolnshire, the opposite was the case in Grimsby. In the 1840s it was still a small town but then the Manchester, Sheffield and Lincolnshire Railway company arrived and started to build large new docks. The town grew into the greatest fishing port in the world and, with Cleethorpes, was the largest urban area in Lincolnshire. The joint population in 1841 was 4,702 but by 1901 it had risen to 75,716. After Smedley retired William Robertson's Lincoln company started visiting Grimsby in the 1840s and his youngest daughter, Margaret, was born there in 1848. The theatre was then near the Ropery works in Riby Square, off Cleethorpe Road.[73] By the 1850s Grimsby was expanding and in December 1852 a new theatre was opened in the town, 'in the presence of about 700 persons of all classes'. The theatre was said to be 'under the control of the few proprietors who think that in this peculiar department of amusement the town is not up to the mark'.[74] This theatre was in Loft Street North (now Victoria Street) near its corner with Freeport Wharf (now Corporation Road). It was a wooden building coated with tar and only lasted two years before it burnt down on the morning of 22 January 1855. Grimsby soon had another theatre and from these beginnings the town managed to support the popular theatre, and later music hall as well, right into the twentieth century.[75]

After the loss of nearly all theatres in Lincolnshire the well-to-do could take the train to playhouses elsewhere, but the audience from the pit and gallery was still

---

[70] *SM*, 30 August 1850.
[71] *SM*, 25 July 1845.
[72] White, William, *Directory of Lincolnshire*, Sheffield (1856), p.433.
[73] Chapman, Peter, *Grimsby. The Story of the World's Greatest Fishing Port*, Grimsby (1991), pp.137, 138.
[74] *SM*, 31 December 1852.
[75] Gillett, Edward, *A History of Grimsby*, London (1970), p.240.

there to be entertained, and for them new and cheaper premises were needed. Strolling players had set up temporary theatres in the mid eighteenth century before permanent playhouses were erected and as towns lost their theatres in early Victorian times the players had to resort once more to primitive replacement venues and tents at fairs. There are references to temporary theatres in use for a while, such as Market Deeping in 1842, Louth in 1843, Alford 1847 and Brigg 1849.[76] In Spalding Mr R. Kelley, the landlord of the New Bell inn, Bridge Street, erected a temporary theatre in his inn yard in March 1853. The 'substantial place' was built by Mr Dawson, and the theatre would be occupied by Mr S.H. Bell of the theatre at Bury in Lancashire.[77] The landlord must have thought it a worth-while venture, for in September 1854 he repeated the exercise. On the latter occasion the building, said to be 84 feet by 36 feet and capable of seating 1000 people, was erected by Mr Stainton, builder of Boston, and was expected to take only a week to set up. Mr Bell also described himself as a well-known marine painter and scenic artist. Seat prices were really low: Boxes 1s, Pit 6d, and Gallery 3d.[78] This second effort may not have paid off, for it appears that Kelley had left the New Bell inn by 1856.

After Boston theatre closed a large temporary wooden building was erected in the Pen Yard in Wide Bargate, next to the Cross Keys inn, now a car park next to the Mayflower hotel, where theatricals were performed for a few weeks each year in the 1850s. Mr Douglas built the theatre and his touring melodrama company attracted large audiences and visited for several years, usually during the May fair.[79] Pishey Thompson considered the performances to be far below those of earlier years, referring to them in 1856 as 'the degraded drama of the day'.[80] From the mid nineteenth century Corn Exchanges, Temperance Halls, Oddfellows Halls, and similar buildings were being erected in every town and most had stages and proscenium arches where travelling actors and local amateurs could perform, even if they lacked boxes or a gallery.

As the local 'companies of comedians' had all gone from Lincolnshire so new touring companies of strolling players emerged, and where permanent troupes of actors still remained they were referred to as 'stock companies' to distinguish them from these new touring companies. At the same time the word 'comedian' lost its wider meaning of 'actor' and assumed the much narrower modern definition as essentially a single performer telling jokes. In November 1847 J. Robson Daniels of the Lyceum theatre, London, brought a small company

---

[76] *SM*, 3 June 1842, 21 July 1843, 10 December 1847, 2 March 1849.
[77] *SM*, 25 March 1853.
[78] *SM*, 22 September 1854.
[79] Gould, Mervyn, *Boston and Spalding Entertainment and the Aspland Howdens*, Wakefield (2005), p.4.
[80] Thompson, Pishey, *History and Antiquities of Boston*, Boston (1856), p.211.

to Lincolnshire and performed in Boston theatre before going on to Spilsby and then in January 1848 to Sleaford.[81] The programme at Boston included the classic play *She Stoops to Conquer* and the farce *Family Jars* (1822) with a tight-rope walker and the new dance called the Polka. Daniels did not do well because, 'here, as elsewhere, the public taste for the legitimate drama is evidently on the decline'.[82]

A Mr Bennett put on 'minor drama' in a tent in Stamford during the mid-Lent fair in April 1848 and then did the same at Gainsborough during the Mart week in May. At the end there was a fracas at the Black Bull inn when a clown hit the landlord, and that started a general fight.[83] A Mr Edwards also had a theatre in a tent at Stamford Mid-lent fair in 1848, and a year later he appeared at Grantham's Mid-lent fair. As previously mentioned, in April 1849 these tented theatres were not allowed to continue in Grantham during Passion Week. Mr Edwards strongly pleaded for permission to carry on, and he was allowed to open on Monday evening for songs, dances and ventriloquism but not for theatrical performances.[84] A month later at Boston May Fair Mr Edwards actually rented the theatre, even though it was in the process of being sold by that date. His company were still there for the 'fortnight' market two weeks after Boston Fair, and they paraded the streets in a van in full costume to drum up business.[85]

Another new company arrived in Newark in August 1848, Messrs Eaglesfield and Wakeman of Aston, near Birmingham, and it was described as 'another attempt to revive the drama' in the town. The season would start on 4 September 1848 with the ever popular *The Stranger* and the new melodrama of *The Bottle* (1847) which exposed the evils of drink.[86] From there they went on to Lincoln. One of the last companies mentioned in the *Stamford Mercury* was not actually touring within Lincolnshire. Mr W.T. Simpson 'from Wellingborough, Leighton Buzzard, etc' took his company of comedians to Oakham in July and August 1850, and it was said he had visited that town some eleven years previously. They were there for at least five weeks and then went on to Uppingham and Melton, but at the latter place they got very little encouragement with only half a dozen patrons present for one performance.[87]

A few years later, in March 1853, another company appeared. It was managed by Miss Faukland (late of the Theatres Royal, Edinburgh, Glasgow and

---

[81] Lincolnshire County Archives, ref:3/ANC/7/23/49, letter No.13a.
[82] *SM*, 28 January 1848.
[83] *SM*, 7 April, 12 May 1848.
[84] *SM*, 7 April 1848, 30 March, 6 and 20 April 1849.
[85] *SM*, 11 and 18 May 1849.
[86] *SM*, 25 August 1848.
[87] *SM*, 23 and 30 August 1850.

Newcastle) with actors from London and provincial theatres. Stamford theatre had been closed for dramatic performances for three or four years and was now let to Henry Johnson, bookseller, and he arranged with Miss Faukland to bring her company there for a short season. It was said that she had been at Sleaford before coming to Stamford. The latter theatre was being redecorated and would be thoroughly ventilated and warmed.[88]

Fanny Robertson had retired to Wisbech in 1843 but by the end of the decade her nephew William was too poverty-stricken himself to give her much financial help. In May 1847 when Mr Davenport, lessee of several Norfolk theatres, opened a season in Wisbech theatre he kindly proposed a benefit for Fanny Robertson, the former lessee.[89] In April 1848 the *Stamford Mercury* reported that a public subscription would be raised for her support and Mr Caple had consented to give all the help he could. Subscription lists were opened in the towns of the former company's circuit.[90] On 9 May 1848 a concert was put on in Wisbech theatre for Fanny's benefit, with the printing, the gas, and the services of the Wisbech Harmonic Society given for free. At the same time an artist called Hunter contacted other actors who had known Fanny during her career. He received donations from William Charles Macready who had often played with the Lincoln company, Henry Compton who had performed with the company in his youth, and other London actors, to help set up an annuity for Fanny.[91]

Fanny Robertson lived another seven years and died at Wisbech on the night of 18/19 December 1855 at the great age of 87. She and her husband had experienced the ups and downs that arose from a theatrical life, and frequently had to struggle against financial hardship. However, during the course of their long connection with the towns of the circuit they had made many kind friends, who it was said had on more than one occasion extricated them from ruin. Her husband had died at Huntingdon on 31 August 1831 and she survived him for over 24 years, and had chosen Wisbech as her home after retiring from the stage. One of her early and kindest friends, Dr John Whitsed, had professionally attended her for some days before her death.[92] Whitsed had been Mayor of Wisbech in 1845 and 1851 and a play he had written, *The World's Slippery Turns, Or, Mind How You Wed* (1845), had been performed by the Lincoln company and was still available in print in 2015.

With the death of Fanny the connection of the Robertson family to the theatres of Lincolnshire and adjacent parts came to an end after a period of over seventy years.

---

[88] *SM*, 4 March 1853.
[89] *SM* 21 and 28 May 1847.
[90] *SM*, 7 and 21 April 1848.
[91] *SM*, 12 May 1848.
[92] *SM*, 28 December 1855.

Truly it could now be said of the Georgian theatre in Lincolnshire, as Shakespeare wrote in *The Tempest*, act 4, scene 1:

> *Our revels now are ended. These our actors,*
> *As I foretold you, were all spirits and*
> *Are melted into air, into thin air,*
> *And, like the baseless fabric of this vision,*
> *The cloud-capp'd towers, the gorgeous palaces,*
> *The solemn temples, the great globe itself,*
> *Yea, all which it inherit, shall dissolve,*
> *And, like this insubstantial pageant faded,*
> *Leave not a rack behind. We are such stuff*
> *As dreams are made on, and our little life*
> *Is rounded with a sleep.*

11
EPILOGUE – WHAT DRAMA DID NEXT

Georgian theatre in Lincolnshire had died in the middle of the nineteenth century after a long and painful fight against the coming of the dark. When Fanny Robertson breathed her last in 1855 there were only a few theatres in the county still struggling to stay open. Drama continued to prosper in London where the number of theatres doubled between 1850 and 1890, and Fanny Robertson's nephew William left the county in 1849 to take on the Marylebone theatre in London and then other theatres in Bristol and Bath.[1] William Robertson's children continued to work in his theatres and later two of them took important places on the national scene. His son, Thomas William (1829-71) wrote plays that changed the direction of British drama. T.W. was a robust and convivial creature with red hair and beard and a brilliant flow of conversation.[2] In 1854 he took the job of prompter at the Lyceum Theatre in London, then acted at the Theatre Royal, Richmond, before joining his father briefly at the Marylebone Theatre. He never succeeded as an actor at the national level, but from 1851 he had been writing numerous plays, mostly comedies and adaptations of the novels of Charles Dickens, and songs for comedians.[3]

In 1864 T.W. Robertson had his first notable playwriting success with *David Garrick* (1864) and the following year found fame with the production of his comedy *Society* (1865) which came to be regarded as a milestone in Victorian drama because of its realism in sets, costume, acting and dialogue. All of his popular plays, except for *David Garrick*, were produced by the actor-managers Squire and Marie Bancroft at the Prince of Wales' Theatre. His plays became known as 'problem plays' because they dealt seriously and sensitively with issues of the day, and were notable for their 'cup and saucer' realism. Robertson also helped to develop the role of the director as someone who was neither an actor nor a prompter.

He was not a great playwright and Henry James described his plays as 'infantile' but George Bernard Shaw referred to them as a 'theatrical revolution'. They broke the mould, showed new ways for drama to develop and prepared the public for better plays than his own. His plays were small and neat, and these attributes were striking in an age used to declamation, melodrama, spectacle and romantic acting.

Thomas William Robertson (1829–71). Playwright who changed the direction of drama, bringing new realism and developing the role of the director.
From T.W. Robertson (junior), The Principal Dramatic Works of Thomas William Robertson (1889).

---

[1] Donaldson, Walter, *Recollections of an Actor*, London (1865), p.208.
[2] Hartnoll, Phyllis (ed), *The Oxford Companion to the Theatre*, London (3rd edn 1967), p.802.
[3] Donaldson, *op. cit.*, p.27-28.

Dame Madge Kendal (1848–1935), born Margaret Robertson in Grimsby. Younger sister of T.W. Robertson the dramatist. She and her husband became stars of the theatre in Canada and the United States as well as in Britain.
Old White Lodge

They were light comedies that brought the English stage closer to more simple and normal life, and under the Bancrofts and Robertson's direction they introduced modern scenic effects.[4] His work now seems old-fashioned, but he replaced heavy delivery and broad gestures with a quieter and more natural style of acting. After a few years of fame and adulation he died, aged 42, at the height of his success. He left a permanent mark on the theatre of his time and foreshadowed the work of many twentieth century dramatists.[5] His plays are still occasionally seen, such as *Ours* (1866) which was produced in 2007 at the Finborough Theatre, London.

T.W. Robertson's youngest sister achieved international fame, in her case as a leading actress. Margaret (or Madge) Shaftoe Robertson (1848-1935) was born in Grimsby at the Royal Dock tea and coffee rooms at the corner of Railway Street and Cleethorpe Road, where her parents were lodging while performing in the town. Later the Railway Hotel was built on the site of the tea rooms and a century later a plaque was affixed to the hotel wall commemorating her birth.[6] Madge made her first appearance on stage in 1854 at the Marylebone Theatre in London under her father's management. In 1867 Madge and her parents made a brief return visit to Lincolnshire and, with the assistance of some local performers, put on two dramatic entertainments in Boston's Corn Exchange. She returned to the town in 1868 and gave some dramatic readings. It was also in 1867 that she had played at the Haymarket theatre and met William Hunter Kendal whom she married two years later. Madge Kendal became best known for her roles in Shakespeare and English comedy. In 1889 the Kendals toured Canada and the United States and they continued to be active in popular plays on both sides of the Atlantic until 1908 when they both retired. They were held up as the very model of partnership, both on and off the stage. Madge was created a Dame Commander of the British Empire (DBE) in 1926 and the following year awarded the Order of the Grand Cross (GBE).[7]

Meanwhile in another time and place, back in the Lincolnshire that the Robertsons had left behind, the only old theatres still in business in the 1850s were in Stamford and Lincoln, with Sleaford perhaps being used at the start of the decade and Grimsby developing anew. Stamford theatre, like much of the town, was owned by the Marquess of Exeter, who was reluctant to change, and this may be one of the reasons why that theatre survived as long as it did. In an effort to save its flagging fortunes, in 1864 it offered 'Entertainments for the People', including band concerts with minstrels, for which admission was only 1d for the circle, 2d for the pit and 3d for the boxes. By a kind of perverse logic, as the theatre declined in status it adopted a grander title, and so by 1865 it was listed in playbills as 'Theatre Royal, Stamford'.

---

[4] Sampson, George, *The Concise Cambridge History of English Literature*, Cambridge (1941), pp.755-56.
[5] Hartnoll, Phyllis and Found, Peter (eds), *The Concise Oxford Companion to the Theatre* (New Edition), London (2nd edn 1992), p.422; Sampson, *op. cit.*, p.755.
[6] Chapman, Peter, *Grimsby. The Story of the World's Greatest Fishing Port*, Grimsby (1991), pp.137, 138.
[7] Donaldson, Frances, *The Actor Managers*, London (1970), p.28.

By that date the title Theatre Royal no longer signified a patent from the crown, but had become a generic title for a playhouse.[8] The programme in Stamford was still similar to that of fifty years earlier, with 'historical dramas' and 'laughable farces', though in 1866 it also included a 'celebrated Burlesque Extravaganza' as performed at the Theatre Royal, St James'. On 23 June 1871 the theatre finally closed and was converted to the Stamford Chess, Billiards and News Club that opened on Boxing Day, 1871. It was another hundred years before it became a theatre again.

Similar fates befell even larger theatres that had been part of the same circuit as Stamford, with Nottingham and Derby theatres closing in the 1860s. John Faucit Saville purchased Nottingham theatre in 1854 and made a number of improvements inside and out. He died on 31 December 1855 at the age of 48 but his widow kept the theatre going until April 1865. It re-opened later the same year as the Alhambra concert rooms and changed to a restaurant in the 1880s. The restaurant later closed as it became a haunt of prostitutes and the building was then adapted as a Lace Warehouse around the turn of the century. It was destroyed by a German bomb on the night of 8/9 May 1941.[9] Derby Theatre declined in the face of competition from other entertainment houses and closed in 1864, reopening as a Gospel Hall in 1865, with an intermediate floor inserted. At that time the Green Room fireplace was said to be one of the last relics of the old theatre. Later it became a magistrates court, but by 1992 it was disused and shabby., though the basic brick shell and pitched roof remained largely intact. It was demolished in 2002 when a complex of new magistrates courts was built around the historic Shire Hall in the adjacent St Mary's Gate. Chesterfield theatre closed in the 1870s, and was later used to house the generators for the town's street lighting, the first electric street lighting in Britain. Halifax theatre, like Lincoln, was one of the few to outlast the nineteenth century and was demolished in 1904 when a new Theatre Royal was erected on the site. Leicester theatre also struggled through the Victorian period into the twentieth century and, as the Theatre Royal, was closed and demolished in 1957.

Some playhouses were demolished as soon as they closed, such as Peterborough and Boston's 1806 theatre. Others like Grantham, Gainsborough and Newark were converted to new uses and their status as theatres became just a part of their history. Yet more endured years without any theatrical use, but could be opened up if a company arrived in the town, as appears to have been the case in Sleaford and Horncastle for some time, and Spalding was not dissimilar. Southwell theatre was on the first floor of commercial premises in the Market Place, and even in the twenty-first century some evocative elements of the theatre remain in the

---

[8] Hartnoll and Found, *op. cit.*, p.505.
[9] Wood, A.C., 'Nottingham 1836-1865; 1.The Borough 1836-1865', *Transactions of the Thoroton Society*, Vol.LIX, Nottingham (1955), p.34; Payne, Michael, 'Mr Whitley and his Company of Comedians: Nottingham St Mary's Gate Theatre, 1761-1865', *Transactions of the Thoroton Society*, Vol.109, Nottingham (2005), p.124.

The former Newark theatre in 2016. The upper windows were probably inserted in 1850 when the building was converted into a shop, and the ground floor facade newer still.

The former Wisbech theatre in 2016. Since 1978 it is again in use as a theatre, known as the Angles Theatre, with the former school to the south as the front of house area.

upper room, probably the nearest that the East Midlands has to the interior of a Georgian theatre.

Part of Newark theatre was demolished in 1884 to allow construction of the covered market (now the Buttermarket) on the site of the butchers' shambles behind the Town Hall. The front part of the old Newark theatre has new windows probably inserted after the 1852 sale but the hipped roof and parts of the walls still remain and the building is occupied in 2015 by Milletts. The shell of the 1772 Boston theatre in the Market Place is now part of a pub/restaurant. The first Gainsborough theatre had closed in 1790 but was converted to other uses and was demolished about 1938 when North Street was widened. After 1848 Wisbech theatre, like Grantham, became a chapel for Wesleyan Reformers and then had other uses, including a Christian Spiritualist church from 1920 until it became a theatre again in 1978.[10] The school in front of Wisbech theatre also had other uses, including being the town library, and was reunited with the theatre in the 1980s. Huntingdon theatre was demolished and a church dedicated to St John the Baptist, now closed, was built on the site.

By 1856 or earlier the Public Hall in Holbeach, which had served as the local theatre, was also being used for meetings of the local Board of Health, the County Court was held there by 1871 and magistrates were still hearing cases there in 1953.[11] It had several other uses in the twentieth century, a cinema in the silent era, a dance hall, auction room, and the Holbeach Youth Club from 1945 until 1983, as well as overflow accommodation for Holbeach Schools. It was used in the 1950s for plays by the Caryl Jenner Mobile Theatre, named after a lady who put on regular performances there. By the late 1970s the Public Hall needed expensive repairs and it was sold for demolition. Semi-detached houses were built on the site.[12]

Sleaford theatre was sold in 1856 for £380 to Kirk and Parry, a local firm of architects and builders, and they then sold it to the Church of England for an infant school for about £1,000. It stayed as a school until the 1930s, became an office of the Department of Social Security from 1948 to 1993 and then returned to being a theatre, now owned by a trust. The building that was Horncastle theatre in Dog Kennel Yard survived for well over 100 years after its closure as a playhouse. In 1859 it was purchased for conversion to a British School but was only used as such from 1863 until 1876.[13] There was then some attempt to

---

[10] Angles theatre website.
[11] White, William, *Directory of Lincolnshire*, Sheffield (1856), p.831; White, William, *Directory of Lincolnshire*, Sheffield (1872), p.742; Satherley, Jeremy, *A neat little town – the history of Holbeach*, Holbeach (2004), p.32.
[12] Satherley, *op. cit.*, p.33.
[13] *Stamford Mercury*, 25 November 1859.

reinstate it as a theatre, but by that time there were other halls in the town. It was instead sold in 1877 for £305 to Alfred Healey for a malt kiln.[14] In 1976 it was still standing and was in use as a vehicle repair shop by Achurch & Sons, agricultural engineers, but it was demolished a few years later and the site is now part of a supermarket car park.

Touring companies from London and the larger provincial cities would occasionally visit Lincolnshire in the mid nineteenth century and they provided 'drama' and 'variety shows' in cheap wooden buildings like the one in the Pen Yard in Boston, that were not usually patronised by the middle classes. Henry Compton, who had spent three years with the Lincoln company in the 1830s, brought his own 'Compton Comedy Company' to the Lincoln Theatre Royal for one night in 1881, and Lord Monson patronised Compton's benefit that night.[15] The son of T.W. Robertson the dramatist, also called Thomas William, had a touring company that visited Northampton in the 1880s to perform his father's comedies. He went back in the 1890s, this time putting on plays other than his father's. It was a heavy expense but the theatre was occupied by a 'numerous and admiring audience' every night.[16]

The form of theatre that died about 1850 was different from anything that had been before and from what came after. It entertained all classes of society except the very poorest and for most of the time was a successful commercial cultural enterprise serving Lincolnshire and a few other towns close by. In the end this county embraced Methodism and the local theatres were condemned to a slow, lingering death, with only Lincoln excepted.

Georgian theatre's legacy was divided and eventually emerged in two forms defined as music hall and the legitimate stage. The theatre-going public was divided between those who patronised serious drama and those who could only afford popular entertainment, and even in the twenty-first century theatres struggle to reunite these distinct strands. After the Georgian theatre had died some entertainment was provided in public houses and the rooms used for that gradually grew into separate buildings, usually with drink and food provided. The Surrey Music Hall, opened in London in 1848, was the first building so named. Music halls flourished in Grantham, Gainsborough and Lincoln, which were growing into industrial towns with large engineering works employing many hands. Even greater growth was seen in the fishing port of Grimsby. Fishermen spent a long tough time at sea, and when they came ashore had only a limited period to spend their wages on drink and entertainment. The 1852 theatre that burnt down in January 1855 was soon replaced by the Royal Adelphi in Newmarket Street which had a season from September to February and could be used by touring companies during the rest of the year. That

---

[14] Robinson, David N., *The Book of Horncastle and Woodhall Spa*, Buckingham (1983), p.160, 164; Clarke, *op. cit.*, p.96.
[15] Warwick, Lou, *The McKenzies called Compton*, Northampton (1977), p.158.
[16] Warwick, Lou, *op. cit.*, pp.109, 124.

closed on 14 May 1864 and was followed by a Theatre Royal in Victoria Street, which opened on 4 February 1865. After 1884 Joseph Curry opened several large variety theatres in Grimsby including the Prince of Wales and the Tivoli.

A 'Theatre Royal' was erected in George Street, Grantham, in 1875, but it was called the Empire when putting on variety shows, blatantly illustrating the division of theatre into two strands. A Masonic hall built in Newland, Lincoln, in 1872 could be used for theatrical performances after 1877 and in 1902 it became the Palace theatre, offering competition to the Theatre Royal. In Gainsborough the King's Theatre was opened in 1885 as a music hall in Trinity Street. Popular entertainment was also provided in the new seaside resorts developing along the sandy Lincolnshire coast. Touring companies visiting other market towns in Lincolnshire had to use corn exchanges, temperance halls and similar buildings as venues.[17]

Lincoln was lucky. Despite the departure of the Robertsons Lincoln theatre did not die, and though for a long time it was a mere shadow of its former self it did survive the wilderness years. In 1856 it could only charge boxes 2/6, upper boxes 1/6, pit 1/- and gallery 6d compared with nearly twice as much in 1840: boxes (two tiers) 3/6 (2/- half price), pit 2/- and gallery 1/-. It is the only playhouse in greater Lincolnshire to have kept going continuously from the Georgian period to the present, a period of over 250 years. The auditorium of the present theatre is on the footprint of the original 1760 building, with later additions on its south side. It prospered again in late Victorian times and by 1872 was called the Theatre Royal.[18] The 1806 building was burnt down on 26 November 1892 and a new one was quickly built on the same site in Kings Arms Yard, opening on 18 December 1893 with the extremely popular *Charley's Aunt* (1892), and is still in use today.[19] In 1907 the management purchased adjacent property fronting onto Butchery Street (now part of Clasketgate) and later made the modern entrance and front of house facilities there.

In the twentieth century the Lincoln theatre supported a repertory company for a few years, but that apart, the county could not sustain a permanent company of actors making their living just by touring Lincolnshire. The vacuum drew in professional actors for occasional visits, and also led to the emergence of several local amateur dramatic societies that have lasted into the twenty-first century. There had been amateur performances by gentlemen during the Georgian period and in 1866 or 1870 an amateur society for the performance of plays, still employing professional actresses for the female parts as before, was formed in Spalding. That society continued until 1928 when an amateur operatic society

---

[17] Wright, Neil R., *Lincolnshire Towns and Indusry, History of Lincolnshire* Vol.XI, Lincoln (1982), pp.242, 243.
[18] White, William, *Directory of Lincolnshire*, Sheffield (1872), p.107.
[19] Warwick, Lou, *Drama that Smelled; Or, Early Drama in Northampton and Hereabouts*, Northampton (1975), p.195.

was formed to present musical plays. The amalgamation of those two societies formed the Spalding Amateur Dramatic and Operatic Society which is still going in 2016 and is the oldest such society in mainland Britain.[20]

In this century there are a few purpose built theatres in Lincolnshire, and some converted from other uses. Theatres in Stamford, Wisbech and Sleaford were created in the late twentieth century in the shells of theatres dated 1768, 1793 and 1826 respectively. King's Lynn theatre in St George's Guildhall ceased to be a theatre in 1814, but in 1945-51 it once more became a theatre and is now owned by the National Trust and leased by an Arts Centre. Stamford theatre is also part of an Arts Centre, as are new theatres in Gainsborough, Grantham and Boston. The Lincoln Performing Arts Centre (LPAC) is part of the University of Lincoln. The Broadbent Theatre in Wickenby was created in 1971 out of an 1878 Methodist chapel – what would those Victorian moralists say to that? It is named after Roy Broadbent whose son is the award-winning, Lincolnshire-born actor Jim Broadbent. Some schools and church halls also have stages that can be used for performances by regional or national touring companies.

However, there are fewer purpose-built theatres in Lincolnshire than there were in the eighteenth century, and there are no longer any local touring companies in the style of Whitley, the Robertsons, Manly, Huggins or Smedley. Entertainments provided in Lincolnshire theatres in the early twenty-first century include plays with professional actors on national tours, plays and musicals by the numerous amateur dramatic and operatic societies, gigs by elderly performers, tribute bands and some younger musicians, and of course the ever popular pantomimes that for over a century have been part of Christmas festivities in this county as elsewhere. The main benefit of the modern situation is that, when we do have the chance to experience live theatre, it is probably of a better quality than that enjoyed two centuries ago. Nowadays it is competition from cinema, television and other forms of recreation that the theatres have to contend with, rather than the moral objections of church and chapel folk. Once again, even clergymen can go to the theatre with a clear conscience and enjoy an entertaining and uplifting night out. Even though so much has changed since the 1760s, live drama is still performed in Lincoln, Stamford and Wisbech in theatres where Fanny Robertson would have appeared two centuries ago. Perhaps her spirit is looking down and encouraging the performers of today.

---

[20] Rush, Jean, 'Putting on an Act', *Lincolnshire Life* (November 2012), p.36.

Appendix 1

Family Tree of the Robertson Family *(Simplified)*

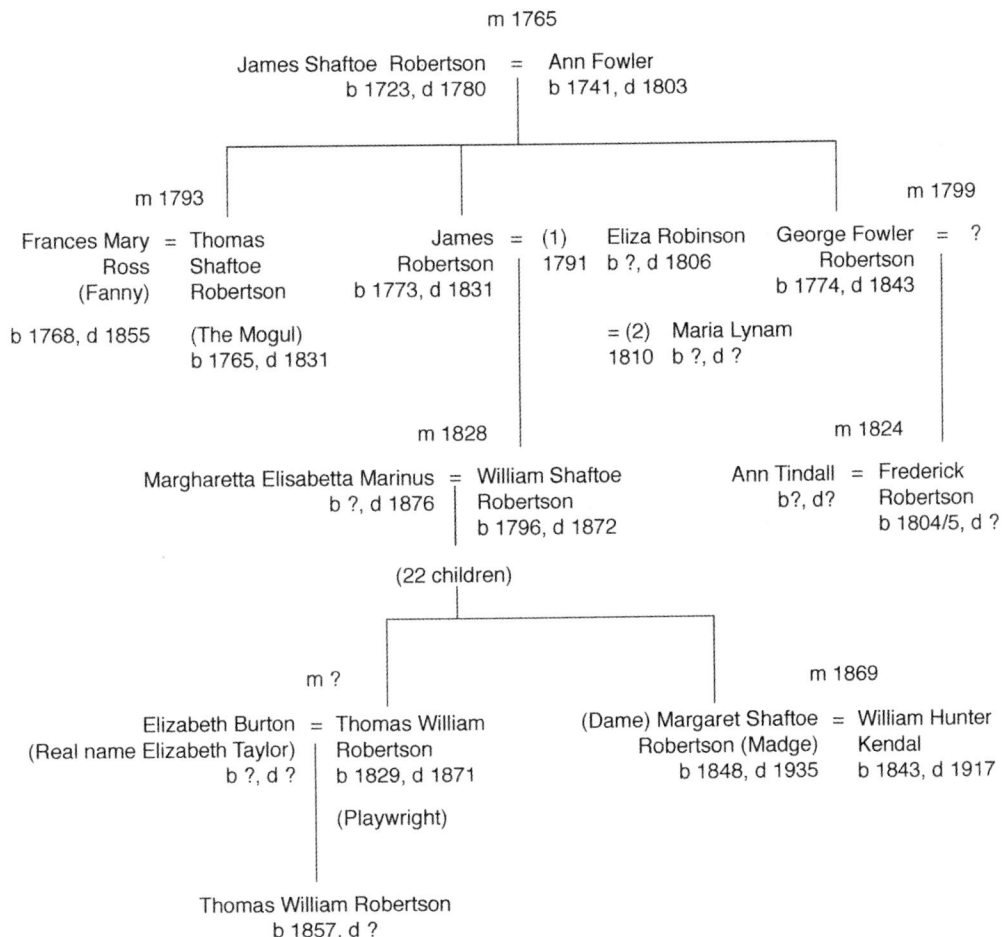

Appendix 2
Some Other Relatives of Fanny Robertson
(born Frances Mary Ross)

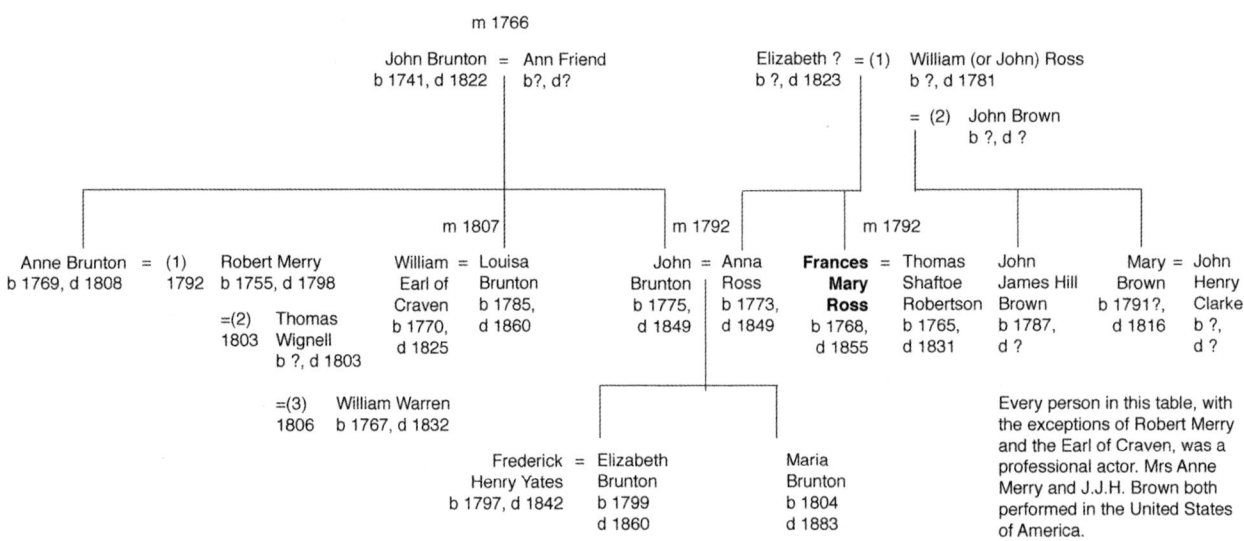

Appendix 3
Family Tree of the Huggins Family

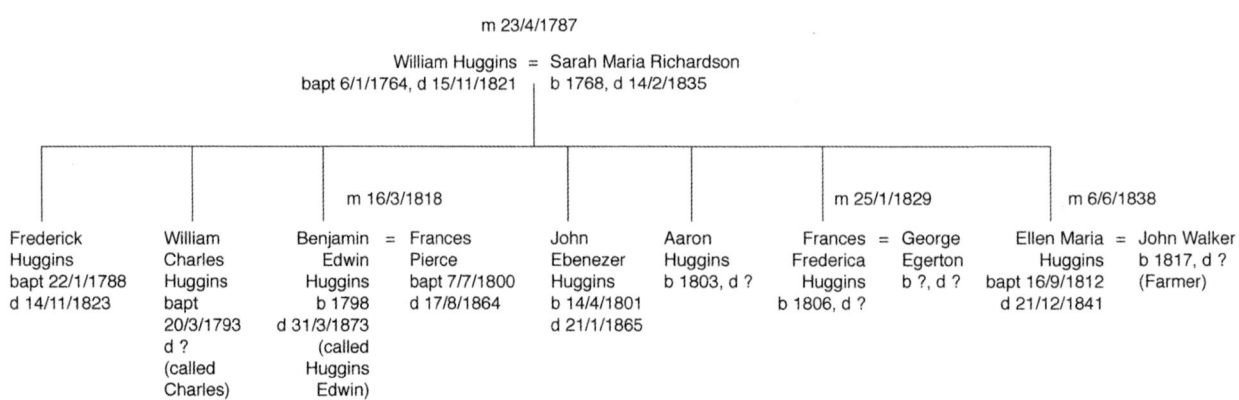

Appendix 4
Managers Of Stamford Theatre 1768-1847

1768-1781	James Augustus Whitley
1782-1783	John Anderson O'Brien
1784-1795	William Pero
1795-1800	William Perkins Taylor and James Robertson
1800-1802	Mrs Hannah Henrietta Taylor and James Robertson
1802-1805	Benjamin Wrench and James Robertson
1805-1806	James Robertson and Mr Adcock
1806-1818	James Robertson and Thomas Hill Wilson Manly
1818-1839	Thomas Hill Wilson Manly
1839-1840	Mr Boddie
1840-1843	Mrs Frances Mary Robertson
1843-1847	William Robertson

Appendix 5
Theatres in the Lincoln Circuit in 1803

Writing from Newark on 1 December 1803, Thomas Shaftoe Robertson sent details to James Winston about all the theatres in the Lincoln circuit, as follows:

LINCOLN: Has been built upwards of 40 years and has undergone very little improvement. It is situated in the Kings Arms Inn yard. Will hold between £60 and £70. The season commences in the Race Week in the beginning of September and continues two months.

NEWARK: Was in its first state temporary where the Methodist Chapel now is in Balderton Gate, only pit and gallery. About 30 years back a new theatre was built by the late John Brough, Esq., with front boxes and which at several times underwent alterations. This year it has undergone a total alteration and enlargement – circular boxes, upper and lower, and allowed to be a most handsome and elegant provincial theatre. It is situated in Middlegate, calculated to contain when filled between £60 and £70. The season six weeks commencing in November.

GRANTHAM: In its first state was a rude temporary building of pit and gallery in Westgate. Thirty years back a more convenient one was built in the Market Place but no boxes. Ten years back front boxes were added. In 1800 the lease being out a handsome new theatre with circular upper and lower boxes was built by Joseph Lawrence. It is situated at the bottom of [Swinegate]. When full will contain about £50. Season five weeks commencing in December.

BOSTON: Was a temporary pit and gallery in a granary in the Market Place. Twenty-six years ago one was built by the Corporation within a few yards of the old temporary one and at that time esteemed handsome, having front boxes but being found for several years past much too small for its improving spirits and population a new one on the most improved plan is about being built by subscription. The present theatre, when filled to inconvenience, will hold about £40. Season six weeks commencing latter end of January.

WISBECH: Was for several years at the end of the town on the road to Spalding and from its inconvenient situation when the lease was out about ten or twelve years back a new one was built in the centre of the town at the back of York Row, the property of Mr Robertson. When full it will hold upwards of £40. The season six weeks commencing in March.

HUNTINGDON: Was for many years temporary in a barn. Four years back an elegant theatre at the back of the George inn was built by subscription with lower and upper boxes, planned by Mr Rowles, nephew of Mr Holland, the architect of Drury Lane. When filled will contain about £50. The Lincoln Co. attends the Race Week and every second year.

PETERBOROUGH: Was for many years pit and gallery noted for being dirty and inconvenient. A handsome commodious theatre was built four years back by subscription within a few yards of the old one. Contains when full about £50. Season seven weeks commencing in June.

SPALDING: Is on the same ground that it has been for upwards of forty years. It has undergone various alterations. Ten years ago boxes were added. It is in the White Hart Inn Yard. When full upwards of £40. Season one month commencing August.

NORTHAMPTON: Still remains as it has been for many years temporary. When full contains upwards of £30, situated in St Giles Street. The season six weeks commencing in May every second year.

Mr Robertson added that prices through his circuit were boxes 3s; pit 2; gallery 1s. Half price, for admission to the latter part of the evening, was taken at every town.

The above list is from Warwick, Lou, *Theatre Unroyal; Or, They called them Comedians*, Northampton (1974), p.30.

STAMFORD THEATRE

Extract from the notes by James Winston, said to have been supplied by Mr Gosli in 1793. That date is not correct as James Robertson did not become manager until 1795, taking over from William Pero. The date was probably 1803, the same year that Tom Robertson supplied information on his theatres, as that would be 35 years after the theatre was built.

> Theatre the property of Mrs Gosle built about 35 years. Robertson (manager). It was recon'd a wonderfully grand place as before that they play'd in barns throughout this part of the Country. It is a pretty Th. now & lately we have much improved it by taking away the Heavy pillars & putting in their place small cast iron ones. business at Races & fair is very good, principal perfs. well rewarded at their Benf. Charges 11 Guineas. The charges here are low as an equivalent for the performers play – Season in Summer holds £60. Earl of Exeter has Private Box his arms under it.

From Mackintosh, Iain and Ashton, Geoffrey, *The Georgian Playhouse: Actors, Artists, Audiences and Architecture*, 1730-1830, (Arts Council, 1975).

Appendix 6

John Caple's *Corps Dramatique*, 1848

In a playbill for a performance at Stamford Theatre on 3 April 1848, John Caple listed all the members of his company, with the other duties some of them undertook, and a few other non-acting staff. This is the only comprehensive list for any company in Lincolnshire in the Georgian period.

He also named the artists who had painted his scenery.

In relation to his actors, he also listed the theatres from which they came to join his company. Miss Goddard heads the list, as his partner and future wife, without indicating the theatre from which she came. Of his 25 actors, most came from the northern half of England, with only three from London, one from Birmingham, two from Leicester, three from Dublin and one from Glasgow. The following numbers had performed at each of the theatres listed (several actors listed more than one theatre): Newcastle 5, Manchester 4, Liverpool 4, London 4 (Olympic 2, Drury Lane 1, Covent Garden 1), Dublin 3, Whitehaven 2, Leicester 2, Birmingham 1, Glasgow 1, Hull 1 and Sheffield 1.

The relevant part of the playbill is set out below.

THE *CORPS DRAMATIQUE*

Has been selected with the utmost care, and will be found adequate to the enactment of the first productions of our National Dramatists, and will consist of the following Ladies and Gentlemen:–

Miss Goddard

Mrs Raymond of the Theatres Royal, Liverpool and Manchester

Mrs Marian Douglas of the Theatre Royal, Liverpool
Miss Scrimshaw of the Theatre Royal, Hull
Miss Connor of the Theatres Royal, Glasgow and Liverpool
Miss Ramond of the Theatres Royal, Liverpool and Manchester
Mrs Lacey of the Theatre Royal, Manchester
Mrs Proctor of the Theatre Royal, Newcastle
Mrs Robins of the Theatre Royal, Whitehaven
Miss Proctor of the Theatre Royal, Newcastle

Mr Lacey of the Theatre Royal, Manchester
Mr Phelerius of the Theatre Royal, Dublin
Mr Henderson of the Theatre Royal, Birmingham
Mr Artaud of the Olympic Theatre, London
Mr Marris of the Theatre Royal, Newcastle
Mr Griffiths of the Theatre Royal, Leicester
Mr Masters of the Theatre Royal, Dublin
Mr Fielding of the Theatre Royal, Leicester
Mr Robins of the Royal Olympic Theatre *[London?]*
Mr Woodridge, from the Theatre Royal, Sheffield
Mr Proctor of the Theatre Royal, Newcastle
Mr Godfrey of the Theatre Royal, Newcastle
Mr Brown of the Theatres Royal, Drury Lane and Covent Garden
Mr Acraman of the Theatre Royal, Whitehaven
Mr Rogers of the Theatre Royal, Dublin

The scenery will be entirely new, and Painted by Messrs Thorne and Dearlove from the Theatres Royal, Liverpool and Norwich.

Acting Manager – Mr Henderson
Stage Manager – Mr Artaud
Prompter – Mr Fielding
Artist – Mr Fisher
Leader of the Orchestra – Mr Rogers
Costumier – Mr Brown
Mechanist – Mr Hurst
The Properties, by Mr Rough

Appendix 7

Southwell Theatre – Surviving Remains

The theatre building at Southwell still stands and contains some evidence of its former use. The theatre was in an upper room and still has the stage, the door to the gallery, the original floor of the pit, and iron posts which seem to mark the position of the front of the boxes on each side, as well as rooms that were doubtless the original dressing room and green room. There is also a narrow passage behind the stage that would have allowed actors to pass from one side to the other, without being seen, and enter from stage right. The building also has a semi-circular bow in the west wall that may have contained a spiral stair to give a separate access to the boxes on that side of the theatre. The theatre does not seem to have had boxes at the far end facing the stage, as the floor of the gallery behind them would appear to have been too low to allow boxes there.

Bibliography

Manuscript Sources

Anonymous, *A lady's diary of a visit to Boston in 1766,* transcript from Christine Waterfield, 2014

British Library – Manly account books, 1820s

Hewings, Richard, *The Public Buildings of Boston 1702–1822,* unpublished paper read to the Association of Art Historians at Sheffield, 9 April 1988

Gainsborough Public Library – Theatre file

Grantham Library – Playbills

Grimsby Library – Skelton Collection

Lincoln Central Library – Abel Collection of Cuttings; Playbills

Lincolnshire Archives – Ancaster papers; Smedley papers; playbills

Louth Naturalists, Antiquarian and Literary Society – Playbills

Wisbech Museum – Playbills

Newspapers

Leicester Journal

Lincoln, Rutland and Stamford Mercury/Stamford Mercury

Nottingham Journal

Theses

Clemenston, Diana W., *The Theatre Royal, Lincoln,* Lincoln (1960)

Hemingway, G., *The Robertson Family and the Lincoln and Nottingham Theatrical Circuits,* Lincoln (1976) [UP 7467]

Parker, B.J., *The Theatre of Gainsborough. From 1772 until 1850,* Gainsborough (1963)

Works of Reference

Andrews, C. Bruyn (ed), *The Torrington Diaries, containing the tours through England and Wales of the Hon John Byng (later Fifth Lord Torrington) between the years 1781 and 1794,* Vol.2, London (1935).

Booth, Michael R.; Southern, Richard; Marker, Frederick and Lise-Lone; and Davies, Robertson, *The Revels History of Drama in English,* Vol.IV 1750–1880, London (1975).

Burnim, Kelman A. and Highfill, Philip H. Jnr, *John Bell, Patron of British Theatrical Portraiture,* Carbondale, South Illinois University Press (1998).

Hartnoll, Phyllis (ed), *The Oxford Companion to the Theatre,* London (3rd edition 1967).

Hartnoll, Phyllis and Found, Peter (eds), *The Concise Oxford Companion to the Theatre (New Edition),* London (2nd edition 1992).

Highfill, Philip H. Jnr, Burnim, Kelman A. and Langhans, Edward, *Biographical Dictionary of Actors, Actresses, Musicians, Dancers, Managers and Other Stage Personnel in London, 1660–1800,* 16 volumes, Carbondale, South Illinois University Press (1973–93)

Jones, Stanley; Major, Kathleen; Varley, Joan; and Johnson, Christopher, *The Survey of Ancient Houses in Lincoln, IV: Houses in the Bail, Steep Hill, Castle Hill and Bailgate,* Lincoln (1996).

Kahrl, Stanley J., *Records of Plays and Players in Lincolnshire 1300–1585,* (The Malone Society, Collections, Vol.VIII), Oxford (1974).

Lincolnshire Family History Society, *Lincolnshire Marriage Index 1700–1837,* Lincoln (2011).

Moody, Jane and O'Quinn, Daniel (eds), *The Cambridge Companion to British Theatre 1730–1830,* Cambridge (2007).

Oxford Dictionary of National Biography (*DNB*).

Robertson, Thomas William, Jnr, *The Principal Dramatic Works of Thomas William Robertson*, Vol.1, London (1889).

Stokes, James (ed), *Records of Early English Drama – Lincolnshire*, Torronto (2009).

White, William, *Directory of Lincolnshire*, Sheffield (1st edition 1842, 2nd edition 1856, 3rd edition 1872).

Winston, James, *The Theatric Tourist*, London (1805, facsimile 2008).

Other Published Works

Atkin, Wendy J., '*A most ingenious Authress* Frances Brooke (1724–1789) and her Lincolnshire connections', *Lincolnshire History and Archaeology*, Vol.32, Lincoln (1997).

Bagley, George S., *Boston Its Story and People*, Boston (1986).

Bailey, Isabel (ed), *Transcript of Pishey Thompson's Boston Diary, 18 October 1842 to 6 April 1844*, Boston (1994).

Beardsley, Martyn and Bennett, Nicholas (eds), *Grateful to Providence. The Diary and Accounts of Matthew Flinders, Surgeon, Apothecary and Man-Midwife 1775–1802*, Vol.1 1775–1784, Vol.2 1785–1802, Lincoln Record Society Vol.95 and Vol.97, Lincoln (2007 and 2009).

Borsey, Peter, *The English Urban Renaissance: Culture and Society in the Provincial Town, 1660-1770*, Oxford (1991).

Brewer, John, *The Pleasures of the Imagination: English Culture in the Eighteenth Century*, Abingdon (2013).

Brown, Susan, 'Manufacturing spectacle: the Georgian playhouse and urban trade and manufacturing', *Theatre Notebook*, Vol.64, No.2, London (2010).

Bull, June and Vernon, *Peterborough Then and Now*, Stroud (2013).

Byrne, Paula, *Perdita, the Life of Mary Robinson*, London (2004).

Carroll, Ray; Martin, Ernie; Tingey, Ray; Tingle, Joyce; and Waltham, Dorothy, *Holbeach Past – Part 1*, Holbeach (1988).

Chapman, Peter, *Grimsby. The Story of the World's Greatest Fishing Port*, Grimsby (1991).

Clarke, J.N., *Education in a Market Town – Horncastle*, Chichester (1976).

Donaldson, Frances, *The Actor Managers*, London (1970).

Donaldson, Walter, *Recollections of an Actor*, London (1865).

Durham, Weldon B. (ed), *American Theatre Companies 1749-1887*, New York (1986).

Earl, John, *British Theatres and Music Halls*, Princes Risborough (2005).

Evans, Rosemary, 'Theatre Music in Nottingham, 1760–1800', *Transactions of the Thoroton Society*, LXXVIII, Nottingham (1984).

Field, Moira, *The Lamplit Stage*, Norwich (1985).

Gillett, Edward, *A History of Grimsby*, London (1970).

Gilliland, Thomas, *The Dramatic Mirror; containing the History of the Stage*, London (1808).

Golland, Jim, 'A Dramatic Discovery or, A Manly Enterprise', *Local History Magazine*, No.42, Nottingham (1994).

Gould, Mervyn, *Boston and Spalding Entertainment and the Aspland Howdens*, Wakefield (2005).

Grice, Elizabeth, *Rogues and Vagabonds*, Lavenham, Suffolk (1977).

Grigg, Erik, 'Lincoln's Lost Medieval Theatre', *Lincolnshire Past and Present*, No.67, Lincoln (2007).

Hance, Frank, 'Stamford Theatre and Stamford Racecourse', *The Story of Stamford*, No.3, Stamford (1970).

Henderson, Mary C., *Theater in America*, New York (1996).

Hill, Sir Francis, *Georgian Lincoln*, Cambridge (1966).

Honeybone, Diana and Michael, *The Correspondence of William Stukeley and Maurice Johnson 1714–1754*, Lincoln Record Society Vol.104, Lincoln (2014).

Honeybone, Michael, *The Book of Grantham*, Buckingham (1980).

Hughes, Glenn, *A History of the American Theatre 1700–1950*, New York (1950).

Langford, Paul, *A Polite and Commercial People, England 1727–1783*. Oxford (1989).

Leacroft, Helen and Richard, *The Theatre in Leicestershire*, Leicester (1986).

Lincolnshire Archivists' Report 25, *Smedley and Sumners Family Papers* (LLHS 38), Lincoln (1975).

McGregor, Michael, *Historic Pictures of Bourne, Lincolnshire*, Bourne (2000).

Mackintosh, Iain and Ashton, Geoffrey, *The Georgian Playhouse: Actors, Artists, Audiences and Architecture, 1730–1830*, London (1975).

Marsden, Walter, *Lincolnshire*, London (1977).

Mayes, Ronald, *The Romance of British Theatres*, articles in theatre programmes in the 1930s.

(The) Mirror of Taste and Dramatic Censor, Vol.1, No.5, London (May 1810).

Molyneux, Frank and Wright, Neil, *An Atlas of Boston*, Boston (1974).

Payne, Michael, 'Mr Whitley and his Company of Comedians: Nottingham St Mary's Gate Theatre, 1761–1865', *Transactions of the Thoroton Society*, Vol.109, Nottingham (2005).

Piercy, John S., *History of Retford*, Retford (1828).

Porter, Herbert, *Boston 1800–1835*, Boston (1941–43).

Richards, John, 'Thomas Shaftoe Robinson and *The Theatric Tourist*', *Theatre Notebook*, Vol.XXIX, No.1, London (1975).

Robinson, David N., *The Book of Horncastle and Woodhall Spa*, Buckingham (1983).

Robinson, David N., *Adam Eve and Louth Carpets, and the Story of Eve & Ranshaw Ltd*, Louth (2010).

Robinson, David and Sturman, Christopher, *William Brown and the Louth Panorama*, Louth (2001).

Rosenfeld, Sybil, 'The Theatrical Notebooks of T.H. Wilson Manly', *Theatre Notebook*, Vol.7, No.1, London (October, December 1952).

Rosenfeld, Sybil, *Georgian Scene Painters and Scene Painting*, Cambridge (1981).

Rosenfeld, Sybil, *The Georgian Theatre of Richmond, Yorkshire*, London (1984).

Sampson, George, *The Concise Cambridge History of English Literature*, Cambridge (1941).

Satherley, Jeremy, *A neat little town – the history of Holbeach*, Holbeach (2004).

Saunders, John, Jnr, *Lincolnshire in 1836*, Lincoln (1836).

Senior, William, *The Old Wakefield Theatre*, Wakefield (1894).

Shilton, Richard Phillips, *The History of Southwell*, Newark (1816 reprinted 2011).

Sissons, Eddie, and The Delvers, *That's Entertainment (Part 1)*, Gainsborough (2001).

Smith, Martin, *Stamford Then and Now*, Stamford (1992).

Southern, Richard, *The Georgian Playhouse*, London (1948).

Stark, Adam, *The History and Antiquities of Gainsborough*, Gainsborough (1st edition 1817, 2nd edition 1843).

Taylor, David, 'Discoveries and recoveries in the laboratory of Georgian theatre', *New Theatre Quarterly*, Vol.27, No.3 (2011).

Tebbs, H.F., *Peterborough – A History*, Cambridge (1979).

Thompson, Pishey, *History and Antiquities of Boston*, Boston (1856).

Townley, C., *Galway's Early Association with the Theatre*, Galway (2010).

Varley, Joan, *The Parts of Kesteven – Studies in Law and Local Government*, Sleaford (1974).

Walker, J. Holland, 'An Itinerary of Nottingham', *Transactions of the Thoroton Society*, Vol. XXXII, Notiingham (1928).

Warner, Tim, 'Newark's first theatre', *Newark: Aspects of the Past*, Nottingham (1994).

Warner, Tim, 'Newark's great forgotten playwright', *Newark: Aspects of the Past*, Nottingham (1994).

Warner, Tim, 'Curtain rises on the town's first theatre', *Newark Civic Trust Magazine*, Issue 68, Newark (February 2013).

Warwick, Lou, *Theatre Unroyal; Or, They called them Comedians*, Northampton (1974).

Warwick, Lou, *Drama that Smelled; Or, Early Drama in Northampton and Hereabouts*, Northampton (1975).

Warwick, Lou, *The McKenzies called Compton*, Northampton (1977).

Warwick, Lou, *Death of a Theatre; History of the New Theatre, Northampton*, Northampton (1978).

Wood, A.C., 'Nottingham 1836–1865; 1. The Borough 1835–1865', *Transactions of the Thoroton Society*, Vol.LIX, Nottingham (1955).

Wright, Neil R., *Lincolnshire Towns and Industry*, History of Lincolnshire Volume XI, Lincoln (1982).

INDEX

*Numbers in **bold** are maps, pictures, playbills or other illustrations. Plays are listed separately after the main index.*

A

Abbott and Harper's company, 192-193
Abbott and Mosley';s company, 193, 194, 214
Accidents, 60
Account books, 57-58
Acts of Parliament, 19, 23-25, 211, 226
Adcock, Mr, 132, 263
Aldridge, Ira Frederick, (1804-67), 63, **64**, 223, 233, 238
Alford, 96, **112**, 215, 249
Alford theatre, 112, 113, 115, 136, 173, 175, 179, 181-183, 196, 215, 233, 249
Amateur Performers, **124, 125**, 156-157, 162, 164, 166, 219, 223, 227, 229, 239, 242, 247, 259-260
America, *see 'United States'*
Ancaster, 3rd Duke of, (1714-78), 122-123
Animal stars, 136
Argand lamp, 32, 72
Armstrong, Mr, 158
Arundell, James Everard, **197**, 199
Assaults in theatres, 42
Audience, 27-28, **38**, 37-42, **214**
Auditorium, 27-28, 36-37, 67-68, **214**
Audley, Erasmus, 80-81

B

Ballet, *The Loves of Mars and Venus*, 22
Baltimore, theatre, 163
Bardney, 202
Barton on Humber, theatre, 177, 179, 182-184, 203, 232
Bath, theatre, 23, 25
Belfast, theatre, 200
Benefits, defined, 58
Bespeaks, defined, 34
Bespeaks, sponsors of, 34, 35, 121-122, 124, 185, 221, 225
Betty, William Henry West, **62**, 62-63 135-136, 175
Beverley, theatre, 181, 189, 197
Beynon, Mr, 114, 132. 171
Bingham (Notts), theatre, 179, 186
Boddie, Mr, 217-218, 263
Boston (Lincs), 18, 19, 23, 26, 172, 249, 250, 254, 260
Boston, first theatre, 39, 90, 91, **102**, 102-104, **148**, 263
Boston, second theatre, 37, 42-44, 62, 67-68, 123, 138-139, 144-145, **148**, 153, 156, 159, 168, 172-173, 203, 209, 215, 220, 221, 225, 228, 232-235, 239, 246, 246-247, 250, 255
Boston, warehouse theatre, 23, 103, **148**, 263
Boston (Massachusetts), 95, 162, 164
Bourne, theatre, 136, 179, 183, **186**, 186-189, 192-194, 196, 201, 204
Boxes, **27, 39, 40**, 38-41, 43-45, 143-144, **149**, 149-150, 264
Box keepers, 45-46, 142, 143, 156
Box offices, 45-46
Bradford, theatre, 187, 189, 195
Brady family, 202
Braham, John, 53
Breeches roles, 64
Bridlington, theatre, 179, 185, 186
Brigg, theatre, 121, 172, 175, 176, 183, **187**,188, 190, 192, 197, 235, 249
Bristol, theatre, 25
Broadbent Theatre, 260
Brooke, Mrs Frances (1724-89), 117-118, **118**
Brown, Mrs Elizabeth, 108, 134, 262
Bruce and Bullen's company, 56, 176, 195-198, 203, 223
Bruce, John, 195-198
Brunton, Mrs Anna (1773-1849), 54-56, 124, 135, 262
Brunton, Anne, *see Merry, Anne*
Brunton, Eliza, 56
Brunton, John (1741-1819), 54, 262
Brunton, John (1775-1849), 54, 56, 124, **134**, 135, 151, 262
Brunton, Louise (1785-1860), Countess of Craven, 56, 66, 262
Buckinghamshire, Albinia, Countess of, 124, **124, 125**
Bullen and Bruce's company, 56, 176,195-198, 203, 223
Bullen, Mr, 54, 195-198
Bullen, Mrs, 54, 196
Bullen, Melinda, *see Smedley*
Bulwer-Lytton, Edward, (1803-73), 210-211
Burghley House, 59
Butler, Mr, 117, 172
Butler and King's company, 114, 118, 171-173
Byng, John (later Lord Torrington), 113-114

C

Caistor, theatre, 50, 179, 183, **201**, 202, 212
Canada, 117
Candles, 37, 150
Caple's company, 203, 232, 237, 264-265
Caple, John (d.1863), 232, 235-242, **251**, 264
Carrighan, Andrew, *see Gosli*
Cawdell, James (1750-1800), 172-173
Centlivre, Susannah (1667-1723), **20**, 20
Charity performances, 137-138
Charleston, South Carolina, 95, 118, 162
Chesterfield, theatre, 69, 86, 132, 164, 165, 255
Chesterton, Mr, 163
Children, reduced prices for, 43-44, 177
Cibber, Colley (1671-1757), 20
Circular boxes, 144
Clarke, Mr, 173, 178
Clifford's company, 203
Closing theatres, 17, 50, 85, 100, 118, 185, 190-191, 213-215, 225, 231-234, 242-243, 245-248, 255-258
Cockpits, 70, 185, 215
Cockfighting, 23
Collier, Mr, 158, **162**, 173
Collier and Huggins company, 115, 118, 152, 163, 173
Comedian, defined, 21, 249
Comedy, defined, 28
Compton, Henry (1805-77), 207, **212**, 212, 251, 258
Costumes, 58, 63, 168
Cowell, Joseph Leathley (1792-1863), **157**, 158, 161-162
Craven, Earl of, 56, 66
Crowland, theatre, 70, 171, 179
Croyland, 22

D

Daniel, J. Robson, 43-45, 249-250
Davenport's company, 213, 229, 251

Death by fire, 134-135
Decoration of theatres, 76-77, 167, 237
Della Cruscans, 123
Denny, William, 23
Derby, theatre, 34, 37, 86, **89**, 90, 110, 112, 114, 132-134, 153, 164-165, 238, 247, 255
Design of theatres, **27**, 28, **38**, 38, **39**, 67, **84**, 87, 147
Dickens, Charles, 190, 210, 253
Doncaster, theatre, 221
Donington, 19, 30, 93-94
Dress Circle, 225, 237
Dublin, theatre, 200
Dunn, Mrs, 135
Durham, theatre, 171, 172-173
Durravan's company, 90, 96

E

Eaglesfield and Wakeman, 250
Elephant on stage, 136
Elizabethan drama, 19
Engravings, 74, 77, 160, 212
Exeter, Earl/Marquess of, 87, 114, 186-187, 237, 254

F

Farce, defined, 28
Farren, Miss, Countess of Derby, 66
Faucit, John, *see Saville*
Faukland's company, Miss, 250-251
Finances, 68-71, 148, 164-165, 168
Fisher, Clara, **165**, 165, 188
Flinders, Matthew, 30, 76, 93-94, 231
Folkingham, 179
Foote, Maria (c1797-1867), 61
Franklin, Robert Henry (1770-1802), **109**, 109, **126**, **129**, 130, 142, 144
Freemasons, 35, 220
French Revolution, 125-126
Fricker, Thomas (1812-58), 228
Fromow, Mr, 59

G

Gainsborough, 174, 250, 259, 260
Gainsborough, first theatre, 39, 67, 92, **96-99**, 99-100, 118, 257
Gainsborough, theatre in Old Hall, 36, 39, 42, 48, 49, 67, **96**, 100, **115-117**, 114-118, 126, 171-172, 174-176, 181-183, 190, 192, 194-195, 201, 204, 207, 221, 222, 227-228, 232, 235, 237, 239, 243-246, 255
Garrick, David (1717-79), 25, 30, 72
Gas lighting, 37, 147
Gifford family, 203
Goddard, Eleanor, 235, 242, 264
God Save the King, 125-127, 212
Gosli, Andrew Joseph Carrigham (1746-1815), 54, 110-112, 134
Gosli, Elizabeth, 54, 110
Grantham, 20, 33, 130, **142**, 250, 258, 259
Grantham, Market Place theatre, 102-104, 143, 263
Grantham, Swinegate theatre, 36, 44, 69, 76, 77, 121-123, 126, 137, **142-144**, 143-144, 148, 153, 156-157, 159, **162**, 166-168, 203, 207, 209, 211, 221, 223, 232, 235-236, 238, **240**, **241**, 242-243, 255, 257, 263
Grantham, Westgate theatre, 39, 90-92, 102-104, 263
Great Driffield, theatre,179, 185

Greatheed, Bertie (1759-1826), 123
Greatheed, Lady Mary, 123
Grimsby, 18, 19, 248, 254, 258-259
Grimsby, theatre, 69, 178, 179, **181**, **182**, 181-183, 232, 248, 258-259
Grist, Thomas (d.1808), **61**, 61, 171
Grose, David, 203
Gurner, Mr J.O., 60, 163, 211

H

Haddelsey, Robert, 81
Half-price, *see Second price*
Halifax, theatre, 37, 69, 112, 133, 153, 164, 216, 221, 247, 255
Hallam, John Springfield, 158, **162**, 164
Hamilton, Mr, 117
Hamilton, Myrton (c1745-1818), 200-202
Harborough, Earl of, 66
Harlequin, The, 29, **79**, 81
Hazlewood, Mr, 235
Hartopp family, 113, 201, 208
Heathcote, Robert, 66
Heating, 36, 144
Henderson, Mr, 200, 203, 238, 241, 245, 265
Henderson and Melvin's company, 203, 238
Herbert, Nathaniel, 54, 69, **73**, **81**, 81, 83, 94-95, 105-106
Herbert, William (c1695-1770), 34, 81, 83-85, 90, 95
Hickman, Henry Bacon (1789-1862), 190, 195, 243-245
Hilton, William (1752-1822), **72**, 74, 76, 160
Holbeach, 18, 20, 200
Holbeach, theatre, 177, 179, 182-183, **184**, 186, 232, 257
Holcroft, Thomas, 32
Horncastle, theatre, 67, **152**, 152, **153**, 172-176, 183, 190, 196, 200, 207, 255, 257
Howden, theatre, 69, 179, 185
Huddersfield, theatre, 189
Huggins (and Clarke's) company, 115, 118, 152, 163-164, 172-176, **174**, **175**, 183, 187, 199, 200, 205-207, 211, 227, 244 *see also Collier and Huggins*
Huggins, Charles (b.1793), 174-176, 205, 262
Huggins, Edwin (1798-1873), 174, 176, 262
Huggins, Sarah (c1768-1835), 54, 56, 171-174, 176, 205, 262
Huggins, William (1764-1821), 54, 56, 60, 171-174, 262
Hull, 179, 202
Hull, Queen's Theatre, 238
Hull, theatre, 23, 25, 197, 199, 221
Huntingdon, 170
Huntingdon, theatre, 92, 110, 114, 122, **140**, **141**, 141, 153, 157, 168, 257, 263-264

I

Immanuel, Mr, 147
Imprisonment for debt, 155-158
Inchbald, Elizabeth, 35
Infant Roscius, 62-63, 135-136, 175
Irnham Hall, **197**, 199-200
Ipswich, theatre, 144-145, **146**, 147

J

Jones, Richard, 199
Jordan, Dorothy, 106-108

K

Kean, Charles, 224
Kean, Edmund (1787-1833), 30, **31**, 32, 61, 63, 164, 209
Kendal, Dame Margaret (Madge) (1848-1935), 220, 248, **254**, 254, 261
Keregan, Thomas, 22
King, William, 56, **73**, 114, 118, 171-172
King's Lynn, theatre, 36, 41, 91, 92, **93**, 96, 107, 151, 260
Knapp, Revd. Henry Ryder, 113
Knight, Mr, 190, 192

L

Laceby, 198
Land, Miss E., 194, 220
Laudanum, 61
Lease of theatre, 68, 69
Leicester, theatre, 37, 90, 96, 99, 114, 140, 164, 175, 189, 201, 215-216, 218, 221, 224, 255
Lewis, 'Monk', 32, 137
Lighting, 32, 37, **38**, 72, 147, 166-167
Lincoln, 17, 18, 203, 258, 259, 260
Lincoln, Asylum, 42
Lincoln circuit, 81, 90-92, 100, 103, 141, 144, 152-154, 175, 206-207, 211
Lincoln company, 91-92, **91**, **93**, **111**, 152-154, **157**, 161-164, 167-169, 176, 178, 187, 203, 209-212, 248, 258
Lincoln, County Hospital, 42
Lincoln, first theatre, 23, 67, **78**, **80**, 80-85
Lincoln, King's Arms yard theatre, 25, 37, 41, 44, 47, 67, 77, **82**, **83**, 85, 90, 92, 115, 121, 122, **126**, 127, 129, 138, **149**, 149-150, **154**, 157-158, 160, 166-167, 169, 175, 176, 198, 199, 206-211, 215-217, 219, 222-225, 228-229, 232, 235-238, 241, 247, 254, 258, 263
Linley, Thomas (1756-78), 122
Little Dalby Hall (Leics), 113, 201-202
Local economy, theatres in, 70
London, Adelphi theatre, 56
London, Covent Garden theatre, 20, 22, 24, 57, 110, 118, 136, 139, 140, 211
London, Drury Lane theatre, 20, 24, 57, 72, 116, 122, 123, 141, 161-162, 194, 201, 211, 239, 245
London, Haymarket theatre, 24, 25, 113, 117, 194
London stars, **31**, 61, **62**, **64**, 123, 135-136, 164, **165**, 188, **208**, 209, 224
Long Sutton, 18-19, 192-193, 196
Lord Chamberlain, 24, 211
Louth, 18, 19, 249
Louth, theatre, 42, 76, 115, 118, **119**, 151, **174**, 172-175, 196-198, 205, 207, 209, **213**, 213, 232
Loutherbourg, Philippe Jacques de (1740-1814), 72, 111, 118
Love, Emma Sarah (1798-1881), 65

M

Macarty, Mr, 50, **201**, 202
Macready, William (1793-1873), 30, 61, 63, 140, 152, 164, **208**, 209, 225, 251
Maddocks, W.H., 238-239
Maddesley, Edward, 81
Malton (Yorks), 203
Manly, Charles, 133, 216
Manly, Thomas Hill Wilson (c1772-1840), 33, 47, 49, 53, 56, 58-60, 69, 71, 94, 131-134, 157, 159-160, 164-167, 169, 216-217, 219, 224, 263
Mansfield, theatre, 172, 174

March (Cambs), theatre, 183-185, 220, 225, 232
Marinus, Miss Margharetta, 60, 161, 163 *see also Robertson, Margaret*
Market Deeping, 19, 26, 172, 177, 179, 189, 192, 196, 212, 232, 249
Market Rasen, theatre, 178, 182, 197, 203, 232
Medieval religious plays, 18
Mellon, Harriet, 65, 66, 121
Melodrama, definition, 31
Melton Mowbray, theatre, 36, 70, 111, 112, 179, 182, 183, 185, 189, 192, 196, 202, 215, 232, 250
Melvin, Mr, 196, 203
Merry, Mrs Anne (1769-1808), **55**, 54-56, 124, 262
Merry, Robert (1755-98), 54, 123-124, 262
Mildenhall, theatre, 179
Miller, James Edward, 54, 106, 107-109, **109**, 130
Monson, Lady, 41, 121
Mosley, John, 188, 189, **193**, 192-195, 214, 227. *See also Rogers and Mosley*
Mosley and Abbott's company, 192-194, 227
Mosley and Rice's company, 194-195, 227
Music, 33, 53
Music Hall, 258-259

N

Negro minstrel shows, 223
Nelson, Lord, 32, 139
Newark, 179, 231, 250
Newark, theatre, 36, 37, 69, 76, 77, 86, 92, 97, **101**, 101-102, 122, 127, 144, **145**, **147**, 153, 157, 159, 160, 163, 166, 167-169, 194, 207, 209, 214, 232, 235, 255, **256**, 257, 263
Newby, Edgar, 227, 228
Newspaper advertising, 35-36, 137, 159, 169
New York, theatre, 162, 163, 233
Norris, Mrs, 60, 139, 158, 162
Northampton, theatre, 76, 110, 112-114, 127, 149, 152-153, 258, 264
Northouse, George (1798-1844), 60, **75**, 76-77, 187, 196, 211-212
Norwich company of comedians, 22, 54, 56, 57, 83, 92, 106, 135, 178, 226
Norwich, theatre, 23, 25, 135
Nottingham, 24, 26, 160, 170, 179, 200
Nottingham, theatre, 23, 24, 37, 41, 44, 69, 86, **89**, 90, 110, 112, 114, 127, 132, 134, 153, 160, 164-165, 218, 231, 238, 255
Novels adapted for the stage, 210-211

O

Oakham, theatre, 193, 250
O'Brien, John Anderson (c1740-1810), 110-111, 129-130, 263
Opposition to theatre, 19-20, 46-50, 168, 205-206, 213, 226, 246-247
Oundle, 92
Oundle, theatre, 122, 154, 167-168, 194, 207, 221, 232
Out of season use of theatres, 69, 185, 186, 215-216
Ownership of theatres, 68-69, 185-187

P

Paganini, Niccolo, 206
Pantomime, defined, 29
Paton, Eliza, 209
Pensions, 135
Pero, William (d.1803), 36, 56, 74, 111-115, 129, 130, 171, 263
Peterborough, 130, 233-234
Peterborough, theatre, 33, 65, 77, 90-92, 100, 122, 127, 136, 141-142, 153, 157, 159, 166-167, 176, 207, 211, 216, 218-219, 221-222, 225, 232-233, 255, 264

Peters, John (1742-97), 59
Philadelphia, theatre, 55, 95, **100**, 118, 162, 163
Pittsburgh, theatre, 163
Playbills, 73, **80**, **109**, **117**, **126**, **154**, **162**, **166**, **174**, **175**, **182**, **187**, **193**, **197**, **201**, **208**, **213**, **239**
Pontefract, theatre, 189
Poverty, 57, 61, 223-224
Prices, 43-45, 136, 206, 224, 249, 259, 264
Proscenium door, **28**, 28
Prostitutes, actresses seen as, 65
Publicity, 33-34

Q
Queen's Jester, The, 212
Quick, John (1748-1831), **136**, 136

R
Railways opened, 226, 231, 246
Railway principle, 221, 225
Rayner, Samuel, 242, 247
Redbourne Hall, 66, 121, 176
Reduced prices, 223, 227, 237
Reeve, Mr, 77, 188
Reeve, Miss, 188
Rent of theatres, 68-70
Repertoire, 28-32
Retford, theatre, 69, 86, 112, 115, 132, 164, 167, 207
Rice, Charles, **193**, 194-195
Richardson, Sarah, *see Huggins, Sarah*
Richmond (Virginia), theatre, 118
Richmond (Yorks), theatre, 67
Riot in Stamford theatre, 169
Road accidents, 94
Robertson, Ann (1741-1803), 54, 105-107, 130, 261
Robertson, Frances (Fanny) (1768-1855), 37, 42, 54, 62-64, 66, 108-109, 129, 130, 134-136, 147, 150, 154, 156-159, 161, 164, 168, 170, 205-207, 209, 213-214, 216, 218-220, 251, 261, 262, 263
Robertson, Frederick, 160-161, 261
Robertson, George Fowler (1774-1843), 97, 131, 142, 160, 261
Robertson, James Shaftoe (1723-80), 35, 52, 54, 95-99, 105, 261
Robertson, James (1773-1831), 33, 54, 56, **73**, 77, 97, 105, 106-107, 114, 130-132, 157-161, 164, 170, 205, 261, 263
Robertson, Margaret Elizabeth (d.1876), 53, 161, 205, 209, 219, 220, 224, 261. *see also Marinus, Miss*
Robertson, Madge, *see Kendal*
Robertson, Thomas Shaftoe (1765-1831), 26, 35, 42, 44, 54, 59, 65, 76, 92, 97, 105-109, 114, 121, 126, 130, 134, 137-38, 144, 147-150, 152-159, 170, 205, 251, 261, 262, 263
Robertson, Thomas William (1829-71), 220, 253-254, 258, 261
Robertson. William Shaftoe (1796-1872), 53, 54, 130, 161, 170, 205-207, 209-210, 213, 215-217, 220-226, 228-235, 242, 246, 248, 251, 253, 261, 263
Rogers and Mosley, 189, 192-193, 227. *see also Mosley, John*
Rogers, Mr, 192-193
Rogues and vagabonds, 19, 24
Roscius, 63 (note)
Roscius, Young, **62**, 62, 135-136, 175

S
St Albans, Duke and Duchess of, 65, 66, 121, 176, 190, 198
Sandon, Stretton, 244

Sankey's company, 227
Sauceman, 66
Saville, John Faucit, 218, 238, 239, 255
Scenery, 23, **27**, 60, **75**, 72-77, 225
Scenery painters, 60, 72-77, 160, 211-212, 236, 244, 265
Scraggs, William, 204
Season tickets, 224, 242
Second-price, 43, 182
Selby, theatre, 70, 185-186
Seymour, Mr E.H. 57, 135
Shakespeare Dinner, Lincoln, 210
Shakespeares' plays, 24, 30-31, 33, 57
Sheath's Bank, 151
Sheffield, theatre, 111, 136, 153, 164, 221, 238
Sibthorp, Colonel, 208, 210
Siddons, Sarah (1755-1831), 57, 61, 65, **123**, 123
Sidney, Mr Scholey (1738-1815), 60
Sidney, Mrs (first), 60
Sidney, Mrs (second) (1762-1840), 60
Simms, Mr J., **197**, 199-200
Skegness, 197, 202
Sleaford, 18, **118**, 118, 191
Sleaford, theatre, 37, 49, 69, 179, **183**, 183, **184**, 189-194, **193**, 199, 203, 232, 248, 250-251, 254, 255, 257, 260
Smedley's company, **180**, **187**, 176-191
Smedley, George, 189, 191
Smedley, Joseph Close (1784-1863), 26, 33-34, 35, 37, 47, 49, 56, 57-60, 69-71, 115, 171, **182**, 176-192, 203, 207, 219, 221, 227, 248
Smedley, Joseph, junior, 189
Smedley, Mrs Melinda (1781-1870), 56, 177-178, 191
Snagg, Thomas (1746-1812), 91, 94
Sock and buskin, 50
Southwell, theatre, **150**, **151**, 150-151, 177, 179, 183, 255-257, 265
Spalding, **22**, 22-23, **138**, **139**, 220, 249
Spalding, theatre, 39, 42, **73**, 74, 90, 104, 106, 107, **109**, 115, 121, 127, 136, **138**, **139**, 140, 153, 157, 166, 167, 175, 198, 218, 225, 232, 249, 255, 264
Spalding, Town Hall used as theatre, **22**, 22, **139**
Spilsby, theatre, 182-183, 190, 196, 198, 207, 232, 250
Sponsors of bespeaks, 34-35, 121-122, 124
Stamford, 18, 19, 21, 22, 32, 33, **228**, 250
Stamford circuit, 86, **89**, 90, 153, 164-165
Stamford company, 59, 65, 66, 107, 114, 116, 129-131, **131**, 134-135, 157, 170-173, 200-201
Stamford, first theatre, 23, **84**, 85-86, 115
Stamford, Guildhall, 22, 33
Stamford, St Mary's St theatre, 25, 32, 34, 36, 37, 42-45, 56, 60, 62-63, 67, 69, 71, 74, **84**, 87-90, 99, 110-112, 121, 125-126, 132, 137. 160, 164-166, **166**, 169, 171, 193, 202, **208**, 216-226, 228-229, **234**, 235, 237-239, 254-255, 260, 264
Stannard family, **162**, 163-164, **175**, 175
Stark, Adam (1784-1867), 46
Stevens, George Alexander (1710-80), 54, **81**, 81, 83, 85, 95
Stock roles, 52
Stoke Doyle, 69-70, 142, 167, 179-181
Style of acting, 28

T
Takings at theatres, 44

Taylor, Mrs Hannah Henrietta (1755-1837), 54, 56, 114, 130-132, 263. *see also Mrs Wrench*
Taylor, William Perkins (d.1800), 54, 56, 114, 130-131, 263
Teasdale, Herr, 247
Tee-totallers, 216
Temporary theatres, 43, 149, 213, 238, 249, 258
Tennyson, Alfred (1809-92), 183, 211
Tennyson D'Eyncourt family, 208
Theatre Royal title, 20, 25, 211, 237, 247, 254-255
Theatres redecorated, 166-167
Thompson, Pishey (1785-1862), 49, 220, 249
Ticket offices, 44, 156 *see also Box Offices*
Ticket prices, 43-45, 136, 206, 224, 249, 259, 264
Times of performance, 42
Torrington, Lord, *see Byng*
Training, 52, 53
Tragedy, defined, 28
Transparencies, 32, 74, 111, 127
Tucket, Captain Harvey, 223
Turner, Rev. Samuel, 183
Tussaud, Madame, 175
Tuxford (Notts), 199

U
United States of America, 32, 54-56, 93, 118, 162-164, 212, 233, 254
Uppingham, theatre, 193, 196, 250

V
Vandenhoff, George (1820-84), 233
Victoria, Queen, 206, 212, 247

W
Wages, 57-58, 187
Waggon accidents, 94
Wainfleet, 197
Wakefield, theatre, 37, 39, 42, 86, 88, 181, 189, 191, 192, 221
Wallack, Fanny and Julia, 233
Wallet, William (1813-92), 212
Warren, Mrs Anne *see Merry, Anne*
Washington (DC), theatre, 163
Waterloo, Battle of, 139
Wemyss, Francis Courtney (1797-1859), 107, **162**, 163, 170
Wesley, John, 46
West family, 115-118
West, James (c1763-1805), **117**, 115 118, 171, 172, **201**
West Indies, 83, 93
Whitfield, John (1752-1814), 106, **107**
Whitley and Herbert company, 69, 97-99, 105
Whitley, Cassandra, 86, **88**, 88
Whitley, James Augustus (Jemmy) (c1724-81), 24, 36, 52, 54, 59, 86-88, **89**, 95, 99, 105, 110, 114, 153, 170, 224, 263
Whitsed, solicitor in Derby, 161
Whitsed, Dr John in Wisbech, 251
Whittlesey, 220
Whittlesey, theatre, 154, 218, 221
Wilkinson, Tate, 34, 47, 72, 88, 96-97, 114
Windmill hotel, Alford, **112**, 113, 115
Wisbech, 179, 220, 251
Wisbech, theatre, 67, 77, 90, 92, 102, 115, **120**, 121, 136, 140, 153, 157, 159, **162**, 167, 168, 213-214, **214**, 216, 219-222, 224-225, 229, 232, 234, 251, 257, 260, 263

Worksop, theatre, 172, 174, **175**, 175, 195
Wragby, 202
Wrench, Benjamin (1778-1843), 56, **131**, 131-132, 263
Wrench, Mrs, 56, 59 131-132
Wright, Thomas (1762-1808), 42, 59, 74

Y
Yates, Mrs Eliza, *see Brunton, Eliza*
York, theatre, 22, 23, 25, 96-97, 164
Young Roscius, *see Betty, W.H.W.*

INDEX OF PLAYS
Titles starting 'A' or 'The' are listed under the second word of the title.

Actress of all Work, The, 165
Adelmorn the Outlaw, 137
Africans, The, Or, War, Love and Duty, **162**
Aladdin, or The Wonderful Lamp, 77, 160
Alfonso, King of Castile, 76
All in the Wrong, 103
Anatomist, The, 114
Apparition, The, **109**
Arrived at Portsmouth, 127
As You Like It, 30, 112, 121, 152, 173
Battle of Trafalgar, The, 77
Bee Hive, The, 165
Beaux Stratagem, The, 113
Beggars Opera, The, 22, 33
Beggars Opera Reversed, The, 65
Bertram, 57
Blind Bargain, 163
Bold Stroke for a Husband, A, 117
Bottle, The, 250
Camp, The, 122
Castle Spectre, The, 32, 77, **126**, 148, 149, 202
Catherine and Petrucio, 202
Christmas Carol, A, 210
Cinderella, 92
Citizen, The, 103
Clandestine Marriage, The, 103, 113
Cozeners, The, 107
Cymbeline, 30
David Garrick, 253
Deaf Lover, The, 30
Death of Captain Cook, The, 74
Democratic Rage, Or, Louis the Unfortunate, 64, 126, 172
Devil upon Two Sticks, The, 30, 107
Distress'd Mother, The, 30, 87
Douglas, Or, The Noble Shepherd, **162**
Earl of Warwick, The, 139
Edward and Eleanora, 107
England Preserv'd, 173
Esmeralda, 210
Every One Has His Fault, 220
Family Jars, **208**, 250
Farmer, The, or Macaroni Staymaker, 108
Farmer's Story, The, 210
Fashionable Levities, Or, The World as it Goes, **117**
Flitch of Bacon, The, 60
Floating Beacon, The, Or, the Norwegian Wreckers, **201**, 202
Forest of Bondy, 136
Forty Thieves, The, 76
Foundling of the Forest, **174**
George Barnwell, 49, 177, **187**

Hamlet, 30, 52, 135, 178, 209, 228, 242, 247
Harlequin Rambler, 114
Heart of Midlothian, The, 210
Henry IV, 30, 81
Henry VIII, 30
Hero of the North, The, 35
Honey Moon. The, 150, **154**, 199
How to Die for Love, 35, 156
Hunt the Slipper, 113
Inkle and Yarico, 108
Invasion, The, Or, A Trip to Brighthelmstone, **73**
Ivanhoe, 60, 77, 168, 178, 210
Jew and the Doctor, The, 157, **162**
John Bull, Or, The Englishman's Fireside, 201
Julius Ceasar, 30
King John, 30
King Lear, 30, 196
Lady of Lyon, The, 210
Lady of the Rock, The, 137
Laugh When You Can, **213**
Law of Java, The, 76
Louis XIII, 108, 207
Louis the Unfortunate, 64, 126, 172
Love in a Village, 24, 33, 87, 88
Love Laughs at Locksmiths, 35, 200
Macbeth, 30, 52, 209
Magician of the Rocks, The, 74
Maid of Normandy, The, Or the Death of the Queen of France, 126
Maid of the Mill, The, 24, 33, 60
Maria Marten, Or, The Murder in the Red Barn, 165
Matrimony, 199
Mayor of Garratt, The, 93, 103
Merchant of Venice, The, 30, **109**, 164, 209, 235
Merry Wives of Windsor, The, 30
Midas, 85
Miller and his Men, The, 60, 77
Monsieur Tonson, 74
Money, 211
Much Ado About Nothing, 30
Netley Abbey, Or, The Wooden Walls of Old England, **126**
Nicholas Nickleby, 190, 210
No Song No Supper, 121
Nun, The, 108, 207
Of Age Tomorrow, **197**, 200
One Hour, Or, The Carnival Ball, 208
Oriental Magic, or Harlequin Sorcerer, 146
Othello, 30, 52, 164, 226, 228, 232, 238, 247
Ours, 254
Padlock, The, 238
Patie and Roger, or, The Gentle Shepherd, 122
Peeping Tom of Coventry, 74
Perfection, **213**
Philoclea, **80**
Pickwickians, The, 211
Pickwick Papers, 60, 210
Pizarro, 181, 220, 228
Plot and Counterplot, Or, The Portrait of Cervantes, **174**
Poor Gentleman, The, 196
Pride Shall have a Fall, **182**

Provoked Husband, The, 157
Purse, The, Or, The Benevolent Tar, 164
Quaker's Wedding, The, 93
Raising the Wind, 139, **166**, 175
Recruiting Officer, The, 113
Regent, The, 123
Reprisal, The, 103
Review, The, Or The Wags of Windsor, **201**
Richard III, 30, 163, 178, 211
Richard Coeur de Lion, 74
Richelieu, 210
Rivals, The, 52, 132, 196, 210
Robin Hood, **162**
Robinson Crusoe, 76
Rob Roy, 220, 227
Roland for an Oliver, A, **187**
Romeo and Juliet, 30, 52, 81, 112
Romp, The, 107
Rosina, or Harvest Home, 117-118
St David's Day, 77
Savoyards and the Monkey, The, **193**
School for Scandal, The, 52, **166**
School for Lovers, The, 103
School of Reform, The, Or, How to Rule a Husband, 200
Selina and Azor, 122
Sergeant's Wife, The, **193**
She Stoops to Conquer, 65, 100, 127, **175**, 250
Slave, The, 76
Society, 253
Soldier's Daughter, The, **197**, 199, 200
Speed the Plough, 142, 144, 158, 177
Stranger, The, 57, 161, 201, 209, 220, 233, 250
Tale of Mystery, A, 32
Taming of the Shrew, The, 30
Tekeli, 58
Tempest, The, 30, 74
Three Weeks after Marriage, 201
Tom and Jerry, 58
To Marry or Not to Marry, 35
Triumph of Liberty, The, Or, The Destruction of the Bastille, 125
True Patriotism, or, Poverty Ennobled by Virture, 127
Twelfth Night, 30, 178
Two Gregories, **193**
Two Strings to your Bow, Or, The Servant of Two Masters, 160
Vampire, The, 77, 160
Venetian Outlaw, The, 108
Venice Preserv'd, 156, 157, 202
Virginius, 165, **208**, 209
Wags of Windsor, The, 199, **201**
Wandering Boys, The, 178
Ways and Means, 142, 144
Weathercock, The, 148, 150, **154**
West Indian, The, 74, 77, 132
Where to Find a Friend, 158
Which is the Man?, 113
Widow of Wicklow, The, 208
Winter's Tale, The, 30
Word to the Wise, A, **73**
World's Slippery Turn, The, Or, Mind How You Wed, 251